英語で読む
シャーロック・ホームズ
珠玉長編４作品

Sherlock Holmes
The Four Stories

原著＝コナン・ドイル
Sir Arthur Conan Doyle

IBCパブリッシング

リライト協力
Raina Ruth Nakamura, David Olivier, Roger Ahlberg
●
ナレーター
John Bell
●
カバー写真
iStock.com/IakovKalinin
●
本文扉イラスト
塩澤 文男
●
本文イラスト
©The Arthur Conan Doyle Encyclopedia (https://www.arthur-conan-doyle.com)

本書掲載タイトルのうち、「緋色の研究」「バスカヴィル家の犬」はラダーシリーズを再録したものです。

はじめに

ロンドンは大きな街です。そしてロンドンはその複雑な通りの構造や郊外にまで伸びる街の広さから、東京と似たところがあるともよくいわれます。18世紀の江戸は世界でもっとも大きな都市だったといわれますが、19世紀中盤から後半にかけてのロンドンは人口が190万人を超えた世界屈指の巨大都市へと成長していました。

今でもロンドンでタクシーに乗れば、熟練された運転手さんは通りと番地をいえば迷うことなく、そこに連れていってくれます。それがロンドンのタクシー運転手のプライドなのです。19世紀末、ホームズが生きていたロンドンの街には、タクシー運転手こそ存在していないものの、同じように街を知り尽くした馭者の操る馬車が縦横無尽に走っていました。ベーカー街の彼のアパートから外に出て、馭者にサマセット・ハウスまで行ってくれといえば、それ以上の会話は必要ありませんでした。馬車に乗り込み、ステッキでトントンとたたけば、馬車はそのまま動き出します。大都会ロンドンは、そんなとても便利で機動的な街だったのです。

もちろん貧富の差はありました。人々は高貴な人はそれらしく、背筋を伸ばし、物腰もやわらかく、穏やかな口調でクイーンズイングリッシュを操ります。そして地方から来て下働きをしている人々や、靴磨きの少年は、彼らならではの労働者のカジュアルな英語を使いながら、活気あるロンドンを支えていました。ホームズのもとを訪れ、彼が巻き込まれてゆく事件で出会う人々はその双方であり、さらにそこに「世界の工場」としてのロンドンを目指し、海の向こうから多くの人々が集まってきます。

今回は、そんなロンドンでホームズと相棒の医師ワトソンが親交を深めるきっかけとなった、記念すべきシリーズ第1作『緋色の研究』から楽しんでいただきます。それはアメリカから復讐のためにロンドンに流れ、馭者に扮した犯人をホームズが見破る一幕が痛快な名作です。まさに、ロンドンを舞台にした作品ならではの解決劇です。

ホームズの物語によく登場するロンドン警視庁の刑事たち。別の名前を「スコットランドヤード」といいます。その昔、ロンドン警視庁があった場所の裏側がグレート・スコットランドヤードという通りに面していたことから、このニックネームがつき、今に至っています。そのためスコットランドヤードといっても、スコットランドとは直接の歴史的つながりはありません。ホームズはあくまで私立探偵。あのアガサ・クリスティの創作した名探偵ポワロなどと同じように、プロフェッショナルなプライドをもつ犯罪刑事との鞘当てもイギリスのミステリーの面白いところです。

この『緋色の研究』の犯罪捜査をきっかけに、ホームズは大英帝国の植民地や、そこで得た財産などが絡む、さまざまな事件を解決します。作者コナン・ドイルは、その一部始終をワトソンが記録するという形で作品にしてゆくのです。ワトソンという一見実直で知的な医師の存在はホームズの物語には欠かせません。そして、ホームズはロンドンやその近郊の自然の中に住むさまざまな人に変装し、時にはワトソンをもからかうかのように騙しながら捜査を続けます。

読者の皆さんにはこうしたホームズの物語を通して、当時のロンドンの富と貧困、そして植民地を通して世界から人々や財産が出入りする大英帝国のありさまを堪能していただけることでしょう。

IBC編集部

●音声一括ダウンロード●

本書の朗読音声(MP3形式)を下記URLとQRコードから無料でPCなどに一括ダウンロードすることができます。

https://ibcpub.co.jp/audio_dl/0789/

※ダウンロードしたファイルはZIP形式で圧縮されていますので、解凍ソフトが必要です。

※MP3ファイルを再生するには、iTunes(Apple Music)やWindows Media Playerなどのアプリケーションが必要です。

※PCや端末、ソフトウェアの操作・再生方法については、編集部ではお答えできません。付属のマニュアルやインターネットの検索を利用するか、開発元にお問い合わせください。

■ラダーシリーズについて

ラダーシリーズは、「はしご（ladder）」を使って一歩一歩上を目指すように、学習者の実力に合わせ、無理なくステップアップできるよう開発された英文リーダーのシリーズです。初心者から中級者までのレベルに分かれており、自分に合ったレベルから学習を始めることができます。

ラダーシリーズの特長は、次のとおりです。

・中学校レベルから中級者レベルまで、５段階に使用する単語を限定して、やさしい英語で書き改められた本です。自分に合ったレベルからスタートできます。

・クラシックから現代文学、ノンフィクション、ビジネスと幅広いジャンルを扱っています。あなたの興味に合わせてタイトルを選べます。

・巻末のワードリストで、単語の意味を確認できます。レベル１、２では、文中の全ての単語が、レベル３以上は中学校レベル外の単語を掲載しています。

・カバーにヘッドフォンマークのついているタイトルは、オーディオ・サポートがあります。ウェブ上から購入／ダウンロードし、リスニング教材としても併用できます。

・弊社ラダーシリーズ特設サイトでは、毎月おすすめタイトルや検索急上昇タイトルを紹介しています。(https://ibcpub.co.jp/ladder/)

■ラダーシリーズを使った英語多読法

ここでは、英語多読を効果的に行うためのコツをご紹介します。

・自分のレベルに合った本を選ぶ：効率的に英語力を向上させることができます。
・速く読む：スピードを重視し、スムーズな読解力を養います。
・訳さず英語のまま読む：直訳に頼らず、英語のまま理解する力を養います。
・辞書を使わずに読む：文脈から推測して理解する力を養います。
・巻末ワードリストで調べる：どうしてもわからない所は、無理せずに調べます。
・毎日少しずつ読む：英語多読は、続けることが大切です。
・発信する：読んだ内容を、英語で話したり書くことで発信力を高められます。

ラダーシリーズを使った英語多読は、英語力を効率的に向上させるための最適な方法です。ぜひ、ラダーシリーズを使って、英語多読を始めてみてください。

Foreword

Whodunit, Howdunit, Whydunit...

Do you know what has been described as the world's most expensive magazine—not when it was published, but today? Well, in fact, it's an annual paperback titled *Beeton's Christmas Annual* that was produced from 1860 to 1890 by Samuel Beeton, the husband of Isabella Beeton, the famous writer of *Mrs. Beeton's Book of Household Management* (1861). If you ever happen to find a copy of the 1887 edition, please treat it very carefully and regard yourself as really lucky, because they are extremely rare: only 11 complete copies are known to have survived. One sold for $156,000 at an auction in New York on June 21, 2007. What does this have to do with Sherlock Holmes? Well, the simple reason for the magazine's value is that it featured *A Study in Scarlet*, the very first Sherlock Holmes story written by the Scottish doctor and writer Sir Arthur Conan Doyle (1859–1930).

A Study in Scarlet was first published in book form in 1888, illustrated by Doyle's father. It was the first of the four Holmes novels, sometimes called 'long stories', which are presented in this book in a skillfully condensed form. They were published over the next four decades along with the 56 short stories that also feature Sherlock Holmes and Dr. John Watson. The other three were *The Sign of the Four* (1890), *The Hound of the Baskervilles* (1901–02), and *The Valley of Fear* (1914–15).

Born in Scotland, and educated in England and Austria, Doyle trained in Edinburgh from the age of 17 to be a physician, and even worked as doctor on a whaling ship as a student. He started work as a

序文

だれが、どうやって、なぜ……

世界で最も高価な雑誌と言われているものが何かをご存知だろうか？　出版された当時ではなく、今日の話だが……。それは、『ビートンのクリスマス年鑑』である。『ビートン夫人の家政読本』(1861年)の著者として有名なイザベラ・ビートンの夫サミュエル・ビートンが、1860年から1890年まで毎年刊行していたペーパーバックの雑誌だ。もしこの1887年版の本誌を見つけたら、自分はなんと運がいいと思って、大切に扱うとよいだろう。現存する無傷の完全版は11部のみであることが確認されており、きわめて稀少なものだからだ。2007年6月21日にニューヨークで開催されたオークションでは、一誌156,000 USドル（当時の円相場で約2,000万円）で落札された。これがシャーロック・ホームズと何の関係があるのか？　それは単純、『緋色の研究』が掲載されていたからだ。スコットランド出身の医師で作家のアーサー・コナン・ドイル卿(1859-1930)が書いたシャーロック・ホームズのいちばん最初の物語が、この雑誌の価値を高めた理由というわけだ。

『緋色の研究』は1888年に初めて単行本として出版され、ドイルの父親が挿絵を担当した。「長編小説」と呼ばれることもあるホームズ4作品の第一作めであり、本書ではこの長編小説のすべてが巧みに凝縮された形で紹介されている。これらの4作品は、同じくシャーロック・ホームズとジョン・ワトソン博士が登場する56作品の短編とともに、その後40年間にわたって出版された。

他の長編3作品は『四つの署名』(1890年)、『バスカヴィル家の犬』(1901-1902年)、『恐怖の谷』(1914-1915年)である。

スコットランドに生まれ、イングランドとオーストリアで教育を受けたドイルは、17歳からエディンバラで内科医としての訓練を受け、学生時代には捕鯨船の船医も務めた。イングランドで開業医として働き始めたが、前々から短編

general practitioner in England, but he had always been a keen writer of both short stories and non-fiction articles. He was also a fan of Edgar Alan Poe's stories and his crime-solving character Dupin, who could put himself into the minds of criminals. Doyle decided he could create an even better detective, and he came up with two of the most famous literary characters in the world today. The 'cases' of Holmes as reported by Watson would eventually bring Doyle great fame.

The persona of Holmes who has considerable skills in interpreting circumstances scientifically was closely based on Doyle's university teacher in Edinburgh, Dr. Joseph Bell, a surgeon who observed minute details in his medical studies. Bell said of Doyle, "His education as a student of medicine taught him how to observe, and he is gifted with eyes, memory and imagination." Dr. Watson was, at least in part, partly a parody of Doyle himself, and, like the author, he was skilled with guns.

Doyle was actually most interested in writing historical novels, medical short stories, and science fiction, such as *The Lost World* (1912). But it was his stories of the great scientific detective that became so popular worldwide and stimulated the development of detective stories, while embodying the Victorian ideals of being logical and rational.

A Study in Scarlet is a thrilling story of murder and revenge. However, it is of great significance to 'Sherlockians' (avid fans of the stories, also known as 'Holmesians') because it introduced the Holmes-Watson team and provided lots of invaluable information about them both.

In this very first story, Watson tells us he is recording Holmes' stories because he was angry that all the credit for solving the case was given to the police: "*I have all the facts in my notebook and I shall*

小説やノンフィクションの執筆にも熱心だった。また、エドガー・アラン・ポーの物語と、犯罪者の心の中に入り込むことができる捜査を行う人物、デュパンのファンでもあった。ドイルは自分ならもっと優れた探偵を創作できると考え、今日世界で最も有名な二人の架空の登場人物を生み出した。ワトソンを語り手とするホームズの「事件」は、やがてドイルに大きな名声をもたらすことになる。

状況を科学的に解釈する能力に長けたホームズの人物像は、エジンバラでのドイルの大学時代の教師で、医学の研究で細部まで観察する外科医のジョセフ・ベルに近い。ベルはドイルについて、「医学生としての教育で観察の仕方を身につけ、観察眼と記憶力と想像力に恵まれている」と話している。ワトソン博士については、少なくとも部分的には、ドイル自身のパロディでもある可能性が高く、しかも作者と同じく、銃の扱いに優れた人物として描かれている。

ドイルが最も興味を持っていたのは、実は歴史小説や医療短編、『失われた世界』(1912年)などのサイエンス・フィクションを書くことだった。しかし、この偉大な科学探偵の物語こそが、世界的な人気を博し、論理的で合理的であるというヴィクトリア朝時代の理想が染み込んだ探偵小説の発展を刺激したのだ。

『緋色の研究』は殺人と復讐のスリリングな話である。しかし、「シャーロキアン」(Holmesiansとしても知られるシャーロック・ホームズの推理小説の熱心なファン)にとっては、ホームズとワトソンというワンチームを紹介し、ふたりに関する貴重な情報をたくさん提供してくれたという意味で、非常に重要な作品である。

この一番最初の物語で、ワトソンは、事件解決の手柄がすべて警察に与えられていることに怒りを覚えたので、自分はホームズの話を記録するつもりだと宣言する。彼曰く「私のノートにはすべての事実が記録されてある、だからこれを

make sure that the public gets to read them." He informs us that he is a Doctor of Medicine who trained to become an army surgeon and was wounded in Afghanistan. When they first meet, he tells Holmes that he smokes, has a dog, is very lazy, and dislikes arguments.

And from Watson's description, we learn that his new flatmate: is tall and thin, with a square chin, a long nose, and an alert expression in his sharp eyes; is an excellent boxer and swordsman; plays the violin, smokes, does scientific experiments at home, goes to bed and gets up early, and may go several days without speaking; and is an expert in crime, law, and some areas of science, especially the 'Science of Deduction', using not just his impressive brain but also cutting-edge scientific methods.

> *"I have some skill in both observation and deduction. The theories which you dismiss as the work of a thinker, are practical. Indeed, so practical that I depend upon them for my living. My own trade, and I fancy I am the only one in the world, is that of a consulting detective."*

From Watson we also learn the surprising fact that Holmes' ignorance is just as remarkable as his knowledge. Here is Holmes' explanation:

> *"You see, I consider that a man's brain is originally like an empty room, and you have to fill it as you see fit. A fool will take in everything that he comes across... The skillful workman... will have nothing but the tools he needs, but all of them will be in perfect working order... There comes a time that for every piece of knowledge you gain you forget something that you knew before. It is of the highest importance therefore not to have useless facts elbowing out the useful ones."*

In the modernized *Sherlock* version (2010), starring Benedict Cumberbatch as Holmes, the story becomes *A Study in Pink*.

世の中の人々が読める物語にするつもりだ」。ワトソンは医学博士で、軍医になるための訓練を受け、アフガニスタンで負傷したと、読者に教える。ふたりが初めて会ったとき、ホームズに、自分はタバコを吸う、子犬を飼っている、とても怠け者である、そして騒々しい言い争いが嫌いである、と告げる。

そしてワトソンの記述から、彼の新しい同居人は、背が高く痩せていて、角張ったあごと長い鼻の持ち主で、目つきが鋭く油断のない表情を浮かべている。そして優れたボクサーで剣士。ヴァイオリンを弾き、タバコを吸い、家で科学実験を行い、早寝早起きで、何日も口をきかないこともある。犯罪、法律、科学のいくつかの分野、特に「推論の科学」の専門家であり、その素晴らしい頭脳だけでなく、最先端の科学的手法も駆使する人物であることがわかる。

「私は多少の観察力と推理力の両方に恵まれている。君が思想家の仕事だとして退けてしまう理論は、非常に実用的なのだ。いや実のところ、非常に実用的だからこそ、それを糧に生計を立てていける。私は自営業で、間違いなく世界で私一人だけだと思うが、専門的助言を与える探偵なのだ。」

私たちは、ワトソンから、ホームズの無知が彼の知識と同じくらい著しいという注目すべき事実も学ぶ。以下はホームズの説明である。

「私は、人の脳はもともと空っぽの部屋のようなものだと考えている。それを自分がいいと思うように埋めなければならない。愚か者は、出会うものすべてを取り込んでしまう……熟練した職人は……自分に必要な道具だけを持ち、そのすべてを完璧に使える状態にしておく……知識を得るたびに、前に知っていたことを忘れる時がいつかはやって来る。ゆえに、役に立たない事実が有用な事実を追い出してしまわないようにすることが最も重要である。」

ベネディクト・カンバーバッチがホームズを演じる現代版『シャーロック』(2010年)では、この物語のタイトルは『ピンク色の研究』だ。

The second novel, ***The Sign of the Four*** (also known as *The Sign of Four*), had an interesting conception. In 1889, J. B. Lippincott, the American publisher of *Lippincott's Monthly Magazine*, invited Doyle and the legendary writer Oscar Wilde to dinner at a London hotel. He wanted British writers to contribute to his magazine and invited them both to produce new stories. They agreed. And so, in February 1890, *The Sign of the Four* was published in the American (25 cents) and British (1 shilling) versions of the magazine.

That's another valuable item for collectors! Incidentally, the May 1890 edition included a love story titled *Karma* by Lafcadio Hearn, and the July edition featured *The Picture of Dorian Gray* by Wilde.

The intricate revenge and murder story involves some mysterious pearls that relate back to an extraordinary treasure chest in India. But the story opens in the flat at 221B Baker Street with Holmes' drug habit and his thoughts on the science of deduction and "the difference between looking and thinking":

> *"He believed he was the only person to have the three qualities necessary for the ideal detective— the power to look, the power to think, and the power of knowledge."*

Another significant feature of the novel is Watson falling in love... but no spoilers about that here! I can, however, quote Holmes' famous comments on love and marriage:

> *"Love is an emotional thing and whatever is emotional is opposed to that true cold reason which I place above all things. I would never marry myself because it would harm my reasoning power."*

The 2014 *Sherlock* version (Series 3-2) is titled *The Sign of Three.*

第二作めの『四つの署名』(The Sign of the Four またはThe Sign of Four)が生まれた背景は興味深い。1889年、『リピンコット・マガジン』という月刊誌を発行していたアメリカ人のリピンコットは、ドイルと伝説の作家オスカー・ワイルドをロンドンのホテルに招いて夕食を共にした。彼はイギリス人作家に自分の月刊誌に寄稿してもらいたいと考え、二人に新作の執筆を依頼したのだ。作家たちは同意した。そして1890年2月、『四つの署名』はアメリカ版(25セント)とイギリス版(1シリング)の雑誌に収められた。

これもコレクターにとっては貴重なアイテムだ！　ちなみに、1890年5月号にはラフカディオ・ハーンの『カルマ』というタイトルの恋愛小説が、7月号にはオスカー・ワイルドの『ドリアン・グレイの肖像』が掲載されている。

この込み入った復讐と殺人の物語には、インドの極めて特別な宝箱にまつわる謎めいた真珠が絡んでいる。しかし、物語はベーカー街221Bの下宿から始まり、ホームズの薬物常用癖や、推理の科学と「観察することと推理することの違い」に関する彼の考えが描かれる。

「彼は、理想的な探偵に必要な三つの資質、すなわち観察する力、推理する力、そして知識という力を備えているのは自分しかいないと信じていた。」

この小説のもうひとつの大きな読みどころは、ワトソンが恋に落ちること……ここではネタバレはしない！　だが、恋愛と結婚に関するホームズの有名なコメントを引用しておこう。

「愛とは情緒的な心のはたらきである。情緒的なものが何であれ、それは私が何よりも重んじる真の客観的な理性に対立するものだ。私は決して結婚はしない。自分の推理力をそこなうことになるからだ。」

2014年のシャーロック版(シーズン3、エピソード2)のタイトルは『三の兆候』だ。

The third novel, ***The Hound of the Baskervilles***, came eleven years later. It's the best known of the four novels and has remained immensely popular, with far more TV and movie versions than any other Holmes story. It was a publishing phenomenon when it appeared serially in the *Strand Magazine* in 1901-2. Why? Because it was the first Holmes story since his apparent death in *The Final Problem* (1893), an event that had basically sent the British nation into mourning! Reluctantly, Doyle had to bring Holmes back from the dead by popular demand.

As he was writing the novel, Doyle told his mother, "I'm going to make it a real creeper", and it's a scary story indeed. It centers around mysterious events on the remote Dartmoor moors in southwest England, complete with an escaped convict. The words that get Holmes interested in the case are: "The footprints of a giant hound!" (Not a 'dog', note, but 'a hound')

The 2012 *Sherlock* version (Series 2-2), titled *The Hounds of Baskerville*, retains the misty, mysterious moors and the hideous hell-hound, but changes 'Baskerville' from a family name into a secret chemical research center. The story was also one of the *Classic Adventures* parodied by the British comedian Spike Milligan in 1998.

Original copies of the *Strand Magazine* containing this story are not so rare, but Doyle's hand-written manuscript pages in dark brown ink are. They were used by the publisher for advertising purposes and only 37 are known to have survived, 12 of them in private hands. One page auctioned in 2012 for $423,000.

The fourth novel, ***The Valley of Fear***, was also first published in the *Strand Magazine* in 1914–15. It's a fascinating saga that has a basic

第三作めの小説The Hound of the Baskervilles『バスカヴィル家の犬』はその11年後に発表された。4作品の中で最もよく知られた小説で、他のどのホームズ小説よりもテレビ化や映画化が多く、絶大な人気を誇っている。1901年から1902年にかけてStrand Magazine（ストランド・マガジン）に連載されたときは、出版界の一大現象となった。なぜか？　それは、The Final Problem『最後の事件』（1893年）でホームズが明らかに死亡して以来、初めてのホームズ物語だったからである！　ホームズの死は基本的に英国民を喪に服させた出来事だった。そのため、不本意ながらも、ドイルは多くの要望に応えてホームズを死から蘇らせなければならなかった。

この小説を書きながら、ドイルは母親に「本当にぞっとするような作品にするつもりだ」と言ったという。その言葉どおり、実に恐ろしい話だ。イングランド南西部の人里離れたダートムーアの荒野で起きた不可解な事件を軸として、脱獄囚がわき筋としてからみ展開する。ホームズがこの事件に興味を持つきっかけとなった言葉がこれだ。「巨大な猟犬の足跡だ！」(dog ではなく、a hound であることに注意)

2012 年のシャーロック版(シーズン2、エピソード2)のタイトルは『バスカヴィルの犬（ハウンド）』で、霧に覆われた不気味な荒野と恐ろしい地獄の番犬はそのままに、「バスカヴィル」が一家の姓から秘密の化学研究所の名前に変更されている。この物語は、1998年にイギリスのコメディアン、スパイク・ミリガンによってパロディ化されたClassic Adventuresにも収められている。

この物語を掲載したストランド・マガジンの原書はさほど珍しいものではないが、ドイルが濃い茶色のインクで手書きした自筆原稿は希少である。出版社が広告用に使用したもので、現存するのは37枚、うち12枚が個人所有であることが知られている。 2012年のオークションでは1枚が423,000 USドル（当時の円相場で約3,300万円）で落札された。

第四作めの『恐怖の谷』も、1914年から1915年にかけてストランド・マガジンに掲載された作品だ。第一部では基本的に「だれが」（犯人）と「どうやって」

'whodunit' (the criminal) and 'howdunit' (the means) story in Part 1. It begins with Holmes cracking a secret code and includes a mystery that hinges on two missing items: a dumb-bell and a wedding ring. And then there is a thrilling Part 2 set in America to delve into the 'whydunit' (the reason) background to the case, the deeper psychological aspects to the crime that fascinate Holmes most, to satisfy his great intellectual curiosity.

In this case, it's actually first editions of the story in book form that fetch a good price.

I hope you will enjoy these novels as much as I continue to do, and that you will then feel energized to read all 60 original versions of the Holmes stories. I wish you happy reading and careful observations and deductions regarding the WHO, the HOW and the WHY!

Stuart Varnam-Atkin
Holmesian/Sherlockian & Trivia Collector

(手段) の話が展開される魅力的な物語である。物語はホームズが秘密の暗号を解読するところから始まり、ダンベルと結婚指輪という二つの紛失物をめぐる謎解きになっている。そして、舞台をアメリカに移したスリリングな第二部では、事件の背景となる「なぜ」(理由) を掘り下げ、ホームズを最も魅了する犯罪の深層心理に迫り、彼の大きな知的好奇心を満足させる。

この場合、高値で取引されるのは、実は書籍化された『恐怖の谷』の初版本である。

私がこれからもそうであるように、皆さんも本書に収めた小説を楽しんでくださることを願っています。そうすれば、ホームズの原作全60編を読む活力が湧いてくるはずです。そして楽しい読書をしながら「だれが」、「どうやって」、「なぜ」と注意深く観察し、鋭い推理を行ってみてください！

ステュウット　ヴァーナム-アットキン
ホームズの熱狂的ファンでトリビア収集家

(訳：とよざきようこ)

CONTENTS

A Study in Scarlet

緋色の研究

読み始める前に

A Study in Scarlet 緋色の研究

「シャーロック・ホームズ」シリーズ最初の作品
1887年の「ビートンのクリスマス年鑑」12月号に初出

［主な登場人物］

Sherlock Holmes シャーロック・ホームズ 鋭い観察眼と推理力、そして犯罪に関する膨大な知識をあわせ持つ私立探偵。ロンドンのベーカー街221Bに下宿している。

John H. Watson ジョン・H・ワトソン 元軍医。戦争中に傷を負い健康を害し、赴任先のアフガニスタンからイギリスへ帰国した。この物語の語り手。

Tobias Gregson トバイアス・グレッグソン ロンドン警視庁の刑事。手に負えない事件があると、ホームズに助言を求めにたびたびやってくる。

Lestrade レストレード グレッグソンと同じくロンドン警視庁の刑事。グレッグソンとは手柄を争い張り合う仲。

Enoch J. Drebber イーノック・J・ドレバー 空き家で死体となって発見された男性。持ち物を見るとアメリカからやってきたらしい。

Joseph Stangerson ジョセフ・スタンガーソン ドレバーが伴っていた私設秘書。

John Ferrier ジョン・フェリアー 砂漠を横断中に遭難した一団の生き残り。移住地を探していたモルモン教徒たちに、改宗を条件に救われる。

Lucy Ferrier ルーシー・フェリアー ジョン・フェリアーと共に砂漠で生き残った少女。血のつながりはないが、彼の養女となり、実の親子のように愛情を持って育つ。

Jefferson Hope ジェファーソン・ホープ ルーシーをある危機から救った青年。ルーシーに恋をした彼は、隣の州で仕事をしておりモルモン教徒ではなかったが、しばしフェリアー家を訪れるようになる。

［あらすじ］

アフガニスタンで軍医として従軍していたワトソンは、怪我を負ったあげくに病気にかかり、すっかり弱りきってイギリス・ロンドンへ帰国した。手ごろな家賃の住処を探しているところに、昔の知人の紹介で、ホームズという奇妙な男に出会う。

二人はすぐにベーカー街の下宿屋でルームシェアの生活を始める。ホームズは持ち前の観察力と推理力、そして勉強の成果による妙に偏った分野の知識を活かして、私立探偵として生計を立てているらしい。ホームズの自信満々の態度と物言いに反感と不信感をぬぐえないまま、ワトソンはホームズと共にロンドン警視庁の刑事が持ち込んだ事件の現場を訪れる。現場の空き家には、恐怖に顔を歪めた男性の死体があった。外傷も凶器もないのになぜかそこには血痕が残されており、さらに壁には血で書かれた文字と、女性ものの金の指輪も見つかった。

遠いアメリカの地で起きた悲しい物語の幕がロンドンで閉じられると同時に、ホームズとワトソンの、名コンビの活躍の幕が開かれる。

Illustrations by Richard Gutschmidt (1902)

［総単語数］20,680語

PART 1

Being a Reprint from the Records of Dr. John H. Watson

01

Chapter 1
Mr. Sherlock Holmes

It was in 1878 that I was first introduced to Sherlock Holmes. I had just returned to London from Afghanistan after leaving the Army because of ill-health. I was lonely, and still quite weak from my illness. London was new to me and I was finding it difficult to make friends. One day I met an old friend, Stamford, and I asked him to join me for lunch at the Criterion, Piccadilly.

I told Stamford that I was staying in a hotel off the Strand, and I was looking for somewhere cheaper and more homely.

"That's strange," he said, "you are the second man I have spoken to today that has that problem."

He explained that the other fellow was doing experiments at the hospital where he worked. "He has found some nice rooms but they are too big and too much money for him. He is looking for someone to share them with."

"We should meet up without delay. I would prefer sharing to living alone anyway," I cried.

My friend looked at me with amusement.

"You have not met Sherlock Holmes yet," he said, "you might change your mind when you do."

"Why? Is there something wrong with him?" I asked.

"I didn't say there was anything wrong with him. He's just a little strange in his ideas. He is an expert in certain areas of science, and you know that scientific men can seem a little strange at times."

"Studying to be a doctor, I suppose?" I said.

"No. I have no idea what he intends to do in the future. He is an expert on the human body but as far as I know, he has never taken any recognized courses. He prefers to follow his own methods of learning. By doing so he has gained knowledge known only to a few people."

"Did you ever ask him why he studied these subjects?" I asked.

"He can be a very difficult man to draw out, although when he warms to his subject he is quite a talker," replied my friend.

"He sounds interesting. Can you arrange for me to meet him?"

My friend nodded, "Come with me to the hospital. Holmes is certain to be there. He is either away for weeks or he is there from morning to night."

As we drove round I asked Stamford whether there was anything else I should know about Mr. Holmes.

"He is so interested in science that he can seem quite cold-blooded and heartless. When he is trying to prove something I feel that he would let nothing stand between him and getting

at the truth." As we spoke we entered the hospital and made our way to the office where Holmes normally worked.

At the far end of the office was a tall, thin man bending over a desk. As we entered he looked up and rushed over to us. "I've found it!" he cried. "I have found a substance which changes color when it is mixed with blood—fresh blood or dried blood. Nothing else causes it to change to this color." He could not have looked happier if he had just discovered how to make gold.

"Dr. Watson, Mr. Sherlock Holmes," said Stamford introducing us.

"How are you?" he said in a friendly manner, shaking my hand more firmly than I had expected. "You have been in Afghanistan, I see."

"How on earth did you know that?" I asked with real surprise.

"Never mind," said Holmes, laughing to himself, "the question now is about blood. No doubt you see the importance of my discovery."

"It is interesting for men of science, but from a practical point of view I do not—"

"It is the most practical discovery for medical law in years. Don't you see that it gives a test for blood stains that cannot fail. Come over here and watch."

He pushed a needle into his finger then, causing it to bleed.

He mixed this drop of blood with a liter of water. He then added a white liquid to the water. The liquid changed color and a dark brown substance sank to the bottom of the water.

"There!" laughed Holmes, "what do you think of that?"

"It seems a most exact test," I remarked.

"Indeed!" cried Holmes, "the other tests for blood are uncertain at best, and useless if the stains are more than a few hours old. This test will work whether the stain is a few hours or a few months old. If this test had been invented, there are hundreds of men who are now walking free who would have been in prison long ago. A man may be suspected of a crime that happened months earlier. His clothing is examined and stains are found. Are they mud stains, food stains or blood stains? This question has puzzled many an expert. Now we have the Sherlock Holmes test to remove any doubts."

Holmes then named half a dozen criminal cases where he felt his test would have put the defendant in prison. It was clear that Holmes was also an expert on police matters.

"Very interesting Holmes," said Stamford, "but we are here on business. My friend needs somewhere to live, and you are looking for someone to share with. I thought that I had better bring you together."

Sherlock Holmes seemed delighted at the idea of sharing his rooms with me. "I have seen some rooms in Baker Street," he said, "which would be perfect for us. You don't mind sharing with a smoker I hope?"

"I smoke myself," I answered.

"Good! I like to do experiments from time to time."

"That's fine by me," I replied.

"I have some other bad points. For example, I sometimes go days without speaking. You must not think I am angry. Just leave me alone and I will be right. It's best that we know the worst of each other before we start to live together."

"Well," I said, "I keep a dog, and I don't like rows because my nerves are still shaken from my illness. I get up at strange hours and I am very lazy. If I am well I have other bad points but these are the main ones at present."

"Do you include violin playing as a row?"

"It depends on the player," I replied, "a well-played one is a treat for the Gods—a badly played one—"

"Oh, that's all right," laughed Holmes. "I think we will be fine together—if you like the rooms, that is."

"When shall we see them?"

"Call for me at noon tomorrow and we'll go together and settle everything," Holmes answered.

We left him working and we walked together towards my hotel.

"By the way, Stamford," I asked suddenly, "how did he know that I had been in Afghanistan?"

"That is his speciality," he said. "A good many people have wondered how he finds things out."

"Oh good," I cried, "a mystery is it? How delightful! I am most thankful to you for bringing us together. I will enjoy studying Sherlock Holmes."

"You will find him a difficult subject to fully understand. I am sure that he will learn more about you than you do about him," said my friend.

02

Chapter 2
The Science of Deduction

We met as arranged the next day and went to 221B, Baker Street to look at the rooms. There were two comfortable bedrooms and a large, light sitting-room. We were so pleased with the apartment that we agreed to the terms and made arrangements to move in at once. Within two days we were both established in our new home.

Holmes was certainly not a difficult man to live with. He went to bed early and had usually breakfasted and gone out before I got up in the morning. When he wanted to work he would do so for weeks without tiring. On other occasions he would lie around the sitting-room without moving or speaking from morning to night. He was so dreamy at these times that if his general attitude was not that of a clean-living gentleman, I would have thought he was under the influence of some illegal drug.

As the weeks went by my interest in Holmes and what he was doing increased. Even his appearance was striking. He was over six feet tall, and so thin that he appeared to be even taller. His sharp eyes and long nose gave his whole face a look of watchfulness. His square chin was the mark of a man of determination.

As to the purpose of his life, that was harder to discover as Holmes said little about himself. He was not studying medicine, that much he had admitted. Whatever he did study, however, he studied in great detail. Although it seemed to me to be without pattern, there must have been a purpose to his hard work. In some areas of science he probably had more knowledge than anyone else in the world. In areas he was not interested in he knew next to nothing. When I explained a well-known fact to him I could barely believe that he really did not know of it.

"You appear to be surprised," he said with a smile. "Now that I know it I shall do my best to forget it."

"To forget it!"

"You see," he explained, "I consider that a man's brain is originally like an empty room, and you have to fill it as you see fit. A fool will take in everything that he comes across. The knowledge that might be useful to him gets crowded out or mixed up with lots of other things and he can never use it when he needs it. Now the skillful workman is very careful about what he takes into his room. He will have nothing but the tools he needs, but all of them will be in perfect working order. It is a mistake to think that you can keep bringing things into the room. Depend upon it, there comes a time that for every piece of knowledge you gain you forget something that you knew before. It is of the highest importance, therefore, not to have useless facts elbowing out the useful ones."

As I thought about what he had said over the next few days I realized that Holmes studied everything for a purpose and, if I looked at what he was studying, I might discover that purpose. I reviewed what I knew about Holmes. He knew nothing of literature or politics. He was an expert in crime, law, and some areas of science. He was an excellent boxer and swordsman. He was also an expert on the strangest things. For example, he could tell what part of London someone had been in by looking at the soil on their shoes. He also knew what plants could be used to make poisons, but very little else about flowers and plants.

When I had considered all of this I still could not understand why Holmes studied what he did.

During the first week or so we had no callers and I had begun to think that my companion was as friendless as I. Soon, however, I found that he knew many people from all levels of society. One, who was introduced to me as Mr. Lestrade, came three or four times each week but most of the others just made a single visit.

I felt that I did not know Holmes well enough to ask him what all these visits meant. One day Holmes brought the subject up himself.

It was the 4th of March, a day I remember well. I had risen somewhat earlier than usual. Holmes was finishing his breakfast and as I waited for mine I looked at a magazine. One of the articles had a pencil mark at the heading and since my interest was aroused, I began to read.

It was called "The Book of Life," and it attempted to show how much an observant man could learn by careful examination of all that came his way. All life was a great chain, argued the author, the nature of which can be deduced by seeing one small part of the chain. He went on to say that the Science of Deduction is one which can only be gotten by long and patient study. On a simple level, the author stated, it was possible to look at a man, at his fingers, his clothes, his face, his shoes and deduce what his job was. I finished reading the article and threw the magazine on the table.

"What nonsense!" I cried.

"What is?" asked Sherlock Holmes.

"This article," I said, "I don't deny that it is well written, but it is clearly the work of a thinker who has very little practical experience of 'deduction' as he calls it. I should like to see him in a train of people. I would wager a thousand to one that he could not tell me the job of one of them."

"You would lose your money," Holmes said quietly. "As for the article, I wrote it myself!"

"You!"

"Yes. I have some skill in both observation and deduction. The theories which you dismiss as the work of a thinker are practical. Indeed, so practical that I depend upon them for my living."

"How?" I asked.

"Well, my own trade, and I fancy I am the only one in the world, is that of a consulting detective. Here in London we have lots of government detectives and many private ones. When these fellows are unable to solve a case they come to me. They give me all the details. Generally, I am able, with the help of my knowledge of crime, to point them in the right direction. If you know the details of a thousand crimes it is rare that you can't solve the thousand and first. Lestrade is a well-known detective. He was having problems with a case and so he came to visit me."

"And the other people?" I asked, my curiosity growing by the minute.

"Most of them are people sent on by private detectives. They have some problem or other and need help. I listen to their story, they listen to my comments, and then they pay me. Sometimes a case turns up that is unusual and I have to go and look at the details myself. That is when the rules of deduction, laid out in the article you have dismissed, are invaluable to me. Observation is second nature to me. For example, you appeared to be surprised that I knew you had come from Afghanistan. No one had told me, but I knew. From long habit, the deductive process ran so quickly through my mind that I could not tell the individual steps along the way. There were such steps, however. The train of reasoning ran, 'Here is a gentleman who looks like a doctor, but with the air of an army man. Clearly an army doctor, then. He has just come from somewhere hot, for his face is dark, and that is not the natural color of his skin for the inside of his arms are white. His face shows he has undergone hardship and sickness and he has injured his left arm which he holds very stiffly. Where could all this have happened to an English army doctor? Clearly in Afghanistan. This whole thought process lasted less than a second."

"It is simple enough as you explain it," I said, smiling.

"I have spent a lifetime studying crimes and I honestly feel that no man alive could match me in my ability to solve them. And what is the result? There is no crime to detect. Or at least no crime worthy of my attention."

No sooner had he spoken this than we heard a loud knock at the door. A few moments later a man was shown into the room.

"For Mr. Sherlock Holmes," he said, handing my friend a letter.

03

Chapter 3
The Lauriston Gardens Mystery

"Now this is more like it," said Holmes. He threw me the letter and asked me to read it aloud.

This is the letter I read:

"My Dear Mr. Sherlock Holmes,

"There has been some bad business at 3 Lauriston Gardens off the Brixton Road. One of our policemen saw a light there at about two in the morning. The house should have been empty so he went inside to see if anything was wrong. The front door was open, and in the front room he discovered the body of a well-dressed gentleman. In his pocket he found cards bearing the name of 'Enoch J. Drebber, Cleveland, Ohio, USA.' Nothing had been stolen, nor is it clear how the man met his death. There are blood marks in the room but no wound on his body. We do not know how he came to be in the empty house, in fact the whole thing is a puzzle to us. I would be very pleased to have your help in this matter.

Yours faithfully,
Tobias Gregson"

"Gregson is one of the smartest at Scotland Yard," my friend commented, "he and Lestrade are the pick of a bad lot. They are both quick and energetic, but have no imagination. They dislike each other, too. They try to outdo each other on any case they both work on. There could be some fun in it if they are both put on this one."

He quickly got into his coat, showing the energy that had been lacking these last few weeks.

"Get your hat," he said.

"You wish me to come?"

"Yes, if you have nothing better to do." A minute later we were in a cab heading for the Brixton Road.

As we drove along my companion seemed very excited. He talked of many things but did not mention the letter.

"I am surprised you are not thinking about the case," I said after a while.

"No information yet. It is a serious mistake to theorize before you have all the evidence."

"Well, we are getting close now so you shall soon have your information."

"So we are. Stop!" he called quickly to the driver.

We were still some way from the house but he insisted on getting out here and walking the rest of the way.

When we got to 3 Lauriston Gardens we found a house with a small garden in front bounded by a three-foot high wall.

I had thought that Holmes would have hurried into the house at once to start looking for clues. Nothing seemed further from his mind. He walked slowly up and down opposite the house, staring at the ground, the sky, the houses opposite and the wall. Finally, he proceeded slowly down the path, or rather down the grass next to the path. He looked carefully at the ground. Twice he stopped, and once I saw him smile in satisfaction. There were many foot marks on the wet ground but the police had been back and forth along the path many times and I could not see how my friend could hope to learn anything from it. He had already taught me, however, that he could see a great deal that was hidden from me.

At the door of the house we were met by a tall, white-faced man with a notebook in his hand. He rushed forward and shook Holmes warmly by the hand. "It is indeed kind of you to come," he said, "I have left everything untouched."

"Except that!" answered Sherlock Holmes, pointing at the pathway. "Any evidence from that area has long since been destroyed by the police. No doubt, Gregson, you had already examined it before you allowed this to happen."

"I have had so much to do in the house, I left the outside to my colleague, Lestrade."

Holmes glanced at me and said with a half-smile, "With two such men as you and Lestrade on the case, there will not be much for a third party to find out."

Gregson looked pleased, although I was sure Holmes was not really praising him.

"I think we have done all that can be done. But I know you like strange cases so I asked you to come over."

"You did not come here in a cab?" asked Sherlock Holmes.

"No, sir."

"Nor Lestrade?"

"No, sir."

"Then let us go and look at the room." With this remark he walked into the house. We followed Holmes through the hall into the room where the death had occurred.

It was a large room, empty of furniture, with the wallpaper hanging off the walls. There was a fireplace opposite the door and on one corner of this there was a red candle. There was a window, but it was so dirty that barely any light got into the room. The dark feeling to the room was increased by the thick layer of dust that covered everything.

All of this I noticed afterwards. At first my attention was drawn to the motionless figure on the floor whose empty staring eyes looked upwards. It was a man in his mid-forties, average build, with curly, black hair and a short beard. He was well-dressed and his clothes were clean. His arms and legs were set as though his death struggle had been a fierce one, and on his face was a look of terror.

Lestrade was standing in the doorway

and greeted my companion and myself.

"This case will be famous, Mr. Holmes," he remarked. "It beats anything I have seen and I've been around a while."

"There is no clue?" asked Gregson.

"None at all," replied Lestrade.

Sherlock Holmes approached the body. He knelt down examining it carefully.

"You are sure there is no wound?" he asked pointing to the many bloodstains around the room.

"Completely!" cried both detectives.

"Then, of course, this blood belongs to a second person—probably the murderer, if murder has been committed."

As he spoke, his fingers were flying here, there and everywhere, examining the clothing and the body. Finally, he smelled the lips of the dead man and then looked at the soles of his boots.

"He has not been moved at all?"

"No more than was necessary for our investigation."

"You can have him taken away now; there is nothing further to learn," said Holmes.

The police lifted the body and carried it out. As they turned in the hall a ring hit the floor. Lestrade picked it up and cried,

"There's been a woman here! This is a woman's wedding ring."

We looked at it.

"This makes things more difficult," said Gregson. "It was enough of a puzzle before this."

"Are you sure it does not make it easier?" asked Holmes. "Show me what you found in his pockets."

Gregson pointed at a collection of items, "They are all here, a gold watch and chain, a gold ring, gold pin, personal cards in the name of Enoch J. Drebber of Cleveland, some money, a book with the name Joseph Stangerson on the flyleaf. Two letters—one addressed to E.J. Drebber and one to Joseph Stangerson."

"At what address?"

"American Exchange, The Strand—to be left until called for. They are both from a Steamship Company, and refer to the sailing of their boats from Liverpool. It is clear that this unfortunate man was about to return to New York."

"Have you made inquiries as to this man, Stangerson?"

"I did it at once, Mr. Holmes," said Gregson. "I have had notices sent to all the newspapers, and one of my men has gone to the American Exchange but he has not returned yet."

"Have you sent a telegram to Cleveland?"

"This morning, sir."

"What did you ask?"

"We told them the situation and asked if they had any information that could help us."

"You did not ask for particulars on any point that seemed more important."

"No, I just asked about Stangerson," said Gregson in a slightly angry voice as Sherlock Holmes laughed to himself.

At that moment Lestrade entered the room looking very

pleased with himself.

"Mr. Gregson," he said, "I have just made a discovery of the highest importance, and one which would have been overlooked if I had not made a careful examination of the walls."

He could barely hide his delight in being able to score a point against his fellow policeman.

We followed him as he hurried back to the room where the body had been found. He lit a match and held it up against the wall.

"Look at that!"

In the corner, in blood-red letters, there was written a single word—

RACHE

"Well, what do you think?" cried Lestrade. "This was not seen before because it is the darkest part of the room and no one thought of looking there. The murderer has written it with his or her own blood."

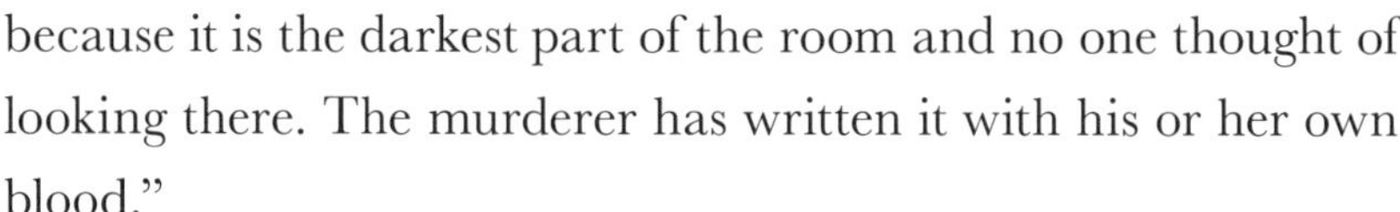

"What does it mean now that you have found it?" asked Gregson, trying to sound unimpressed.

"Mean? Why, it means that the writer was going to put the female name Rachel, but was disturbed before he or she had time to finish. You will see, when this case is finished you will find that a woman named Rachel has something to do with it."

At this point Holmes burst out laughing.

"It's all very well for you to laugh, Mr. Sherlock Holmes. You may be very clever but sometimes good police work is the best way to solve a case."

"I do beg your pardon," said Holmes. "You certainly must take the credit for finding this clue and, as you say, it would appear to have been written by the other party in last night's mystery. I have not had time to examine this room yet, but I will do so now with your permission."

He measured the distance between every point in the room, talking to himself all the while. At the same time he examined every mark he could find with a magnifying glass. For twenty minutes or more he continued his examination. In one place he carefully gathered up a little pile of gray dust from the floor and put it away in an envelope. Finally he examined with his glass the word upon the wall. When he had done this he appeared to be satisfied for he put away his glass and measure.

Gregson and Lestrade had watched Holmes's actions with interest and some amusement. They clearly failed to realize that none of Sherlock Holmes's actions were without reason and that he was moving toward some definite end.

"What do you think of it, sir?" they both asked.

"You gentlemen are doing so well, it would not be fair to help you and take the credit for solving the case." It was clear from Holmes's tone that he did not really think that the detectives were capable of solving the crime. "If you will let me know how your investigations go," he continued, "I shall be happy to give you any help I can. In the meantime, I would like to speak to the policeman who found the body. Can you give me his name and address?"

Lestrade gave him the details of John Rance, the policeman in question.

"Come along, Doctor," he said: "we shall go and look him up. I'll tell you one thing which may help you in this case," he continued, turning to the two detectives. "There has been murder done, and the murderer was a man. He was more than six feet tall, was physically fit, had small feet for his height, wore heavy square-toed boots and smoked a Trichinopoly cigar. He came here with the murdered man in a four-wheeled cab, which was pulled by a horse with three old shoes and one new one. In all probability, the murderer had a red face and the fingernails of his right hand were remarkably long. This is not much for you, but it may help."

Lestrade and Gregson smiled at one another.

"If he was murdered, how was it done?" asked Lestrade.

"Poison," said Holmes quickly, and then walked off. "One other thing, Lestrade," he added, "'Rache' is the German for 'revenge' so don't lose your time looking for Miss Rachel."

With this parting shot he walked away leaving the two detectives open-mouthed in disbelief.

04

Chapter 4
What John Rance Had to Tell

It was one o'clock when we left the house. Sherlock Holmes went straight to a telegram office and sent off a long telegram. We then got a cab to the policeman's address.

"You can't be as sure as you sound about the information you gave those two," I said.

"There is not the slightest chance that I am wrong," he answered. "The very first thing which I noticed on arrival was some wheel marks of a cab which had stopped outside the house. Up to last night we had not had rain for a week, so these marks must have been made last night. The outline of the marks made by the horse's feet had one much clearer than the other three. Since the cab was there after the rain and Gregson says no cabs came during the day, it must have been there in the night and it must have brought those two individuals to the house."

"That seems clear enough," I said, "but how about the man's height?"

"The height of a man, in nine out of ten cases, can be told from the length of his steps. I had two measurements for this man's step, one outside the house and one on the dust in the room. I could then check this against the writing. When a man writes on a wall it is natural for him to write above the level of his own eyes. The writing was just over six feet from the ground."

"And his fitness?"

"Well, if a man can step four and a half feet without effort he must be in good condition. He stepped over the puddle on the path whereas the other man walked around it. Is there anything else that puzzles you?"

"The fingernails and the Trichinopoly," I suggested.

"The writing on the wall was done with a man's forefinger dipped in blood. My magnifying glass enabled me to examine the wall closely and I could see the scratches that would not have been there if his nail had been short. You may have noticed that I picked up some ash. My study of cigar ash enabled me to recognize it as Trichinopoly. It is in just these details that the skilled detective is different from the likes of Lestrade and Gregson."

"And the red face?" I asked.

"Ah, you must wait to find that out, but I have no doubt that I am right in that matter as well."

"I still can't work it out. The more you tell me the more mysterious it becomes. Why did the men come to an empty house? What has become of the cab driver who brought them? How could one man make another take poison? Where did the blood come from? What was the reason for the murder—nothing was stolen? What was the woman's ring doing there? Above all, why should the second man write up the German word RACHE before he left? Even if I knew the answers to these questions, I doubt it would lead me to the murderer."

"You sum up the problem very well," said Holmes with a smile. "There is much that is not clear but I am sure I know the main facts. As to poor Lestrade's discovery, it was a trick to put the police on the wrong track. It was not done by a German. The letter 'A' was written in a way that English people think Germans write 'A's.' In fact Germans write it in a different way altogether. I am not going to tell you much more about this case, Doctor, for fear that if I reveal too many secrets you will not think that I am doing anything out of the ordinary."

"Oh, I am sure I will. You have already shown me things I did not think were possible. It seems to me that you have brought detection as near an exact science as it is possible to do."

Holmes smiled and clearly took a lot of pleasure in my words. It seemed to me that if Holmes had a weakness, it was that he needed other people to recognize his great ability.

"I'll tell you another thing," he said. "The two men came in the same cab, and they walked down the path like two friends, side by side. When they got to the room they walked up and down, or rather the murdered man, Mr. Drebber, walked up and down. I saw that on the dust on the floor and I also

saw that, as he walked, he became more excited. His steps got longer. Then the murder took place. That is all I know, although I could guess at a good deal more." As he finished speaking we pulled up outside John Rance's house.

Rance seemed quite annoyed when we entered his house but he brightened up when he saw the coin in Holmes's hand.

"I shall be happy to tell you anything I can," he said, without taking his eyes from the coin.

"Just let us hear it all in your own words."

"Well, at about two in the morning I was walking down the Brixton Road. I didn't see a soul, although one or two cabs passed me. It was a wet night and I was thinking how warm my bed would be, when suddenly I saw a light in the house in question. Now, as it is my beat, I knew that the house was empty. I went down the path to investigate—"

"There was no one in the street?"

"Not a living soul, sir. Then I went and pushed the door open. All was quiet inside, so I went into the room where the light was burning. I saw—"

"Yes, I know. You walked round the room several times, and you knelt down by the body and then you walked through and tried the kitchen door, and then—"

Rance jumped to his feet looking very frightened and a little angry.

"Where was you hid to see all that?" he cried. "It seems to me that you know a good deal more than you should."

Holmes laughed and threw his card on the table, "Don't go arresting me for the murder," he said. "I am on your side. Mr. Gregson or Mr. Lestrade will answer for that. What did you do next?"

Rance continued, "I went back to the gate and sounded my whistle. That quickly brought two more policemen to the house."

"Was the street empty then?"

"Except for the drunk."

"What do you mean?"

The policeman's face broke into a smile at the memory, "I've seen many a drunk in my time, but never one in the state as that fellow. He was at the gate when I came out, leaning up against the wall and singing at the top of his voice. He could barely stand."

"What sort of man was he?" asked Sherlock Holmes.

"He was an uncommon drunk man," said Rance a little angrily.

"His face, his clothes, did you notice them?"

"Of course I did! I had to hold him up and help him along the road. He was a tall man with a red face, with his coat—"

"That's enough," cried Holmes. "What became of him?"

"We'd enough to do without worrying about a drunk. He got

home all right, I'll wager."

"How was he dressed?"

"A brown top-coat."

"You didn't happen to see or hear a cab after that?"

"No."

"Thank you, Mr. Rance," said Holmes, handing him the coin. "You have been most helpful, but I am afraid you will never make a detective. The man whom you held in your hands is the man who holds the answer to this mystery and is the one we are looking for. Come along, Doctor, we must go." Holmes turned and walked out of the room leaving a speechless Rance staring at his back.

"The fool!" said Holmes angrily, as we drove back to our lodgings. "Just to think of the luck that he had and how he simply wasted it."

"The description of this man does match your idea of the second man. But why should he return to the scene of the crime? Surely that is not the way of criminals?"

"The ring, man, the ring; that was why he returned. If we have no other way of catching him we can always use the ring to bring him out into the open. I will catch him, Doctor, I'll wager you two to one that I will catch him. I have you to thank for this, one of the most interesting studies I have worked on. If it wasn't for you I might never have gone. A study in scarlet! There's the scarlet thread of murder running through this case, and our job is to find it and trace it until we have seen the answer."

Holmes leaned back in the cab singing to himself. He looked happier and more excited than any time I could remember.

05

Chapter 5
Our Notice Brings a Visitor

I was quite weak after our morning's work and lay down to rest, but my mind was racing. Holmes had gone out and I was alone with my thoughts.

The more that I thought about it the more that my friend's theories seemed to be guess-work. I remembered how he had smelled the man's lips and no doubt he had detected something that had caused the idea. But if Holmes was wrong, then what else could have caused the man's death? There were no marks on the body nor signs of a struggle, except the pool of blood on the floor. Here was no weapon to be found that might have been used to cause a wound. I could find no answer to these problems, but Holmes's quiet, confident manner made me think he had already formed a theory which explained all the facts.

Holmes returned quite late.

"Have you seen the evening paper?" he asked cheerfully, "It gives a good account of the crime but does not mention the woman's wedding ring that fell when the body was lifted. It is just as well that it does not."

"Why?"

"Look at this notice," he answered. "I had one sent to every paper this morning."

He threw me the paper, and I glanced at the place indicated. It was the first notice in the "Found" column. "In Brixton Road this morning," it said, "a plain gold wedding ring, found in the roadway between the White Hart Hotel and Holland Grove. Apply Dr. Watson, 221B, Baker Street, between eight and nine this evening."

"Excuse my using your name, but I feared that someone would recognize mine."

"That is all right," I answered. "But if someone does apply I have no ring."

"Oh yes you do," he said, handing me one. "This will do very well. It is almost the same."

"And who do you expect will answer this?"

"Why, the man in the brown coat. If he does not come himself, he will send one of his friends."

"Do you not think that he would consider it too dangerous?"

"Not if my view of the case is correct. I believe he would risk everything to get the ring back. I think he dropped it when he leaned over the body. After leaving the house he discovered his loss and hurried back, but found the police there. He had to pretend to be drunk to get away again. When he has time to think about it he will hope that he lost the ring in the road after leaving the house. If so he would look in the evening papers to see if some honest soul had found it. He will be overjoyed when he sees this notice. Why should he fear a trap? There would be no reason in his mind why the finding of the ring should be connected to the murder. He will come. You will see him within the hour."

"And then?"

"You can leave him to me. Do you have a gun?"

"I have my old army hand-gun."

"You had better clean it and load it. He will be a desperate man, and though I shall take him unawares, it is best to be ready for anything."

I went to my room and prepared my gun, and when I returned Holmes was playing his violin.

"I have just received an answer to my American telegram. I am pleased to say that my view of the case is the correct one."

"And that is—?" I asked quickly.

"My violin would be better for new strings," he remarked. "Put your gun in your pocket. When the man comes, speak to him in an ordinary way. Leave the rest to me. Don't frighten him by looking too hard at him. It's eight o'clock now and he will probably be here in a few minutes. Open the door slightly and put the key on the inside."

As I did so there was a sharp ring at the bell. We heard the servant pass along the hall and the front door opening.

"Does Dr. Watson live here?" asked a clear but rather rough voice.

We heard the door close. Someone began to climb the

stairs with a slow uncertain step. A look of surprise came over Sherlock Holmes's face as he heard it. The footsteps slowly approached the door and we heard a weak knock.

"Come in," I cried.

Instead of the man of violence we were expecting, an old woman walked slowly into the room. I looked at Holmes and could see that he was most upset.

The old woman pulled out a newspaper and pointed at our notice. "It's this that has brought me, a gold wedding ring in the Brixton Road. It belongs to my girl, Sally. She's only been married a year, her husband is a steward on a boat, and what he'd say if he came home and found her without her ring don't bear thinking about. He's bad enough when he's in a good mood."

"Is that her ring?" I asked.

"Thank God!" cried the old woman. "Sally will be a happy woman tonight!"

"And what may your address be?" I asked, taking up a pencil.

"13, Duncan Street, Houndsditch. A long way from here."

"How did she happen to lose her ring in Brixton then," asked Holmes leaning forward.

The old woman turned and looked at Holmes. "The gentleman asked me for *my* address," she said. "Sally lives in Peckham near Brixton."

"And your name is—?"

"Mine is Sawyer, hers is Dennis, married to Tom Dennis and he's a good man if he hasn't had a drink, and he's well thought of at work—"

"Here's your ring, Mrs. Sawyer," I interrupted at a sign from Holmes. "It clearly belongs to your daughter and I am pleased to be able to give it back to the rightful owner."

She thanked me over and over again as she made her departure. When she had left the room Holmes sprang to his feet and rushed to his room. He returned in a few seconds wearing his hat and coat. "I'll follow her," he said. "She must be helping him and will lead me back to him. Wait up for me."

We heard the door close behind the old woman and immediately Holmes was after her. "Either his whole theory is incorrect," I thought to myself, "or else he will be led now to the heart of the mystery."

It was nine when Holmes set out and close to midnight when he returned. One look at his face told me he had not been successful although he burst into a loud laugh shortly after entering the room.

"I wouldn't want the police to know about this, not after all the fun I have had at their expense. I can afford to laugh because I know that I will get my man in the end."

"What happened then?" I asked.

"Well, I'll tell you even if it makes me look like a fool. I followed the old woman a little way when she pulled up as though she had hurt herself. She quickly stopped a cab. I was close enough to hear the address, 13, Duncan Street, Houndsditch. I watched her climb in then jumped up behind without being seen. The driver drove fast and we did not stop until we reached the street in question. I jumped down before we came to the door. I saw the cab pull up a little further on and the driver get down and open the door. No one came out. When I reached it the driver was inside searching high and low and calling the old woman all the names he could think of. We inquired at Number 13 and found that they had never heard of a Sawyer or a Dennis at that address."

"You don't mean to say," I cried in amazement, "that a weak, old woman was able to get out of a moving cab without either you or the driver seeing her?"

"Old woman! We were old women to be so taken in. It must have been a young man, and an active one at that. He saw that he was followed and used the cab trick to lose me. It shows that the man we are after has friends who are quite prepared to endanger themselves for him. Now, Doctor, there is nothing more we can do tonight. You are looking worn out. Take my advice and get some sleep."

Holmes was right. It had been a long, tiring day for me. I left Holmes in the sitting-room playing his violin, clearly deep in thought about the strange problem which he had decided he must solve.

06

Chapter 6
Tobias Gregson Shows What He Can Do

The papers were full of the "Brixton Mystery" as they called it. I read them together with Holmes and found they had uncovered some information unknown to me. Here is what one said:

"The dead man had stayed at the boarding-house of Madame Charpentier, in Torquay Terrace, Camberwell. He had a companion on his travels, a Mr. Joseph Stangerson, his private secretary. The two left their landlady on Tuesday the 4th for Euston Station, intending to get the Liverpool train. They were seen together at the station. Nothing more is known of them until Mr. Drebber's body was discovered in an empty house in Brixton Road, many miles from Euston. How he came there, or how he met his death, are questions still surrounded in mystery. We are glad to hear that the famous detectives from Scotland Yard, Mr. Lestrade and Mr. Gregson, are both working on the case."

Holmes was smiling when he finished reading.

"I told you that Lestrade and Gregson would look good no

matter what happened."

"Surely that depends on how it turns out."

"That doesn't matter in the least. If the man is caught, it is *because* of their work; if he is not, it is *in spite* of their work!"

As he spoke I heard a terrible row from downstairs and the sound of small feet on the stairs.

"It's my own team of detectives," said my companion; as he spoke, half a dozen dirty street children rushed in.

"Line up!" cried Holmes, in a sharp tone and they immediately obeyed. "In future you shall send up Wiggins alone to report, and the rest of you must wait in the street. Have you found it, Wiggins?"

"No sir!"

"You must keep on until you do. Here are your wages," and he gave each of them a coin. "Now off you go and come back with a better report next time."

They ran off and a few moments later I heard their voices in the street below.

"There's more work to be gotten out of one of those street kids than out of a dozen policemen. The mere sight of a man in uniform closes men's lips, but those youngsters go everywhere and see and hear everything," said Holmes.

"Are they working on the Brixton case?" I asked.

"Yes. There is one thing I would like them to find out. It is merely a matter of time. Look!" cried Holmes as he was looking out of the window. "Here comes Gregson and by the look of him, he thinks he has got some good news."

A few moments later Gregson burst into our room.

"My dear fellow," he cried, shaking Holmes by the hand, "I've done it. I've made the whole thing as clear as day."

At this Holmes appeared to look slightly worried.

"Well?" he asked.

"We have the man in question under lock and key."

"And his name is?"

"Arthur Charpentier, a ship's officer," cried Gregson, looking very pleased with himself.

Holmes breathed a sigh of relief and relaxed into a smile.

"Take a seat and try one of these cigars," he said. "We are anxious to know how you managed it. Will you have a drink?"

"I deserve one," the detective answered. "It's been hard work these past two days. Not physically but mentally. You will understand that, Mr. Holmes, for we are both brain workers."

"You do me too much honor," said Holmes humbly. "Tell us how you arrived at this most interesting result."

The detective made himself comfortable, then suddenly burst out laughing.

"The fun of it is," he cried, "that the fool Lestrade, who thinks himself so clever, has gone off on the wrong track altogether. He is after the secretary, Stangerson, who had as much to do with the crime as you or I. No doubt he has caught him by now."

The idea was so funny to Gregson that he laughed until I

thought he would do himself an injury. Finally Holmes asked, "And how did you get your clue?"

"I'll tell you all about it. Of course, Dr. Watson, this is in confidence. Well, the first problem was to uncover this American's background. Do you remember a hat next to the body?"

"Yes," said Holmes; "by John Underwood and Sons, 129 Camberwell Road."

Gregson was taken aback.

"I had no idea that you had noticed that," he said. "Have you been there?"

"No."

"Ah!" cried Gregson, brightening up at once, "you should follow every chance, Mr. Holmes, however small it may seem. I went to Underwood and asked him if he could recall who had bought that hat. He looked up his records and found it straight away. He had sent the hat to a Mr. Drebber, staying at Charpentier's Boarding House, Torquay Terrace, Camberwell. Thus, I had his address."

"Smart, very smart!" said Holmes quietly.

"I next called upon Madame Charpentier," continued the detective. "When I was shown to her room, she was with her daughter and both of them looked very upset. They were nervous and I began to think that I might be on the right track. I asked them if they had heard about the mysterious death of Mr. Drebber who had boarded with them. The mother nodded and the daughter burst into tears. I knew then that I was on to something.

"'At what time did Mr. Drebber leave your house for the train?' I asked.

"'At eight o'clock,' she replied. Her voice was little more than a whisper. 'His secretary Mr. Stangerson said that there were two trains, one at 9:15 and one at 11:00. He was to catch the first.'

"'And was that the last you saw of him?'

"An awful change came over her face as I asked that question. She went bright red and seemed unable to breathe. It was some seconds before she said the single word 'Yes.'

"There was silence for a moment and then the daughter spoke in a calm, clear voice.

"'No good can come from telling lies. We must tell the truth to this gentleman. We *did* see Mr. Drebber again.'

"'May God forgive you,' cried Madame Charpentier. 'You have done for your own brother.'

"'Arthur would rather that we spoke the truth,' the girl answered firmly.

"'Now that you have started,' I said, 'you'd best continue.'

"'I will tell you all, sir,' said the mother. 'Do not think that I avoided telling you because I feared my son was guilty, it is just that the circumstances do not look good for him. Despite his good character and his good job, he will appear guilty in some people's eyes.

"'Mr. Drebber has been with us nearly three weeks. He and his secretary, Mr. Stangerson, had been traveling abroad, and they arrived here from Copenhagen. Stangerson was a quiet man, but his employer, I am sorry to say, was not a gentleman at all. He was rude in his ways and his habits. The night he arrived he became the worse for drink, and most days he was in the same condition by the afternoon. His manners towards the maids was far too familiar, and worst of all, he soon came to treat my daughter the same way. He even threw his arms around her once and had to be held back by his own secretary.'

"'But why did you put up with this?' I asked.

"'I wish I had given him notice to leave on that first day. But he paid well, for both of them, and I needed the money. I thought that once he had gone everything would get back to normal. However, after the upset with my daughter I'd had enough and gave him notice. That was why he left.'

"'Well, why did he return?'

"'When I closed the door behind them I felt a great sense of relief. My son was due back on leave. I knew that he would not have stood by and let that man treat us so. As Arthur is a man of action I feared that there might be a scene. I was pleased that we had been spared that.

"'But in less than an hour Mr. Drebber had returned. He had missed the train and had been drinking heavily. He forced his way into the room where I was sitting with Alice, and in front of me, proposed that she should run away with him. Alice backed away from him but he caught her by the arm and tried to drag her with him towards the door. I screamed, and at that moment my son Arthur came into the room. What happened next I do not know for I was too afraid to look. I heard the sounds of a struggle. When I did look up I saw Arthur standing in the doorway laughing, with a stick in his hand. "I don't think that fine fellow will trouble us again," he said, "but I will just go after him to see where he is heading." With those words he went out. The next morning we heard of Mr. Drebber's death.'

"That's her story—I made shorthand notes to make sure I missed nothing."

"It's all very exciting," said Holmes sleepily. "What happened next?"

"Well, I saw that the whole case rested on one point. I asked her what time her son had returned.

"'I do not know,' she answered.

"'You don't know?' I asked again.

"'No. He has a key and he let himself in.'

"'After you went to bed?'

"'Yes.'

"'When did you go to bed?'

"'About eleven.'

"'So your son was gone at least two hours?'

"'Yes.'

"'Possibly four or five?'

"'Yes.'

"'What was he doing in that time?'

"She was silent for a moment and she had turned very pale.

"'I do not know,' she finally whispered.

"Of course there was little more to be done. I found out

where Arthur Charpentier was, took two officers with me and arrested him. When we caught him he said straight away, 'I suppose you are arresting me for the murder of that no-good Drebber.' We had said nothing about it, so his mentioning it seemed to be another thing pointing to his guilt."

"Oh, of course," said Holmes.

"He still had with him the stick that his mother had spoken about."

"You have a theory, then?"

"Yes. I think he followed Drebber to the Brixton Road where a fresh argument broke out. In the course of this Drebber received a blow to the stomach from the stick which killed him without leaving a mark. As no one was about, Charpentier dragged the body into the empty house. As to the candle, and the blood and the writing on the wall, these were all tricks to put the police on the wrong track."

"Well done!" said Holmes. "Gregson, you are getting there! We shall make something of you yet."

"I am rather pleased with myself," the detective answered with some pride. "Charpentier gave us a statement in which he said that he followed Drebber out of the house, then Drebber saw him and took a cab in order to get away. On his way home he met an old shipmate and took a long walk with him. He does not know where that shipmate lives. I don't believe his story and neither, I think, will a judge. What I find most funny about the whole thing is that Lestrade has followed completely the wrong track. Why! Here is the fellow himself."

It was indeed Lestrade, who had climbed the stairs as we talked. He did not look at all comfortable. He was clearly disturbed about something and the presence of Gregson seemed to upset him even more. Finally, he spoke. "This case is beyond understanding, it really is."

"Do you think so, Mr. Lestrade?" asked Gregson happily. "I thought you might. Have you managed to find the secretary, Stangerson?"

"The secretary, Mr. Joseph Stangerson," said Lestrade, "was murdered at Halliday's Private Hotel about six o'clock this morning."

07

Chapter 7
Light in the Darkness

This news was so unexpected that all three of us were taken aback. I stared at Holmes, whose lips were tight and his face lined with the effort of thinking.

"Stangerson too!" he said quietly. "The story moves on."

"Are you sure of this?" asked Gregson.

"I discovered the body."

"We have been hearing Gregson's view of the matter," said Holmes. "Perhaps you could tell us what you have seen and done."

"By all means," said Lestrade. "I admit that I thought Stangerson played some part in the death of Drebber. I now see that I was completely mistaken. Drebber and Stangerson had been seen together at Euston Station about half-past eight on the evening of the third. At two in the morning Drebber had been found in the Brixton Road. I needed to know what Stangerson had been doing between these two times and what had become of him afterwards.

"I sent a telegram to Liverpool asking the police to watch for a man of Stangerson's description coming from London and possibly heading for America. I then investigated all the hotels and boarding houses in the Euston area, in case Stangerson was unable to get the train that night. Finally, at eight o'clock this morning I tracked him down to Halliday's Private Hotel. The manager told me that he had been waiting for someone for two days.

"'Where is he now?' I asked.

"'He is upstairs in bed. He wished to be called at nine.'

"I went up to see him straight away, as I hoped that my sudden appearance might cause him to say something unguarded. When I got to his room I saw something that made me feel sick to my stomach. From behind the door came a ribbon of blood which formed a pool in the middle of the hall. I forced the door, which was locked on the inside. The window of the room was open and beside the window lay the body of a man in his night clothes. He had been dead for some time as his limbs were stiff and cold. I called the manager and he recognized him as Joseph Stangerson. The cause of death was a deep knife-wound to the heart. And now here is the strange part; what do you think was on the wall?"

"The word RACHE, written in blood," Holmes answered.

"That was it," said Lestrade, looking at Holmes in some surprise. Then he continued. "A man was seen. A milk boy passing the back of the hotel noticed a ladder up against one of the windows on the second floor. He saw a man coming out and down the ladder. The man was so open about it that the boy thought that he must be a workman at the hotel. He thinks that the man was tall, had a reddish face, and was wearing a long brown coat. He must have stayed in the room for a while after the murder, for we found bloodstains in the sink where he washed the weapon."

I looked across at Holmes when I heard the description of the murderer which so exactly matched his own. He did not look at all pleased though.

"Did you find anything in the room which might give a clue to the murderer?" he asked.

"Nothing. Stangerson had Drebber's purse in his pocket, but as he did all the paying this is not unusual. There was a lot of money in it, so whatever the reasons for these crimes, stealing is not one of them. There were no papers on the man except an unsigned telegram from America sent the month before which simply said, 'J.H. is in Europe.'

"And there was nothing else?" asked Holmes anxiously.

"Nothing of importance. A book and a pipe on the table by the bed, and a small box containing a couple of pills."

Sherlock Holmes jumped from his chair. "That's it," he cried, "my case is complete."

The two detectives looked at him as if he were crazy.

"I now know all the details that have caused you so many problems. There are of course some fine points to be filled in, but I am now certain of all the main facts, from the time that Drebber parted from Stangerson at the station up to the discovery of Stangerson's body. It's as if I had seen them with my own eyes. I will give you proof of my knowledge. Do you have those pills?"

"Yes, I do," said Lestrade, "but I must say I do not attach any importance to them whatsoever."

"We shall see," said Holmes as he took them from Lestrade. "Now, Doctor," he continued, turning to me, "are those ordinary pills?"

They certainly were not. I did not recognize them. "From their appearance," I said, "I would imagine that they are to be mixed with water."

"Exactly," said Holmes. "Now would you be kind enough to go down and get that old dog that the landlady wanted to put out of its pain yesterday?"

I went downstairs and carried up the poor thing. It was clearly in some discomfort and it would be a mercy to end its life quickly. I placed it on the floor. Holmes then cut one of the pills in two and mixed one half with some milk which he placed in front of the dog and he returned the other half to the box.

"Now watch, gentlemen. You will see that the dog drinks it quickly enough."

The dog finished the milk and we continued to watch for some minutes but could see no change in the creature's appearance. Holmes looked puzzled. Suddenly, he jumped up and cried, "I must be right, and if I am there is only one answer." He rushed to the box and took the remaining tablet, cut it in half and again offered it to the dog mixed with milk. This time the dog seemed hardly to have tasted it before it gave a violent shake and lay still on the floor.

Holmes was delighted, "I knew it," he cried. "All my reasoning told me this must be the answer." He looked around at us. "All this seems strange to you," he continued, "because you missed the only important clue at the beginning. I was lucky enough to recognize it and since then every turn that has puzzled you has served to strengthen my theories."

Gregson could contain himself no longer. "Look here, Mr. Sherlock Holmes," he said, "we all know that you are a clever man with your own way of working. But we must have something more definite than just your theories. We must catch the man. I know now that I was wrong. Young Charpentier could not have been involved in this second affair. Clearly, the late Mr. Stangerson was not the criminal either. You seem to know more than Lestrade or I, but the time has now come for you to name the man who did it, if you know his name."

Lestrade nodded his agreement and I said that I felt they were right, for any delay now might enable the murderer to commit further crimes.

With the three of us pressing him Holmes looked unsure of himself. He walked up and down the room then said, "There will be no more murders, so you need not worry on that account. You have asked me if I know the name of the murderer. I do. More importantly, I expect to lay my hands on him very shortly. But he is a desperate and clever man and to catch him we need to fool him into thinking he is safe. If he gets any idea that we are onto him, he would change his name and disappear in the city. You have my word that as soon as I can let you have more details without endangering my plan, I will."

Gregson and Lestrade seemed most unhappy with this but before they could speak there was a knock at the door. It was young Wiggins.

"Please, sir," he said, "I have the cab downstairs."

"Good boy," said Holmes and immediately went to his desk from which he took a pair of handcuffs. "The cabman may as well help me with my boxes. Just ask him to step up, Wiggins."

I was surprised to learn that my friend was about to make a journey. Holmes picked up a bag and was trying to get it shut properly when the cabman came in.

"Just give me some help with this bag, cabman," he said, without lifting his head.

The fellow came forward and put out his arms to help. At that moment Holmes jumped up and fastened the handcuffs on him before he could move.

"Gentlemen," cried Holmes, with his eyes bright with excitement, "let me introduce to you Mr. Jefferson Hope, the murderer of Enoch Drebber and Joseph Stangerson."

The whole thing had happened so quickly that I had no time to take it in. I can still picture the scene, though. Holmes's expression was one of victory, the cabman's one of puzzlement, anger and disbelief. He looked at the handcuffs, which had

appeared as if by magic, at the end of his arms. For a moment none of us moved. Then with an angry roar the prisoner reacted. Pulling himself free of Holmes he threw himself at the window. Before he got through however, Holmes, Lestrade and Gregson reached him and pulled him back into the room. There then followed a mighty struggle. So strong and powerful was the man that even in handcuffs it took the four of us to finally contain him. Only when we tied his feet did we feel confident that we had him.

"Now, gentlemen," said Holmes, "we have reached the end of this little mystery. You are very welcome to ask me any questions that you like and, of course, I will answer them in full."

PART 2

The Country of the Saints

08

Chapter 1
On the Great Salt Plain

In the center of the North American Continent is a wild land of deserts and rocks. Nothing grows there, apart from a few bushes. Many people have crossed this plain heading West, and from above one would see a trail crossing this desert. Here and there one would see white objects along this trail. A closer examination would reveal that these white objects were bones— the bones of men and beasts that have failed in their attempt to cross the fifteen hundred miles that this lifeless plain stretches.

Looking down on this scene, on the 4th of May, 1847, was a man. He had a thin face and clothes that hung off his bony body. The man was dying from hunger and thirst. He had climbed this hill above the trail in the hope that he might see some water. When he saw the lifeless plain stretching out all around him he realized the truth. It was here that he was going to die. He put his rifle down, and placed next to it the large object he was carrying in a blanket. The movement caused a cry to come from the blanket and soon a little frightened face with bright brown eyes appeared.

"What's happening?" asked a childish voice, "Where's my mother?"

"Mother's gone," answered the man unwrapping the blanket to reveal a little girl of about five years old.

Although the child was dirty, she was well-dressed and her strong body showed that she had suffered less than her companion.

"It's funny that she didn't say good-bye," said the little girl. "Say, it's awful dry. Isn't there any water or something to eat?"

"No, there isn't anything dearie. You just need to wait for a while, then everything will be all right." He looked down at her trusting face and shook his head, "I guess I'd better tell you things straight," he continued. "You remember when we left the last river?"

"Oh, yes."

"Well, we thought we'd find another river soon. But something went wrong, the maps or something. The river didn't turn up and the water ran out. Then—then well, we kept a little for you but the others—. Mr. Bender was the first to go, then Pete, then Mrs. McGregor and Johnny, and then, dearie, your mother."

"Then mother's dead, too," cried the little girl burying her face in her hands.

"Yes, they've all gone except you and me. I thought there might be some water over here so I carried you up this hill. But there's nothing. We haven't got much of a chance now, dearie."

"Do you mean we're going to die, too?" asked the child, lifting her tear-stained face.

"I guess we are."

"Why didn't you say so before?" she said breaking into a happy laugh. "You gave me such a fright, but now I know I'll be with my mother again soon, so I'm not at all worried. How long have we got to wait before we get to heaven and see mother?"

"I don't know—not so very long. Let's try and rest now." The child got close to him and soon her regular breathing told him that she was asleep. He tried to keep awake but his head nodded and his eyes slowly closed until he too was asleep.

If the traveler had been able to stay awake another half an hour a strange sight would have met his eyes. Far away on the extreme edge of the salt plain there rose up a little cloud of dust. It approached the hill where the man and girl lay. It was the dust caused by a great number of moving creatures. As it reached the hill a great many wagons and figures of armed horsemen could be seen. The front of this group were at the hill but the rest stretched out behind as far as the eye could see. At the head of the party rode a number of serious men all armed with guns. They stopped at the hill as they discussed their next move. As they were about to move off one of the sharper-eyed among them uttered a cry and pointed up the hill. A little piece of pink cloth blew in the wind behind a rock. The men took up their guns fearing that this might mean trouble. "Whatever or whoever it is, I don't think there will be many of them out here," said one, who looked as though he were a leader.

"Shall I go forward and see, Brother Stangerson?" asked one of the band.

"And I," cried a dozen other voices.

"Leave your horses here and we will wait for you," replied the leader.

The younger men went up the hill quickly but carefully. When they reached the rock they saw the thin, half-starved man and next to him the healthy looking young child. The noise of the young men woke the sleeping pair and the man got unsteadily to his feet. When he had fallen asleep the plain below him had been empty. Now it was covered with people and wagons. He thought he was dreaming.

The rescuing party quickly convinced him that they were real, and helped the pair back down to the wagons.

"My name is John Ferrier," the wanderer explained; "Me and that little one are all that's left of a party of twenty-one people. The others died of thirst and hunger down in the south."

"Is she your child?"

"I guess she is now," cried Ferrier. "She's mine because I saved her. No man will take her from me. She's Lucy Ferrier from now on. Who are you people anyway? There seems to be a mighty number of you out here in this desert."

"There are nearly ten thousand of us. We come from Nauvoo

in Illinois where we founded our church. We have been driven out of there by non-believers."

The name Nauvoo was familiar to John Ferrier. "I see," he said, "you are the Mormons."

"We are the Mormons," answered his companions with one voice.

"And where are you going?"

"We do not know. The hand of God is leading us in the person of our prophet. We will take you to him. He will say what is to be done with you."

They reached the foot of the hill and pushed through the crowd that had gathered until they reached the largest wagon. It was pulled by six horses whereas the rest were pulled by two or four. Beside the driver sat a man of about thirty years of age, far younger than many of the others, yet he was clearly the leader. He listened carefully as one of them told him of the rescue. Then he turned to the two weary travelers.

"If we take you with us," he said, "it can only be as believers in our religion. We cannot have non-believers who might turn others against us. It would be better for you to stay here than to be the one bad fruit which destroys the harvest. Will you come with us under those terms?"

"Guess I'll come with you on any terms," replied Ferrier.

"Take him, Brother Stangerson," he said, "give him food and drink, and the child likewise. Let it be your task to teach him our beliefs. We must now move on. We have delayed long enough."

The Mormon who had been made responsible for the two took them to his wagon where a meal was already awaiting them.

"You can remain here until you have recovered. Meanwhile remember that now and forever you are of our religion. Brigham Young has said it, and he speaks with the voice of Joseph Smith our founder, which is the voice of God."

09

Chapter 2
The Flower of Utah

The Mormons suffered many hardships in their journey across the desert. Although they were brave and hardy, there was not one among them who was not thankful when they caught sight of the broad valley of Utah and learned from their leader, Brigham Young, that this untouched land was to be theirs.

Young quickly proved to be a good administrator as well as a strong leader. Maps were drawn and the land divided into farms and given out in proportion to the importance of each individual. A town was built with streets and squares and the land all around was farmed so quickly that by the next summer there was golden wheat in every field. Above everything towered the great temple that was built in the center of the city.

John Ferrier and his adopted daughter, Lucy, accompanied the Mormons to the end of the journey. Lucy spent most of her time in the wagon which she shared with Stangerson's three wives and his son, who was a few years older than her. As they traveled, John Ferrier made himself useful as a guide and hunter. So quickly did he win the respect of his new companions, that when they reached the end of their wanderings he was given a piece of land the equal of anyone except Young himself, Stangerson, Kemball, Johnston, and Drebber, who were the four elders of the church.

Over the years Ferrier worked hard. He built a good size house and his farm did well. After ten years he was one of the richest and best known men in Utah.

The one way that Ferrier upset his Mormon companions was in his attitude to setting up a family. No amount of persuasion could make him take a wife even though most Mormon men had several wives. Some felt that he was not a true believer and others that he was too mean to go to the expense of setting up a large household. Whatever the reason, Ferrier did not marry but in all other ways took part in the Mormon way of life.

Lucy grew into a beautiful young woman and with her good looks and her father's wealth soon began to attract attention. Neither father nor daughter really noticed the change in Lucy, but others did.

She was riding her horse into town one fine June day. The roads into and out of the city were full of travelers heading West as there was talk of gold in the mountains out there. When Lucy reached the edge of town she found her way blocked by a herd of cattle. She tried to force her way through by pushing her horse into a gap but the

beasts closed in around her and there was no way out. Soon she was in serious trouble. It was all she could do to hang on. The heat and the dust were starting to weaken her when she heard a kind voice at her shoulder. One of the cattlemen had reached her. He caught hold of the horse and led her to safety.

"You're not hurt, I hope, miss," said her rescuer, respectfully.

She looked up into his handsome face and laughed, "No, I'm safe now," she said. "I never would have thought that my horse would get so frightened."

"Thank God you kept your seat," said the man. "You are the daughter of John Ferrier, aren't you?" he continued. "When you see him ask him if he remembers the Jefferson Hopes of St. Louis. He and my father were pretty good friends."

"Why don't you come and ask for yourself?" replied Lucy.

The young man seemed pleased at the suggestion. "I'd like to but I've been in the mountains for two months and I'm not really fit to visit folk."

"He won't mind. After what you've just done he's got a good deal to thank you for, and so have I," she answered. "I must push on now as I have to attend to some business for my father. See you again. Good-bye!" She turned her horse and rode off in a cloud of dust.

Young Jefferson Hope rode on with his companions quietly and thoughtfully. They had been in the mountains looking for silver and were returning to Salt Lake City, the biggest town in Utah. If they could raise some money, they would go back to the mountains and mine for the silver they had found. He had thought this a good idea until the moment he had rescued Lucy Ferrier. Now he could not stop thinking about her. He was in love. He was a strong-willed man and was used to succeeding in whatever he attempted. He decided he wanted to marry Lucy Ferrier and swore that, if it was humanly possible, he would do it.

He called on John Ferrier that night and many other nights until he became a familiar face at the farm house. He told Ferrier, who had not left his farm for twelve years, news of the outside world. Lucy listened eagerly to all he had to say. He had traveled widely in America and told of many exciting adventures. He soon became a favorite with the old farmer who often praised his honesty and bravery. At such times Lucy felt a warmth inside and she realized that she was in love.

One summer evening he came riding up to the house. Lucy went out to greet him but he did not come in.

"I am going, Lucy," he said taking her two hands in his. "I won't ask you to come with me now, but when I return will you be ready to leave with me?"

"And when will that be?" she asked.

"A couple of months at the most. I will come for you then my darling. There's no one that can come between us now."

"And how about father?" she asked.

"He's given his consent, provided we get these mines working all right. I have no fear on that point."

"Oh well! If you and father have arranged it, there is nothing else to be said," she whispered as he held her close.

"Thank God!" he cried. "It is settled. The longer I stay the harder it will be to leave. My companions are waiting for me. Good-bye, my darling—good-bye. In two months you shall see me."

He rode off at a fast pace, never once looking round. Lucy watched him until he was out of sight then walked back to the house the happiest girl in Utah.

10

Chapter 3
John Ferrier Talks with the Prophet

Three weeks had passed since Jefferson Hope and his companions had left Salt Lake City. John Ferrier knew he would lose Lucy when the young man returned, but her happy face told him that it was for the best. Moreover, he had decided long ago that she would not marry a Mormon. Such a marriage he regarded as no marriage at all. No matter what else he felt about the Mormon beliefs, on that point he was fixed. He told no one of this, for he knew that it was a dangerous matter to question the beliefs of the church, or the decisions of the elders.

Utah was run by the Mormons. Almost the entire population was Mormon and the leaders of the church had total power. These men safeguarded their power very carefully. People who questioned the faith or the decisions of the prophet would suddenly disappear. Whoever carried out these actions seemed to be all-seeing and all-powerful. But they, themselves, were never seen or heard. Few people would tell anyone of their doubts as they were fearful that whoever they told might report them.

At first this power was used only against people who, having taken the Mormon faith, now wished to give it up or change it. Soon, however, it took a wider range. Camps of travelers were found with all the men murdered and the women gone. Stories were told that they had been taken by the Mormons who needed more women as wives. These stories were told and retold until many people knew of the dangers of traveling in Mormon country.

The secret organization was given a name—The Avenging Angels. No one knew who belonged to this secret society, so no one trusted anyone. People were afraid to say anything which might be taken the wrong way.

One morning John Ferrier was about to set out to his fields when he heard his gate shutting. He looked through his window and saw a short, well-built, middle-aged man coming up the path. Ferrier was worried, for this was none other than Brigham Young himself, the prophet of the Mormons. He ran to the door to greet Young and became more anxious when he saw the cold, unsmiling face of his leader. Young entered the sitting-room and took a seat.

"Brother Ferrier," he said, "the true believers have been good friends to you. We saved you when you were starving in the desert, and we shared our food with you. We led you to the Chosen Valley and gave you good land. You have become rich under our protection. Is this not so?"

"It is so," answered John Ferrier.

"In return for all this we asked but one condition: that you should take our faith, the true faith, and follow in every way our beliefs. This you promised to do, and this, if common report is true, you have not done."

"What have I not done?" asked Ferrier. "Have I not given to the common fund? Have I not attended the Temple? Have I not—"

"Where are your wives?" asked Young. "Call them in, so that I might greet them."

"It is true that I have not married," answered Ferrier, "but women were few, and there were many who needed a wife more than I. I am not a lonely man. I have my daughter to look after me."

"It is of your daughter that I want to speak," said the leader of the Mormons. "She has become the flower of Utah, and has found favor with many who are high in the land.

"There are stories, which I would prefer not to believe, that say she is promised to a non-believer. The thirteenth rule in the laws of the holy Joseph Smith states, 'Let every woman of the true faith marry one of the chosen, for if she marries a non-believer she commits a sin.' This being so, it is impossible that you, who say you follow our beliefs, should make your daughter break them."

John Ferrier could not answer.

"Upon this one point shall your faith be tested," continued Young. "It has been decided by the Holy Council of Four. The girl is young so she will not marry an old man, nor would we give her no choice at all. Brother Stangerson has a son, as does

Brother Drebber. Both of them would welcome your daughter to his house. They are young and rich, and of the true faith. Let her choose between them. What do you say to that?"

Ferrier thought for a few minutes.

"You will give us time," he said at last. "My daughter is very young—she is not yet old enough to marry."

"She shall have a month to choose," said Young, rising from his seat, "at the end of that time she shall give us her answer."

As he went out the door he turned to Ferrier and said angrily, "Remember this, John Ferrier, it would have been better for you and she if you had died in that desert, than that you now stand against the might of the Holy Council of Four."

After Young had left, Ferrier just sat at his table with his head in his hands. He felt a touch on his shoulder. He turned and saw from his daughter's white face that she had heard everything.

"Oh father, father what shall we do?" she cried.

"Don't be afraid," he answered, "we'll work something out. I'll get a message to your young man. If I'm any judge, he'll be back here before we know it. He'll know what to do for the best."

"But we cannot go against Young. You hear such awful things that happen to the people who disagree with the Prophet," cried Lucy.

"But we haven't quarreled with him yet and we have a month before we need to. But I guess we'd better think about getting out of Utah."

"Leave Utah! What about the farm?"

"We'll sell what we can and leave the rest. I've been thinking about it for a while now. It doesn't suit me to be bowing down to any man the way these Mormons do to their Prophet. I'm a free-born American and it goes against my upbringing."

"But they won't let us leave," said Lucy.

"Wait till Jefferson comes. If anyone can get us out of this territory safely, it'll be him. In the meantime there's nothing to worry about so don't get yourself upset."

Although John Ferrier tried to sound confident he was extra careful about locking up that night, and he cleaned and loaded the old gun which he kept in his bedroom.

11

Chapter 4
A Flight for Life

The next morning John Ferrier went into Salt Lake City. He found an old friend who was going towards the mountains where Jefferson Hope was mining. His friend agreed to take a message to him.

On his return to the farm he was surprised to see two horses at the gate. He was even more surprised to find two young men in his sitting-room. One, with a long, pale face was sitting in a chair with his feet up on a table. The other, a thick-necked youth with a rough, red face was standing by the window. Both of them nodded to Ferrier as he entered the room and the one in the chair said,

"Perhaps you don't know us, this is the son of Elder Drebber and I'm Joseph Stangerson."

John Ferrier nodded coldly.

"We have come," continued Stangerson, "at the advice of our fathers to ask for the hand of your daughter for whichever of us may seem good to you and to her. As I only have four wives and Brother Drebber has seven, I would say that my case is the stronger."

"No, no, Brother Stangerson," cried the other, "the question is not how many wives we have, it's how many we can keep. I am richer than you."

"But my future looks better," argued Stangerson heatedly. "When the Lord takes my father I will be the richer then, and I am your elder and higher in the Church."

"It will be for the girl to decide," answered Drebber, "we will leave it all to her decision."

During all this John Ferrier had stood in the doorway, his anger rising.

"Look here," he said at last, "when my daughter asks to see you, you can come, but until then stay away from this house."

The two young Mormons stared at him in disbelief. They thought that Lucy and her father should be proud that both of them wanted her.

Ferrier walked over to them threateningly, "Now get out before I throw you out."

The two young men left quickly but when they were safely out of reach they turned.

"You'll pay for this!" Stangerson cried. "You have gone against the Prophet and the Council of Four."

"The Hand of the Lord shall be heavy on you," cried young Drebber.

Ferrier reached for his gun but Lucy, who had come in as they left, stopped him.

"The young devils," he cried, "how dare they use God's name against me. I would sooner see you in your grave, my girl, than see you marry either of them."

"And so should I, father," Lucy said quietly. "But Jefferson will be here soon."

"It's as well that he is, for we don't know what their next move will be, but you can be sure that they will not let this go."

The next morning Ferrier realized the danger he was in. He awoke to find a note pinned to the sheet above his chest. On it was printed:

"Twenty-nine days are you given to mend your ways and then—"

The unspoken threat was more worrying than any named danger. He realized that twenty-nine days were what was left of the month that Young had given him. What made his blood run cold however was the thought that these people were able to enter his house, and put this on his bed, without anyone hearing. If they had wanted to, they could have killed him as he slept.

He was even more shaken the next day. They were having breakfast at the table when Lucy cried out and pointed upwards. In the center of the ceiling was written the number 28. That night he sat up with his gun. He did not see or hear anything but the next morning found a great 27 had been painted on his door.

Each new day there was a reminder for him of the passing of his time. Sometimes the number appeared in the house, sometimes pinned to the gate. Try as he might, he could not catch them in the act. Slowly but surely his nerves began to wear, until he had but one hope left—the arrival of Jefferson Hope.

Twenty had changed to fifteen, and fifteen to ten, and still there was no sign. One by one the numbers went down. In the end, when four had given way to three, he lost heart. Single-handed and with little knowledge of the surrounding mountains, he could never escape. The main roads were guarded, and none could pass without an order from the Council. He knew it was hopeless but still he would not allow his daughter to wed a Mormon.

The next day he was still desperately trying to think of a way to escape, when he heard a noise at the door. Rushing to it, he threw it open hoping to catch the men who left the numbers. There was no one there. Just as he turned to go back in he saw a movement at his feet. A man lay there face down and without getting up he went past Ferrier into the cabin. It was Jefferson Hope.

"Give me food and water," he cried. "I have had nothing to eat for two days.

"How is Lucy?" he said as soon as he recovered his strength.

"She is bearing up well, but she does not fully know the danger we are in."

"Good," replied the young hunter. "The house is watched, that is why I came in that way. They may be sharp but they're not sharp enough to catch Jefferson Hope."

"Tomorrow is our last day, what are we to do?" asked the old man.

"Unless we move tonight we are lost. I have three horses hidden a couple of miles from here. We must get to them. How much money do you have?"

"Two thousand dollars in gold, and five in cash."

"That will do. We'll head for Carson City through the mountains. Wake Lucy and I'll get ready."

In the time it took for Ferrier to get Lucy, Jefferson Hope had packed all the food he could carry and filled a container with water. The lovers greeted each other warmly.

"We must start at once," said Jefferson Hope. "The front and back are watched, but if we take care we can get out the side window and across the fields."

John Ferrier took one last look around. He thought about all that he was leaving behind. His mind was set, however, and when he saw the determined look in Jefferson Hope's eyes and the happiness of his daughter, he knew he had made the right choice.

They silently opened the window and climbed out. Bending low they ran to the fence which they followed to a gap that led to the field. Just as they reached this point, the young man got hold of his two companions and threw them to the ground.

His hunter's ear had heard something which both Lucy

and her father had missed. Within a few seconds a man came through the gap to which they had been heading and was joined a moment later by another.

"It has been decided," said the first, "tomorrow at midnight."

"Good," said the second man. "Shall I tell Brother Drebber?"

"Yes, and tell him to tell the others. Nine to seven."

"Seven to five."

When they had exchanged these words they went off in different directions. As soon as their footsteps had died away Jefferson Hope leapt to his feet and pulled the other two up and through the gap.

"Hurry!" he whispered. "Everything depends on speed. We have passed the guards."

Once on the road they made fast progress. Just before the town, Jefferson Hope led them down a track which soon disappeared, but the young man pressed on without a doubt. Finally, in a well hidden spot, they came upon the three horses.

Hope led the way along a dangerous route with a mighty drop on one side of them and the mountain face on the other. Despite these dangers the travelers' spirits rose for each step they took brought them one step closer to safety.

They were not yet out of danger, though. At the most lonely part of the mountain pass, Lucy gave a worried cry as she pointed up. There stood a single guard holding a gun.

"Who goes there?" he cried.

"Travelers for Nevada," said Jefferson Hope.

"By whose permission?" he asked looking at them carefully.

"The Council of Four," replied Ferrier.

Thinking quickly, Jefferson Hope said, "Nine to seven."

When he heard the password the guard replied, "Seven to five," and allowed them to pass. Beyond him the path widened and they were able to move quickly. Looking back they could see the guard and realized they had passed the last post of the chosen people, and that freedom lay before them.

12

Chapter 5
The Avenging Angels

The three of them rode all night through the mountain passes trying to put as much distance between themselves and the Mormons as possible. As the sun came up they found themselves in a scene of breathtaking beauty. They were surrounded by snow-capped mountain peaks and as each one in turn caught the morning sun it took on a rosy color.

They rested briefly but when Lucy and her father wanted to stop again Hope urged them on.

"They'll be on our track by now. We must get to Carson City where we will be safe. You can rest all you want when we get there."

Through the whole of that day they struggled on. At night they stopped for some food and a rest. They got a few hours sleep but were up and on their way before daybreak. Jefferson Hope had seen no sign of anyone behind them. He began to hope that they had passed beyond the reach of the powerful organization which they had dared to oppose. He little knew how far that iron hand could reach, or how soon it would close upon them and crush them.

In the middle of the second day the food began to run out but Jefferson was not worried. He had hunted in these mountains many times and knew that he would find something sooner or later.

He picked a hidden spot and made camp. When Lucy and her father were comfortable he set off to hunt. It took him longer than he expected but just before nightfall he caught and killed a beast. He hurried back to the camp but took a couple of wrong turns which cost him more time. Finally, he recognized where he was and called out a greeting to his companions. There was no reply, just the sound of his own voice as it came back from the hills.

Fear swept over him. He started to run. When he turned the corner to where he had left his friends there was no sign of life. Ferrier, his daughter, the horses, all had disappeared. The campfire was almost out but he picked up some smoking wood and blew on it until it burned brightly. He looked around the camp and saw that the ground was all stamped down. It was clear that a large party of horsemen had caught up with the escapers. Their tracks showed that they had returned in the direction of Salt Lake City.

Turning the light around Jefferson Hope saw something he would never forget. On one side of the camp was a freshly dug grave. There was a stick in it with a piece of paper in the top. The writing on the paper was brief but to the point.

JOHN FERRIER
FORMERLY OF SALT LAKE CITY
Died August 4th, 1860

The proud old man he had left just a few hours ago was no more. Jefferson Hope looked wildly round for another grave but finding none he realized that Lucy had been taken back. She was to live out the future that John Ferrier had given his life trying to prevent.

For a moment Jefferson wished he was dead. But soon his active spirit stirred him. His face hardened as he thought of what the Avenging Angels had done. He could think of only one thing—revenge! Pausing only to cook some food, he set off on the tracks of the Avenging Angels back to Salt Lake City.

For five days he traveled, sleeping only when overcome by tiredness, and pressing on again after a few hours. On the sixth day he was into Mormon territory and could look down upon Salt Lake City. He saw that there were flags in the main streets and the signs of some celebration. He was still wondering what this might be when he heard the sounds of a rider approaching. He recognized the man as a Mormon named Cowper whom he had helped out on several occasions.

As Cowper approached he called out to him, "I am Jefferson Hope. Do you remember me?"

The Mormon clearly had not recognized the thin and dirty man that stood before him. When he realized who it was, he looked around himself nervously.

"You are mad to come here," he cried. "It is more than my life is worth to be seen talking to you. The Holy Four want to arrest you for helping the Ferriers to escape."

"Tell me what has happened to Lucy. You and I were friends once, so please tell me."

Cowper once again looked all around. With a worried look he answered, "She was married yesterday to young Drebber. What's up with you man? You look like you're about to pass out."

"Tell me more," said Hope in barely a whisper, as he leaned heavily on his gun.

"That's what the flags in the streets are for. There were some words between Stangerson and Drebber as to who should marry her—Stangerson felt that as he had killed the father he had the strongest claim. But the council decided that Drebber had the stronger claim. He won't have her very long though. The girl's dying. I could see it in her face. Are you off then? Where are you going?"

"Never mind," said Jefferson Hope who had risen from his seat and shouldered his gun. He headed off for the heart of the mountains to gather his thoughts.

Cowper's prediction came true only too quickly. Whether it was seeing her father's death or being forced into a hateful marriage, Lucy never recovered her spirit and was dead within a month. Her husband did not miss her. He had married her for her father's property and he did not even pretend he was upset when she died.

His other wives took care of the burial arrangements and stayed up the night before the funeral as is the Mormon way. They were grouped around the body in the early hours of the morning when the door flew open and a thin, wild-looking man burst in. He went straight to the body of Lucy Ferrier and taking her hand he pulled off the gold wedding ring.

"She shall not be buried in that," he cried then left the room as quickly as he had entered. He was gone before anyone had moved.

For some months after that, Jefferson Hope tried to get his revenge. After a couple of near misses, his targets, Stangerson and Drebber, became very careful about leaving the house at night, and were accompanied everywhere by guards. They also took armed men into the mountains to try and find him, but without success.

After a while, when no further attacks were made on them, they started to relax and hope that time had cooled their enemy's desire for revenge.

If anything, it had hardened his determination. But Jefferson Hope was a practical man. The only thing he now lived for was revenge but he knew that he would not live to see it if he continued to push his body to the limits in the mountains. He returned to Nevada to recover his health and get some money.

He thought he would be away just a year but several years

passed before he was ready to take on the Mormons again.

He changed his appearance and name and he returned to Salt Lake City. He found that the church had divided and many had left Utah. Among them were Drebber and Stangerson. Drebber had managed to sell most of his property before leaving, but Stangerson had left Utah with very little money. No one had any clues as to their whereabouts.

Many men would have given up there and then, but not Jefferson Hope. Over the next few years he traveled widely in the West looking for Stangerson and Drebber. His hair turned gray and the hard life told on his features. Finally, his patience was rewarded. In Cleveland, Ohio he recognized Stangerson and Drebber through a shop window. He returned to his room unable to really believe he had found them. But he too had been recognized, and before he could do anything, Drebber persuaded a local lawman that his and Stangerson's lives were in danger, and Jefferson Hope was arrested. When he was let go after a few days, he found that Drebber and Stangerson, who was then working as Drebber's secretary, had gone to Europe.

He had to start all over again, but he would not give up. He worked in whatever job he could find, saving his dollars until he had enough to follow them to Europe.

He missed them in Russia, France and Denmark, but in London he caught up with them. As to what happened there, we should tell his story as taken down by Dr. Watson.

13

Chapter 6
A Continuation of the Records of John Watson

Once he had stopped struggling the prisoner calmed down quickly. He looked at Holmes and shook his head.

"I can't believe that you have caught me. You must be the finest detective in England, if not the world. I've a good deal to say," he continued slowly, "and I want to tell you gentlemen about it. I might not last until my trial and I want to set the record straight. Is there a doctor among you?" he asked.

"Yes," I answered.

"Then put your hand here," he said pointing to his chest.

I did so; straight away I could feel an unnaturally strong, irregular beat.

"Why, you have a serious heart condition!" I cried.

"Yes," he replied calmly. "I went to the doctor last week and he told me that it was sure to burst in the next few days. I got the condition from the hard times I had in the Utah mountains. I've done my work now and I am prepared to go at any moment. I'd like to leave the true story behind me."

Gregson and Lestrade decided that under the circumstances they would take his statement there and then.

"I'll sit down if I may, gentlemen, as I feel tired after our struggle. I will die soon. Every word I speak will be the truth."

Gregson took the man's statement word for word and I reproduce it here:

"It doesn't matter to you why I hated those men, but take it from me, they were guilty of the death of two people — a father and daughter. No court on earth would have found them guilty, but I knew they were. I decided to take the law into my own hands. You'd have done the same in the circumstances.

"The girl that I have spoken of was to have married me twenty years ago. She was forced to marry Drebber, and broke her heart over it. I took the wedding ring from her dead finger and swore that his dying eyes should look upon it, and that his last thoughts should be of the crime for which he was punished. I have chased him and his companion Stangerson, who murdered her father, across America and over the seas to Europe. They thought they could outrun me but they couldn't.

"They were rich and I was poor, so it was not easy for me to follow them. When I got to London I had no money. I managed to get a job as a cabdriver and just about got by.

"It was some time before I found out where they were staying. Finally, I located them in Camberwell, south of the river. I had grown a beard and knew they would be unlikely to recognize me. They would not escape me again.

"I followed them everywhere either on foot or in my cab. They were always together. No doubt they knew they were in danger, and they did not go out after nightfall. Drebber was drunk most of the time, but Stangerson was very careful. I started to worry that my heart would give up before I had taken my revenge.

"One evening I was driving up and down their road when I saw another cab pull up outside their house. Their bags were brought out and then Drebber and Stangerson got in and the cab drove off. I followed them.

"They got out at Euston Station, and I went in behind them. With all the people around I could get close to them and hear what they were saying. They were going to Liverpool but had just missed one train and would have to wait for the next. Stangerson seemed very upset, but Drebber was pleased. I heard him say that he had some business of his own to attend to and that he would meet Stangerson back at the station at 11:00 that night. Stangerson argued that they had agreed to stay together, but Drebber reminded him that he was his paid servant. Stangerson gave in and arranged that if Drebber missed the last train, they would stay at Halliday's Private Hotel near Euston.

"The moment I had been waiting for had finally come. I had my enemies in my power. Apart they were at my mercy. But I did not want to just kill them—they had to know why they were dying.

"I had been lucky enough to find a key in my cab for an empty house I had taken a gentleman to look at some days earlier. It was here that I planned to bring justice to Drebber. Getting him there was the problem that I had to solve.

"Drebber's nature helped me here. He visited a drinking shop and came out looking very unsteady. He got a cab which I followed closely. To my surprise it pulled up outside his former lodgings. Shortly after he had gone in, he was thrown out by an angry young man who followed him into the street. Drebber saw my cab and called to me. A moment later he was in my cab wanting to go to Halliday's Private Hotel.

"I was desperately trying to think how I could get him to the empty house. As I drove along slowly he called out for me to stop. He got out at another drinking shop and asked me to wait for him. He stayed until closing time and when he came out he was so far gone that I knew I could do what I wanted.

"Don't think that I wished to kill him in cold blood. I would give him a chance. I knew about poison from a job I had taken in America. I had made up four pills, two with deadly poison in, and two harmless. They all looked the same. I got two containers and put one poisonous pill and one harmless pill in each. The time had now come for me to use them.

"I pulled up outside the house in Brixton Road. I suppose that Drebber thought he was at the hotel. I had to help him up the path, and I swear that I saw old John Ferrier and my lovely Lucy leading the way.

"We got inside and I lit a candle so he could see. Before he

realized anything was wrong I closed the door and asked him if he knew who I was. He looked closely and when I saw the fear in his eyes I knew he had recognized me. He fell back. At last, after twenty years, I could enjoy my sweet moment of revenge. I could feel the blood pounding in my head and I was sure my heart would burst but for the blood suddenly pouring from my nose.

"I told him how I had followed him all those years. 'What do you think of Lucy Ferrier now?' I asked. 'Punishment has been slow in coming but it has caught up with you at last.'

"'Would you murder me?' he whispered fearfully, his lip trembling.

"'Murder? Who talks of murdering a mad dog? What mercy did you show when you dragged my poor darling away from her murdered father?'

"'It was not I who killed her father,' he cried.

"'But you broke her poor heart,' I pushed the pill box toward him. 'Let God judge between us. Choose and eat. There is death in one and life in the other. I shall take what you leave. Let us see if there is justice or whether we are ruled by chance.'

"He tried to back away, but I drew my knife and forced him to take a pill. When he had eaten it I took the other and we stood facing each other for a minute to see who had taken the poison. I will never forget the look on his face when he realized it was he. I held Lucy's wedding ring in front of his eyes in the few seconds it took for the poison to work. He fell to the ground. I bent down and felt for his heart. There was no movement. He was dead!

"Suddenly I noticed all the blood that had poured from my nose. I thought I would leave a false clue for the police so I drew the word RACHE on the wall in my blood. I had read of a case in New York where this had happened and thought that the police might think it was the work of a German. I walked out to my cab and drove off. After some distance I felt in my pocket for Lucy's ring. It was not there! Straight away I returned to the house. It was the only possession I had of hers and I wanted it back at any cost. When I got back a policeman was there and I only got away by pretending to be completely drunk.

"That's how Enoch Drebber met his end. I then had to deal with Stangerson. I knew he was at Halliday's Private Hotel so I went there and waited outside. He must have thought that something was up when Drebber did not arrive, for he stayed in his room all day. However, I discovered which room he was in and early the next morning got in through the rear window. I woke him and told him the hour had come for him to pay for murdering John Ferrier. I described Drebber's death to him and offered him the same choice. Instead of taking his chance with the pill he attacked me and, in defending myself, I stabbed him in the heart.

"There is little else to say. I continued to cab for a few days, hoping I could save enough to get back to America. I was standing in the yard when a youngster came in and asked for

Jefferson Hope saying that a gentleman wanted a cab. He led me round here. As far as I knew no one in London could possibly think I had anything to do with these crimes, but before I knew it this young man had slipped the handcuffs on me and I was caught. You gentlemen may consider me a murderer, but I think I am as much an officer of justice as you are."

When he had finished no one spoke for a minute. Finally Holmes said,

"There is just one thing I would like to know. Who was your helper, the one who collected the ring from us?"

The prisoner nodded at Holmes and smiled, "I will tell you my own secrets but I am not prepared to say anything that might get others into trouble. He did well enough though."

"He did indeed," said Holmes, smiling back.

Lestrade and Gregson then took their prisoner and we heard that he would be brought before the judge in three days time.

14

Chapter 7
The Conclusion

We never did get to court. On the night of his arrest Jefferson Hope's heart gave up and he died peacefully with a smile on his face.

"Gregson and Lestrade will be angry at his death for they will miss out on their big moment in court," said Holmes, with a smile.

"I don't see that they had much to do with catching him," I answered.

"It is not what you do, but what you can make people think that you have done that is important," said Holmes. "Never mind," he continued. "I wouldn't have missed this case for the world. Simple as it was, there were some good lessons in it."

"Simple!" I cried.

"Well, what else could you call it? Without any help I managed to solve it in three days."

"That's true," I replied, hoping that he would tell me more of his methods.

"This was a case in which you were given the result and had to find out everything else yourself. To begin at the beginning. I approached the house on foot. I examined the roadway and saw the marks of a cab. By asking Gregson I found out that no one else had used a cab that morning, so the marks were made in the night. Point one.

"I then walked along the path. No doubt all you could see was a mass of foot marks, but to my trained eye I could picture what had happened and in what order. I saw the marks of the policemen, but I also saw the marks of the two men who had first passed through the garden. It was easy to see that they had been there first for in places their marks were completely covered by those of the police. Point two—there were two visitors on the night of the murder. One, I could tell from the length of his step, was tall, and the other was well-dressed. I could tell this from the mark his boot had made.

"On entering the house the well-booted fellow lay in front of me. The tall one then had done the murder. I knew it was murder by examining the body. The fearful expression on his face showed me he had foreseen his end, but there was no wound. I smelt his lips and knew then that he had been poisoned.

"And then I needed to discover the reason why. Nothing had been taken. If not for money, was it politics, then, or love? Political murderers do not stay at the scene of their crime. They kill quickly then leave. I knew that the man had been there for some time, so it must have been a personal wrong that called for such a revenge. When the letters were found on the wall I was even more certain, as it was clear that this was an attempt to put the police off the track. When the ring was found, it settled the question. Clearly, it had been used to remind the murdered man of some dead or forgotten woman. It was at this point that I questioned Gregson about his telegram to Cleveland. He had not asked about anything unusual relating to Drebber and a past wife. But I did in the one I sent.

"I continued to examine the room and discovered the cigar ash. From the letters on the wall I knew that the murderer had long nails. I also had decided that the blood must have come from the murderer's nose as the stains matched with his walking around the room. This would only happen to someone very full-blooded, which in turn would mean that he would have a red face.

"When the answer to my telegram came, the puzzle was solved. It told me that Drebber had applied for protection against Jefferson Hope, who had been in love with one of his wives many years before. They told me that Hope had recently traveled to Europe.

"I had already realized that the man who had walked into the room with Drebber was also the man that had driven the cab. The marks outside had shown me that the cab had wandered on a little in a way that was impossible if someone was in charge of it. Also, no one would carry out a murder with a cab driver waiting outside for them. I also realized that if someone wanted to follow a man in London, what better way than to be a cab driver. I knew then that I would find Jefferson Hope amongst the cabdrivers of London. I also guessed that he would probably stay in his job for a few more days as he would not want his sudden departure to be noticed.

"I therefore organized my street kids to search him out. How well they did and how quickly I ended the case you still remember well. You see the whole thing is one unbroken line of reason."

"That is quite remarkable," I cried. "You should be famous for it. You should publish your records. Indeed, if you don't, I will."

"You may do what you like, Doctor," he answered calmly, as he handed me the evening paper.

In it there was an account of the case praising Gregson and Lestrade to the sky but with no mention of Holmes's name, apart from saying that Jefferson Hope was arrested in Holmes's apartment.

"Didn't I tell you when we started?" laughed Holmes. "The result of our 'Study in Scarlet' has been to earn praise for those two."

"Never mind," I said. "I have all the facts in my notebook and I shall make sure that the public gets to read them."

The Sign of the Four

四つの署名

読み始める前に

The Sign of the Four 四つの署名

「シャーロック・ホームズ」シリーズの第2作目
1890年の「リピンコット・マガジン」2月号に初出

[主な登場人物]

Sherlock Holmes シャーロック・ホームズ 鋭い観察眼と推理力、そして犯罪に関する膨大な知識をあわせ持つ私立探偵。ロンドンのベーカー街221Bに下宿している。

John H. Watson ジョン・H・ワトソン 医師。ホームズの相棒でこの物語の語り手。ベーカー街221Bでホームズと同居している。

Mary Morstan メアリー・モースタン 本件の依頼人。父のモースタン大尉が失踪した後、毎年同じ日に真珠が差出人不明で届くようになる。

Captain Morstan モースタン大尉 メアリーの父。アンダマン島囚人警備隊の将校。休暇のためにロンドンに帰国後、謎の失踪を遂げる。

Major John Sholto ジョン・ショルトー少佐 モースタン大尉の友人。かつて同じ連隊に所属していた退役軍人。

Thaddeus Sholto サディアス・ショルトー ショルトー少佐の息子。メアリーに面会を求める手紙を送り、同行したホームズたちにモースタン大尉とショルトー少佐の因縁話を聞かせる。

Bartholomew Sholto バーソロミュー・ショルトー サディアスの兄。ポンディシェリー荘で毒矢を受けて死亡しているのが見つかる。

Jonathan Small ジョナサン・スモール 義足の男。モースタン大尉の遺品とポンディシェリー荘の現場に残されていた「四つの署名」の筆頭にあった名前。

Athelney Jones アセルニー・ジョーンズ ロンドン警視庁の刑事。

[あらすじ]

この数ヵ月ろくな事件が起きず暇を持てあましていたホームズのもとに、若い女性が訪ねてくる。

メアリー・モースタンという彼女の父親はインドで従軍していたが、10年ほど前に休暇でロンドンに帰国した後、行方不明となってしまった。そして6年前から、毎年同じ日に正体不明の人物から彼女のもとへ大粒の真珠が送られてくるようになった。さらに「未知の友」を名乗る謎の人物から面会を求める手紙が届いたことから、ホームズに相談をしにきたのだ。

彼女に同行したホームズとワトソンは、手紙の差出人から彼女の父親の過去にまつわる話を聞き、そして真珠の持ち主が判明する。しかし持ち主を訪ねてみると、すでに殺されており、そこには「四つの署名」が残されていた。テムズ河で繰り広げられる犯人とその正体を突き止めたホームズとの追走劇の末に明かされる、「四つの署名」の真相と過去から現在へとつながる事件の全貌とは——。

Illustrations by Richard Gutschmidt (1902)

[総単語数] 16,020語

Chapter 1
The Science of Deduction

Sherlock Holmes took his cocaine bottle from the shelf and his needle from the case. He pulled up his sleeve and put the needle in his arm. I had wanted to stop him from doing this many times but could not say anything. He knew taking this drug was bad for his body, but it excited his mind. He liked his mind to be very active and said that was why he chose to be the world's only unofficial consulting detective.

He thought that deduction should be an exact science. He believed he was the only person to have the three qualities necessary for the ideal detective — the power to look, the power to think, and the power of knowledge. He told me, for example, how important it is to be able to know the difference among the ashes of the various tobaccos and the tracing of footsteps.

I did not quite understand the difference between looking and thinking. He explained by telling me that this morning I went to the post office and sent a telegram.

"How did you know?" I asked.

"By looking, I see you have some red dirt on your shoe," he started. "Workmen are repairing the street near the post office where such red dirt is found. I also know that you have not written a letter or used any of my postcards or stamps. The only reason for going to the post office, then, was to send a telegram—this was the thinking part."

I then tested him by showing him my watch and asking him to tell me about the man who had owned it before me. I was sure I could prove that he was not as clever as he thought. But by examining the details of the watch he was, indeed, able to tell me that it had belonged to my elder brother and, moreover, what kind of man he was. I couldn't believe my ears! Before I could ask him more about it, there was a knock on the door—someone to see Holmes, a Miss Mary Morstan.

16

Chapter 2
The Statement of the Case

Miss Morstan came in. She was a young, blonde lady and was well dressed. She seemed very upset. She said she was in a very strange situation, almost impossible to explain.

"My father was in the army in India and he sent me home to England when I was still a small child," she began. "My mother was dead and she had no family here, so I was placed in a boarding house owned by a Mrs. Forrester. In 1878 my father returned to England for a year. I received a telegram from him telling me to meet him at his hotel in London. It had been many years since I had seen him and I was very excited. But when I got there he was not there. He had checked into the hotel, but he went out the day before I arrived and never came back. The date was December 3, 1878."

Holmes was listening carefully and

nodded his head for her to continue. “Even stranger,” she said, “was about six years ago—to be exact, on May 4, 1882—an ad appeared in the newspaper asking for the address of Miss Mary Morstan, stating that it would be to her advantage to come forward.”

She told us that she published her address in the ad column and on the same day a box arrived in the mail. It contained a very large and beautiful pearl, but no note or any letter. Since then every year on the same date a box has always arrived, always containing a similar pearl, without any clue as to the sender. The pearls were said to be of a rare variety and of great value. She showed us the six pearls and the wrapping they arrived in. She was sure the writing on the wrapping was not her father’s.

“This is very interesting,” said Holmes. “Has anything else happened to you?”

“Yes, just today. That is why I have come to you. This morning I received this letter, which you will perhaps read for yourself.” Holmes examined the envelope carefully. The letter read:

> Be at the third pillar from the left outside the Lyceum Theatre tonight at 7:00. If you are distrustful, bring two friends. You are a wronged woman and shall have justice. Do not bring police. If you do, it will all be for nothing.
>
> Your unknown friend.

She needed help, so Holmes and I decided to go with her to the theater. She said she would be back at 6:00 and left.

"What a very pretty woman!" I said, turning to Holmes.

"Is she?" he replied. "I did not look."

Holmes had to go out for a while. I sat in his chair thinking about the young lady. I was charmed by her beauty and thought she must now be 27 if she had been 17 at the time of her father's disappearance. But what was I but a poor doctor with an even poorer leg? Not a great match for a woman like her.

17

Chapter 3
Looking for a Solution

Holmes Came back at 5:30 and he was in a good mood. He thought that he already had an important clue to the mystery. Mary's father had only one friend in London, a Major Sholto. They had been together in India. Holmes checked the back files of the Times and learned that Sholto had died on April 28, 1882.

Within a week of this date, Mary got the package with the pearl and this was repeated every year. He wondered if one of Sholto's relatives was sending the presents and had now sent the letter.

Mary arrived and the three of us went out for our strange meeting. Holmes asked her more about Sholto. She said he and her father had spent time in the Andaman Islands, just off the coast of India. She also said that a strange piece of paper had been found in her father's desk which no one could understand. She showed it to Holmes, who examined it carefully. It seemed to be a map of a large building. At one point there was a red cross and above it was written '3.37 from left' in pencil. In the left-hand corner was a strange symbol, like four crosses in a line with their arms touching. Beside it was written 'The sign of the four—Jonathan Small, Mahomet Singh, Abdullah Khan, Dost Akbar.' Holmes did not know what it meant but thought it was important.

There were many people at the Lyceum Theatre and just as we reached the third pillar, the place of the meeting, a small, dark man came up to us.

"Are you the people who came with Miss Morstan?" he asked.

"I am Miss Morstan and these two gentlemen are my friends," she said.

He asked if we were policemen and she replied we were not.

"Then you must come with me to meet my employer."

A horse-drawn cab pulled up and we got in and raced away through the foggy streets. We drove and drove and did not know where we were going, except Holmes, who knew every area that we went through.

We came to a poor neighborhood and stopped at a house which was dark inside except for a little light in the kitchen window. All of the neighboring houses were dark and looked empty. On knocking, a Hindu servant opened the door.

"The sahib awaits you," he said.

We heard a high-pitched voice from an inner room which said, "Show them in, quickly."

18

Chapter 4
The Story of the Bald-Headed Man

We Followed the Indian down a dark hall until he opened a door on the right. Inside the room was a small man with almost no hair at all. His teeth were yellow and, as he spoke, he tried to cover his mouth with his hand. The furniture, paintings, and decorations inside his room did not match the rest of the house. They were clearly those of a rich man.

The bald man introduced himself as Mr. Thaddeus Sholto. "I will tell you everything that happened. My father was Major John Sholto, once of the Indian Army. He retired 11 years ago and came back to England to live with my twin brother Bartholomew and me. We read about the disappearance of Captain Morstan, but we did not know our father was keeping a secret about what had really happened to him." Holmes and Mary and I were paying close attention to his every word.

"Early in 1882," Thaddeus said, "my father received a letter from India which was a great shock to him. My brother and I did not know what the letter said, but it made our father very sick. His condition got worse, and towards the end of April he wished to say some last words to us. He confessed that he had a treasure, that he had kept it all for himself but should have given at least half to Morstan's daughter, Mary. He felt very bad about what he had done. He asked us to send Mary a fair share of the treasure, but only after he had died."

"My father and Captain Morstan had discovered this treasure in India. My father brought it to England, and when Captain Morstan returned to London he came to our house to get his share. He and my father argued about how much each should get. Morstan yelled in anger, fell backward and cut his head on the corner of the treasure chest. He died right there in the room."

I looked over at Mary and saw tears in her eyes. But she nodded for Thaddeus to continue.

"Of course, my father knew people would think he killed his friend. His servant and he decided to hide the body, and within a few days the London newspapers were full of the mysterious disappearance of Captain Morstan. Now, as he was dying, he wanted to do the right thing by giving Mary her part. He asked my brother and me to put our ears down to his mouth and said, 'The treasure is hidden in—'

"At this moment his face became filled with fear and he said in a very loud voice, 'Keep him out!' We turned our heads in the direction he was looking, and through the window we could see a wild, angry face looking in. We ran over to the window, but the man was gone. When we returned to the bed, our father was dead."

Thaddeus then told us more about the mystery. "We found one footmark outside the window, so we knew we had not imagined the face. In the morning the same window was open and we saw that someone had opened all the boxes and cupboards in the room. On top of our father's chest was a torn piece of paper with the words 'The sign of the four' written on it. We did not know who had come inside or what the words meant. It did not look like anything had been stolen."

After listening to all of this Mary turned white, but when I offered her some water, she recovered somewhat.

Thaddeus told us how excited he and his brother were about the treasure. For years they had looked for it in the garden but could not find it. The only part of the treasure they had seen were the pearls their father kept in his room. Bartholomew was like his father and did not want to part with the pearls. They both thought that, by sending them to Mary, they might get in trouble.

Finally, they decided to send one pearl a year. Still, they could not agree completely, so Thaddeus decided to live separately from his brother. Then, yesterday, he learned that the treasure had been found, and he wrote the letter to Mary to meet him.

Now Thaddeus asked us to drive to his father's house with him and demand a share of the treasure from Bartholomew. Thaddeus thought it was valued at £500,000. Our eyes went big upon hearing this amount. Even with just half of this, Miss Morstan would become the richest lady in England.

19

Chapter 5
The Tragedy of Pondicherry Lodge

It Was nearly 11:00 when we reached the final stage of our night's adventures. We had come to Pondicherry Lodge in Norwood, where Bartholomew lived. The doorman didn't want to let us in, but, after much conversation we were allowed to go inside the garden. The house was big and dark, and gave one a cold feeling. Thaddeus pointed up at Bartholomew's window, but there was no light.

Holmes said, "But I see a little light in the window beside the door."

"Ah, that is the housekeeper's room. That's where old Mrs. Bernstone stays. But perhaps you should wait here for a minute or two, because if we all go in together, she may be surprised. But, quiet! What is that?"

Thaddeus held up the light. From the great black house there sounded through the silent night the saddest of sounds—the crying of a frightened woman. Thaddeus hurried to the door, which was opened by an old woman.

"Oh, Mr. Thaddeus, sir, I am so glad you have come!" He went inside with her.

Holmes had the lantern now and was swinging it around, looking at the house and at the big piles of dirt in the garden.

Mary and I were both very frightened and stood there holding hands. Though I was frightened, I thought how romantic it was.

"What a strange place!" said Mary. "It looks as though all the moles in England have been here."

"These are the holes of the treasure-seekers," said Holmes. "You must remember that they looked for it for six years."

At that moment, Thaddeus came rushing out of the house. "There is something wrong with Bartholomew!" he cried. "Oh, I am frightened!" He looked like a terrified child.

"Come into the house," said Holmes in his firm way. We all went inside and into the housekeeper's room. She also looked scared, but was calmed when she saw Mary's face.

"Master has locked himself in and will not answer me," explained the old lady. "I waited for him all day, and then about an hour ago I feared something might be wrong so I went up and looked through the keyhole. It was horrible! You must go up and see for yourself."

Holmes took the lamp and led the way. Thaddeus was shaking violently. Mary stayed below with the frightened housekeeper.

Up on the third floor, Holmes knocked on Bartholomew's door, but there was no answer. He tried to open the door, but it was locked on the inside. He looked through the keyhole and stood up with a sharp intake of breath.

"There is something devilish in this, Watson," he said, more emotional than I had ever seen him. "What do you think?"

I also looked and jumped back in horror. Looking straight at me and floating in the air, for all beneath was in shadow, hung a face—the very face of our companion, Thaddeus. The face was set in a horrible smile, fixed and unnatural, more frightening than an angry face. The face was so like our bald friend that I had to turn around to make sure he was still with us. I then remembered that he and his brother were twins.

We broke open the door and went inside Bartholomew's room. It looked like a chemical laboratory. One of the containers had broken and the air had a strange smell. By the table in a wooden chair sat the master of the house with that smile on his face. He was stiff and cold and clearly had been dead for many hours.

By his hand on the table there was a torn sheet of paper with the words 'The sign of the four' written on it.

"My God, what does it all mean?" I asked.

"It means murder," said Holmes, bending over the dead man. "Ah! I expected it. Look here!" He pointed to what looked like a long dark thorn stuck in the skin just above the ear.

"It looks like a thorn," I said.

"It is a thorn. You may take it out, but be careful because it is poisoned."

To me, the mystery was growing darker and darker, but to Holmes it was getting clearer and clearer. He needed only a few missing links to have an entirely connected case.

We had almost forgotten about Thaddeus. He was standing in the doorway in horror.

Suddenly he cried out, "The treasure is gone! They have robbed him of the treasure. There is the hole in the ceiling through which we lowered it last night. I helped him do it! I was the last person who saw him. I left him here last night, and I heard him lock the door as I came downstairs."

"What time was that?" asked Holmes.

"It was ten o'clock. And now he is dead, and the police will be called in, and they will think that I did it. Oh, yes, I'm sure of it. But you don't think so, do you gentlemen? Surely you don't think that it was I? Oh, dear! Oh, dear! I know that I will go crazy!"

"You have no reason for fear, Mr. Sholto," said Holmes kindly, putting his hand upon his shoulder. "Take my advice and drive down to the station to report the matter to the police. Offer to assist them in every way. We shall wait here until your return."

He nodded in agreement and went down the stairs slowly, as if he were drunk.

20

Chapter 6
Sherlock Holmes Gives a Demonstration

"Now, Watson," said Holmes, rubbing his hands. "We have half an hour to ourselves. Let us make good use of it. Simple as the case seems now, there may be something deeper underlying it."

"Simple?" I cried.

"Yes. In the first place, how did these people come and how did they go? The door has not been opened since last night. How about the window?"

He walked across to it, talking to himself rather than to me. The window was locked on the inside, there was no water pipe to climb up on the outside of the building, and the roof was out of reach. But a man climbed up to the window. There was a footprint on the edge and also a round muddy mark, and the same marks were on the floor and by the table.

"That round mark is not a footmark," I said.

"No, it is something much more valuable to us. It is the mark of a wooden stump."

"From a wooden-legged man."

"Yes. But there has been someone else—a very able helper. Could you climb that wall, Watson?"

I looked out of the open window. It was about 60 feet (18 meters) from the ground and there were no footholds for climbing. "It would be impossible," I said.

"But if you had a friend up here who lowered you this strong rope which I see in the corner, tying one end to this big hook in the wall, then maybe you could, even with a wooden leg. You could leave in the same way. Your friend would pull up the rope, untie it from the hook, shut the window and lock it on the inside, and leave the way that he came. The wooden-legged man, however, was not accustomed to climbing with ropes. I see more than one blood mark on the rope, telling me he slipped down with such speed that he took the skin off his hands."

"But how did the mysterious friend come into the room?" I asked.

"Ah, yes, the friend. He is interesting and he makes this an unusual case."

Holmes thought it must have been through the hole in the roof, where the treasure was hidden. We went up a ladder and into the secret room. It was very small. We found a trapdoor which led out onto the roof. This is how the helper entered. Holmes looked at the dusty floor of the room and saw the prints of a

shoeless foot but it was only half the size of an ordinary man.

"Has a child done this terrible thing?" I asked, confused. Holmes did not answer, but went down again to the lower room and continued to look for clues.

"We are in luck," he said. "We ought to have very little trouble now. The helper stepped in the creosote and you can see the outline of his small foot here. We have got him now because I know a dog that would follow that smell to the end of the world. Ah, but wait, the police have arrived."

"Before they come up," said Holmes, "just put your hand here on this poor fellow's arm, and here on his leg. What do you feel?"

"The muscles are as hard as a board," I answered.

"Quite so, much harder than usual. What does it suggest to your mind?"

"Death from some very powerful poison."

"That's what I thought when I saw the face, and as you saw I found a thorn which had been driven or shot into the head. Now look at this thorn."

I looked closely at the thorn. It was long, sharp and black. Near the point it looked as though something sticky had dried upon it. The opposite end had been cut and rounded off with a knife.

"Is that an English thorn?" I asked.

"No, it certainly is not."

Just then the police came into the room. One of the policemen, Detective Athelney Jones, remembered Sherlock Holmes from a previous case. Holmes had, as usual, used theories to solve the case, but the policeman thought his success was only good luck.

"But what is all this?" said Jones. "Bad, bad. Now let's have the facts—no room for theories. What do you think this man died of?"

"Oh, I'm sure you don't want any of my theories, detective," said Holmes dryly.

"No, no. Still, we can't deny that you are exactly right sometimes. Oh, dear. Door locked. I understand jewels worth half a million missing. How was the window?"

"Locked, but there are footprints on the sill."

"Well, well, if it was locked the footprints could have nothing to do with the matter. That's common sense. The man might have died from shock; but then the jewels are missing. Ha! I have a theory. These flashes come upon me at times. Sholto was, by his own confession, with his brother last night. He killed his brother in anger and then walked off with the treasure. How's that?"

"On which the dead man very kindly got up and locked the door on the inside," Holmes said jokingly.

"Hmm, I see your point. Let us use common sense. Thaddeus was with his brother. There was a fight. This we know. The brother is dead and the jewels are gone. This we also know. No one saw the brother from the time Thaddeus left him. His bed had not been slept in. Thaddeus is in a troubled state of mind. You see that I am making a case against Thaddeus."

"You do not yet have all the facts," said Holmes. "This thorn, which I think was poisoned, was in the man's head, where you still see the mark. This piece of paper with the writing on it was on the table. How does all that fit into your theory?"

"Confirms it in every way," said the man confidently. "If this thorn is poisonous, Thaddeus may as well have used it as any other man. The paper is some kind of trick, to lead us away from the facts. The only question is how did he leave? Ah, of course, here is a hole in the roof."

He went up to examine the secret room, found the trapdoor and came down to say that facts are better than theories and that his view of the case was confirmed. He called for Thaddeus to come into the room.

"Mr. Sholto, it is my duty to inform you that anything which you may say will be used against you. I arrest you in the Queen's name as being concerned in the death of your brother."

"You see? Didn't I tell you?" cried the poor little man, throwing up his hands and looking from one to the other of us.

"Don't worry, Mr. Sholto," said Holmes. "I think I can clear you of the charge."

"Don't promise too much, Mr. Theorist!" said Jones in an angry voice.

"Not only will I clear him, sir, but I will tell you the name and description of one of the two people who were in this room last night.

His name is Jonathan Small and he's got a wooden leg which is worn away on the inner side. He is a middle-aged man, very sunburned, and he has been in jail before. These few things may help you, together with the fact that there is a lot of skin missing from the palm of his hand."

The policeman was not happy that Holmes knew all these things because he wanted to be the clever one, but he listened carefully.

"The other man is a rather strange person," continued Holmes. "I hope to be able to introduce you to both of them soon."

At this point Holmes took me out in the hall and asked me to take Miss Morstan home and then return. He also wanted me to drop by a friend's place to pick up a dog named Toby, and bring him back with me.

"Toby has an amazing sense of smell and can surely lead us to the killers. I would rather have Toby's help than the whole detective force of London."

It was 1:00 in the morning and I hoped to be back by 3:00. In the meantime, Holmes would question Mrs. Bernstone and Bartholomew's Indian servant, Lal Rao.

21

Chapter 7
The Episode of the Barrel

The Police had brought a cab with them and I took Miss Morstan home in it. She had been calm until now, but in the cab she started crying because of the adventures of the night. I wanted to do something. I wanted to speak my words of affection, but two thoughts stopped me. She was weak and helpless that night and it would have been wrong to show my love at such a time. Worse still, she was rich and she might look upon me as a mere fortune seeker. I dropped Miss Morstan off at her home and made my way over to get Toby.

On the way I thought about everything that had happened and how wild and dark it all was to me. There was the original problem: the death of Captain Morstan, the sending of the pearls, the ad in the newspaper, the letter—we had some light upon all those events. They had only led us, however, to a deeper mystery. The Indian treasure, the curious paper found among Morstan's things, the strange scene at Major Sholto's death, the rediscovery of the treasure immediately followed

by the murder of the discoverer, the things connected with the crime—the footsteps, the strange thorn, the words upon the piece of paper which were the same as those on Captain Morstan's paper. I thought that only a man like Holmes could begin to understand these things.

I found the house where Toby's owner lived and asked to borrow the dog for a short time. The owner was a friend of Holmes's and agreed quickly. Toby was an ugly, long-haired dog, with ears that hung down loosely, a mixed breed, brown and white in color and walked like a duck. We got back to Pondicherry Lodge at three in the morning. I found that Thaddeus, the gatekeeper, the housekeeper and the Indian servant had been taken to the police station, all under arrest.

Holmes said he wanted to check something on the roof. I waited in the garden with Toby while he followed a path where the tiles of the roof had come loose. This took him to a corner where there was a water pipe going up the wall. It looked strong and he came down to the ground on this pipe. He showed me what he had found on the roof – something which looked like a cigarette case. Inside this case were six sharp pieces of wood, the thorns like that which had struck Bartholomew. This was good news because if we found the killer, we didn't want him to shoot any poison thorns at us.

"Are you ready for a long walk, Watson?"

I said yes and Holmes put a handkerchief he had dipped in

creosote under Toby's nose. He then threw the handkerchief far off and tied a rope to the dog's neck, leading him to the place where he had come down the water pipe.

Toby instantly started barking, and with his nose on the ground and his tail in the air, ran off at a fast pace.

It was starting to get light. Toby reached the wall of the garden, ran along it and finally stopped in a corner. Holmes climbed the wall, took the dog and dropped it over the other side. We found a little blood on the white wall and thought it was the handprint of the man with the wooden leg.

The creosote clue was just one of the ways Holmes could trace the criminals, but it was the strongest. But to me it was all still very mysterious and I asked Holmes how he could have described the wooden-legged man with such confidence.

"It was very simple. Two officers, Captain Morstan and Major Sholto, who are in command of a prison learn an important secret as to buried treasure. A map is drawn for them by an Englishman named Jonathan Small. You remember that we saw the name on the map which Captain Morstan had. He had signed it on behalf of himself and his associates—the sign of the four, as he called it. Aided by this map, the officers, or one of them, gets the treasure and brings it to England. But probably he got it without keeping some promise. Why didn't Jonathan Small get the treasure himself? Jonathan Small did not get the treasure because he and his associates were themselves in prison and could not get away."

"But you must be just guessing," I said.

"It is more than that. It is the only idea which covers the facts. Let us see how it fits with what follows. Major Sholto remains at peace for some years, happy with his treasure. Then he receives a letter from India, which frightens him. What was that?"

"A letter to say that the men whom he had wronged had been set free."

"Or had escaped. What does he do then? He guards himself against a man he believes is coming for his treasure. Now, from Jonathan Small's point of view, he came to England with two purposes in mind—to get his part of the treasure and to get revenge on the man who wronged him. He finds out where Sholto lives but he does not know where the treasure was hidden. Suddenly, Small learns that Major Sholto is about to die, so he rushes to the house and appears at the window but does not enter because his two sons are with him. Crazy with hate, however, he enters the room that night, searches his private papers in hopes of finding information about the treasure and finally leaves the message on the piece of paper we found. Later he finds out about the secret room from someone inside the house. Small, with his wooden leg, cannot possibly reach the third floor and get into Bartholomew's room, so he takes another person with him—the one who steps in the creosote."

"So it was the other person and not Small who did the crime."

"Yes. But Small did not wish for Bartholomew to die. It happened because of the wild character of his companion and the

poison did its work so quickly. Small then lowered the treasure box to the ground and came down off the roof himself. As to his personal appearance, he must be middle-aged and must be sunburned after being in prison in such a hot place as the Andamans. His height is easily known from the length of his step."

We had during this time been following Toby down the roads which led to the city. It was getting lighter and people were beginning to appear. Toby paid no attention to them and kept his nose to the ground, barking from time to time, which meant he was getting closer to the goal. At one point Toby stopped, turned backwards showing doubt and looked up to Holmes and me, as if to ask for sympathy for not knowing what to do.

"What's the matter with the dog?" said Holmes.

"Perhaps they stood here for some time," I suggested.

"Ah, it's all right! He's off again," said Holmes.

Toby was indeed off. After smelling again, he suddenly made up his mind and ran with an energy and determination which he had not yet shown. He did not now need to put his nose to the ground. By the look in Holmes's eyes, I thought we were getting near the end of the journey.

We had come to a large lumber yard. Here the dog was very excited and went in through the gate, raced through the yard, went between two wood piles and finally, with a loud bark, jumped at a large container. With his tongue hanging out and his eyes blinking, Toby stood there looking from one to the other of us for some kind of thanks. The container had the color and strong smell of creosote. Toby had brought us to one of the many construction yards that use creosote. We looked at each other and then burst into laughter.

22

Chapter 8
The Baker Street Irregulars

"What Do we do now?" I asked. "We can see that Toby is not quite perfect."

"Well, there is a lot of creosote carried around London. Poor Toby is not to blame."

"We must get on the main track again, I suppose."

"Yes, and luckily we have not far to go. It seems that what puzzled the dog back there was that there were two different trails going in opposite directions. We took the wrong one. It only remains to follow the other."

We went back to the place where Toby had gotten confused. He went around in a wide circle and finally ran off in a new direction. It seemed that we were on the real path now. We went down towards the riverside and finally to the water's edge, where there was a small wooden wharf. Toby took us to the very edge of this and stood there crying, looking out on the dark water beyond.

"We are out of luck," said Holmes. "They have taken a

boat from here."

Nearby was a small house with a sign on it reading 'Boats to hire by the hour or day.'

We went to the house and spoke to the woman inside, a Mrs. Smith. Holmes asked for her husband, but was told he had been away since the morning of the day before and that she was feeling frightened about him.

He had gone off in the steamboat, but without much fuel. She went on to say she didn't like that wooden-legged man who went with him. She described him as a brown, monkey-faced man who had come to see her husband more than once. He had come about 3:00 in the morning and her husband had known that he was coming.

She knew it was the wooden-legged man by his voice. Her husband and her eldest son, Jim, went away with him in the boat. She wasn't sure if the wooden-legged man had come alone. Holmes got a description of the boat from the woman—the name, the color and so on. It was called the Aurora.

We wondered what to do next, how to proceed and look for the men. There were so many places along the river to look. It would take a very long time to check every possibility.

We did not want to tell the police how far we had come or ask people along the river. We were afraid this would make the men aware they were being chased. If they did not think anyone was looking for them, they would feel safe and not be in a hurry to go anywhere, like a foreign country.

We decided to go home, have some breakfast and get an hour's sleep. We kept Toby, thinking he might still be of use to us. Holmes stopped by a post office on the way to send a telegraph.

It was now between eight and nine o'clock in the morning and I was feeling weak in mind and body. I had a bath and changed my clothes, while Holmes prepared breakfast. The morning paper had an article about the murder. It reported that the most clever mind of the police force, Jones, had solved the crime and had arrested four people. There was more praise for the police officer than information about the case.

Holmes laughed about the article, but I said we were lucky not to have been arrested ourselves! At that moment the doorbell rang and we could hear a lot of noise downstairs. I again wondered if we would now be arrested.

"No, it's not quite so bad as that," Holmes said. "It is the unofficial force—the Baker Street irregulars." In came 12 dirty and ragged little street children.

"Got your telegram, sir," said the one called Wiggins, "and brought everyone quickly."

Holmes paid them for the money they had spent to come. He told them that he wanted to find the steamboat called the Aurora and described what it looked like. He wanted the group to search both sides of the river. One person was to go and wait near the Smith house. He gave them some money in advance and they were on their way.

"Are you going to bed, Holmes?" I asked.

"No, I'm not tired. I'm rather strange. I never remember feeling tired by work, though doing nothing makes me very tired. I am going to smoke and to think over this strange business. This ought to be an easy job. Wooden-legged men are not so common, but the other man must be very unique."

"That other man again!"

"Yes, you must have formed your own opinion of him—very small feet, able to move very quickly, small poisoned thorns—what do you think?"

"A wild man!" I said.

"Perhaps. The little thorns could only be shot in one way. They are from a blowpipe. Now, then, where are we to find our wild man?"

"South America," I guessed.

"I think not," said Holmes as he took a big book from the shelf.

He found the entry for the Andaman Islands and the people who live there. The book said they may be the smallest race upon this earth. They are a very wild people but able to have close friendships when their confidence has been gained. Among other features, their feet and hands are extremely small. They shoot poisoned thorns when facing their enemies.

I was very tired. Holmes told me to lie down on the sofa and he would put me to sleep by playing the violin. I soon found myself in dreamland, with the sweet face of Mary Morstan looking down upon me.

23

Chapter 9
A Break in the Chain

It Was late in the afternoon before I woke, strengthened and refreshed. Sherlock Holmes still sat exactly as I had left him, except that he had laid aside his violin and was deep in a book. He looked across at me as I moved, and I noticed that his face was dark and troubled.

"You have slept well," he said. "I feared that our talk would wake you."

"I heard nothing," I answered. "Have you had fresh news, then?"

"Unfortunately, no. I must say that I am surprised and disappointed. Wiggins has just come to report. He says that no trace can be found of the boat. It bothers me because every hour is important."

"Can I do anything? I am perfectly fresh now, and quite ready for another adventure tonight."

"No, we can do nothing. We can only wait. If we go ourselves, a message might come in our absence and that would cause a delay. You are free to do what you wish, but I must remain on guard."

"Then shall I go over to see Miss Morstan? She asked me to, yesterday."

"Oh, Miss Morstan?" asked Holmes with a smile in his eyes.

"Well, yes. She was anxious to hear what had happened. I will be back in an hour or two," I said.

"All right! Good luck! But, if you are crossing the river, you may as well return Toby, for I do not think that we shall have any use for him now."

I took the dog back and paid the owner for the use of him. When I reached Miss Morstan's place I found her a little tired from the previous night, but she wanted to hear the news. Mrs. Forrester, the landlady, was also very interested. I told them all that they had done.

"It's a romance!" cried Mrs. Forrester. "An injured lady, a half million in treasure, a black wild man and a wooden-legged criminal."

"And two heroes to the rescue," added Miss Morstan, looking at me with a bright face.

"Mary, I don't think that you are nearly excited enough. Just imagine what it must be to be so rich. You could do anything," Mrs. Forrester said.

"I am only worried about Mr. Thaddeus Sholto," Mary said. "Nothing else is important. He has been very brave and honorable from the beginning. We must help clear him."

I was happy to notice that Mary was not interested in

becoming rich. It was evening before I left the two ladies, and quite dark by the time I reached home.

Holmes's book and pipe lay by his chair but he had disappeared. I asked our landlady Mrs. Hudson about him.

"Well, after walking up and down, up and down in the study, he finally went to his room. I'm quite worried about his health."

"I don't think you need to worry," I told her. "I have seen him like this before. He has some small matter on his mind which makes him restless."

I tried to speak lightly to the landlady but I myself was somewhat uneasy when through the long night I still heard from time to time the sound of his footsteps. I knew how Holmes was struggling against not being able to take any action.

At breakfast he looked very tired and as though he had a slight fever. "You are making yourself too tired," I said. "I heard you walking around in the night."

"I could not sleep," he answered. "This problem is burning me up. It is too much to be stopped by such a small thing; everything else has gone well. I know about the men, the boat, everything! The whole river has been searched on both sides, but there is no news, nor has Mrs. Smith heard from her husband."

"Perhaps Mrs. Smith gave us the wrong information."

"No, I don't think so. I asked around and there is a boat of that description."

"Could they have gone up the river?"

"I have thought about that, too, and there is a search party who will work up as far as Richmond. If no news comes today, I will go off myself tomorrow and look for the men rather than the boat. But, surely, surely, we will hear something."

We did not, however. Not a word came to us either from Wiggins or from other people. There were articles in most of the newspapers about the murder. They all seemed to be against poor Thaddeus Sholto. There were no fresh details in any of them, except that a hearing was to be held on the following day.

I went to see Mary and Mrs. Forrester again that evening and on my return I found Holmes to be very depressed and quiet. He would hardly talk. He did not sleep again that night.

Early in the morning I woke with a start and was surprised to find Holmes standing by my bedside.

"I am going down the river," he said. "I have thought about everything and can see only one way. It is worth trying."

"Surely I should go with you!" I said.

"I don't want you to go because it's quite possible that some message may come during the day. I want you to open all notes and telegrams and use your own judgment if any news should come. Can I rely on you?"

"Most certainly."

"I may not be gone very long and I will have some sort of news before I get back."

That morning there was some fresh news in the paper. It

had been shown that Thaddeus and the housekeeper, Mrs. Bernstone, were not involved in the murder and had been released. The police now had a clue as to the real criminals and the case was being checked further. For me it was good to know that Sholto was safe and I wondered what the new clue may be. It was, I thought, just a cover-up for the mistake the police had made.

It was a long day. Every time that a knock came to the door or a person passed in the street, I thought it might be Holmes or one of the children. At three o'clock I was surprised to be paid a visit by Detective Jones, the one who had arrested Thaddeus Sholto. He was not now the master of common sense that we had met before. He was no longer so confident. His expression was sad, like he was sorry for something.

I invited him in and offered him a cigar and a glass of whisky. Jones accepted, with thanks. I told him that Holmes had gone out.

He nodded his head. "You know my theory about this case?" he said.

"I remember that you said something."

"Well, I have to reconsider it. I thought it was Sholto who did it but there was a hole in my net. He was able to prove where he was at the time of the murder. It is very bad to be wrong and I need a little help."

"We all need help, sometimes," I said.

"Your friend, Mr. Sherlock Holmes, is a wonderful man. He's a man who cannot be defeated. I have seen him go into many cases and he has always been able to make things clear. He sent me a telegram saying that he has got some clue to the case."

Jones handed the message to me and it read:

> Go to Baker Street at once. If I have not returned, wait for me. I am close on the track of the Sholto gang. You can come with us tonight if you want to be there at the finish.

"This sounds good. It looks like he is on the trail again," I said.

"I don't think so. Even the best of us make mistakes sometimes. But it is my duty not to miss any chances. Ah, there is someone at the door."

It was an old man, wearing the same kind of clothes that Holmes was wearing when he went out. His back was bent, his knees were shaking and his breathing was rough. He had a scarf around his chin and little of his face could be seen. He had dark eyes and hairy eyebrows and long, gray sideburns. He looked like an old sailor.

The old man asked for Mr. Sherlock Holmes.

"He is not here now but I am acting for him and you can give me your message. Is it about the Smith boat?"

"Yes, I know where it is. I know where the men are. And I know where the treasure is. I know all about it."

"Then tell me and I will let him know."

"I should tell Mr. Holmes."

"Well you must wait for him."

"No, no. I can't stay here and wait. If Mr. Holmes isn't here, then he'll have to find out about it by himself. I don't like the looks of you two and I won't say a word."

The old man went toward the door but Jones got in front of him.

"Wait a while, my friend," he said. "You have important information and you must not go away. We will keep you here until Holmes returns."

"Some treatment this is!" he said. "I come here to see a gentleman and you two, who I never saw in my life, treat me in this way." The old man finally sat down and Jones and I continued talking. Suddenly, however, Holmes's voice broke in upon us.

The old man was gone but Holmes was there. "Holmes!" I exclaimed. "You are here! But where is the old man?"

"Here is the old man," he said, holding out some white hair. "I thought my disguise was pretty good, but I didn't think I could fool you."

Jones and I were delighted by the performance. Holmes explained that he had been working in the disguise all day because some members of the criminal world might recognize him.

"You got my telegram?" asked Holmes.

"Yes, that is what brought me here," said Jones.

"Now, Jones, you must do as I say. You can take all the credit, but you must act on the lines that I point out. Is that agreed?"

"Entirely, if you will help me find the men."

"All right, in the first place, I want a fast police-boat to be at the Westminster Stairs at 7:00."

"That is easy."

"Then I want two strong men in case of resistance."

"There will be two or three in the boat. What else?"

"When we find the men, we will find the treasure." Pointing to me, Holmes continued, "I think my friend here would like to take it first to the young lady to whom half of it belongs. Let her be the first to open it. Eh, Watson?"

"It would be a great pleasure," I agreed.

Jones said the treasure would afterwards have to be taken to the police station until the case was closed.

"One other point," said Holmes. "I would like to talk to Jonathan Small himself. May I have an unofficial interview if he is well guarded?"

Jones agreed.

"Is there anything else?" asked Jones.

"Yes, please have dinner with us."

24

Chapter 10
The End of the Islander

Holmes Was in a good mood during dinner, and Jones and I also were feeling merry, mostly because we thought we were coming to the end of our task.

Holmes looked at his watch after the meal. He filled three more glasses with wine and said, "To the success of our journey. And now it is time to go. Do you have your gun, Watson?"

"It's in my desk."

"You had better take it, then. It is good to be prepared. I see that the taxi is at the door. I ordered it for 6:30."

It was a little past 7:00 when we reached Westminster Stairs and found the police boat waiting for us. There were four other men on the boat.

"Where to?" asked Jones.

"To the Tower. Tell them to stop opposite Jacobson's Yard."

I asked Holmes how he knew where to go.

"I put myself in the position of Jonathan Small. He would need the boat for his escape, somewhere nearby, but he could not leave it on the river because it might be found if the police were looking for the boat. I thought the only way to have both things was to put it in a repair yard. It would be hidden and yet available at short notice."

Holmes had disguised himself as a sailor and asked at all the yards down the river. He had no luck at 15 yards but at the 16th—Jacobson's—he learned that the Aurora had been handed over to them two days ago by a wooden-legged man, telling them to do something about the rudder.

Holmes put a guardman on the boat, who was to stand at the water's edge and wave his handkerchief when Small was getting on the boat. Holmes thought we would be able to take the men, the treasure and all.

We waited and waited and finally saw a white handkerchief moving. And then we saw the Aurora, moving very fast.

Jones looked worried and shook his head. He didn't think we could catch them. We increased our speed to the maximum. The Aurora sped on and we followed closely on her track.

"Faster, faster!" cried Holmes.

"I think we're gaining a little," said Jones with his eyes on the Aurora.

Just then another boat came between us and almost caused an accident. This allowed the Aurora to pull ahead by about 200 yards (180 meters). But we could still see her clearly. We followed every move of the boat ahead, and when we turned on the spotlight we could see the men on the deck.

The men on the Aurora now knew without a doubt that they were being chased and they tried to increase their speed.

We were gaining again. This was the most thrilling chase that I had ever experienced. Closer and closer we came. Jones yelled to them to stop. We were not more than four boat-lengths behind.

A man on the back end of the Aurora stood up and shook his fists at us, cursing in a cracked voice. It was Jonathan Small, a powerful-looking man. There was also a little black man on the deck, the smallest I had ever seen, with a big, oddly shaped head. His face looked like a cruel beast. We took out our guns.

"Shoot if he raises his hand," Holmes told me.

We were within a boat-length by this time and almost within reach of our target. It was good that we had so clear a view of the small black man, the islander. As we looked at him, he took out a short, round piece of wood and put it between his teeth. We shot at the same time, Holmes and I, and the man fell dead into the river.

Just then, the wooden-legged man turned his boat sharply toward the shore. Jones's men also turned quickly, but by then the Aurora was almost at the shore. With a bumping noise, it ran into the mud on the shore. Small jumped off the boat, but his wooden leg sank down into the muddy soil and he could not move no matter how much he tried, not forward, not backward. The more he moved, the deeper his wooden leg sank.

We came near him and threw the end of a rope over his shoulders. We were then able to pull him out and drag him over the side of our boat.

The two Smiths, father and son, sat on the Aurora, but came on our boat when ordered to do so. The Aurora herself we tied to the back of our boat.

A solid iron chest of Indian workmanship stood upon the deck. This, there could be no question, was the same that had contained the treasure of the Sholtos. There was no key, but it was very heavy, so we took it carefully to our cabin. As we went slowly up the river again, we flashed the searchlight in every direction, but there was no sign of the little black man.

25

Chapter 11
The Great Agra Treasure

Our Prisoner sat in the cabin opposite the iron box which he had done so much for and waited so long to gain. He was a sunburned man with frightening eyes. He had many lines and wrinkles on his face, which showed that he had had a hard, open-air life. He looked to be about 50 years old. He sat now with his handcuffed hands upon his legs and his head hanging down, while he looked at the box.

It seemed to me that there was more sorrow than anger in his face. He even once looked up with an expression of humor in his eyes.

"Well, Jonathan Small," said Holmes, lighting a cigar, "I am sorry that it has come to this."

"And so am I, sir," he answered frankly. "But I never did anything against Mr. Sholto. It was that little black devil, Tonga, who shot one of his thorns into him. I had no part in it, sir. I was as sad as if it had been my blood-relation. I beat the little devil with the end of a rope for it, but I could not undo it again."

"Have a cigar," said Holmes, "and you had better take a drink from my bottle because you are wet. How could you expect such a small man as Tonga to overpower Mr. Sholto and hold him while you were climbing the rope?"

"You seem to know as much about it as if you were there, sir. The truth is that I hoped to find the room empty. I knew the habits of the house pretty well, and it was the time when Mr. Sholto usually went downstairs for dinner. With Bartholomew Sholto I had no problem at all, so I had no intention of harming him."

"You are in the hands of Mr. Jones. He is going to bring you to my place and I will ask you to tell us the whole story. You must be completely truthful. If you are, I may be able to help you. I think that I can prove that the poison acts so quickly that the man was dead before you even reached the room."

"Yes, he was already dead, sir. I was never so surprised in my life as when I saw him smiling at me with his head on his shoulder as I climbed through the window. It really shook me. The truth is," he added with a bitter smile, "it was a bad day for me when I first saw the merchant Achmet and got mixed up with the Agra treasure, which never brought anything but evil to the man who had it. To Achmet it brought murder, to Major Sholto it brought fear and guilt, and to me it has meant prison for life."

At this moment Jones came into the tiny cabin.

"Well, I think we may all congratulate each other," he said. "Pity we didn't take the other alive but there was no choice. It was just lucky that we could overtake the Aurora."

"All's well that ends well," said Holmes.

"We will soon be landing," said Jones, "and we shall put you ashore, Dr. Watson, with the treasure box. But this is most irregular and, as a matter of duty, I must send a police officer with you, since you will have such a valuable thing. It is a pity there is no key, so that we could see what's inside first. You will have to break it open. Where is the key, my man?"

"At the bottom of the river," said Small.

"Why did you give us this extra trouble? We have had enough work already because of you. Anyway, Dr. Watson, be careful. Bring the box back with you to the Baker Street rooms."

They put me, the police officer and the box ashore. A quarter of an hour's drive took us to Mrs. Forrester's place. The servant told us that Mrs. Forrester was out, but that Miss Morstan was inside. The police officer waited in the cab while I went in with the box.

Mary was seated by the open window. When she heard me come in, she jumped to her feet and smiled with surprise and pleasure.

"I heard a cab drive up," she said. "I thought that Mrs. Forrester had come back very early but I never dreamed that it might be you. What news have you brought me?"

"I have brought something better than news," I said, putting down the box upon the table and looking at her joyfully, even though my heart was heavy within me. "I have brought you something which is worth all the news in the world. I have brought you a fortune."

She looked at the iron box. "Is that the treasure, then?" she asked, coolly enough.

"Yes, this is the great Agra treasure. Half of it is yours and half is Thaddeus Sholto's. You will be one of the richest young ladies in England. Isn't it glorious?"

I thought that she noticed an empty ring in my congratulations because I saw her eyebrows rise a little and she looked at me in a strange way.

"All I have," she said, "I owe to you."

"No, no." I answered, "not to me but to my friend, Sherlock Holmes. With all the will in the world, I could never have followed up a clue which was difficult even for him. As it was, we very nearly lost the thieves at the last moment."

"Please sit down and tell me about it, Dr. Watson," she said.

I told her briefly what had happened since I last saw her—Holmes's new method of search, the discovery of the Aurora, the joining with Jones, and the wild chase down the river. She listened with parted lips and shining eyes to my tale of adventure. When I spoke of the dart which had so narrowly missed us, she turned so white that I feared that she was about to faint.

"It is nothing," she said, as I hurried to pour her out some water. "I am all right again. It was a shock to me to hear that I had placed my friends in such horrible danger."

"That is all over," I answered. "It was nothing. I will tell you no more bad details. Let us turn to something brighter. There is the treasure. What could be brighter than that? I was allowed to bring it with me, thinking that it would interest you to be the first to see it."

"What a pretty box!" she said, bending over it. "This is Indian work, I suppose?"

"Yes, it is Benares metal-work."

"And so heavy," she exclaimed, trying to lift it. "The box alone must be of some value. Where is the key?"

"Small threw it into the river," I answered. "I must borrow Mrs. Forrester's poker." I forced open the lock and with trembling fingers opened the lid. We both stood looking in astonishment. The box was empty! Not one piece of metal or jewelry lay in it.

"The treasure is lost," said Miss Morstan calmly.

As I listened to the words and realized what they meant, a great shadow seemed to pass from my soul. I did not know how much this Agra treasure had weighed me down until now that it was finally removed. I thought it was selfish, disloyal, and wrong, but I could only think that now nothing separated us.

"Thank God!" I said from my very heart.

She looked at me with a quick, questioning smile. "Why do you say that?"

"Because you are within my reach again," I said, taking her hand. She did not withdraw it. "Because I love you, Mary, as truly as ever a man loved a woman. Because this treasure, these riches, kept me quiet. Now that they are gone I can tell you how I love you. That is why I said, 'Thank God.'"

"Then I say 'Thank God,' too," she whispered as I drew her to my side.

Whoever had lost a treasure, I knew that night that I had gained one.

26

Chapter 12
The Strange Story of Jonathan Small

I went back to Baker Street, where Holmes, Jones and Small had only just arrived. When I showed them the empty box, Small leaned back in his chair and laughed aloud.

"This is your doing, Small," said Jones angrily.

"Yes, I have put it away where you will never find it. It is my treasure and if I can't have it, no one can. No living man has any right to it, unless it is three men who are in the Andaman prison, and myself. All the time I have acted for them as much as for myself. It's been the sign of the four with us always. Well, I know that they would have had me do just what I have done, and throw the treasure into the river rather than let it go to the family of Sholto or Morstan."

"You are lying to us, Small," said Jones; "if you had wished to throw the treasure into the river, it would have been easier for you to have thrown it box and all."

"Easier for me to throw and easier for you to find," he answered. "The man who was clever enough to hunt me down is clever enough to pick an iron box from the bottom of a river. Now that they are scattered over five miles (eight km) or so, it may be a harder job."

"This is a very serious matter, Small. If you had helped us, you would have had a better chance at your trial."

"Help?" Small said angrily. "What help should I give to those who have never earned it? Look how I have earned it! I spent 20 long years working hard under the hot sun, chained up at night like a dog, burning with fever, bullied by black policemen who loved to beat a white man. That was how I earned the Agra treasure."

Small had lost all of his control in this outburst of anger. I could understand the fear that Major Sholto had when he first learned that Small was on his track.

"You forget that we know nothing of all this," said Holmes quietly. "We have not heard your story and we cannot tell if perhaps justice may have been on your side at one time."

"Well, sir, if you want to hear my story, I have no wish to hold it back. What I say to you is God's truth, every word of it. I am from Worcestershire, born near Pershore. My family were all steady church-going folk, small farmers, well-known and respected, but I was always different. When I was about 18, I joined the army and went to India.

"I was not destined to be a soldier for long, however. I had just learned to march and handle my gun, when I was fool enough to go swimming in the Ganges. A crocodile took me just as I was halfway across and bit off my right leg as clean as a doctor could have done it, just above the knee. With the shock and the loss of blood, I fainted, and might have died if my sergeant had not caught hold of me and swam for the shore. I got this wooden leg and found myself out of the army and not suitable for any active job.

"I was down on my luck, and not yet 20 years old. However, my misfortune soon proved to be a blessing in disguise. A man named Abel White, who had come out there as an indigo-planter, wanted someone to look after his workers. Since most of the work was to be done on a horse, my leg was not a problem. I had to ride over the plantation to keep an eye on the men as they worked, and to report those who were not working. The pay was fair, I had a small but nice place to live and altogether I was happy to spend the rest of my life there.

"Well, I was never lucky for long. Suddenly, there was a great uprising against the British. One month India was peaceful and the next there were 200,000 black devils let loose and the country was a perfect hell. I'm sure you read about it in the newspapers. My boss did not think it was so serious, so we didn't leave with the other Europeans on their way to Agra, the closest army fort.

"One day I was riding home from another plantation when I saw Abel White's house in flames. From where I stood I could see hundreds of black people, dancing and screaming around the burning house. Some of them pointed at me and a couple of bullets went past my head. So I ran away on the horse across the fields and found myself late at night safe within the walls of Agra.

"The old fort of Agra. is a very strange, very big place. There is a modern part, which held all of us and the supplies, with plenty of room to spare. But the modern part is nothing like the size of the old quarter, where nobody goes, and which is full of poisonous insects. It is full of great deserted halls, and winding passages, so that it is easy enough for someone to get lost in it.

"The river flows along the front of the old fort, and so protects it, but on the sides and behind there are many doors and these had to be guarded, of course. We were short-handed, so it was impossible for us to post a strong guard at every one of the many gates. I was chosen to take charge of a small isolated door on the southwest side of the building. There were two Sikh soldiers under my command and I was told to fire my gun if anything went wrong.

"Well, I was pretty proud at having this small command, since I was so new to the army, and a wooden-legged man at that. For two nights I kept the watch with my two Sikhs. Their names were Mahomet Singh and Abdullah Khan and they were both tall and fierce-looking,

"The third night of my watch was dark and rainy. I took out my pipe and laid down my gun to strike a match. In an instant the Sikhs were upon me. One of them took my gun and pointed it at my head, while the other held a knife to my throat, saying that he would kill me if I moved a step.

"Mahomet said 'Don't make a noise. The fort is safe enough.' I waited in silence to see what it was that they wanted from me.

"'Listen to me,' said the one called Khan. 'You must either be with us now, or you must be silenced forever. The thing is too great a one for us to hesitate. Either you are heart and soul with us or your body will be thrown into the river. There is no middle way. Which is it to be—death or life?'

"'How can I decide?' I asked. 'You have not told me what you want of me.'

"Khan explained, 'We ask you to be rich. If you choose to help us, we promise that you will have your fair share of the treasure. A quarter of it will be yours.'

"'But what is the treasure, then?' I asked. 'I am as ready to be rich as you can be if you will show me how it can be done.'

"'Do you promise, then,' he said, 'to raise no hand and speak no word against us, either now, or afterwards?'

"'I promise,' I answered, 'only if the fort is not in danger.'

"'Then, my friend, I promise you that you will have one quarter of the treasure, which will be equally divided among the four of us.'

"'There are but three,' I said.

"'No. Dost Akbar must have his share. We can tell you the tale while we wait.'

"Then Khan told me a story that was hard to believe, but his eyes told me it was true, every word.

"'There is a rajah in the northern provinces who has much wealth, though his lands are small. Much has come to him from his father and more still he has made by himself. He keeps his gold rather than spending it.

"'Being a careful man, he made plans to keep his treasure safe. The most precious stones and the best pearls, he put in an iron box and sent by a trusted servant, posing as a merchant, to the fort at Agra, to be hidden there until India is at peace.

"'This so-called merchant whose name is Achmet, is traveling with my foster brother, Dost Akbar, who knows his secret. Dost Akbar has promised to lead him to a side gate of the fort, and has chosen this one for his purpose. He will come soon and here he will find Singh and myself waiting for him. The place is lonely and no one will know of his coming. Then the great treasure of the rajah will be divided among us. What do you say?'

"'I am with you heart and soul,' I said.

"'It is well,' he answered, handing me back my gun. 'You see that we trust you, because your word, like ours, is not to be broken. We have now only to wait for my brother and the merchant.'

"The rain was still falling steadily because it was just the beginning of the wet season. Brown, heavy clouds were going across the sky and it was hard to see very far. Suddenly I saw a light on the other side of the moat. It was coming slowly in our direction.

"'There they are!' I exclaimed.

"'You will stop him, as usual,' whispered Abdullah. 'Give him no cause for fear. Send us in with him and we shall do the rest while you stay here on guard.'

"The light kept coming, and I could see two dark figures on the other side of the moat. I let them come down the sloping bank, splash through the mud, and climb halfway up to the gate before I challenged them.

"'Who goes there?' I called.

"'Friends,' came the answer. The first was a very big Sikh with a black beard which nearly came down to his waist-belt. The other was a little fat, round fellow with a great yellow turban and a bundle in his hand. He seemed to be shaking with fear and his head kept turning to left and right with two bright twinkling eyes,

"'I am so happy because I am once more safe—I and my poor things,' he said to me.

"'What have you in the bundle?' I asked.

"'An iron box,' he answered, 'which contains one or two little family matters, which are of no value to others but which I would be sorry to lose. I will reward you, young man, and your commander also if he will give me the shelter I ask.'

"'Take him to the main guard,' I said. The two Sikhs closed in upon him on each side, and the giant walked behind, through

the main gateway. I remained at the gateway with the lantern.

"I could hear their footsteps going through the lonely passages. Suddenly, they stopped and I heard voices and a struggle, with the sound of blows. A moment later there came, to my horror, a rush of footsteps in my direction. I turned my lantern down the long passage, and there was the fat man, running like the wind. I put my gun between his legs as he raced past and he fell, then rolled twice over like a shot rabbit. Before he could get to his feet the Sikh was upon him and buried his knife in his side. The man did not cry out or move a muscle but lay where he had fallen."

Small stopped and held out his hands for the whisky and water which Holmes had made for him. To me this was a horrible man and whatever punishment he might get, he would get no sympathy from me.

"Go on with your story," said Holmes.

"Well, we carried him in, Khan, Akbar and I. Singh was left to guard the door. We took him to a place which the Sikhs had already prepared. The earth floor had sunk in at one place, making a natural grave, so we left Achmet the merchant there, having first covered him over with loose bricks. This done, we all went back to the treasure.

"It lay where he had dropped it when he was first attacked.

The box was the same as that which now lies open upon your table. We opened it and the light of the lantern shined upon a collection of gems such as I have only dreamed of. It was blinding to look upon them. We took them all out and made a list of them. There were 143 diamonds, all first class, including one which has been called, I believe, 'the Great Mogul,' and is said to be the second largest stone in the world. Then there were 97 very fine emeralds and 170 rubies. Also, 210 sapphires, 61 agates, and a great quantity of other stones. Besides this, there were nearly 300 very fine pearls, 12 of which were set in a gold crown.

"We agreed to hide our treasure in a safe place until the country was at peace again, and then to divide it equally among ourselves. There was no use dividing it at that time, because if gems of such value were found on us, it would cause suspicion, and there was no place in the fort where we could keep them near us. We carried the box into the same hall where we had buried the body, and there, under certain bricks in the best-preserved wall, we made a hole and put our treasure in it. We made careful note of the place and the next day I drew four maps, one for each of us, and put the sign of the four of us at the bottom, because we had promised that we would each always act for all.

"Well, there's no use in telling you gentlemen what came of the Indian rebellion. It was broken by the English forces after a few months. Peace seemed to be settling upon the country, and we four were beginning to hope that we might safely go off with our shares of the treasure. However, our hopes were destroyed by our being arrested as the murderers of Achmet.

"It happened in this way. The rajah who sent Achmet with the box of jewels also sent a second person to follow him. This man saw Achmet go into the fort but never saw him come out. We were found guilty in court, though the treasure was never mentioned. because the rajah had left India and no one else knew about it. The murder, however, was clearly made out, and it was certain that we must all have played a part in it. We were to spend the rest of our lives in prison.

"So there we were all four in prison, with little chance of ever getting out again, while we each held a secret which could have made us richer than the richest of men. It might have driven me crazy, but I was always very stubborn so I did my best to endure the situation.

"At last my chance to escape seemed to have come. I and the three Sikhs were moved from Agra to Blair Island in the Andamans. There were very few white prisoners there and since I did nothing bad from the beginning, I soon found myself a kind of special person. I was given a small hut in Hope Town and I learned to pass out medicine for the doctor. I was even able to pick up a little of his knowledge. All the time I was on the lookout for a chance to escape; but the island was very far from any other land and there was little or no wind in those seas, so it was a very difficult job to get away.

"The doctor was a young man and he and the other young officers would meet in his rooms in the evening to play cards.

The place where I worked to make the medicine was next to his sitting room, with a small window between us. I watched these games almost every night. Among the players were Major Sholto and Captain Morstan.

"Well, there was one thing which I soon noticed. The soldiers always used to lose and the civilians always used to win. Major Sholto was the hardest hit. He played for big sums and would sometimes win a few times, and then the bad luck would set in against him worse than ever. All day he would be in a black mood and began to drink more than was good for him.

"One night he lost even more heavily than usual. I was sitting in my hut when he and Captain Morstan were on the way to their rooms. They were very close friends, those two, always together. The major was shouting about his losses.

"'It's all over, Morstan,' he was saying as they passed my hut. 'I shall have to send in my papers to quit the army. I am a ruined man.'

"'Nonsense, old friend!' said the other, 'I've had a bad time myself, but—' That was all I could hear but it was enough to set me thinking.

"A couple of days later Major Sholto and Captain Morstan were walking on the beach so I took the chance to speak to them.

"'I wish to have your advice, please,' I started.

"'Well, Small, what is it?' Sholto asked.

"'I wanted to ask you, sir,' I continued, 'who is the proper person to whom a hidden treasure should be handed over? I know where half a million lies and, as I cannot use it myself, I thought the best thing would be to hand it over to the proper person and then perhaps he would get my sentence shortened for me.'

"'Half a million, Small?' he said with excitement, looking hard at me to see if I was telling the truth.

"'Yes, sir—in jewels and pearls. It lies there ready for anyone. And the strange thing about it is that the real owner has been forced out of India and cannot have it, so it belongs to whoever finds it first.'

"'To the government, Small, you mean it belongs to the government.' But he said this in a halting way and I knew in my heart that I had got him.

"'You think, then, sir, that I should give the information to the governor-general?' I asked.

"'Well, well, you must not do anything too quickly, or that you might be sorry for later. Let me hear all about it, Small. Give me the facts.'

"I told him the whole story, with small changes, so that he could not know the places. When I had finished, he stood very still and his face was full of thought.

"'This is a very important matter, Small,' he said at last. 'You must not say a word to anyone about it, and I shall see you again soon.'

"The next night, Sholto and Morstan came to see me in my hut.

"'Listen, Small,' said the major. 'We've been talking it over,

my friend here and I, and we are sure that this secret of yours is not really a government matter, but is a private concern of your own. The question is, what price would you ask for it? We might be able to help, and at least look into it, if we could agree to something.' He tried to speak in a cool, careless way, but his eyes were shining with excitement and greed.

"'Well, for that matter, gentlemen,' I answered, trying also to be cool but feeling as excited as he did, 'there is only one bargain which a man in my position can make. I shall want you to help me to my freedom, and to help my three friends to theirs. We shall then make you partners and give you a fifth share to divide between you.'

"'Oh,' he said. 'A fifth share! That is not very much.'

"'It would come to 50,000 each,' I said.

"'But how can we gain your freedom? You know very well that what you ask for is impossible.'

"'Not at all,' I answered. 'I have thought it all out to the last detail. The only thing stopping our escape is that we can get no boat for the trip, and no food to last us for so long a time. There are plenty of little boats at Calcutta or Madras which would be just fine. You bring one over. We will get on board at night, and if you will take us to any part of the Indian coast, you will have done your part.'

"'It would be so much better if there were only one person to escape,' he said.

"'None or all,' I answered. 'We have promised each other. The four of us must always act together.'

"'You see, Morstan,' Sholto said, 'Small is a man of his word. He does not go back on his friends. I think we may very well trust him.'

"'It's a dirty business,' the other answered, 'but I think you're right.'

"'Well, Small,' said the major, 'we must, I suppose, try to help you. We must first, of course, test the truth of your story. Tell me where the box is hidden, and I will get time off my job and go back to India in the monthly supply-boat to check into things.'

"'Not so fast,' I said, growing colder as he got hot. 'I must get the OK of my three friends. I tell you that it is four or none with us.'

"'Nonsense!' he broke in. 'What do three black men have to do with our agreement?'

"'Black or blue,' I said, 'they are in with me, and we all go together.'

"Well, the matter ended at a second meeting, at which Singh, Khan and Akbar were all present. We talked the matter over again, and at last we came to an agreement. We were to give both officers a map of the part of the Agra fort, and mark the place where the treasure was hidden. Major Sholto was to go to India to test our story. If he found the box, he was to leave it there, to send out a small boat supplied for a trip, which was to lie off Rutland Island and to which we were to make our way, and finally to return to his duties. Captain Morstan was then to take time off duty, to meet us at Agra and there we were to have a final division of the treasure, he taking the major's share as well as his own.

"All this we sealed by the strongest promises that the mind could think of. I sat up all night with paper and ink, and by the morning, I had the two maps all ready, signed with the sign of the four—that is, of Abdullah, Dost, Mahomet and myself.

"Well, gentlemen, the evil Sholto went off to India, but he never came back again. He had stolen the treasure without keeping the promises on which we had sold him the secret. From that time I lived only for revenge. I thought of it all day and night. I cared nothing for the law—nothing for prison. To escape, to track down Sholto, to have my hand upon his throat—that was my one thought. Even the Agra treasure had come to be a smaller thing in my mind than the killing of Sholto.

"Well, I have set my mind on many things in this life, and never one which I did not carry out. But it was many years before my time came. I had told you that I had learned something of medicine. One day, when Dr. Somerton was down with a fever, a little Andaman Islander was picked up by some prisoners in the woods. He was sick to death and had gone to a lonely place to die. But I gave him some medicine and after a couple of months he got better and was able to walk. He took a liking to me then, and was always staying around my hut. I learned a little of his language from him, and this made him like me all the more.

"Tonga was his name. He was a very good boatman and owned a big canoe of his own. When I saw that he was so thankful and would do anything for me, I saw my chance of escape. I talked it over with him. He was to bring his boat around on a certain night to a place which was never guarded, and there he was to pick me up. I told him to bring lots of food and water.

"He was very true to me. No man ever had a better friend than Tonga. On the night we had named, he was waiting for me with his boat. I went to the boat and in an hour we were well out at sea. Tonga had brought all of his personal things with him. For 10 days we were at sea, trusting in luck and on the 11th we were picked up by a trading ship which was going from Singapore to Jiddah.

"Well, if I were to tell you all the adventures that my little friend and I went through, you would not thank me, because I would have you here until tomorrow morning. Here and there we went around the world, but something always kept us from going to London.

"All the time, however, I never forgot my purpose. I would dream of Sholto at night. I have killed him 100 times in my sleep. At last, however, some three or four years ago, we found ourselves in England. I had no great difficulty in finding where Sholto lived. I made friends with someone who could help me—I name no names because I don't want to get anyone else in trouble—and I soon found that he still had the jewels. Then I tried to get at him in many ways; but he was clever and, besides his sons, always had two bodyguards near him.

"One day, however, I got word that he was dying. I hurried at once to the garden, angry that he might slip out of my hands like that and, looking through the window, I could see he was close to death. I got into his room that same night, and I searched his papers to see if there was any record of where he had hidden our jewels. There was not a line and I came away as bitter as a man could be. Before I left I thought that if I ever met my Sikh friends again, they would be glad to know that I had left some mark of our hatred. So I wrote down the sign of the four of us, as it had been on the map and I put it on his chest.

"Then I heard that the treasure was being hunted for and, after some time, that it had been found. It was up at the top of the house in Mr. Bartholomew Sholto's chemical laboratory.

"I went at once and had a look at the place, but I could not see how, with my wooden leg, I could make my way up to it. I learned, however, about a trapdoor in the roof and also about Mr. Sholto's supper hour. It seemed to me that I could do it easily with Tonga's help. I took him with me and tied a long rope around his waist. He could climb like a cat and he soon made his way through the roof, but by bad luck, Bartholomew Sholto was still in the room. Tonga thought he had done something very clever in killing him.

"He was surprised when I got angry at him for killing the man. I took the treasure box and let it down, and then slid down myself, having first left the sign of the four upon the table to show that the jewels had come back at last to those who had most right to them. Tonga then pulled up the rope, closed the window and went out the way he had come in.

"I don't know if I have anything else to tell you. All this is the truth, and if I tell it to you, gentlemen, it is not to amuse you, but it is only to let all the world know how badly I have myself been served by Major Sholto, and that I did not kill his son."

"A very interesting story," said Sherlock Holmes. "A suitable end to a very interesting case. There is nothing at all new to me in the last part of your story, except that you brought your own rope. That I did not know. By the way, I had hoped that Tonga had lost all his darts but he shot one at us in the boat."

"He had lost them all, sir, except the one which was in his blow-pipe at the time."

"Ah, of course," said Holmes. "I had not thought of that."

"Well, Holmes," said Jones, "I will feel more at ease when we have our storyteller here safe under lock and key. I thank you both for your help. Of course, you will be wanted at the trial. Good-night to you."

"Good-night, gentlemen," said Jonathan Small.

"Well, and there is the end of our little drama," I said, after Holmes and I had sat some time smoking in silence. "I fear it may be the last time I shall have the chance of studying your

methods. Miss Morstan has done me the honor of accepting me as a husband."

Holmes groaned. "I feared as much. I really cannot congratulate you."

I was a little hurt. "Have you any reason to not like my choice?" he asked.

"Not at all. I think she is one of the most charming young ladies I have ever met. But love is an emotional thing and whatever is emotional is opposed to that true cold reason which I place above all things. I would never marry myself because it would harm my reasoning power."

I laughed. "I think my reasoning will be all right. But you look very tired."

"Yes, I'm feeling it. I think I will be this way for a week."

"It all seems unfair," I said. "You have done all the work in this business, I get a wife out of it, Jones gets the credit, but what is there for you?"

"For me," said Sherlock Holmes, "there still remains the cocaine bottle." And he stretched his long white hand up for it.

The Hound of the Baskervilles

バスカヴィル家の犬

読み始める前に

The Hound of the Baskervilles バスカヴィル家の犬

「シャーロック・ホームズ」シリーズの長編3作目
1901年の「ストランド・マガジン」8月号に初出

［主な登場人物］

Sherlock Holmes シャーロック・ホームズ　鋭い観察眼と推理力、そして犯罪に関する膨大な知識をあわせ持つ私立探偵。ロンドンのベーカー街221Bに下宿している。

John H. Watson ジョン・H・ワトソン　医師。ホームズのよき相棒でこの物語の語り手。ベーカー街221Bでホームズと同居している。

James Mortimer ジェームズ・モーティマー　本件の依頼人。死亡したチャールズ・バスカヴィル卿の主治医であり、友人。

Charles Baskerville チャールズ・バスカヴィル卿　デボンシャー州の富豪、バスカヴィル家の当主。ある日、死体で発見される。

Hugo Baskerville ヒューゴ・バスカヴィル　チャールズの数代前のバスカヴィル家の統治者。残酷な荒くれ者。

Barrymore and his wife バリモアとその妻　バスカヴィル家の使用人。先代からこの屋敷に勤めている。

Henry Baskerville ヘンリー・バスカヴィル　バスカヴィル家の現当主。チャールズ卿の弟（若くして死亡）の子ども。唯一の遺産相続人。

Frankland フランクランド　ラフターホール（Lafter Hall）の住人。趣味は望遠鏡で星をみること。結婚したローラ（Laura Lyons）という娘がいる。

Jack Stapleton ジャック・ステープルトン　博物学者。メリピット・ハウス（Merripit House）に美しい妹ベリル（Beryl）と住む。

Rodger Baskerville ロジャー・バスカヴィル　チャールズ卿の一番下の弟。荒くれ者でヒューゴに似ていた。イギリスから南米に逃れ、家族もなく亡くなった。

Cartwright カートライト ホームズの手伝いをする少年。

James Desmond ジェームズ・デスモンド バスカヴィル家の遠縁にあたる聖職者。

Selden セルデン ノッティングヒル殺人事件の犯人。脱獄して逃走中。

Perkins パーキンス バスカヴィル家の御者。

Lestrade レストレード ホームズの長年の知り合いで警部。

［あらすじ］

ホームズをモーティマー医師が訪ねてくる。聞けば友人のチャールズ・バスカヴィル卿の死に際し、その財産の相続人であるヘンリー・バスカヴィルをロンドンに迎えにきたのだが、バスカヴィル家にまつわる恐ろしい伝説のこともあり、そのままデボンシャーの屋敷に連れていっていいものか迷っているというのだ。他の事件もありロンドンを離れられないホームズの代わりに、ワトソンが事件解明とヘンリー保護のためデボンシャーに赴くことになった。

500年続く名家には、チャールズに仕えていた使用人のバリモア夫妻が住んでおり、ほかに近隣住人のステープルトン兄妹、フランクランド親娘らが登場するが、誰もがいわくありげに見える。正体不明の男の存在も浮かび上がり、ホームズに報告するかたちでワトソンの推理が展開される。そしてワトソンも予期せぬところから、ついにホームズが登場する。

突然のホームズの出現に驚くワトソンだったが、ここから2人の謎解きが最終段階に入る。本当にバスカヴィル家の不幸は、魔犬伝説のせいなのか？　真相解明に乗り出すホームズとワトソンだったが、それには危険を伴う大きな賭けに出なければならなかった。

Illustrations by Sidney Paget (1901-1902)

［総単語数］23,420語

27

Chapter 1
Mr. Sherlock Holmes

Mr. Sherlock Holmes was sitting at the breakfast table. I was holding the walking stick which a visitor had forgotten the night before. It was a good, thick piece of wood with a large, round head. There was a silver band around it on which was written, "To James Mortimer, M.R.C.S., from his friends of the C.C.H. 1884." Family doctors often carried such a stick.

"Well, Watson, we missed the visitor last night. We know his name but don't know why he came. Let's see what we can understand about him by studying his stick."

Holmes took the stick, walked to the window, and studied it closely.

"I think he is a young doctor who worked at Charing Cross Hospital, but left the city to work in the country. I think he is friendly, not interested in success, and forgetful. And he has a dog of average size."

I couldn't believe Holmes knew these things by looking at

a stick. From my bookcase I took down the Medical Directory and found the name Mortimer. I read to Holmes.

"Mortimer, James, M.R.C.S., 1882, Grimpen, Dartmoor, Devon. House-doctor, from 1882 to 1884, at Charing Cross Hospital. Author of several papers about disease. Medical Officer for the counties of Grimpen, Thorsley, and High Barrow."

Holmes smiled knowingly. "In my experience only a friendly man receives gifts from co-workers; only a man not interested in success leaves a London practice for the country; and only a forgetful one leaves his stick."

"And the dog?"

"The dog often carries the stick behind his master. Here are his teeth marks. They are about the size of a—yes, it is indeed a spaniel."

"My dear Holmes, how can you possibly know that?"

"Because I see the dog now on our door-step, and his master is ringing our bell. Let's find out what Dr. James Mortimer, a man of science, wants from Sherlock Holmes, the detective."

Our visitor didn't look like a country doctor. He was a young man, very tall and thin, with a long nose like a bird. He wore eyeglasses. His clothes were old. He walked with his head forward in a kind, curious manner. As he entered the room, he noticed the stick in Holmes's hand, and ran towards it

with joy. "Oh, I'm so very glad," he said. "I couldn't remember where I left it. I love that stick."

"Well, you are as we imagined you," said Holmes, glancing at me. "And now, how can we help you?"

"I assume that you are Mr. Sherlock Holmes."

"That's correct. And this is my friend, Dr. Watson."

"I have heard of you both and am very glad to meet you. I am a humble man of science, Mr. Holmes. I have a particular interest in the brain."

Sherlock Holmes pulled up a chair for our strange visitor. "Did you come here last night and again today only to talk about brains?"

"No, sir, no. I came to you because I am faced with a very serious problem and you are a great detective."

"Tell me about your problem, Dr. Mortimer."

28

Chapter 2
The Curse of the Baskervilles

"I have a manuscript in my pocket," said Dr. James Mortimer.

"Yes, I can see a corner of it. I'm very good at dating manuscripts. I'd say that one is from 1730," said Holmes.

"Well done, Mr. Holmes. The exact date is 1742." Dr. Mortimer took it from his coat pocket. "Sir Charles Baskerville gave me this family manuscript. His death three months ago in Devonshire was very sudden and sad. I was his personal friend as well as his doctor."

Holmes reached for the manuscript and opened it. At the top was written: "Baskerville Hall, 1742."

"It appears to be a story."

"Yes, it is a tale about the Baskerville family. But it will help you to understand why I came here. I'd like to read it to you."

Holmes leaned back in his chair and listened. Dr. Mortimer began to read the following, strange tale:

"My sons, I come in a direct line from Hugo Baskerville. My father told me about the Hound of the Baskervilles, as his father had told him. I write this story now believing what I was told. I want you to believe that the evils of the past can be forgiven and changed. Learn from this tale so that the past tragedy of our family will not come again in our future.

"Many years ago this Manor of Baskerville was owned by Hugo. He was a wild and godless man, like others in the region, and he was also a very cruel man. Hugo fell in love with the daughter of a farmer who lived in the area. But the good, kind, young lady was afraid of him. One holiday the girl's father and brothers were away from home. Hugo knew this, so he went with a few of his bad companions to the farm and carried off the girl. They brought her to the Hall and locked her in an upstairs room. They then went downstairs to get drunk, as they did every night. The poor girl upstairs was afraid but brave. She climbed out the window and escaped. Then she ran towards home across the moor.

"A short time later Hugo discovered she was gone. He was crazy with anger. He ran downstairs, jumped up on the table, and shouted that he would give his soul to the devil in return for catching the girl. His drunken friends were surprised. One of them said they should let the hounds chase the girl. Hugo then ran outside and let the hounds go. He got on his horse and followed them across the moor in the moonlight.

"A while later his drunken friends got on their horses and rode toward the farmer's house. On the moor they passed one of the night watchmen. They asked him if he had seen the hunt. The man was so afraid that he could hardly speak. He said that he had seen the unhappy girl, the hounds chasing her, and Hugo Baskerville on his black horse. 'But I have seen more than that,' he said. 'Running silently behind the horse was a huge hound. It must have been from hell because God could not have created such an animal.' At first the drunken men didn't believe him. But later they saw the frightened black horse without a rider. Soon, they also saw the hounds standing together on a hilltop, making crying sounds.

"Now the riders were afraid. Finally, they rode down the valley until they came to a broad open space. They saw two large stones, placed there hundreds of years ago by ancient people. The moon was shining brightly. The poor farm girl lay near the stones. She had died of fear. Near her lay the body of Hugo Baskerville. Standing over Hugo and tearing at his throat was a terrible black beast. It looked like a hound, but was larger than any dog alive. As they watched, the beast ate the neck of Hugo Baskerville.

> Then, with fiery eyes, it turned towards the men. They rode screaming across the moor. Their lives were never again the same.
>
> "This is the tale, my sons, of the hound which has cursed our family ever since. I tell you this because I believe that it is better to know the truth than to hide from it. It is true that many in our family have died sudden, bloody, mysterious deaths. However, we must be good people and trust God to remove this curse from our family. Finally, my sons, please don't cross the moor at night when the powers of evil are greatest."

Dr. Mortimer finished reading this story and looked at Holmes.

"Very interesting," said Holmes.

Dr. Mortimer then took a newspaper article from his pocket.

"Now, Mr. Holmes, here is something more recent. This is the *Devon Newspaper* of May 14th of this year. It is a short account of the facts of Sir Charles Baskerville's death."

Our visitor began to read:

> "The recent sudden death of Sir Charles Baskerville is a tragedy for the county. The baronet was a very likable and generous person who had many friends. He made his money in South Africa. Two years ago he brought that money to Devonshire when he moved into the family home. He had many ideas to improve Baskerville Hall and

the county. Sir Charles had no children. He wanted to share his wealth with others.

"Sir Charles probably died of natural causes and was not murdered. There are old tales about the family history, but they had nothing to do with his death. He was a man of simple tastes. He had only two housekeepers, Barrymore the butler and his wife. They said that Sir Charles was not very healthy. Dr. James Mortimer, his friend and doctor, also said he had a weak heart.

"The facts of the case are simple. Sir Charles Baskerville took a walk along the path of yew trees every night. On May fourth, Sir Charles told Barrymore that he was going to London the next day. That night he went out for his usual evening walk, smoking his usual cigar. He never returned. At midnight Barrymore became worried and went to search for him. He could follow Sir Charles's footprints on the wet path. Halfway down the path there is a gate which leads out onto the moor. It appeared that Sir Charles had stood at the gate for some time. His body was discovered at the end of the path. Barrymore says that his master's footprints changed after he passed the moor gate. There were no marks of any kind on the dead man's body. However, there was a terrible look

> of fear on his face. Both Dr. Mortimer and the police doctor believe that he died of a heart attack. Now the foolish tales of evil can be ended and the next heir can move into Baskerville Hall. That person is Mr. Henry Baskerville, son of Sir Charles Baskerville's younger brother. The young man lives in America."

Dr. Mortimer said, "Those are the public facts of Sir Charles's death."

"I see," said Sherlock Holmes. "Now please give me the private facts."

Dr. Mortimer seemed emotional. "There are few people who live on the moor. Everyone there knows each other. I often saw Sir Charles Baskerville. Only two other men who live there, Mr. Frankland of Lafter Hall, and Mr. Stapleton, the natural scientist, are well-educated. Sir Charles and I became friends because of his illness, and because we love science.

"In recent months Sir Charles's nervous condition became worse. He truly believed this tale and the terrible curse of his family. He was afraid to walk on the moor at night and never left his own property. Often, he thought he heard strange creatures at night.

"I suggested that Sir Charles go to London because he needed a city holiday. And then came this terrible night.

"The night Sir Charles died, Barrymore the butler sent for me. I got to Baskerville Hall less than an hour after he found the body. I checked all the facts, including the footsteps down the path. I was also the first one to examine the body. His face was so changed by fear that I hardly recognized him. There were no marks on his body. I also clearly saw something near the body that no one else saw—the footprints of a giant hound!"

29

Chapter 3
The Problem

I could see the excitement in Holmes's eyes at these words.

"You said nothing? Why did no one else see it?"

"The marks were about twenty yards from the body. I'm sure I noticed them only because I'd heard the tale. The prints were huge."

"But it did not come near the body?"

"No."

"What kind of night was it?"

"Wet and cold."

"What is the path like?"

"There are two lines of old yew trees. They grow like a wall and are about twelve feet high. The path in the center is a strip of grass on both sides between the trees and path. There is a gate which leads to the moor about halfway along the path."

"Is there any other opening to the path?"

"None. Only from the house."

"Tell me, Dr. Mortimer, were the footprints you saw on the path or the grass?"

"The path. You can't see any prints on the grass."

"Were they on the same side of the path as the moor gate?"

"Yes, they were on the edge of the path on the gate side."

"Very interesting. Was the gate closed?"

"Closed and locked."

"How high was it?"

"About four feet high."

"Then anyone could climb over it?"

"Yes."

"And what marks did you see by the wooden gate?"

"It seems that Sir Charles had stood there for several minutes."

"How do you know that?"

"Because the ash from his cigar had dropped twice."

"Good detective work, Doctor. But I wish I had been there. I would know exactly what happened."

"However, Mr. Holmes, there are some things even you cannot know."

"Do you believe that this thing is supernatural?"

"I don't know anymore. Before Sir Charles died, several people said they saw a huge, devilish creature on the moor. People are very afraid and nobody will cross the moor at night."

"You are a scientist. Do you think it comes from hell?"

"I honestly don't know."

Holmes sighed. "Dr. Mortimer, if you believe such

supernatural stories then why did you come to me?"

"It's about the young heir, Sir Henry Baskerville."

"Is he the only heir?"

"Yes. Sir Charles had two younger brothers. The second brother died young. He was the father of Henry. The third, Rodger Baskerville, was the family bad boy. They tell me he looked and acted like old Hugo. He had to escape from England and ran to Central America. He died there in 1876 of disease. Henry is the last of the Baskervilles. I must meet him at Waterloo Station in one hour. Now, Mr. Holmes, what should I do?"

"I think he should go to his family home."

"Yes, he probably should. The well-being of the entire county depends upon the wealth of the family. But every Baskerville who goes there meets an evil fate. This young man is the last heir. I need your advice."

Holmes thought for some time.

"I suggest that you take a cab to Waterloo and meet Sir Henry."

"And then?"

"Say nothing to him until I make a decision about the matter."

"How long will that be?"

"Twenty-four hours. Please return here with Sir Henry at ten o'clock tomorrow."

"All right, Mr. Holmes." He began to leave.

"Only one more question, Dr. Mortimer. Did anyone see this creature on the moor after Sir Charles died?"

"I don't think so."

"Thank you. Good morning."

Holmes returned to his seat with a satisfied look on his face.

I knew that my friend needed to be alone. He wanted to smoke tobacco and think about the case. I spent the day at my club and returned to Baker Street at nine o'clock that evening. The room was completely filled with smoke.

"I see you have been inside all day," I said.

"My body remained in this armchair, but my mind went to Devonshire. Here is a large map of the area, and here is Baskerville Hall in the middle."

"There are woods around it?"

"Yes. This is the small village of Grimpen, where Dr. Mortimer lives. As you see, there are only a few other buildings in the area. These are farmhouses. Here is Lafter Hall and there is a house which may be the home of Stapleton, the natural scientist. Then fourteen miles away is the great prison of Princetown. All around these points is the lifeless moor. It's the kind of place a devil would enjoy—"

"Then you, too, believe in this supernatural idea?"

"No. I believe that people can be devils. There are two questions to begin with. The first, whether or not there has been any crime; the second, what is the crime and how was it done? Have you thought about the case?"

"Yes, all day long. It's very strange, indeed. For example, why do you think his footprints changed down the path?"

"He was running, Watson—running for his life. He ran until his heart stopped and he fell dead."

"Running from what?"

"I don't know yet. But I think he was very afraid of something that came from the moor. I also think he was waiting for someone."

"Why do you think so?"

"The man was old and not healthy. The weather was bad. Why would he stand in one place for five or ten minutes?"

"But he went out every evening."

"Yes, but he usually avoided the moor and probably the gate. That night he waited there. It was the night before he went to London. This case interests me, Watson."

30

Chapter 4
Sir Henry Baskerville

Our guests arrived at almost exactly ten o'clock the next morning. The young heir was a small man with dark, intelligent eyes, about thirty years old. He had a strong-looking body and face. He appeared to be both a man of the outdoors, and an English gentleman.

"This is Sir Henry Baskerville," said Dr. Mortimer.

"Yes," he said, "and I'm glad to meet you, Mr. Holmes. I understand that you enjoy puzzles. I've already had one this morning."

"What happened?"

"Nothing very important, Mr. Holmes. It was this letter I received this morning."

He put the letter on the table. The address, "Sir Henry Baskerville, Northumberland Hotel," was printed with a rough hand. It was postmarked, "Charing Cross," with yesterday's date.

"Who knew that you were going to the Northumberland Hotel?" asked Holmes, looking at our visitor.

"Nobody. Dr. Mortimer and I decided to stay there only after we met."

"Hmmm! Someone seems to be interested in where you go." He unfolded the letter. In the middle of the paper was a single sentence made up of printed words placed together. It said:

> If you value your life or your reason, keep away from the moor.

Only the word "moor" was written by hand.

"What does this mean, Mr. Holmes?" asked Sir Henry Baskerville.

"Well, Dr. Mortimer, there seems to be nothing supernatural about it."

"What are you talking about?" asked Sir Henry sharply.

"I promise you, Sir Henry, that you will know as much as we do before you leave this room," said Sherlock Holmes. "For now, let's think only about this very interesting note. It must have been put together and posted yesterday evening. Do you have yesterday's *Times* newspaper, Watson?"

"Yes, here it is."

His eyes quickly ran up and down the pages. "I see that the words in this letter and the print in the newspaper are the same. Someone cut out those words from yesterday's paper."

"You're right! That's very clever!" cried Sir Henry.

"Well, this is my special interest. I have studied the differences in newspaper type for years. The *Times* is like no other print."

"But why was the word 'moor' written by hand?" asked Sir Henry.

"Because the other words were all simple to find in a newspaper. But 'moor' is less common, and this person could not find it in print."

"What else do you see in this message?"

"There are one or two other clues. The address, for example, is written in rough characters. I think the writer is trying to hide his own handwriting because you may recognize it. Also, the *Times* is a paper usually read by educated people. So I assume that the letter was created by an educated man. Further, you see that the words are not arranged in a straight line. I believe he was in a hurry when he did this because he wanted it to reach Sir Henry quickly."

"Surely, Mr. Holmes, you are only guessing now," said Dr. Mortimer.

"I don't like the word guess. Rather, I begin with real facts and use science in my thinking. And one more thing; I feel certain that this address was written in a hotel."

"How on earth can you say that?"

"Look closely and you will see that the writer had difficulty with the pen. A private pen is usually full and working well. But as you know, in hotels it is uncommon to find a good pen. Yes, I really think that we should look in the hotel waste-baskets around Charing Cross until we find the same copy of the *Times*. Then we could easily find our writer. Whoa! What's this?"

He was examining the letter paper, holding it close to his nose.

"Well, what is it?" I asked.

"Oh, nothing," he said suddenly, putting it down. "I think there is nothing more to learn from this strange letter. So, Sir Henry, what else has happened to you since you came to London?"

"Well, there is one small matter. I've lost one of my shoes."

"Please tell me about it," said Holmes.

"Well, yesterday I went shopping because I needed new clothes. Among other things, I bought some expensive brown shoes. They needed a special oil to make them soft so I put them outside my door last night. This morning there was only one. The man who cleans them didn't know anything about it. The worst part is that I never had a chance to wear them."

"Interesting," said Holmes. "Perhaps you'll find the missing shoe when you return to the hotel."

"I hope so. Now, gentlemen," said Sir Henry, "please keep your promise and tell me what's going on here."

"All right," Holmes answered. "Dr. Mortimer, I think you ought to explain the story to Sir Henry as you did to us."

Then our friend of science took his papers from his pocket and repeated what he had told us. Sir Henry Baskerville listened closely until he finished.

"Well, I'm in an interesting situation. Of course, I've heard of the hound since I was a young boy. It's a favorite family story. But I never thought it was serious. My uncle's death is a real mystery, isn't it?"

"Yes," answered the doctor.

"And now someone sent this letter to me at the hotel."

"Perhaps someone is kind enough to warn you of danger," said Holmes. "Or they may be trying to frighten you for their own purposes. But now we must decide, Sir Henry, whether or not you should go to Baskerville Hall."

"I've already decided. There is no devil in hell, Mr. Holmes, and there is no man on earth who can stop me from going to my home. And that is my final answer." He had the forceful voice and strong temper of the Baskervilles. "Right now," he said, "I would like to have an hour or two to think about all that has happened. Mr. Holmes, why don't you and Dr. Watson come have lunch with us at two o'clock? We can talk further then."

"Fine. You may expect us at two. Shall I call a cab for you?" Holmes asked.

"I'd prefer to walk in the fresh air. Good day."

Our visitors left the house. Instantly, Holmes said, "Quick, get your hat and coat, Watson! We must follow them!" We hurried down the stairs and into the street. Dr. Mortimer and Baskerville were about two hundred yards ahead of us.

"It is a very fine morning for a walk, Watson. I want to follow our friends but I don't want them to see us."

We continued into Oxford Street and down Regent Street. That's when Holmes noticed the cab across the street with a man inside. When our friends stopped, the cab stopped. When they moved, it moved.

"He's our man, Watson! Come on! We'll have a good look at him."

At that instant I saw a face with a large black beard inside the cab. He looked at us through the window. He then shouted to the driver, and the cab drove quickly down Regent Street. Holmes looked quickly for another cab but saw none. He then chased the cab down the street, but was already too far behind.

Holmes was upset. "Bad luck and bad planning, too. It was my fault! I should have stayed behind the cab. Now we have lost him."

"Who was the man?"

"I have no idea. But I knew that someone was following Baskerville. That's how this person knew they were at the Northumberland Hotel. This man is very clever, Watson, and I don't know yet whether he wants to hurt or to help us."

"Too bad we didn't get the cab number!"

"My dear Watson, it was number 2704."

We were standing on Regent Street. Dr. Mortimer and Sir Henry were no longer in sight.

"There's no point in following them now," said Holmes. "The mystery man is gone. Did you see his face inside the cab?"

"Only that he had a large beard."

"Yes, and it was probably a false beard to hide his face. Come in here, Watson!"

Holmes walked into one of the local messenger offices. He was greeted by the manager.

"Ah, Mr. Holmes, how can I help you?"

"Does that boy named Cartwright still work for you?"

"Yes, sir, I'll get him."

"Thank you! And I would like to change this five-pound note."

A boy of fourteen with a bright face was called in by the manager. He stood looking with great respect at the famous detective.

"Let me have the Hotel guide book," said Holmes. "Thank you! Now, Cartwright, there are the names of twenty-three hotels here, all in the area of Charing Cross. Do you see?"

"Yes, sir."

"Here is what I want you to do. You will visit each hotel. You will give the doorman one shilling. Here are twenty-three shillings."

"Yes, sir."

"Tell him that you want to see yesterday's waste-paper. Tell him that an important telegram was lost and that you are looking for it. But you are really looking for a page of the *Times* with some holes cut in it. Here is a copy of the *Times*. Can you recognize it?"

"Yes, sir."

"It will be a difficult job and you probably won't find it. But try your best. Here are ten extra shillings in case you have any problems. Send me a report at Baker Street before the evening. And next, Watson, we will send a wire to find out who was cab driver number 2704."

31

Chapter 5
Three Broken Threads

At two o'clock we arrived at the Northumberland Hotel.

"Sir Henry Baskerville is expecting you," said the front desk man.

We walked up the stairs. Sir Henry was standing in front of his room, his face was red with anger. He was holding an old, dirty shoe.

"What's the matter?" asked Holmes.

"These hotel people must think I'm a fool," he cried. "This is a bad joke. If that man can't find my missing shoe there will be trouble."

"Are you still looking for your shoe?"

"Yes, sir, but this time it's an old black one."

"What! You don't mean—?"

"That's just what I mean. I only had three pairs of shoes in the world—the new brown ones, the old black ones, and the special leather ones which I'm wearing now. Last night they took one of my brown ones, and today they took one of the black. Well, have you got it? Speak, man!" said Sir Henry to a nervous German worker.

"No, sir. I have asked all over the hotel, but nobody knows about it."

"I'm going to tell the manager."

"Please be patient, sir. I promise we will find it."

"Excuse my anger, Mr. Holmes. This is one of the strangest things that has ever happened to me. What do you think of it?"

"Well, Sir Henry, I'm not sure yet. I've handled many cases, but yours is one of the most difficult I've faced. Sooner or later we will know the truth."

The four of us talked during lunch in the hotel dining room.

"I'd like to go to Baskerville Hall at the end of the week."

"I think that's a good idea," said Holmes. "Did you know that someone was following you and Dr. Mortimer?"

Dr. Mortimer sat up surprised.

"Followed! By whom?"

"I don't know. Do you know anyone in Dartmoor who has a full, black beard?"

"No—or, um, let me see—why, yes. Barrymore, Sir Charles's butler, has a full, black beard."

"Ha! Where is Barrymore?"

"He is in charge of the Hall."

"We should find out if he is really there, or if he is in London."

"How can you do that?"

"Give me a telegraph form." Holmes then wrote: 'Is all

ready for Sir Henry?' "That will do. What's the nearest town? Grimpen? Good, we will send this to the postmaster in Grimpen and ask him to deliver it directly to Barrymore at Baskerville Hall. If he's not there, then the postmaster will return the message here to Sir Henry."

"Very well," said Baskerville. "Dr. Mortimer, who is this Barrymore?"

"He is the son of the old housekeeper, who is dead. He and his wife are respected in the county."

"Did Sir Charles leave any money to Barrymore?" asked Holmes.

"He and his wife received five hundred pounds each."

"Ha! Did they know that they would receive this?"

"Yes. Sir Charles was very happy to talk about his will. Please don't think of everyone who received money from Sir Charles as a suspect. He also left a thousand pounds to me."

"Really! And anyone else?"

"There were many smaller amounts that went to different people. The rest went to Sir Henry."

"And how much was the rest?"

"Seven hundred and forty thousand pounds."

Holmes raised his eyes in surprise. "My, that's a large amount!"

"Sir Charles was richer than we knew. The total value of his possessions was nearly one million."

"Dear me! That's enough to make someone play a serious game. I must ask one more question, Dr. Mortimer. If anything happened to our young friend here, who would become heir to the property?"

"Well, Sir Charles's younger brother, Rodger Baskerville, died unmarried. So the property would go to the Desmonds, who are distant cousins. James Desmond is an old churchman in Westmoreland. I have met him. He is an intelligent, honest man. I don't think he cares about money. But he would be the heir unless Sir Henry wants to change the will."

"And have you made your will, Sir Henry?"

"No, Mr. Holmes, I've had no time. But my uncle believed that the money should go with the title and the property. I feel the same."

"Well, Sir Henry, I agree with you about going to Devonshire without delay. However, you must not go alone."

"Dr. Mortimer will return with me."

"But Dr. Mortimer is busy with his practice. And I am very busy here in London. You need a trusty man who will always be near you. My friend Watson is perfect for the job. Well, Watson, what do you think?"

I was very surprised. But before I had time to answer Baskerville was shaking my hand.

"Well, that is really kind of you, Dr. Watson," he said. "I will be very grateful to have your company at Baskerville Hall."

I have always enjoyed adventure. I also felt pleased by Holmes's words and the eagerness of Sir Henry.

"I will come, with pleasure," I said.

"And please report very carefully to me," said Holmes. "Then let's meet at the ten-thirty train from Paddington on Saturday."

We walked back up to the room with the two men. When Baskerville opened the door, he gave a little cry of joy. He pointed to his bed and walked over to it. He reached under the bed and picked up a new brown shoe.

"My missing shoe!" he cried.

"That's very strange," Dr. Mortimer remarked. "I searched this room carefully before lunch."

"And so did I," said Baskerville. "There was no shoe then."

"Probably the worker found it and put it there while we were eating."

We sent for the German, but he said he knew nothing about the shoe. No one else in the hotel knew either. Here was another mystery which had happened in the past two days. The others included the printed letter, the black-bearded man in the cab, the loss of the new brown shoe, and the loss of the old black shoe.

We said good-bye and got into the cab. Holmes sat in silence in the cab. I knew he was thinking deeply about all these odd facts.

Just before dinner two telegrams were brought to us. The first said:

> Have just heard that Barrymore is at the Hall.
>
> BASKERVILLE.

The second:

> Visited twenty-three hotels as directed, but sorry to report no *Times* paper with cut-outs.
>
> Cartwright.

"There go two of my clues, Watson. We must look around for others."

"We still have the cab driver."

"Exactly. I have already sent for him."

At that moment, the doorbell rang. A rough-looking man entered. He was indeed the cab driver.

"In the office they told me that a gentleman at this address was asking about No. 2704," he said. "Is something wrong?"

"There's nothing wrong, my good man," said Holmes. "In fact, I have half a pound for you if you will give me a clear answer to my questions."

"Well, what was it you wanted to ask, sir?" said the cab driver with a smile.

"First of all, what's your name?"

"John Clayton."

"Now, Clayton, tell me all about the passenger who came and watched this house at ten o'clock this morning, then followed two gentlemen down Regent Street."

The man looked very surprised. "Well, sir, he told me he was a detective, and that

I was to say nothing about him to anyone."

"Did he say anything more?"

"He mentioned his name."

Holmes glanced happily at me. "Oh? That was foolish. What was his name?"

"His name," said the cab driver, "was Mr. Sherlock Holmes."

Never have I seen my friend more surprised. For a moment he sat in shock. Then he began to laugh.

"Ah, Watson, he certainly fooled us this time, didn't he? So, his name was Sherlock Holmes. Excellent! Tell me where you picked him up and all that happened."

"He got in my cab this morning. He offered me two pounds if I would do exactly what he wanted all day. I agreed. We went to the Northumberland Hotel. Two gentlemen came out and we followed them here. We waited an hour and a half. Then we followed them again along Regent Street until the man told me to drive quickly to Waterloo Station. There he paid me, and told me, 'By the way, I'm Mr. Sherlock Holmes.' Then he walked into the station."

"And how would you describe Mr. Sherlock Holmes?" asked Holmes.

The cab driver seemed uncertain. "Well, I'd say he's about forty years old, of average height—shorter than you, sir. He was dressed like a rich man, and he had a black beard. His face was pale. That's all I can remember."

"Well, then, here is your half-pound. Thank you and good night!"

"Thank you, sir!"

John Clayton departed happily. Holmes turned to me with a slightly disappointed smile.

"There goes our third clue. We end where we began. Our bearded friend is very clever. He knew about us, so he told the driver that he was me. I tell you, Watson, this case will not be easy. Please be very careful in Devonshire."

32

Chapter 6
Baskerville Hall

Sir Henry Baskerville and Dr. Mortimer were ready to take the train to Devonshire on Saturday. Mr. Sherlock Holmes drove with me to the station.

"I will not tell you my theories of the case, Watson," he said. "Rather, I want you to simply report the facts to me, as completely as possible."

"What kind of facts?" I asked.

"Anything which may affect the case. I am quite sure that Mr. James Desmond is not a part of this case. That leaves the people who live with or near Sir Henry Baskerville on the moor. We have a list of suspects. There are the Barrymores. There is our friend Dr. Mortimer, whom I believe is perfectly honest. There is this scientist, Stapleton, and his sister, a young lady. There is Mr. Frankland, of Lafter Hall, who is also unknown to us, and there are one or two other neighbors. These are the people whom you must study."

"I will do my best."

"Do you have your guns?"

"Yes."

"Good. This may be a dangerous case. Always be careful."

Our friends were waiting for us outside our first-class car.

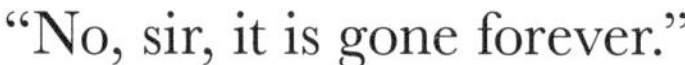

"No, we have no news of any kind," said Dr. Mortimer when Holmes asked him. "I am sure that nobody followed us these past two days."

"Did you find your other shoe?" Holmes asked Sir Henry.

"No, sir, it is gone forever."

"Indeed. That is very interesting. Well, good-bye." As the train began to move away he added, "Sir Henry, remember one of the sentences in that queer old tale which Dr. Mortimer read to us—avoid the moor in those hours of darkness when the powers of evil are strongest."

I looked back and watched the tall, straight figure of Holmes standing at the station.

The journey was fast and pleasant. In a very few hours we were in the rich, green farmland of Devonshire. The cows were eating the tall grass in the fields. Young Baskerville was excited by the scenery.

"I've seen a lot of the world since I left here, Dr. Watson," he said, "but I've never seen a prettier place."

"And I never met a Devonshire man who didn't love his county," I said.

"When was the last time you saw Baskerville Hall?" asked Dr. Mortimer.

"I've never been there. I was a teenager when my father died. We lived on the South Coast. From there I went straight to a friend in America. This is all new to me. I can't wait to see the moor."

"Well, wait no longer, for there is your first sight of the moor," said Dr. Mortimer, pointing out of the train window.

We looked out over the green squares of the fields and trees. In the distance was a gray, dark hill with a strange shape. It looked like scenery in a dream. Baskerville stared at it eagerly for a long time. It was his first sight of the land where his family had lived for centuries. He sat there in his American suit, with his American manners and way of speaking. But I knew that he was truly of this land. He had the family in his blood. There was pride and strength in his green eyes, his Celtic nose, and firm mouth. The moor might be dangerous, but he would be brave.

The train arrived at a pretty country station. The staff helped us carry our bags to a waiting wagon. Our driver was an old, small man. Soon we were driving down the wide white road. We passed farms, animals, houses and gentle hills in the warm afternoon sun. But behind that quiet countryside were those dark, rocky, evil-looking hills in the distant moor.

The wagon turned into a narrow, curving road. Autumn leaves fell from the many trees. The sun was setting. There was a steep curve in the moor road. On the point above us stood a horse and rider watching. He was a serious-looking soldier with a rifle.

Dr. Mortimer asked the driver, “Who is he?”

“There’s a criminal who escaped from Princetown Prison a few days ago. He’s a really dangerous villain. The guards watch every road. No one has seen him yet.”

“Who is he, then?”

“He’s Selden, the Notting Hill murderer.”

I remembered the case well because Holmes was interested in it. The killer was a truly hateful, evil person with no respect for life. Our wagon came to the top of the rise and we could see the moor clearly. A cool wind began to blow. Somewhere out there was an evil murderer hiding like a wild beast.

The farmland was now behind us. The scenery in front of us grew wilder and darker. There were huge rocks on the hillside. Occasionally, we passed a house built of stone. Suddenly, we saw two high, narrow towers above the trees.

“Baskerville Hall,” said the driver, pointing.

Sir Henry stood up and stared with shining eyes. A few minutes later we passed through the iron gate into the tree-lined

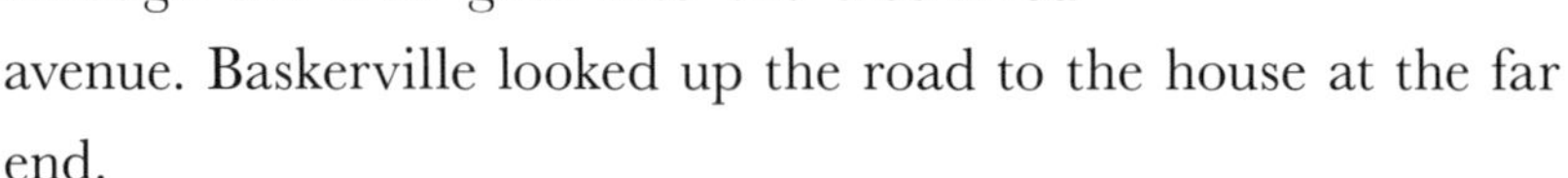

avenue. Baskerville looked up the road to the house at the far end.

“Was it here?” he asked in a low voice.

“No, no, the yew path is on the other side.”

The young heir glanced around with a sad face. "It's dark here. I'll soon brighten this place with electric lights."

We came to Baskerville Hall. The center of the house was a heavy, old building with ancient twin towers. To the right and left of the towers were more modern wings of black stone. A soft light was shining through the windows.

"Welcome, Sir Henry! Welcome to Baskerville Hall!"

A tall man stepped from the entrance to open the wagon door. A woman also came out to help with our bags.

"Sir Henry, my wife is expecting me at home," said Dr. Mortimer. "I'll say good-bye and leave you with Barrymore."

The wagon drove back out to the road while Sir Henry and I turned into the hall. The heavy door closed behind us. It was a fine building, we were in with large, high rooms of black oak. A warm fire was burning in the great old fireplace. It felt good because we were cold from the long drive. On the oak walls were family signs and animal heads.

"It's just as I imagined it," said Sir Henry with a big smile. "My family has lived in this same house for five hundred years. It makes me very proud."

Barrymore returned from taking our bags to the rooms. He stood in front of us now with the manner of a well-trained butler. He was a very good-looking man, tall with a square black beard and pale, strong features.

"Would you like dinner at once, sir?"

"Is it ready?"

"In a very few minutes, sir. You will find hot water in your rooms. My wife and I will be happy, Sir Henry, to stay with you until you have found new housekeepers. I'm sure that you will be needing more people to work."

"What do you mean?"

"Well, sir, Sir Charles led a quiet life. My wife and I were enough to care for the house. I'm sure you will want to have more company and will need more housekeepers."

"Do you mean that you and your wife wish to leave?"

"Only when it is convenient to you, sir."

"But your family has been with us for many, many years. I would feel badly if you left."

I could see the emotion on the butler's white face.

"My wife and I also feel that way, sir. But we were both very attached to Sir Charles. His death shocked us and made this house very painful to us. I'm afraid we shall never again feel comfortable in Baskerville Hall."

"But what do you intend to do?"

"I'm sure we shall succeed in one business or another. Sir Charles was very generous and we have enough money to live. And now, sir, may I show you to your rooms?"

Two sets of stairs went up to the second floor. There, two long hallways continued the whole length of the building. All the bedrooms opened on to these hallways. My room was near Sir Henry's in the same wing. This part of the house was newer and brighter.

But the dining room was a shadowy, unhappy room. It was too big for just two people. We were both silent. Old portraits of family members stared down at us from the walls. I was glad when the meal ended and we moved to the smoking room.

"Well, it isn't a very cheerful place," said Sir Henry. "Perhaps I will get used to it. I understand why my uncle was nervous living here alone. I think we should go to sleep early tonight and start fresh in the morning."

I tried to sleep but turned in my bed, awake for a long time. I heard the wind blowing outside. Then suddenly, in the dead of night, I heard the clear sound of a woman crying. She couldn't control her sorrow. She was certainly inside the house. When it stopped I waited for half an hour, my nerves wide awake. But there was no other sound except the wind.

33

Chapter 7
The Stapletons of Merripit House

The following morning was fresh, beautiful and sunny. We felt much better about Baskerville Hall.

"I guess we were just tired and cold from the drive last night!" said Sir Henry as we ate breakfast together.

"Probably," I answered. "Tell me, did you hear a woman crying in the night?"

"Actually, I thought I heard something when I was half asleep."

"I clearly heard a woman crying."

"We must ask about this right away." He rang the bell and asked Barrymore if he knew anything about the crying. The housekeeper's face seemed to turn more pale as he listened to the question.

"There are only two women in the house, Sir Henry," he answered. "One is the kitchen-maid, who sleeps in the other wing. The other is my wife, and I can tell you that it was certainly not her."

But he was lying, for after breakfast I met Mrs. Barrymore in the bright hallway. She was a large woman with heavy features. Her eyes were red and larger than normal. It was she who cried long and hard in the night. Her husband must have known, yet he denied it. Why? There was already an air of mystery around this pale, handsome, bearded man. He was the one who discovered the body of Sir Charles. Was it Barrymore we saw in the cab? The cab driver had described a shorter man, but he might have been mistaken. I decided to go see the Grimpen postmaster, and find out if Barrymore had received the test telegram.

Sir Henry was busy with papers and work after breakfast. I took a pleasant walk of four miles along the moor's edge to a very small village. The postmaster was also the village storekeeper. He remembered the telegram.

"Certainly, sir," he said. "This is my son James. He delivered it to Mr. Barrymore."

"Into his own hands?" I asked the boy.

"Well, he was upstairs at the time, so I could not put it into his own hands. But I gave it to Mrs. Barrymore, and she promised to deliver it."

"Did you see Mr. Barrymore?"

"No, sir. I told you he was upstairs."

"If you didn't see him, how do you know he was upstairs?"

"Well, surely his own wife should know where he is," said the postmaster, somewhat upset. "Didn't he get the telegram? If there is any mistake, it is for Mr. Barrymore himself to tell me."

I decided not to ask any more questions. Clearly, we could not be certain that Barrymore was at home and not in London. I walked back thinking about the case.

Suddenly, I heard the sound of running feet behind me and heard a voice call my name. I turned around. I didn't know this person. He was a small, thin, clean-faced man with golden hair, between thirty and forty years of age. He was dressed in a gray suit and country hat. He carried a net for catching insects and a box to put them in.

"Please excuse me, Dr. Watson," he said. "I am Stapleton, of Merripit House. I was visiting Mortimer when you walked by his house. I wanted to introduce myself."

"How do you do?" I said.

"I trust that Sir Henry is feeling fine after his journey?"

"He is very well, thank you."

"We were all afraid that Sir Henry might not want to live here after the tragedy of his uncle. Of course, you know the tale of the devil dog which attacks the family?"

"I have heard it."

"Surprisingly, many country people here believe the story. Some say they have seen the creature on the moor. I think Sir Charles believed the tale and died because of it. Maybe he really saw something that night in the yew path. What do you think?"

"I honestly don't know."

"What about Mr. Sherlock Holmes?"

I was greatly surprised to hear my friend's name.

"Dr. Watson, everyone around here knows about your great detective friend. Your name is also well known. If you are here then it follows that Mr. Holmes is interested in the matter. I am curious to know what he thinks."

"I can't answer that question because he's busy in London with other cases."

"What a pity! I would like to talk to him. Please tell me if I can be of any help to you in this case."

We came to a narrow, grassy path that crossed the road into the moor. There was a sharp hill with many large rocks to the right. In the distance was a house.

"That is Merripit House," he said, "where I live with my sister. Would you like to meet her?"

I knew that Holmes wanted me to meet the neighbors, so I agreed.

"It's a wonderful place, the moor," he said, looking around the hills and rocks and plants. "It contains so many secrets."

"You know it well, then?"

"I've only been here two years. We came shortly after Sir Charles moved in. Because of my interest in nature, I have walked around almost every part of this country. I'm sure that few men know the area better than I do."

"Is it hard to know?"

"Very hard. That is the great Grimpen Mire. A mire is a place of wet, soft, bottomless ground," he said. "A wrong step

there means death to man or beast. Today I saw a young moor horse die in there. It is always dangerous to cross it. But I have found one or two paths across the mire."

"Why do you want to go there?"

"Because the most uncommon plants and insects are in those hills."

"Perhaps I shall try one day."

"Dear God, don't even think of it," he said. "You would be lucky to come back alive."

"Whoa!" I cried. "What is that?"

A long, low, animal-like cry swept over the moor. It became a roar filling the air, then slowly ended.

"The country people say it is the Hound of the Baskervilles calling for its food."

I looked around, a great fear in my heart.

"Surely you don't believe those tales. What do you think made such a sound?"

"I really don't know," said Stapleton. "The moor is a strange place."

As we continued walking on the path I saw a hill covered with unusual stone circles.

"What are those?"

"They are the stone huts of ancient men who lived here thousands of years ago. There are walls but no roofs."

"What did those ancient people do?"

"They raised sheep and cows on these hills. They learned to

dig for metal. Look at the great hole they dug on the other hill."

Just then a small insect flew by, and Stapleton chased after it with great speed. I watched him running, jumping, and hopping across the mire. Then I heard the sound of footsteps behind me. I turned and saw a woman near me. She had come from the Merripit House path.

I was sure that this was Miss Stapleton. She was a very beautiful woman, and very different from her brother. He was of light color, fair hair, and gray eyes. She was tall, with dark eyes and very dark hair. And her dress was also beautiful. She walked quickly towards me.

"Go back!" she said. "Go straight back to London, immediately."

I stared at her in stupid surprise. She was very serious.

"Why?" I asked.

"I cannot explain," she quickly whispered. "Please God, I'm warning you. Leave and never come back here."

At that moment Stapleton returned from chasing the insect and his sister became quiet.

"Hello Beryl!" he said. His voice was not very friendly.

"Hello Jack," she answered. "I was just saying hello to Sir Henry."

"No, no," I said. "I'm only his friend. My name is Dr. Watson."

A puzzled look came over her face. "Well, excuse my error," she said.

Her brother looked at us with questioning eyes.

"Perhaps Dr. Watson would like to see our house," she then suggested. A short walk brought us to it. It was an old farm house recently rebuilt. The outside of the house seemed lonely and cold but the inside was much nicer. The butler greeted us. He was a strange, very old man in a reddish coat. I looked out the window at the boring moor. I could not understand why this well-educated man and this beautiful lady wanted to live there.

"It's a strange place for a house," said Stapleton as if reading my mind. "And yet we're quite happy here, aren't we Beryl?"

"Quite happy," she said, but her words sounded empty.

Stapleton said, "I had a school in the north. I loved teaching young people. However, we had some bad luck. There was a serious disease that occurred in the school and three of the boys died. The school closed and I lost a great deal of money. I miss teaching but I feel very lucky to live in this natural place."

"Isn't life a little dull for you here?" I asked Miss Stapleton.

"No, no, we are never bored," her brother answered.

"We have our studies, our books, and we have interesting neighbors like Dr. Mortimer. Poor Sir Charles was also an excellent companion. We were hoping to meet Sir Henry today."

"I'm sure he would be delighted."

"Meanwhile, please come upstairs and look at my excellent insect collection. Then we shall have lunch."

But I was eager to return to my duties. The sadness of the moor, the strange roar we heard earlier, and the serious

warning from Miss Stapleton all made me uneasy. I excused myself and said good-bye.

To my surprise I saw Miss Stapleton waiting for me along the path. She had taken a shorter route to meet me.

"I must tell you quickly, Dr. Watson, that I'm sorry for my mistake," she said. "Please forget what I said."

"But I can't forget, Miss Stapleton," I said. "I'm Sir Henry's friend. What danger is there to him? Please be honest with me."

For a moment I could see in her eyes that she wanted to tell me something important. But then she said, "Oh, it's nothing; just a feeling I have. We were very shocked by Sir Charles's death, Dr. Watson. When he died I thought the tales of the hound might be true. I was upset when Sir Henry came here because I don't want him to be hurt."

"I don't believe those tales. Tell me, Miss Stapleton, why are you worried that your brother will see you talking to me?"

"My brother is very anxious for someone to live in the Hall. He thinks it will be good for the poor people in this county. He would be very angry if he knew I wanted Sir Henry to leave. Now I must say good-bye." She turned and walked quickly toward the house. With my soul still full of uneasy fears I returned to Baskerville Hall.

34

Chapter 8
First Report of Dr. Watson

Baskerville Hall, October 13th.

My Dear Holmes:

Here on the moor I feel as if I have left modern England behind. It's a place with many ancient huts, graves, and temples. I think there are many strange mysteries here.

I am writing this report to tell you what I have observed until now.

There is a dangerous criminal on the moor who escaped from prison two weeks ago. It seems impossible that this villain could live on the moor alone all this time. Most people believe he is no longer in the area.

Our friend, Sir Henry, is showing great interest in his lovely neighbor, Beryl Stapleton. She is very different from her brother. On the outside, Stapleton seems very cool and without emotion, but I think there is a fire burning inside him. He has much control over his sister.

He came over to visit Baskerville that first afternoon. The

next morning he took us to see where the story of the evil Hugo took place. The scene was just as we heard it described in the story. There was a grassy area in a small, rocky valley with two old, tall stones that looked like the teeth of a beast. Sir Henry was very interested in all of it.

On our way back we stopped for lunch at Merripit House. That is when Sir Henry met Miss Stapleton for the first time. Both of them appeared to like one another. Since then we have seen the sister or the brother almost every day. Stapleton should be happy about a match between his sister and Sir Henry. However, I feel certain that he doesn't want them to fall in love. By the way, it will be very difficult for me to always stay with Sir Henry if a love affair develops.

On Thursday Dr. Mortimer and the Stapletons lunched with us. Sir Henry asked the doctor to take us to the yew path and show us exactly what happened that night. We all still have many questions about Sir Charles's death.

I have met one other neighbor since I last wrote, Mr. Frankland of Lafter Hall. He is an older man, red-faced and white-haired. His passion is for the British law, and he spends most of his time and money in court. He's a queer old character who makes us laugh. His hobby is studying the stars with a telescope. Lately, he likes to use his powerful telescope to search for the escaped criminal on the moor.

Now, let me end by telling you about the most important development.

It concerns Barrymore. We can't be certain that he was here when you sent the test telegram. However, Sir Henry and I spoke to him and we believe that he was at the Hall and not in London. Sir Henry was kind to him and even gave him a gift of clothing.

Mrs. Barrymore is of interest to me. She is a heavy, hard-working woman who seems unemotional. Yet I have seen tears on her face several times. Something troubles her deeply.

You know that I am a light sleeper. Last night, at about two in the morning, I heard someone walking in the hallway near my door. I quietly looked out and saw a man holding a candle. He was walking softly, without shoes. From behind he looked like Barrymore.

I followed him. He entered one of the rooms at the end of the hallway. These rooms are completely empty. I quietly looked into the room.

Barrymore was standing near the window with the candle held against the glass. He seemed to be staring out onto the moor, waiting for something. Several minutes passed and then he put out the light. I returned quickly to my room. This morning I talked to Sir Henry about it. We have a plan to uncover the truth about this mysterious business. I will tell you about it in my next report.

35

Chapter 9
Second Report of Dr. Watson

THE LIGHT UPON THE MOOR

Baskerville Hall, October 15th.

MY DEAR HOLMES:

I know I didn't send you much news in the first days of my visit. But now things are happening quickly and there is much to tell.

The following morning I went to the room where I had seen Barrymore that night. The window in that room has the best view of the moor in the house. Therefore, I believe that Barrymore was looking for something, or someone, out on the moor. The night was very dark, however, so I doubt that he could see anyone.

I told the baronet about it. He was less surprised than I expected.

"I knew that Barrymore walked around at night," he said. "Two or three times I have heard his steps in the hallway at that hour."

"Perhaps he goes to that room every night," I suggested.

"If so, we should follow him and see what he's doing."

"But surely he would hear us."

"The man does not hear well. Besides, we must take a chance. We'll sit up in my room tonight and wait until he passes." Sir Henry rubbed his hands with pleasure. I could see he enjoyed the adventure.

These days the baronet is talking with designers and builders from London. He plans to spend a lot of money to restore the glory to Baskerville Hall. Then he will only need a wife to make it perfect. It's clear that he is very interested in Miss Stapleton. And yet, the road to love is not always smooth.

Today, for example, Sir Henry prepared to go out and I did the same.

"What, are *you* coming, Watson?" he asked, looking at me strangely.

"Well, you know that Holmes was serious when he told me to stay with you on the moor."

Sir Henry put his hand on my shoulder and smiled. "My dear fellow," he said, "I'm going to see Miss Stapleton and I prefer to go alone. I hope you understand." Before I could answer he opened the door and was gone.

I was in a difficult position. I decided it was best to follow him at a distance.

I hurried along the road toward Merripit House and turned

onto the moor path. I climbed a small hill and saw him about a quarter mile away. He was talking to Miss Stapleton. I felt badly about spying on him, but I also had to protect him.

I watched Sir Henry put his arm around Miss Stapleton. It looked like he wanted to kiss her but she put up her hand to stop him. Then I noticed someone else walking towards them on the same path. It was Stapleton with his insect net. They both quickly turned around when they heard Stapleton approaching. He was angry. I guess that Sir Henry tried to explain the situation. The lady stood by silently. Finally, Stapleton turned quickly and ordered his sister to follow him. She obeyed her brother and walked away. Stapleton appeared to be angry with her, too. The baronet watched them leave, then walked back down the path, his head hanging sadly.

I ran down the hill and met the baronet at the bottom. His face was red.

"Hello, Watson! Where did you come from?" he asked.

I explained everything to him. How I felt wrong about letting him go to the moor alone, how I followed him, and how I had seen everything. For a moment his eyes burned with anger, but my honesty softened him and he laughed a bit.

"I never thought it would be so difficult to carry on a private love affair here on the moor. I think her brother is crazy, don't you?"

"Not really."

"No, he probably isn't. But now I don't understand anything. What's wrong with me, anyway? Do you think I would make a good husband to the woman I love?"

"Certainly."

"Then why is he against me? It can't be my title or my house. I would never hurt his sister. He won't even let me hold her hand."

"Did he say so?"

"That, and more. Watson, I know she's the right woman for me. We make each other happy. But he will never let us be alone together. This was the first time we tried. She was glad to see me but she didn't want to talk about love. She kept telling me that this was a place of danger and that I should escape. I said I might agree to leave only if she came with me. That is when her brother arrived like a madman. He was white with anger. I told him that I had true and honorable feelings towards her, and wanted to marry her. That made him angrier. I, too, was angry. It ended badly, as you saw. I just don't understand it, Watson."

Neither did I. Everything about our friend—his fortune, his title, his age, his character, his appearance—is positive. However, later that same afternoon Stapleton came to the house to tell the baronet that he was sorry for his actions. They had a long talk in Sir Henry's study and came out friends once more. We are invited to dinner at Merripit House next Friday.

"He may be a bit crazy," said Sir Henry, "but he was kind to come and say sorry."

"Did he explain why he got so angry?"

"He said his sister is everything in his life. They've always been together and he doesn't like the thought of losing her. He didn't know that we were falling in love and he was shocked when he saw us together. He now feels very badly for his actions. He thinks I am a good match for his sister, but he needs some time to get used to the idea. So he wants me to wait three months before I ask to marry her. I promised to wait."

So, there is one of our mysteries cleared up. I've also learned the secret of the Barrymores, which I will now report to you.

Sir Henry and I sat quietly in my room last night with the lights very low. The hours passed slowly. Shortly after two o'clock we heard someone walk by in the hallway. We waited a moment, then opened the door and followed him very quietly to the same room as before. For several minutes we watched him hold a candle to the window, moving it slowly back and forth.

Sir Henry walked across the room. Barrymore jumped up in great surprise, his eyes full of fear.

"What are you doing here, Barrymore?"

"Nothing, sir." He was so nervous that he could hardly speak. The candle was shaking in his hand. "I was just closing the window, sir."

"Don't lie to us, Barrymore!" said Sir Henry without patience. "Why were you holding a candle to the window?"

"Please don't ask me, Sir Henry—don't ask me! I give you my word, sir, that it is not my secret, and I cannot tell it."

A sudden idea occurred to me and I took the candle from him.

"I think the candle is a signal to someone out there," I said. "Let's try it." I held the candle and slowly moved it as I stared into the dark night. And then I saw a tiny yellow light from far off.

"There it is!" I cried.

"No, no, sir, it is nothing!" the butler broke in. "Believe me, sir—"

"Now, Barrymore," demanded the baronet, "speak up! Who is that person and what is going on?"

The man refused to talk. "It is not my business and I cannot tell."

"Then you no longer work for me as of now. You have broken our trust and must leave without honor."

"Very well, sir. If I must, I must."

"No, no, sir! Please, it's not his fault, it's mine!" It was the voice of Mrs. Barrymore standing at the door in her nightclothes. She looked pale and afraid. "Sir Henry, my husband only wanted to help me because I asked him."

"Speak up, then! What does it mean?"

"My unhappy brother is living on the moor without food. We cannot let him die at our very gates. This candle is a sign to him that food is ready, and his light tells us where to bring it."

"Then your brother is—"

"The escaped criminal, sir—Selden."

"That's the truth, sir," said Barrymore.

Sir Henry and I both looked at her in shock. Could this good woman really have the same blood as one of England's worst criminals?

"Yes, sir, my name was Selden, and he is my younger brother. We were too nice to him when he was a boy and spoiled him badly. He grew up thinking everything was for him. Later, he met some really evil companions. He became a criminal, broke my poor mother's heart, and ruined our good name. But to me, sir, he was always my curly-haired little brother. He escaped from prison because he knew I was here at Baskerville Hall and that I would help him. He came one night hungry, cold and wet, with the prison guards after him. What could I do? We brought him in and took care of him. Then you returned, sir, and my brother thought he would be safer out on the moor. So he has been hiding out there since. Every second night we take out bread and meat for him. I want him to go away, but as long as he is there I have to help him."

We believed the woman and felt sorry for her.

"Well," said Sir Henry, "I cannot blame you for defending your own wife. Forget what I have said. We shall talk again in the morning."

When they were gone we looked out of the window again. Sir Henry had opened it and the cold night wind blew on our faces. Far away in the blackness there burned the tiny candle.

"How far do you think it is?" asked Sir Henry.

"Not more than a mile, I think."

"That villain is waiting by the candle. By God, Watson, I'm going to get that man!"

I was thinking the same thing. The Barrymores had admitted their secret to us, though not because they wanted to. This man was a danger to society. It was our duty to help put him back in prison before he hurt someone else.

"I will come, too," I said.

"Then get your gun and your coat."

In five minutes we were outside the door. The falling leaves were blowing in the autumn wind. Occasionally, we saw the moon through the clouds. The candle light in front still burned.

"Are you armed?" I asked.

"I only have this hunting whip."

"We must take him quickly and by surprise."

"Watson, do you remember what Holmes said about the hour of darkness when the power of evil is strongest? Could this be it?"

Suddenly, at that moment, we heard that strange, ungodly, animal cry which I had heard near Grimpen Mire. It was a long, deep sound followed by a great roar, which slowly disappeared. The baronet took my arm and his face was white.

The night became silent again.

"Dear God, Watson! That was the cry of a hound," said the baronet.

My blood ran cold for there was fear in his voice.

"What do people here call this sound?" he asked.

"Oh, they are simple people. Does it really matter?"

"Tell me, Watson. What do they call it?"

I could not escape the question. "They say it is the cry of the Hound of the Baskervilles."

He sighed deeply and was silent for a few moments.

At last he said, "My God, can these old tales be true? Is it possible that I am really in danger from a supernatural evil? You don't believe it, do you Watson?"

"No, no."

"Well, I laughed about it in London, but out here in the darkness on the moor, it's quite different. There was the footprint of the hound near my uncle's body. I don't think I'm easily frightened, Watson, but that sound really scared me."

"Shall we turn back?"

"No! We came to get our villain, and we shall do it. Come on!"

We moved slowly forward in the darkness. The tiny yellow light burned in front of us. At last we came to a group of rocks and saw the candle between them. Then we saw the criminal sitting on top of the rock. He didn't see us. He was an awful man to look at. He had the face of a hungry animal, with animal passions. His clothes, beard and hair were very dirty. His body was short and strong. His eyes

moved back and forth like an animal who has heard the hunter.

Then he stood up, and I could read the fear on his face. Sir Henry and I jumped out from behind the rock. At that moment the criminal screamed, then turned and ran away over the rocks. We began to chase him, but he was too fast. We watched him run in the moonlight until he disappeared in the distance.

Then a strange and unexpected thing occurred. We had turned to go home. The moon was low to the right. The tip of a rocky hill was between us and the moon. When I looked that way, I clearly saw the figure of a tall man standing on the rock. His legs were slightly apart and his arms were folded on his chest. It was not the convict. I turned to tell the baronet but when I turned back, the man was gone. Another mystery on the moor.

Well, Holmes, today we plan to talk to the people at Princetown Prison and tell them what happened. It's just bad luck that we didn't catch him. I hope my reports are useful to you. It would be nice if you could come here yourself. I will write again soon.

36

Chapter 10
Parts of the Diary of Dr. Watson

October 16th. A dull and foggy day with some rain. The baronet is still upset after last night's excitement. My heart feels heavy with a sense of coming danger—a danger which I don't really understand.

But there are many good reasons to be afraid. There is the death of Sir Charles, just as in the ancient family tale. There are the reports by local people of a strange creature on the moor. Twice I have heard the sounds of a hound with my own ears. However, I will never believe that this is a supernatural devil dog. Perhaps there is a large dog living out there. But where could such a dog hide? Where would it find food? Why did no one see it in the daytime? And what about the people in this case? There was the man in the cab in London, the missing shoes, the letter warning Sir Henry against the moor. And who was that stranger on the rocks last night?

I know he is nobody I have met from here. He was taller than Stapleton and thinner than Frankland. A stranger is following us, just as in London. I will do everything I can to find this man.

There was a problem this morning after breakfast. Barrymore asked to speak privately with Sir Henry. I heard loud voices several times as they talked in the study. A while later the baronet opened the door and called for me.

"Barrymore is upset," he said. "He thinks it was unfair for us to hunt his wife's brother after he told us his secret. And I think that this villain is a public danger. No one is safe until he is back in prison."

The butler was standing very pale but calmly before us.

"I can promise you he will never trouble anyone in this country again. Sir Henry, in a few days he will take a ship to South America. Please don't tell the police, sir. They have stopped looking for him there. He can wait quietly until the ship comes. He won't hurt anyone now."

"What do you think, Watson?"

"Well, if he were out of the country it would save us some tax money."

"All right, Barrymore. We won't say anything," said Sir Henry.

"God bless you, sir, and thank you! My wife will be so happy."

Barrymore turned to go, but then he stopped and came back.

"You've been so kind to us, sir, that I would like to help you in return. I know something, Sir Henry, which I haven't told to anyone. It's about Sir Charles."

The baronet and I were both on our feet. "Do you know how he died?"

"No, sir, I don't know that."

"What then?"

"I know why he was at the moor gate at that hour. It was to meet a woman."

"To meet a woman! Him?"

"Yes, sir."

"And the woman's name?"

"I can't give you the name, sir, but I can tell you the letters of her name. They are L.L."

"How do you know this, Barrymore?"

"Well, Sir Henry, your uncle had a letter that morning. I noticed that it came from the village of Coombe Tracey, and was written by a woman."

"Well?"

"I forgot about it until my wife cleaned his study a few weeks after he died. She found pieces of a burned letter in his fireplace. Everything was burned except one bit at the end of the page. It said: 'Please, please, as you are a gentleman, burn this letter, and be at the gate by ten o'clock.' Beneath it were signed the letters L.L."

"Do you know who L.L. is?"

"No, sir. But I think that lady could tell us a lot about Sir Charles's death."

"Why didn't you say anything before, Barrymore?"

"Well, sir, immediately after this is when we started to have our own problems with Selden. Also, we both liked Sir Charles very much and this seemed like a personal matter between him and a lady—"

"I understand. Thank you, Barrymore, you can go."

When the butler left us Sir Henry turned to me. "Well, Watson?"

"I will inform Holmes at once. This may be the clue he's looking for."

I went to my room and wrote the report of that morning to Holmes. I knew that he had been very busy lately with his other cases. I wished that he was here.

October 17th. It rained all day today. I thought of the criminal out on the cold, wet moor. I'm sure he is suffering for his crimes.

In the evening I put on my raincoat and went for a walk up on the moor. On the way back, I met Dr. Mortimer who had come in his small wagon from Foulmire. He gave me a ride to the Hall. The man is very upset about his dog, a spaniel, which disappeared on the moor several days ago. I thought about that poor horse in the Grimpen Mire. I don't think he'll see his little dog again.

"By the way, Mortimer," I said, "does anyone live around here whom you don't know?"

"Hardly anyone."

"Can you think of a woman whose names begin with L.L.?"

He thought for a few minutes.

"No, I can't," he said. "Oh, wait a moment," he added. "There is Laura Lyons—her initials are L.L.—but she lives in Coombe Tracey."

"Who is she?" I asked.

"She is the daughter of that odd fellow, Frankland. She married an artist named Lyons. He wasn't a very honest man and later he left her. Her father didn't like the marriage and made life difficult for them."

"How does she live?"

"I think old Frankland gives her a little money, but he hasn't got much more to give. Some people around here knew of her troubles and tried to help her. Stapleton for one, and Sir Charles for another. I myself gave a small amount to help her start a business."

Tomorrow morning I will go to Coombe Tracey to try and find this Mrs. Laura Lyons.

I have only one other thing to report on this stormy day. This is the talk I had with Barrymore when he brought me coffee in the library.

"Well," I said, "has your wife's brother departed, or is he still out on the moor?"

"I don't know, sir. I hope to God he is gone! I haven't heard from him since I left food for him three days ago."

"Did you see him then?"

"No, sir, but the food was gone when I went back."

"Then he was certainly there?"

"I suppose so, sir, unless it was the other man who took it."

I sat with my coffee cup halfway to my mouth and stared at him.

"There's another man on the moor?"

"Yes, sir, there is."

"Have you seen him?"

"No, sir."

"How do you know about him then?"

"Selden told me about him more than a week ago. He's hiding too, but he's not a criminal. I don't like it, Dr. Watson. There's danger and evil out there." He spoke with true feeling.

"But what are you afraid of?"

"Look at Sir Charles's death! And the sounds on the moor! No local man would cross it after dark. Look at this stranger watching and waiting on the moor. What does it all mean? It means no good to the name of Baskerville. I'll be happy to leave here when the new housekeepers arrive."

"But what about this stranger?" I asked. "Where is he hiding, and what's he doing?"

"Selden saw him once or twice, but the stranger said nothing. He said the man seemed like a gentleman, but Selden doesn't know why he's there."

"Where does he live?"

"Among the ancient huts on the hillside."

"What about food?"

"Selden found out that he has a boy who works for him and brings all he needs from Coombe Tracey."

When the butler left I walked over to the window and looked into the blackness. I think the key to the mystery is there on the moor, and I will do all I can to find it.

37

Chapter 11
The Man on the Tor

The earlier chapter was taken from my diary up to October 18th when I learned two important things. The one was that Mrs. Laura Lyons of Coombe Tracey arranged to see Sir Charles on the day and the hour of his death. The other was that the stranger on the moor was living in the ancient stone houses on the hillside.

The next morning the family driver, Perkins, took me to Coombe Tracey. I had no trouble finding the lady's house. A maid showed me in. Mrs. Lyons was sitting in front of a typewriter. She was indeed beautiful. Her eyes and hair were the same rich, light brown color. She asked me what I wanted.

I didn't have a plan so I said, "I know your father."

It was not a good start.

"My father and I do not speak anymore," she said. "He didn't care about me. Other people like Sir Charles Baskerville kindly helped me."

"Actually, I came to see you about Sir Charles."

"What can I tell you about him?" she asked, a bit nervous.

"Did you write to him?"

The lady looked up quickly. "Why are you asking these questions?" she asked sharply.

"It is better that I talk to you in private than have others talk to you publicly."

She was silent and her face was pale. "Well, all right," she said. "Yes, I wrote to him once or twice to thank him."

"Do you have the dates of those letters?"

"No."

"Have you ever met him?"

"Yes, a couple times when he came into Coombe Tracey. He was a very shy, private man."

"But if you were not close friends, then how did he know enough about your personal matters to help you?"

"There were several gentlemen who knew my sad history and helped me. One was Mr. Stapleton. He was very kind and he told Sir Charles about my problems."

"Did you ever write to Sir Charles asking him to meet you?" I continued.

Mrs. Lyons became slightly angry.

"Really, sir, this is a very personal question. The answer is no."

"Not on the very day of Sir Charles's death?"

The redness in her face became very white. Her dry lips could barely speak the word "No".

"Perhaps you've forgotten," I said. "I can tell you part of what you wrote. It said, 'Please, please, as you are a gentleman, burn this letter, and be at the gate by ten o'clock.'"

She looked shocked.

"I thought he was a gentleman!" her voice cried.

"That is not fair to Sir Charles. He did burn the letter. But sometimes it is possible to read them even when burned. Do you admit that you wrote that letter?"

"Yes, I wrote it!" she cried. "I won't deny it. I wanted to ask him for help. So I asked him to meet me."

"But why at that hour?"

"Because I had just learned he was going to London the next morning and might be gone for weeks and months. There were reasons I couldn't get there earlier."

"But why meet in the garden instead of in the house?"

"Do you think a woman could go alone at that hour to a gentleman's house?"

"Well, what happened when you got there?"

"I never went."

"Mrs. Lyons!"

"No, I honestly never went."

"Why not?"

"It is a private matter. I cannot tell you."

"You admit that you asked to meet with Sir Charles at the very hour and place of his death, but you deny that you went there?"

"That is the truth."

Again and again I questioned her on that point, but her answer was always the same.

"Mrs. Lyons," I said, "I may have to go to the police if you don't tell me everything. Why did you deny writing to Sir Charles on that date?"

"Because I was afraid that I might be falsely blamed."

"And why was it so important for him to destroy the letter?"

"You read the letter so you know why."

"I did not say that I had read all the letter. That was only the last line or two. The letter had been burned and most of it was impossible to read. Again, why was it so important to destroy this letter?"

"I will tell you, then. Perhaps you already know that I made a bad decision to marry, and am very sorry for it."

"I had heard that."

"My life has been a continuous problem with a husband I hate. The law is on his side, and I may be forced to live with him. In order to be free of him and be happy again, I had to pay certain expenses. I knew Sir Charles was a generous man and that he might help me if I told him my story."

"Then why didn't you go to see him?"

"Because someone else helped me in the meantime. I was going to write and tell him until I read about his death the next morning."

The woman's story seemed to fit. I believe she did not go to Baskerville Hall. I had a feeling, however, that she wasn't telling me everything.

Driving back to the Hall in the carriage, I saw hill after hill with hundreds of ancient huts. Barrymore told me that the stranger lived in one of them. I planned to start looking on Black Tor, the place where I saw him standing that night. I was going to search until I found him.

Our bad luck in this case was beginning to change for the good. We passed the home of Mr. Frankland who was standing by the road.

"Good day, Dr. Watson," he cried with good cheer. "Give your horses a rest and come have a glass of wine with me."

My feelings towards him were not very friendly after what his daughter had told me. But I sent Perkins and the carriage ahead with a message to Sir Henry that I would walk home in time for dinner. Then I followed the white-haired, red-faced man into his dining room.

"This is one of the better days of my life," he said laughing. "I have won a double victory in court. One for the rights of the common man against the rich; the other to protect our public parks from the dirty people of Fernworthy."

"What do you gain by winning these court cases, Mr. Frankland?"

"Nothing, sir, nothing. I am proud to say that I act only from a sense of public duty. Although I'm sure that the people in Fernworthy will be angry with me tonight. Last time, they made a wooden figure of me and burned it in public. I'm also angry with the police for not protecting me better. I don't think

I'll tell them that I know something very important."

"How do you mean?" I asked.

"It's about that criminal on the moor."

"You mean you know where he is?" I said.

"No, not exactly. But I'm quite sure I could lead the police to him if I wanted. The best way to catch that man is to find out where his food is, and follow him."

He was getting uncomfortably close to the truth. "Perhaps," I said, "but what makes you think he's on the moor?"

"Because I have seen a messenger bring him food."

Poor Barrymore! This nosy old man could bring serious trouble to the butler. However, his next remark made me feel better.

"Surprisingly, the messenger is a child. I see him every day through my telescope up on the roof. He passes along the same path at the same hour. He must be going to the criminal!"

What luck! A child! Barrymore said that our mystery man was helped by a boy. So it was the stranger, not the criminal, that Frankland knew of. I needed to find out what else he knew.

"Are you sure it's not a farmer's son taking dinner to his father?"

"Indeed, sir!" said the old man with fight in his eyes. "Do you see the hill beyond Black Tor over there? It is the rockiest part of the whole moor. There are no farms or animals there."

I admitted I was wrong. This seemed to please him and he was happy to continue.

"I've seen the boy again and again with his package. Every

day, and sometimes twice a day. I am able—wait a moment, Dr. Watson. Do you also see something moving on that hillside?"

It was several miles off, but I could see a small dark dot against the dull green.

"Come!" cried Frankland, running upstairs. "You will see with your own eyes."

The telescope was a large and expensive one standing on three legs. Frankland looked through it and smiled.

"Quick, Watson, quick, before he passes over the hill!"

There he was, a small boy carrying a little package over his shoulder. I could see he was dressed in dirty clothes. When he got to the top he looked around carefully, then disappeared over the hill.

"Well! Am I right?"

"Certainly, there is a boy who seems to have some secret duty."

"Even our foolish police chief could guess what that duty is. But I will tell them nothing, Dr. Watson, and you won't either. Not a word!"

"Just as you wish."

"Those police have treated me shamefully. They don't care about me one bit. When the facts of my next case come out in court, the rest of the county will take my side. Surely you are not going, Dr. Watson? Won't you help me finish the rest of this wine in honor of this occasion?"

But I was able to excuse myself and said good-bye. I stayed on the road until I was away from the old man's sight, then I turned and crossed the moor. I felt very lucky.

The sun was already setting when I reached the hilltop. There was no sound and no movement except for one bird high above. He and I were the only living things between heaven and earth. I couldn't see the boy anywhere. But I looked down the hill into a group of stone huts and I saw one that still had a roof. This must be where the stranger is hiding.

I walked slowly up to the hut, as Stapleton would do when chasing an insect with his net. I could see a tiny path that led to the door and I knew the house was being used by someone. All was silent inside. The stranger might be in there, or he might be outside. I could feel my nerves shaking from the adventure. I threw down my cigarette, put my hand on my gun, and walked quickly to the door. I opened it, but the place was empty.

However, someone was using the house. The ashes of a fire were on the ground. Beside it was a bowl for cooking and some water. There were several empty metal cans nearby, and a half bottle of wine. There were also blankets and a raincoat. I could see the cloth bag the boy had brought containing some bread, meat and fruit. Then I saw a sheet of paper with writing on it and my heart jumped. I raised it to my eyes and read: "Dr. Watson has gone to Coombe Tracey."

So it was I, and not Sir Henry, who was being followed by this mystery man. Perhaps I was being watched at this same moment.

I searched around the hut for more information but found none. Nor could I find any clues about the man who lived here. It was clear that he needed very little and didn't care much about comfort. Was he our evil enemy or our protecting friend? I decided to find out. I sat in the darkest corner of the little hut and waited.

Then at last I heard him. Far away came the sharp sound of a shoe against a stone. Then another, nearer and nearer. I took out my gun and held it tightly. I was ready to shoot. There was a moment of silence as he stopped outside the house. Then he took two more steps and a shadow fell across the door.

"It is a lovely evening, my dear Watson," said a well-known voice. "I really think that you will enjoy the view from out here."

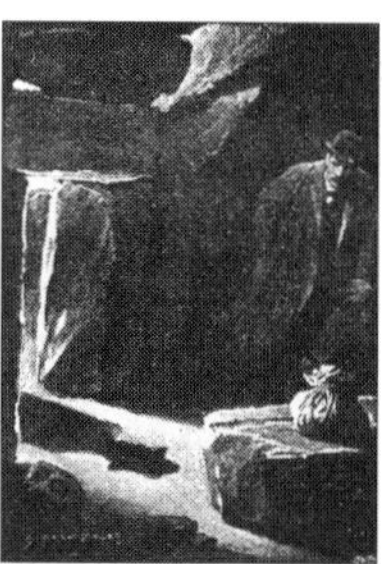

38

Chapter 12
Death on the Moor

For a moment or two I sat in shock, unable to believe my ears. At the same time I felt a huge relief. That voice could only belong to one person in the world.

"Holmes!" I cried—"Holmes!"

"Come out," he said, "and please be careful with the gun."

I walked out under the short door and there he sat sitting on a stone. His eyes were dancing with enjoyment as he looked at me. He was thin and tired, but looked clean and healthy. His face was browned from the sun.

"I'm so happy to see you," I said, as I shook his hand.

"And surprised?"

"Very."

"The surprise was not just yours. I had no idea that you had found my little country house until I was just a few steps from the door."

"My footprints?"

"No, Watson, your tobacco. I saw the end of a cigarette marked Bradley, Oxford Street, next to the path. I knew that you were nearby. And knowing you as well as I do I was sure you were inside waiting for me with your gun. Did you think that I was the criminal?"

"I didn't know who you were but I was certain to find out."

"Excellent, Watson! And how did you find me? Was it that night you went looking for the criminal, when I foolishly stood in front of the moon?"

"Yes, I saw you then. And today I saw your boy coming here so I knew where to look."

"Ha! I see that Cartwright has brought up some supplies. What's this paper? It says you've been to Coombe Tracey?"

"Yes."

"To see Mrs. Laura Lyons?"

"Exactly."

"Well done! Our detective work has been very similar. I'm sure that when we compare our results, we shall uncover this mystery."

"Well, I am very, very glad that you are here, for my nerves were becoming rather weak. But how did you get here, and what have you been doing? I thought that you were in Baker Street working on another case?"

"That is what I wanted you to think."

"Then you used me, and you do not trust me!" I cried, with just a bit of anger.

"My dear fellow, you are always of very great value to me.

Please forgive me if you are feeling tricked. Honestly, it was necessary for the case that you come here alone. It was important that our enemies didn't know I was here."

"But why not tell me you were here?"

"Because I might have been discovered if you tried to help me. That's why I brought Cartwright with me. He brings me food and clean clothes. My needs are simple. He also gives me an extra pair of eyes and feet."

"Then my reports have all been wasted!" I said with hurt feelings.

Holmes took a pile of papers from his pocket.

"Here are your reports, my friend. I've read all of them more than once. I arranged with the mails to receive them one day later. You've done an excellent job."

Holmes's kind words removed the anger from my mind.

"And now, Watson, tell me about your visit to Mrs. Lyons."

It had become cool and dark so we went into the hut. I told Holmes of my talk with the lady. He was very interested in every word.

"This is most important," he said when I had finished. "It makes the situation much clearer. Did you know that this lady and Mr. Stapleton have very close relations?"

"I had no idea."

"There can be no doubt. They meet, they write, there is a complete understanding between them. Now, this puts a powerful piece of information in our hands. If I could only use it to separate his wife—"

"His wife?"

"Yes, Watson. The lady who you know as Beryl Stapleton is really his wife, not his sister."

"My God, Holmes! Are you sure of that? How could he allow Sir Henry to fall in love with her?"

"Sir Henry's falling in love will only hurt Sir Henry."

"But why this trick?"

"Because he knew that she would be much more useful to him in the character of a free woman."

Suddenly I had a terrible feeling about that naturalist with his insect net. Stapleton was a man of great patience with a smiling face and a murderous heart.

"Then he is our enemy—he followed us in London?"

"I believe so."

"And the warning—it must have come from her?"

"Exactly."

Now I began to see the evil which I had only guessed at before.

"How can you be sure, Holmes, that the woman is his wife?"

"Because he told you that he was once a schoolmaster in the north of England. There are very good records on schools and it is easy to find former teachers and masters. I found out that there was a school in the north that had closed in very bad circumstances, and that the man who owned it had disappeared with his wife. His name was different then, but you described the same man, especially his interest in insects."

The darkness was rising from the shadows.

"If this woman is really his wife, then what about Mrs. Laura Lyons?" I asked.

"Your talk with the lady has helped me. I did not know that she planned to leave her husband. She thought Stapleton was unmarried and hoped to become his wife."

"And when she learns the truth?"

"Why, then she may be of service to us. We must both go visit her tomorrow. Don't you think, Watson, that it's time for you to return to the Hall?"

All the color in the sky was gone, and a few stars were shining.

"One last question, Holmes," I said as I got up. "What does he want?"

Holmes's voice sank as he answered.

"It is murder, Watson—cold-blooded, terrible murder. One more day, perhaps two, and he will be our prisoner. The danger is that he will strike at Sir Henry first. You must protect Sir Henry as a mother protects her child. What's that?"

A long, terrible scream broke the silence of the moor. My blood turned to ice.

"Oh, my God!" I cried. "What is it?"

Holmes had jumped to his feet, and I saw his dark, thin figure at the door of the hut. His head was leaning forward into the darkness.

"Sshh!" he whispered. "Sshh!"

The cry had been loud, but from a distant place. Now it seemed nearer, louder.

"Where is it, Watson?" Holmes whispered. I knew from the tone of his voice that my strong friend was shaken to the soul.

"There, I think." I pointed into the darkness.

"No, there!"

The scream came again, even louder and nearer. And a new sound mixed with it. A deep roar, like the low sound of the sea.

"The hound!" cried Holmes. "Come, Watson, come! God, I hope we're not too late!"

He started running at top speed over the moor, and I followed. We heard one last cry of despair, and then a dull, heavy hitting sound. We stopped to listen. There was no wind, only silence.

I saw Holmes put his hand to his head like a man in pain. He kicked his foot into the ground.

"He has beaten us, Watson. We are too late."

"No, no, surely not!"

"I was a fool to wait so long. And you, Watson, see what happens when you forget your duties! But, by Heaven, we will get him!"

We ran blindly through the night, pushing through plants and bushes, up and down the hills. At every rise we stopped to look around, but it was dark and nothing moved.

Finally, Holmes cried, "Look, what's that?"

We heard a very low murmuring sound to the left. There was a group of pointed rocks where the hill suddenly dropped off. We could see a body among the rocks below, and ran towards it. It was a man lying face down on the rocks, his head

bent under him in a terrible curl. Now there was only silence. Holmes struck a match. The dead man's head was crushed. Blood flowed into the ground. And in the light we saw something else which made our hearts sick—the body of Sir Henry Baskerville!

He wore the same wool suit which he had when he first came to Baker Street. We saw it clearly and then the match died, as the hope went out of our souls. Holmes made a painful sound and his face was terribly white.

"That devil! That devil!" I cried in pain and anger. "Oh, Holmes, I shall never forgive myself for leaving him to this fate."

"I am more to blame than you, Watson. In order to complete my case, I have killed the man I tried to help. It is the greatest blow of my working life. But why did he come alone out here on the moor?"

"Oh God, we heard his terrible screams but we couldn't save him! Where is this hound which chased him to his death? It may be around here now. And Stapleton, where is he? He shall pay for this tragedy."

"He will, Watson. I will make sure of that. Uncle and nephew have been murdered. The one frightened to death by the sight of the beast, the other killed trying to run from it. But now we must prove that there really is a beast. Sir Henry died from the fall. We have no evidence of an animal. Stapleton may be clever but he will be in my power by tomorrow!"

We stood with shocked, saddened hearts on either side of the body. The moon rose and we climbed to the rocks from where our poor friend had fallen. Across the moor was a single light coming from the lonely Stapleton house. I cursed it.

"Why don't we get him right now?"

"Our case is not complete. The fellow is intelligent and clever. We must first prove the facts. If we make one mistake, he might escape."

"What can we do?"

"We must wait for tomorrow. Tonight we can only see to our poor friend."

We went back down the steep hill to the body. It was a truly painful sight. My eyes filled with tears.

"Good heavens, Holmes, are you crazy?"

My friend was suddenly dancing and laughing and shaking my hand. I didn't understand.

"A beard! The man has a beard! It is not the baronet—my God, it is my neighbor, the criminal!"

We quickly turned over the body. It was the bloody face of Selden, the criminal.

Instantly, I remembered the baronet had given some of his old clothes to Barrymore as a gift when his new clothes arrived. Barrymore had then given some to Selden. Shoes, shirt, coat, hat—they were all Sir Henry's. This was still a tragedy, but this man deserved to die. My heart jumped with joy and thanks.

"Then it was the clothes that killed this poor devil," he said. "The hound was trained to follow a piece of Sir Henry's clothing—probably that shoe taken from the hotel. But how did Selden, in the darkness, know that the hound was after him?"

"He heard him."

"I don't think that would make a hard man like this scream wildly for help. He probably ran a long way after he knew the animal was following him. How did he know?"

"Well, what shall we do with the poor man's body?" I asked.

"Let's carry it to one of the stone huts until we can talk to the police. Look, Watson, what do I see? Oh my, it's our man himself, walking this way! Wonderful. Say nothing to make him suspect us."

A figure was approaching us in the moonlight. He stopped briefly when he saw us.

"Why, Dr. Watson, is that you? I certainly didn't expect to see you out here at this time of night. But, dear me, what's this? Is somebody hurt? Not—oh no, is it our friend Sir Henry?" He ran past me and bent down to look at the dead man. I heard a shocked sound in his throat.

"Who—who's this?" his voice shook.

"It is Selden, the man who escaped from Princetown."

Stapleton turned a sick color. But with great effort he was able to control his shock and disappointment. He looked at us.

"Dear me! What a terrible affair! How did he die?"

"He appears to have broken his neck after falling onto these rocks. My friend and I were taking a walk on the moor when we heard a cry."

"I heard a cry also. That's why I came out. I was uneasy about Sir Henry."

"Why?" I asked.

"Because I asked him to come to our house for a visit. When he did not come I was surprised. I worried about his safety when I heard screams on the moor. By the way," his eyes moved back and forth from Holmes to me, "did you hear anything else besides a cry?"

"No," said Holmes, "did you?"

"No."

"What do you mean, then?"

"Oh, you know the stories that the country people tell about a devil hound at night upon the moor."

"We heard nothing of the kind," I said.

"How do you think this poor fellow died?"

"I believe that the man's bad mental and physical condition made him crazy. He ran around the moor in a wild manner and fell over here, breaking his neck."

"That seems reasonable," said Stapleton, as he breathed easier. "What do you think about it, Mr. Sherlock Holmes?"

"Ah, you know my name," he said.

"We have been expecting you around here since Dr. Watson came down. You are in time to see a tragedy."

"Yes, indeed. I'm sure that my friend is correct about what

happened here. I will take an unpleasant memory back to London with me tomorrow."

"Oh, you return tomorrow?"

"That is my plan."

"I hope your visit has shined some light on those mysteries which have puzzled us."

Holmes lifted his shoulders.

"One cannot always be successful. A detective needs facts, not ancient stories. It has not been a very satisfying case."

My friend spoke in a direct and unconcerned manner. Stapleton still gave him a hard look. Then he turned to me.

"I think that if we cover his face he'll be safe until morning."

And that's what we did. Holmes and I set off to Baskerville Hall, and the naturalist returned alone. Looking back we saw him walking slowly away over the moor. Behind him lay that small black spot where the man's life came to a terrible end.

39

Chapter 13
Fixing the Nets

"We've almost got him," said Holmes as we walked together across the moor. "What nerve that fellow has! Did you see how quickly he recovered from the shock of finding he had murdered the wrong man? I tell you again, Watson, this man is dangerous."

"I'm sorry that he saw you, Holmes."

"Me too. But it can't be avoided."

"Do you think he will change his plans knowing that you're here now?"

"Perhaps. Most clever criminals believe they are too intelligent to get caught."

"Why shouldn't we take him to the police right now?"

"My dear Watson, you are certainly a man of action. However, you must understand that we have to prove he is guilty in court. At the moment we can prove nothing, mainly because he is using a dog."

"What about Sir Charles's death?"

"Found dead without a mark on his body. Where is the evidence of a hound? Where are the marks of his bite?"

"Well, what about tonight?"

"Same situation. There is no direct relation between the hound and the man's death. We never saw the hound. We heard it, but we can't prove that it was chasing this man. No, my friend, we have no case yet, but we will."

"How do you plan to do that?"

"I have great hopes that Mrs. Laura Lyons will help us when we tell her the truth. Tomorrow will be an important day for us."

He said nothing else, and walked in thought to the Baskerville gates.

"Are you coming in?"

"Yes, I see no further reason to hide. But, Watson, say nothing of the hound to Sir Henry. Let him think that Selden's death was an accident. He will need his nerve when he goes to the Stapleton house tomorrow for dinner."

"I am dining with him there."

"Then you must excuse yourself and he must go alone. We can easily arrange that. Now, shall we go in and eat?"

Sir Henry was very surprised and pleased to see Sherlock Holmes. During our late dinner we told the baronet as much about our experience as we thought he should know. But first it was my duty to tell Barrymore and his wife about Selden. She cried. To everyone else he was an evil man, but to her he would always be her sweet little brother.

"I've been here alone in the house all day since Watson left this morning," said the baronet. "In fact, Stapleton invited me to dinner but I had promised Watson I wouldn't leave the house alone, so I didn't go."

"By the way," said Holmes, "you might want to know that we have been crying over your broken neck?"

Sir Henry opened his eyes, "How do you mean?"

"The poor criminal was dressed in your clothes. Barrymore may get into trouble with the police for that."

"That's unlikely. There was no mark on any of them, I'm sure."

"That's lucky for Barrymore—in fact, it's lucky for all of you, since you are all on the wrong side of the law in this matter. As a good detective perhaps I should take you all into the police."

"But how about the case?" asked the baronet. "Watson and I have learned some things, but not enough. Have you uncovered this great mystery?"

"It has been a very difficult case, but I think it will soon be finished."

"Watson probably told you we heard the hound on the moor. I'm sure there is some creature out there. If you can find that animal, then I'll say you are the world's greatest detective."

"With your help I think I can do that."

"Tell me what to do and I'll do it."

"Very good; and you must do exactly as I say. I think—"

Holmes stopped suddenly and stared over my head into the air.

"What is it?" we both cried.

When he looked down at us I could see an excitement in his eyes. "I love portraits," he said pointing towards the wall, "and you have some fine ones. I'll bet that lady in the blue dress was painted by Kneller. And the gentleman with white hair was painted by Reynolds. Are they all family portraits?"

"Every one."

"Who is the gentleman with the telescope?"

"That is Admiral Baskerville, who served in the West Indies. The man with the blue coat is Sir William Baskerville, who was in the House of Commons."

"And this man on the horse?"

"Ah, he is the cause of our problems. That's Hugo, the one who started the Hound of the Baskervilles. That was painted in 1647."

I looked with interest at the portrait.

"Dear me!" said Holmes, "he looks like a quiet, weak man. I had imagined him as a stronger, more powerful person. But I can see a bit of the devil in those eyes."

Holmes said little more, but the picture of the old Baskerville clearly interested him. He often looked at it during the meal. Later, when Sir Henry had gone to his room, he took me back to the dining room. He held a candle up to the portrait.

"Do you see anything there?"

I looked at the broad hat with feather, at the curly hair, the white silk shirt, and the straight, serious face. He was not ugly or handsome, just hard and firm of character.

"Is it like anyone you know?"

"Well, his mouth is like Sir Henry's."

"Wait a moment!" He then stood on a chair and with his arm he covered the hat and other clothes so that I could see only the face.

"Good heavens!" I cried in surprise.

The face of Stapleton jumped out of the portrait.

"Ha, now you see it. My detective eyes are trained to examine faces."

"They almost look the same."

"Yes, it is unbelievably similar, both physically and in spirit. Stapleton is a Baskerville, I'm sure."

"Do you think he wants to become the baronet?"

"Exactly. This good bit of luck is an important missing piece of the puzzle. We have him, Watson, we have him. Tomorrow night he will be in our net just like one of his insects. Then we will put him in our Baker Street collection!" Holmes then burst into great laughter.

I woke up at my usual hour in the morning, but Holmes was already outside.

"Yes, we have a full day today," he remarked and he rubbed his hands with joy. "The nets are in place, and now we begin to pull them in."

"Have you been on the moor already?"

"I have sent a message from Grimpen to Princetown as to the death of Selden. I can promise that none of you will be troubled by the police. I also sent word to my faithful boy, Cartwright."

"What is the next move?"

"To see Sir Henry. Ah, here he is!"

"Good morning, Holmes," said the baronet. "You look like a general who is planning a battle."

"That is the exact situation. Watson was asking for orders."

"And so am I."

"Very good. I understand that you are dining with the Stapletons tonight?"

"I hope that you will also come. They are very nice people and would be happy to see you."

"I'm afraid that Watson and I must go to London. I think we can be more useful there than here at this moment."

"To London?" The baronet seemed disappointed. "I hoped that you would stay here with me. This is not a very pleasant place when one is alone."

"My dear fellow, you gave me your word that you would do what I told you. Now you must trust me. Please tell your friends that we would like to see them, but we have immediate business in London. We hope to return to Devonshire very soon."

"If you insist."

"There is no choice, I promise you."

The baronet looked hurt by our leaving him.

"When do you desire to go?" he asked coldly.

"Immediately after breakfast. We will drive to Coombe Tracey. Watson, you will send a note to Stapleton to tell him you're sorry you can't come."

"Sir Henry, this evening I want you to drive to Merripit House. Then send back your carriage, and tell them that you intend to walk home."

"To walk across the moor?"

"Yes."

"But that is what you have always told me not to do."

"This time you may do it with safety. I trust your nerve and bravery. It's important that you do this."

"Then I will do it."

"And please stay on the path that goes straight from Merripit House to the Grimpen Road. It is your usual way home."

"I will do just what you say."

"Very good. I would like to get away right after breakfast and reach London in the afternoon."

I was very much surprised by this program. I could only obey Holmes, however, so we said good-bye to our sad friend. Two hours later we were at the station of Coombe Tracey. A small boy was standing at the station.

"Any orders, sir?"

"You will take this train to London, Cartwright. The moment you arrive you will send a wire to Sir Henry Baskerville, in my name. Tell him that if he finds the pocketbook which I have dropped he is to send it by registered post to Baker Street."

"Yes, sir."

"And ask at the station office if there is a message for me."

The boy returned with a telegram, which Holmes handed to me. It said:

> Wire received. Coming down with unsigned police papers. Arrive five-forty.
>
> LESTRADE.

"He is a very good police detective, and we may need his help. Now, Watson, I think that we should visit Mrs. Laura Lyons."

Holmes's plan was becoming clear. He would use the baronet to assure the Stapletons that we were really gone. Then we would return when we were really needed. The telegram from London, if Sir Henry mentioned it to the Stapletons, would remove the last doubt from their minds. Already I could feel our nets drawing closer.

Mrs. Laura Lyons was in her office. Sherlock Holmes was very direct with her.

"I am examining the circumstances of the death of Sir Charles Baskerville," he said. "Yesterday you spoke with Dr. Watson. You admit that you asked Sir Charles to be at the gate at ten o'clock. We know that was the place and hour of his death. You have not told us about the relation between these events."

"There is no relation."

"In that case, the timing is quite unbelievable. However, I think we shall prove that there was a relation. I wish to be perfectly honest with you, Mrs. Lyons. We regard this case as murder. The evidence may point to your friend Mr. Stapleton and his wife."

The lady jumped from her chair.

"His wife!" she cried.

"The fact is no longer a secret. The person who has passed for his sister is really his wife."

Mrs. Lyons sat back down. Her hands were holding tightly onto the chair. Her fingers were turning white from the force.

"His wife!" she said again. "His wife! He is not a married man."

Sherlock Holmes lifted his shoulders.

"Prove it to me! Prove it to me! And if you can—!" The flash of her eyes said more than any words.

"I am prepared to do that," said Holmes, taking several papers from his pocket. "Here is a photograph of the couple taken in York four years ago. It is written 'Mr. and Mrs. Vandeleur,' but you will easily recognize him, and perhaps her also. Here are three witnesses who described Mr. and Mrs. Vandeleur when they owned St. Oliver's private school. Read them and see if you can doubt who these people are."

She glanced at them, then looked up at us with the face of a woman in despair.

"Mr. Holmes," she said, "this man has offered to marry me on the condition that I get a lawful separation from my husband. He has never told me the truth, only lies. I thought he loved and wanted me, but he only used me. He is an evil man. I feel hurt and dishonored. I will tell you anything you like. But please believe that I never dreamed of harming that dear old gentleman, Sir Charles. He was a kind friend."

"I believe you, madam," said Sherlock Holmes. "This must be very painful for you. The sending of this letter to Sir Charles was Stapleton's idea?"

"He told me what to write."

"And he told you that you could receive help for your separation expenses from Sir Charles?"

"Exactly. Later he changed his mind about asking another man to help me. He said that somehow he would help me himself. Then he told me not to keep the appointment. The next day I read the reports of the death in the newspaper. He made me promise to say nothing about my appointment with Sir Charles. I did what he told me because I loved him."

"I think that you are very lucky to be alive," said Sherlock Holmes. "We must say good-bye now, Mrs. Lyons. You will probably hear from us again very soon."

Later that afternoon the London train arrived at the station. We greeted Lestrade. He was a small but powerful looking man. He and Holmes had known each other many years.

"Ah, the country air feels fresh," he said. "What's the plan?"

"We have two hours before we need to start," said Holmes. "Let's get some dinner, shall we?"

40

Chapter 14
The Hound of the Baskervilles

Sherlock Holmes never told anyone else his full plans until a case was finished. He liked to be in control and to surprise others. As we rode the carriage in the cold night air, I could only guess at our plan of action. Finally, we arrived near the path to Merripit House. We started walking.

"Do you have a gun, Lestrade?"

"Always," said the little detective, smiling. "Tell me, Holmes, what do we do now?"

"That light ahead is Merripit House. We'll walk very quietly towards it then we'll wait."

We stopped about two hundred yards from the house.

"This is close enough," he said. "We will hide among these rocks. Watson, you know the house. Move forward very quietly and see what they are doing inside."

I stood behind the low wall next to the fruit trees and looked straight into the window.

Stapleton and Sir Henry were in the room but Miss

Stapleton was not. They were smoking cigars, and drinking wine. Stapleton was talking in a lively manner, but the baronet did not look very happy.

As I watched them, Stapleton got up and left the room. I heard the sound of a door opening and shoes walking on a path. I saw the naturalist walk to a small garden house and unlock the door. Something moved inside as he entered it. A minute later he locked the door and went back to the house to rejoin Sir Henry. I walked quietly back to my companions and told them what I had seen.

"It's very strange that the lady is not there. I wonder where she is," Holmes said.

Above the great Grimpen Mire there was a thick, white fog. The moon was shining on it. It looked like an ice field. Holmes was looking at it.

"It's moving toward us, Watson."

"Is that serious?"

"Very serious. It is the one and only thing which could hurt my plans. I hope Sir Henry leaves soon before the fog gets here."

Every minute we waited brought the fog in closer and closer. As we watched, it slowly surrounded the house. Holmes was worried and impatient.

"If he isn't out in fifteen minutes, the path will be covered and we won't be able to see anything."

Gradually, the fog flowed forward and covered us. We could only see a short distance.

Holmes suddenly dropped to his knees and put his ear to

the ground. "Thank God. I think I hear him coming."

There was a sound of quick steps along the path. The steps grew louder. Then we saw Sir Henry walk by in the fog. He looked back nervously. He didn't see us behind the rocks.

"Psst!" cried Holmes, as he took out his gun. "Look out! It's coming!"

There was the sound of a running animal. All three of us stared into the fog. Suddenly, we saw something very shocking. It was a hound, a huge, dark black creature, like nothing I'd ever seen before. Fire came from its open mouth, its eyes glowed with light, and flames seemed to come from its body. It looked like the devil himself. For a moment we were all too frightened to move. Then Holmes and I both fired our guns. The creature gave a terrible cry. However, it continued forward after Sir Henry.

But the animal's cry of pain gave us hope. If he was hurt, then he was not supernatural. We could kill him. We ran after the hound as fast as we could. In front of us on the path we heard screams of fear from Sir Henry. Then the hound roared and leaped at the baronet, knocking him to the ground, and going for the throat. At that same instant Holmes fired five shots from his gun into the side of the

beast. With a last scream of pain it rolled onto its back, all four feet moving crazily. Then it stopped moving. The giant hound was dead.

Sir Henry was laying on the ground. He was not hurt, but he was in shock. Lestrade put a small bottle of whiskey between the baronet's teeth. Two frightened eyes looked up at us.

"My God!" he whispered. "What was it?"

"It's dead, whatever it is," said Holmes.

The terrible creature was the largest, strongest dog we'd ever seen. It was dead but a blue flame came from its mouth and eyes. I placed my hand on the mouth and my fingers also glowed in the darkness.

"The substance is called phosphorous," I said.

"A very clever, very evil idea," said Holmes, looking at the hound. "Sir Henry, we are very, very sorry that this happened to you. I never expected a creature like this."

"You've saved my life."

"But we almost killed you first. How are you feeling?"

"Oh, I think I'll be all right. What do you plan to do now?"

"To leave you here. You are not ready for another adventure tonight."

He tried to stand on his feet, but it was difficult. We helped him to a rock where he sat shaking, his face in his hands.

"We must leave you now for a short while," said Holmes, "and find our man."

We began walking back along the path. "I'm sure he's not in the house. He probably followed the hound but ran away when he heard the shots." The front door was open, so we ran into the house. The old servant was quite surprised to see us. We looked in every corner, but saw no sign of Stapleton. On the upper floor, however, one of the bedroom doors was locked.

"There's someone in here," cried Lestrade. "I can hear a movement. Open this door!"

Holmes kicked the door with his foot just above the lock and it flew open. We did not find the cruel and clever Stapleton, but we were greatly surprised.

The room was where Stapleton kept his insect collections. In the center of the room was a wooden pole used to support the old roof. There was a person tied to this pole and covered in sheets so that we could not tell who it was. We began to remove the sheets from around the face and neck. Seconds later we were looking into the dark, sad, fearful eyes of Mrs. Stapleton. At that moment her beautiful head fell upon her chest. She had fainted. I saw the clear red mark on her neck where she had been beaten.

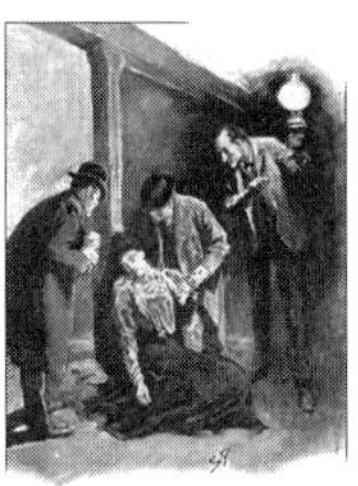

"The devil!" cried Holmes. "Lestrade, give me your whiskey bottle!"

She opened her eyes again a moment later.

"Is he safe?" she asked. "Did he escape?"

"He cannot escape from us, madam."

"No, no. I did not mean my husband. Sir Henry? Is he safe?"

"Yes."

"And the hound?"

"It is dead."

She gave a long grateful sigh.

"Thank God! Oh, this villain! See how he treated me!" She showed us her arms which were covered with marks from being beaten. "But this is nothing, nothing! It is my mind and soul that he has destroyed. Now I know that I have only been used and fooled by him. He never really loved me." She began to cry passionately.

"You have good reason to hate him, madam," said Holmes. "Tell us where he is."

"There is only one place where he can run," she answered. "There is an old mine on an island in the heart of the mire. That's where he kept his hound. It's also his hiding place. I'm sure he's there."

The fog lay like white cotton against the window. Holmes held the light towards it.

"See," he said. "No one could find his way into the Grimpen Mire tonight."

"He may find his way in, but never out," she cried happily. "We marked the path to the mine with guiding sticks. He won't be able to see them."

We knew that we couldn't follow him in this fog. We left Lestrade to guard the house while Holmes and I went back with the baronet to Baskerville Hall. We had to tell him the shocking truth about the Stapletons, and the woman he loved. The night's adventures had broken his nerve. By morning he was in bed sick with a fever under the care of Dr. Mortimer. The two of them later traveled around the world together so that Sir Henry could fully recover his health.

And now I quickly come to the end of this most unusual case. Mrs. Stapleton took us to the path through the mire the next morning. The fog had lifted. She now hated her husband and was eager to help us. We followed the dry-land marker sticks through the wet, dangerous mire. The water and plants had a strong smell. Once or twice we took a wrong step and our legs sank into the mire. Then we spotted a dark object near the path and picked it up. It was Sir Henry's old black shoe.

"Well," said Holmes, "Stapleton probably first let the hound smell the shoe, then he dropped it here as he ran away from us. At least we know that he safely came this far."

But we would never know more than that. There were no footprints in that terrible place. Only the earth itself knows what happened to Stapleton in the fog last night. We believe that the body of that cruel man lies at the bottom of Grimpen Mire.

We found the old mine and the place where he kept his hound. There was a dog chain and a pile of bones. There were also the remains of what looked like a little brown animal.

"A dog!" said Holmes. "By God, I believe the hound ate poor Mortimer's little spaniel. Well, I don't know if this place has any more secrets for us. Stapleton could hide his hound, but not its voice. He wanted to create a hell-hound from the ancient Baskerville family story. Here is the can of phosphorous mix he used. It certainly frightened old Sir Charles to death; the escaped criminal, too. It also stopped the farmers and country people from walking on the moor and asking questions. Very clever, indeed. I said it in London, Watson, and I say it again now. This is the most dangerous man we have ever hunted down. And now he lies there in the green mire."

41

Chapter 15
Looking Back

It was the end of November. Holmes and I sat in front of a warm fire in our Baker Street sitting room. Since returning from Devonshire he had been busy, and successful, with other important cases. He was in a good mood. Sir Henry and Dr. Mortimer were in London on their way to the sea voyage to restore the baronet's health. They visited us earlier at Baker Street. I asked my friend to talk about the case.

"Sometimes when my mind is fixed on one case, it is easy to forget the details of another," said Holmes. "But I'll try to remember what I can. I have had two long talks with Mrs. Stapleton and I now believe that every question has been cleared up. I learned that Stapleton was the son of Rodger Baskerville who was Sir Charles's younger brother. Rodger got into trouble and escaped to South America where they said he died unmarried. He did, however, marry and have one child. This child later married Beryl Garcia, a Costa Rican beauty. He stole a lot of public money, then left for England.

He changed his name to Vandeleur and opened a school in Yorkshire. He hoped to make money, but the school failed badly. Then they changed their name to Stapleton and moved to the south of England.

"Now we come to the interesting part. The fellow knew that there were only two people keeping him from becoming a rich baronet. He badly wanted the ancient family manor and would do anything to get it. He decided to use his wife in the character of his sister. Then he found a place to live near Baskerville Hall. There he began a friendship with Sir Charles Baskerville and the neighbors. Stapleton learned about the family hound, and about Sir Charles's weak heart. Then he made a plan to kill the baronet.

"And the plan worked perfectly. He bought the strongest and most deadly hound he could find. He decided to hide it in Grimpen Mire, which he knew very well from his insect hunts. His idea to put a phosphorous substance on the hound was especially clever and evil. He then waited for his chance.

"It took a long time because the old gentleman never wanted to leave the manor grounds at night. Later, he had an opportunity because of Mrs. Laura Lyons. She thought he was a single man and had fallen in love with him. He promised her that he would marry her if she could get a divorce from her husband. Then he learned that Sir Charles was about to leave for London. He had to act quickly. That's when he told Mrs. Lyons to write the letter to the old man asking to talk with him.

He then lied and stopped her from going to the Hall to see Sir Charles.

"That night Stapleton took his dog to a hiding place near the gate. When he saw Sir Charles he let the hound loose. It jumped over the gate and chased the poor baronet who died of fear. The idea was so clever because the real murderer could not be proven guilty. His only help came from an animal who couldn't talk.

"Dr. Mortimer told Stapleton about the heir coming from America. Stapleton's first idea was to possibly kill Sir Henry in London before he ever came to Devonshire. He brought his wife with him to London because he didn't trust her alone. She was the one who sent the letter of warning to the new baronet.

"It was very important for Stapleton to get some piece of clothing belonging to Sir Henry so that he could later use it for the dog. He went to the hotel. There he paid money to a servant who helped him. The first shoe was new and had no smell, so he had to get a second one.

"The next morning our friends came to visit, followed by Stapleton in his cab. That's when he realized that I was taking the case. He decided to return to Dartmoor and wait for the baronet."

"One moment," I said. "What happened to the hound when its master was in London?"

"For many years the Stapletons had an old servant named Anthony. He recently disappeared and escaped from England. He is the one who took care of the dog when the master was away.

"You may remember that I closely examined the newspaper letter. It's because I could smell a lady's perfume. That's when I began to suspect the Stapletons.

"It was my plan to watch Stapleton. I knew, however, that I had to be alone to do that. So it was necessary to trick everyone, including you, Watson. I told everyone I was busy in London and came there secretly. Actually, I only spent a few nights on the moor in that stone hut. I was in Coombe Tracey most of the time, and Cartwright was there to help me.

"In one of your reports, Watson, you told me about Stapleton's days as a schoolmaster. I then knew exactly who they were. However, I needed to catch Stapleton in the act of murder in order to prove the case in court. That's why I had to use Sir Henry, alone and unprotected. I am truly sorry for the shock to his nerves. He will be fine again soon. I also hope his feelings recover from being tricked by Mrs. Stapleton.

"I believe that Stapleton controlled his wife with both love and fear. She really didn't want anyone to be hurt. She tried to warn Sir Henry while also protecting her husband. The night that Sir Henry came to dinner, she tried to stop her husband. They had a terrible fight. He told her about another woman, and she hated him. He tied her up so that he could carry out his murder. He hoped that later she would forgive him. But she never would.

"Watson, without my notes I can't give you many more details."

"There is just one more question. If Stapleton had become

the heir to Baskerville Hall, how could he suddenly tell people who he really was after all this time?"

"With great difficulty. I really don't have the answer, but I believe there were three choices. He might return to South America and claim the property from there through the British government; or he might try to change his appearance and name completely; or, he might pay a companion to take his place at Baskerville Hall, while he kept most of the money. I'm sure this cruel and clever man would have found some way to do it. And now, my dear Watson, perhaps we should go out and have a nice dinner."

The Valley of Fear

恐怖の谷

読み始める前に

The Valley of Fear 恐怖の谷

「シャーロック・ホームズ」シリーズの長編4作目
1914年の「ストランド・マガジン」9月号に初出

［主な登場人物］

Sherlock Holmes シャーロック・ホームズ 鋭い観察眼と推理力、そして犯罪に関する膨大な知識をあわせ持つ私立探偵。ロンドンのベーカー街221Bに下宿している。

John H. Watson ジョン・H・ワトソン 医師。ホームズのよき相棒でこの物語の語り手。ベーカー街221Bでホームズと同居している。

Professor Moriarty モリアーティ教授 ホームズの宿敵。ロンドンで暗躍する悪党一味を束ねる犯罪者。

Fred Porlock フレッド・ポーロック モリアーティ教授の部下。ホームズに宛てた手紙で使用しているペンネーム。

Inspector MacDonald マクドナルド警部補 ロンドン警視庁の刑事。事件現場にホームズたちを連れていくためにやってくる。

White Mason ホワイト・メーソン サセックス州警察の刑事。

Sergeant Wilson ウィルソン巡査部長 バールストン警察の刑事。

John Douglas ジョン・ダグラス バールストン荘の主人。アメリカの金鉱で成功した資産家。銃殺されて顔が原形をとどめていない状態で発見される。

Mrs. Douglas ダグラス夫人 ジョンより20歳ほど若くて美しい妻。夫の過去のことをよく知らないらしい。

Cecil Barker セシル・バーカー ダグラス夫妻と親しい資産家。度々バールストン荘に宿泊しており、事件当日も居合わせていた。

Ames エームズ バールストン荘の老執事。

Mrs. Allen アレン夫人 バールストン荘の家政婦。

Jack McMurdo ジャック・マクマードー シカゴからヴァーミッサ渓谷にやってきた。のちに秘密結社「自由民団（Order of the Freemen）」の「スカウラーズ（Scowrers）」の団員となる。

Mike Scanlan マイク・スキャンラン スカウラーズの団員。

Jack McGinty ジャック・マギンティ スカウラーズの支団長。

Morris モリス スカウラーズの団員。

Teddy Baldwin テディ・ボールドウィン スカウラーズの団員。エティーの婚約者。

Ettie Shafter エティー・シャフター 若いドイツ人女性。下宿屋の娘。マクマードーと恋に落ちる。

James Stanger ジェームズ・ステンジャー 地元新聞の編集長。スカウラーズに批判的な記事を掲載する。

Captain Marvin マーヴィン警部 シカゴからヴァーミッサ渓谷にやってきた。

Birdy Edwards バーディ・エドワーズ ピンカートン探偵局員。随一の腕利きで、スカウラーズの調査に乗り出す。

Steve Wilson スティーヴ・ウィルソン バーディが調査のために使っている偽名。

［あらすじ］

ホームズはポーロック（偽名）という男から届いた、数字とアルファベットが羅列された暗号文の解読に当たっていた。そこに書かれていたのは、バールストン荘に住むダグラスという金持ちに危険が迫っているという内容だった。そこへ時を同じくして訪ねてきた刑事から、暗号通りの殺人事件が発生したと聞かされたホームズは、事件の背後に宿敵モリアーティ教授が絡んでいると疑い捜査に乗り出す。

顔がめちゃくちゃになった銃殺死体、部屋に置かれていた片方だけの鉄アレイ、堀に囲まれた館からの脱出トリック、過去を語りたがらないダグラスが口にした「恐怖の谷」という言葉——。謎多き館に残された数少ない証拠からホームズが探り出した驚くべき事件の真相とは。そしてこの事件から20年前、数千マイル離れたアメリカの地で繰り広げられた闘いの果てに、恐怖の復讐劇は劇的な結末を迎える。

Illustrations by Frank Wiles (1914-1915)

［総単語数］15,250語

PART 1

The Tragedy of Birlstone

42

Chapter 1
The Warning

Sherlock Holmes and I were in his study. He was leaning his head on his hand and staring at a letter which he had just received, studying it very carefully.

"It's Porlock's writing," he said, thoughtfully. "There's no doubt, though I've seen it only twice before. But if it is Porlock, then it must be of the greatest importance."

"Who then is Porlock?" I asked.

"Porlock, Watson, is a nom-de-plume. Porlock is very important, not for himself, but for the great man with whom he is in touch. You have heard me speak of Professor Moriarty?"

"The famous scientific criminal—?"

"Famous among criminals, yes, but greatly respected as a professor and author by most people who do not know of his other activities."

"But you were speaking of Porlock."

"Ah, yes, Porlock is the only weakness in Moriarty's organization that I have been able to find so far. Encouraged by a

little money, he has once or twice given me valuable information in advance. I cannot doubt that, if we had the cipher, we would find that this message has something to do with Moriarty's darker dealings."

I rose, leaned over Holmes and looked at the strange paper, which read:

534 C2 13 127 36 31 4 17 21 41
DOUGLAS 109 293 5 37 BIRLSTONE
26 BIRLSTONE 9 127 171

"What do you think, Holmes?"

"It is clearly a secret code, the numbers representing the pages of some book. Until I am told which book and which page, however, I am powerless. It's likely we will receive some more information soon."

Holmes was right, and within a few minutes Billy the page appeared with the very letter we were expecting.

"The same writing," remarked Holmes, as he opened the letter, "and actually signed," he added, in a happy voice. But, as he read the note his tone became more serious. "Dear me, I trust that the man Porlock will come to no harm."

"Dear Mr. Holmes,

"I can no longer help you. It is too dangerous. He came to me suddenly and almost saw the letter I was writing to you. I cannot send you the cipher. Please burn the previous message, which is now of no use to you.

"FRED PORLOCK"

"Friend Porlock is clearly scared out of his senses."

"Then why did he write at all?" I wondered.

"Because he feared that I would come around asking questions about him."

"Of course," I said. "But it is maddening to think that an important secret lies here undiscovered."

Sherlock Holmes lit his pipe and leaned back, staring at the ceiling, thoughtfully. "I wonder!" he began. "The book Porlock writes of, what do we know about it?"

"Nothing," I said simply.

"Well, well, it's not that bad. The first message begins with a large 534, does it not? We may suppose that this is a page number; so our book must be a long one. The next sign is C2. What do you think of that, Watson?"

"Column!" I cried.

"Wonderful, Watson. So, now we must think of a long book, printed in double columns. One more thing, my dear Watson; if the book had been an unusual one, Porlock would have sent it to me. Therefore, it must be a very common one."

"A Bible!" I cried excitedly.

"Good, Watson, but not good enough. I can't imagine a book less likely to be used by one of Moriarty's associates. And besides, there are so many different volumes of the Bible and they all have different page systems."

"An almanac!"

"Excellent, Watson! It is in common use, has the right number of pages and has double columns."

He picked up the almanac he always keeps on his desk.

"Here is page 534, column two. Write down the words, Watson! Number thirteen is 'there,' number one hundred and twenty-seven is 'is'—'There is'"—Holmes's eyes were shining with excitement as he counted the words—"'danger.' Ha! Wonderful! Put that down, Watson. 'There is danger—may—come—very—soon—one.' Then we have the name 'Douglas'—'rich—country—now—at—Birlstone—sure—is—urgent.' There, Watson! The meaning is quite clear. Some evil is intended against one Douglas, a rich country gentleman."

Holmes was still smiling at his success as the door opened and Inspector MacDonald of Scotland Yard entered. He was a physically strong man but clever and quiet-natured. Twice in his work Holmes had helped him to succeed. For this reason the Scotsman showed a deep respect for Holmes.

"Ah, Mr. Mac," he said. "I fear that this means there is some problem."

The inspector was about to answer Holmes when he stopped suddenly, and stared with a look of surprise at the paper on the table.

"Douglas!" he cried. "Birlstone! What's this Mr. Holmes? Where on earth did you get these names?"

"It's a coded message that Watson and I have just solved. But why? What's wrong with the names?"

The inspector looked at us in a strange way. "Just this," he said, "that Mr. Douglas of Birlstone was murdered last night!"

43

Chapter 2
Sherlock Holmes Discourses

It Was one of those moments for which my friend existed.

"Remarkable!" he said. "Remarkable!"

"You don't seem surprised."

"Interested, Mr. Mac, but hardly surprised. I receive word warning that a certain person is in danger, and, within the hour I learn that the person is dead. I am interested, but, as you see, not surprised."

"I was going down to Birlstone this morning. I wanted to see if you would come with me. But from what you say perhaps we might be doing better work in London."

"I rather think not," said Holmes. "Though the coded message comes from one in Moriarty's circle, we would waste our time trying to find anything about it here."

"Ah, Moriarty," the inspector said. "He's the professor I've heard you talk about?"

"Exactly!"

Inspector MacDonald smiled. "I will not hide from you, Mr.

Holmes, that I have looked into the man and have even had a talk with him. He seems very respectable and clever."

Holmes laughed softly. "Tell me, Friend MacDonald, this pleasing meeting was, I suppose, in the professor's study?"

"That's so."

"A fine room, is it not? Did you happen to see a picture over the professor's head?"

"Yes, I saw the picture—a young woman with her head on her hands."

"That painting was by Jean Baptiste Greuze, a famous French artist who lived between 1750 and 1800."

MacDonald smiled weakly. "Your thoughts move a bit too quick for me, Mr. Holmes. What is the connection between this painter and the affair at Birlstone?"

"See if this helps you. In the year 1865, a picture by Greuze was sold for more than forty thousand pounds, and may I remind you that the professor's salary is only seven hundred a year."

"Then how could he buy—"

"Exactly! How could he?"

"That's remarkable," said the inspector thoughtfully.

Holmes smiled, as he always enjoyed being admired. "Yes, the picture shows him to be a very wealthy man. But how did he become so wealthy?"

"You mean he has a large income and must earn it outside the law?"

"Exactly. Of course, I have dozens of reasons for thinking so—"

Before my friend could go on about Moriarty's crimes, Inspector MacDonald brought him back to the matter of Porlock.

"Anyhow, what is really important is that there is some connection between the professor and the crime at Birlstone. You got that from the warning received through the man Porlock. Can we get any further than that, Mr. Holmes?"

"We may look at the reasons for the crime. Firstly, I must tell you that Moriarty has very strict control over his people. He uses only one punishment, death. Perhaps Douglas had in some way angered the chief and he was punished to put the fear of death into the other men.

"Another suggestion is that the death was planned by Moriarty as part of his business." Holmes continued. "Was there anything stolen?"

"I have not heard."

"Well, whatever it may be, we must look for the solution down at Birlstone. While we are on our way, Mr. Mac, I will ask you to tell us all about the case so far."

As we traveled by cab to Birlstone, the inspector told us of a letter he had received early that morning from White Mason, a local Sussex detective.

"The official report gives the name John Douglas as the murdered man. It mentioned that the man had been shot in the head by a shotgun and that the hour of the alarm was close to midnight last night. It added that the case was clearly one of murder, but no arrest had been made, and that the case was certainly a very strange one. That's all that we have at the moment, Mr. Holmes."

"Then we shall leave it at that, Mr. Mac. I can see only two things at the moment—a great criminal brain in London, and a dead man in Sussex. It's the connection between them that we are going to find."

44

Chapter 3
The Tragedy of Birlstone

Now, for a moment I will describe the events that took place before we arrived on the scene.

The village of Birlstone is a small and very old group of houses in the north of Sussex. Recently, a number of wealthy families have moved there to enjoy its beauty and natural country charm.

About half a mile from the town, standing in an old park, is the ancient Manor House of Birlstone, parts of which date back to the seventeenth century. A moat forty feet wide, but only a few feet deep, surrounds the house. The ground floor windows are within a foot of the water. The only approach to the house is over a drawbridge, which is pulled up at night—a very important fact to the case.

The house had not been lived in for some years when Mr. John Douglas and his wife moved in. Douglas was a remarkable man, about fifty, with a strong face and a youthful figure. He soon became popular among the villagers, attending their concerts where he sang in a rich voice. He seemed to have a lot of money, gained from the California gold fields. His wife, a beautiful, tall, dark woman, was some twenty years younger than him, but they appeared to have a very happy family life. It was noticed, however, that Mrs. Douglas knew little of her husband's past life in America and seemed quite nervous if her husband was ever late in returning home.

One other person was present at the time of the murder, Cecil Barker of Hampstead. He was a frequent and welcome visitor at the Manor House, an Englishman, who had met Douglas in America. He appeared to be a rather wealthy man, unmarried and somewhat younger than Douglas, forty-five at the most. A tall man, he had a handsome face with sharp black eyes. He was friendly with Douglas and no less friendly with his wife—a friendship that more than once seemed to anger the husband, the servants had noticed.

It was at eleven forty-five on the night of January 6th that the first alarm reached the small local police station. On arriving at the Manor House, Sergeant Wilson, the local policeman, had found the drawbridge down and the whole house in a state of shock. Only Cecil Barker seemed in control of himself and had asked the sergeant in. The village doctor had just arrived and the three men entered the study together.

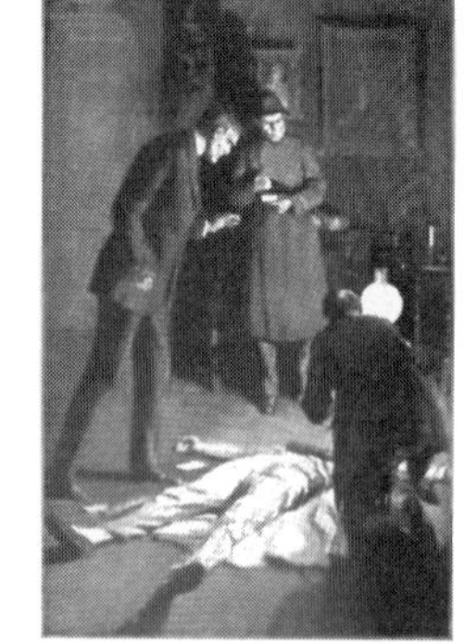

The dead man lay on his back in the center of the room. He was wearing a pink dressing gown and carpet slippers. One look at the body was enough to show the doctor that he was not needed. The man had been terribly hurt. Lying across his chest was a strange gun—a shotgun with the barrels cut to a foot in length. It was clear that it had been fired at close range as his head and face were not recognizable.

"Nothing has been touched up to now," said Cecil Barker. "You see it all exactly as I found it."

"When was that?" The sergeant had drawn out his note-book.

"It was just half-past eleven. I was sitting by the fire in my bedroom when I heard the shot. I rushed down quickly."

"Was the door open?"

"Yes. Poor Douglas was lying as you see him. The candle was burning on the table and I lit the lamp some minutes afterwards. Then I heard Mrs. Douglas coming downstairs and I rushed out to stop her from seeing this terrible sight. She went back upstairs with Mrs. Allen, the housekeeper, and then I went back into the room with Ames, the butler, who had just arrived."

"But I have heard that the drawbridge is kept up all night, so how could the murderer have gotten away?" the sergeant asked.

"Look at this!" Barker drew aside the curtain and held the lamp down to show a mark of blood on the window sill shaped like the bottom of a boot.

"You mean that someone used the window to get to the moat and escape?"

"Exactly!"

"Well, how did he get into the house if the bridge was up? What time was it raised?"

"It was nearly six o'clock," said Ames.

"Well then," said the sergeant, "if anyone came from the outside, they must have gotten in across the bridge before six and been in hiding until Mr. Douglas came into the room after eleven."

The sergeant picked up a card which lay beside the dead man. The letters V.V. and the number 341 were written on it in ink. "What's V.V.? Someone's name, perhaps?" The puzzled policeman walked slowly around the room. "Hello!" he cried excitedly, pulling the curtain to one side. "Someone has been hiding here, sure enough." The sergeant held down the lamp and the marks of muddy boots were able to be seen. "It is likely that his main idea was to rob the house, but Mr. Douglas found him. The thief murdered him and escaped through the window."

The doctor had taken the lamp and was carefully looking at the body. "What's this mark?" he asked. About halfway up the dead man's right arm was an odd brown design, a triangle inside a circle. "The man has been branded at some time. What is the meaning of this?"

"I don't know the meaning of it," said Cecil Barker; "but I have seen the mark on Douglas several times in the last ten years."

"It's a strange thing," said the sergeant. "Everything about this case is strange. Well, what is it now?"

The butler had given a cry of surprise and was pointing at the dead man's hand.

"They've taken his wedding ring!" he exclaimed. "Yes, indeed. Master always wore his plain gold wedding ring on the little finger of his left hand and that ring with the rough nugget above it."

"Are you saying," asked the sergeant, "that the wedding ring was below the other?"

"Always!"

"Then the murderer first took off this ring you call the nugget ring, then the wedding ring, and afterwards put the nugget ring back again."

The country policeman shook his head. "Seems to me that the sooner we get London on this case the better. It won't be long now before White Mason is here to help us. Anyway, I'm not afraid to say that it is a bit too difficult for the likes of me."

45

Chapter 4
Darkness

AT twelve o'clock the chief Sussex detective, White Mason, arrived at the Birlstone police station to welcome us. He was a quiet, comfortable man, who looked more like a small farmer than a criminal officer.

"Your room is at Westville Arms," he said. "This way gentlemen, if you please." And in ten minutes we had all found our rooms and were seated downstairs, listening to the events of the Birlstone mystery which have been described in the last chapter.

"Remarkable!" Holmes said as the story unfolded, "most remarkable!"

"I thought you would say so, Mr. Holmes," said White Mason, in great delight. "Sergeant Wilson had all the facts. I checked them and added a few of my own. I examined the gun. It was not more than two feet long—it could easily be carried under a coat. And the letters P-E-N were printed between the barrels."

"Pennsylvania Small Arms Company—a well-known

American firm," said Holmes.

"Wonderful!" exclaimed Mason, clearly impressed. "No doubt it is an American shotgun. There is some evidence, then, that this man who entered the house and killed its master was an American."

"May I ask whether you examined the far side of the moat to see if there were any signs of the man having climbed out of the water?"

"Yes, I did, and there were no signs, Mr. Holmes."

"Would you mind if we went down to the house at once? There may be some small points which can help us."

"Not at all, Mr. Holmes. I'm sure we are honored to show you all that we know."

"That's the study window," said Mason, as we neared the Manor House, "the one to the right of the drawbridge."

We walked across the drawbridge and were met by the butler Ames. The poor old man was white from the shock. The village sergeant, a tall, formal man, was still in the study.

"You can go home, Sergeant Wilson," said Mason. "You've had enough. Now, gentlemen, we must ask ourselves whether the murder was done by someone outside or inside the house. If it were someone from inside, why would they use the strangest and noisiest weapon in the world, a weapon that was never seen in the house before? Besides that, only a minute after the

alarm was given the whole household was on the spot. It's not possible that in that time the guilty person had time to make footmarks in the corner, open the window, mark the sill with blood, take the wedding ring off the dead man's finger and the rest of it."

"You put it very clearly," said Holmes, "I agree with you."

"Well then, it must have been done by someone from outside the house. The man got into the house before the bridge was raised and hid behind the curtain. There he remained until Mr. Douglas entered the room. There was a very short interview, as the candle shows."

"The candle shows that how?" I asked.

"The candle was a new one, and has not burned more than half an inch," Mason explained. Then, he continued, "So, Mr. Douglas entered the room, put down the candle and the man appeared from behind the curtain. He was armed with a gun and demanded the wedding ring—why, I do not know—then shot Douglas in this terrible way. He dropped his gun and this strange card—V.V. 341—and made his escape through the window and across the moat at the very moment Cecil Barker was discovering the crime."

"Very interesting, but not very likely."

"Come, Mr. Holmes!" cried MacDonald. "You must give us a lead if you think Mr. Mason's story isn't likely."

"I need a few more facts before I suggest my own story. Can we have the butler in for the moment? ...Ames, I have observed that there is a small cut on Mr. Douglas's jaw. Did you notice it before?"

"Yes sir, he cut himself while shaving yesterday morning."

"Did you ever know him to cut himself shaving before?"

"Not for a very long time, sir."

"He may have known he was in danger," Holmes said.

"He was a little nervous, sir."

"Ha! The attack may not have been entirely unexpected. We seem to be making a little progress, do we not? Now, what about this card? Can you make anything of the writing—V.V. 341—Ames?"

"No, sir."

"What do you think, Mr. Mac?"

"Perhaps it's a secret society of some sort, as with the mark upon the arm."

"That's my idea too," said White Mason.

"Well, we can suppose that an agent from such a society makes his way into the house, waits for Mr. Douglas, kills him, and escapes across the moat, after leaving a card beside the dead man, which will tell other members of the society that the death was in revenge. But why this gun, of all weapons? And why the missing ring?"

While talking, Holmes had gone to the window and was closely looking at the bloodmark on the sill. "It is clearly the mark of a shoe, but it is a rather broad one. Strange, because,

as far as I can see, the footmarks behind the curtain seem to be made by a thinner shoe. However, they are not very clear. What's this under the table?"

"Mr. Douglas's dumb-bells," said Ames.

"Dumb-bell—there is only one. Where's the other?"

"I don't know, Mr. Holmes."

"One dumb-bell—" Holmes said seriously, and then there was a knock on the door.

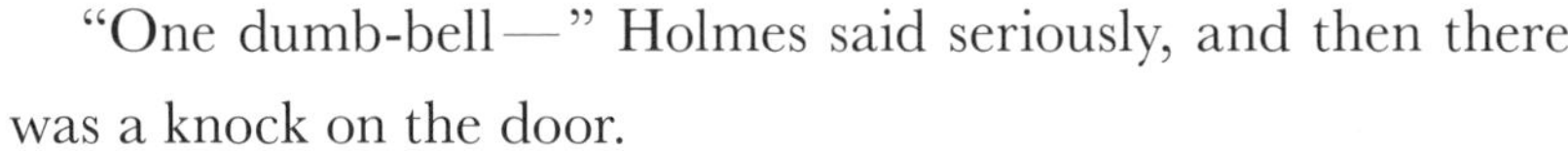

A tall, confident-looking, clean-shaven man looked in at us. I guessed that it was Cecil Barker of whom we had heard.

"Sorry to interrupt your meeting," he said, "but you should hear the latest news."

"Has someone been arrested?"

"No. But they've found his bicycle. It is within a hundred yards of the front door."

We inspected the bicycle, which had been pulled out of some bushes near the house. It was dirty and well used, but there was no clue as to the owner.

"But what made the fellow leave it behind?" the inspector asked. "And how has he gotten away without it? We don't seem to be getting far in the case, Mr. Holmes."

"Don't we?" my friend replied thoughtfully. "I wonder!"

46

Chapter 5
The People of the Drama

"Now that we've finished with the study, perhaps you would like to hear the evidence of some of the people of the house, gentlemen," said White Mason. "We could use the dining room, Ames. Please come yourself first and tell us what you know."

The butler's story was simple and clear and he seemed truthful. He had started working for Mr. Douglas five years ago, when his master had first come to Birlstone. He never saw any signs of fear in Mr. Douglas, but on the day of the murder, he (Ames) had noticed something different about Mr. Douglas. Ames had not gone to bed, but was in the pantry at the back of the house when he heard the bell ring violently. He heard no shot; there were several passages and doors between the pantry and the study. The housekeeper, Mrs. Allen, had come out of her room when she heard the bell and they had gone to the front of the house together.

As they reached the bottom of the staircase, they had seen Mrs. Douglas, who was quite calm, coming down it. Then Mr.

Barker had rushed out and begged her not to go into the study.

"For God's sake! Go back to your room!" he cried, "Poor Jack is dead! You can do nothing."

Mrs. Douglas did not scream or cry, and, after a short time, went with the housekeeper back upstairs to her bedroom. Ames and Mr. Barker had returned to the study. The candle was not lit, but the lamp was burning on the table. They had looked out of the window, but nothing could be seen or heard.

The evidence of Mrs. Allen seemed to fit in with that of her fellow servant. She had been in her room a little nearer to the front of the house when she had heard the ringing of the bell. She was a little hard of hearing, and perhaps that was why she had not heard the shot. She remembered hearing some sound which she thought was the slamming of a door about half an hour before the bell. As for the other servants, they had all gone to bed at the back of the house and could not have heard anything.

Cecil Barker was the next witness. He had very little to add to what he had told the police. He was sure that the murderer had escaped by the window because of the bloodstain on the window sill. Besides, as the bridge was up, there was no other possible way of leaving the house.

Barker said that Douglas was a quiet man, and there were some parts of his life of which he never spoke. He had gone to

America when he was a young man and Barker had first met him in California, where they had become partners in mining. They had done very well, but Douglas had suddenly sold out and left for England. Barker had returned to England and they had renewed their friendship.

Douglas had given Barker the feeling that he was in some danger and he always saw the sudden departure as being connected with this danger. He guessed that some secret society was chasing Douglas and would never stop until it killed him. He thought that the card had something to do with this secret society.

"How long were you with Douglas in California?" asked the inspector.

"Five years, altogether."

"Have you ever heard where his first wife came from?"

"I remember him saying that she was German. She died a year before I met him."

"You don't associate his past with any particular part of America?"

"I have heard him talk of Chicago and he also knew of the coal and iron districts."

"Was there anything unusual about his life in California?"

"He liked best to stay and work in the mountains. He would never go where other men were. That is why I first thought that someone was after him. Within a week of his leaving a dozen men were inquiring after him, a mighty hard-looking crowd."

"These men were Americans—Californians?"

"They were Americans, all right, but not from California."

"That was five years ago and you spent five years with him in California. It seems this business must have been very serious to have continued for ten years. Why didn't he go to the police for protection?"

"Maybe it was some danger that he couldn't be protected against."

"Mr. Barker, did you know Mrs. Douglas before her marriage?"

"No, I did not."

"But you have seen a lot of her since?"

Mr. Barker looked a little angrily at the inspector. "I have seen a lot of him since. If you imagine there is any connection—"

"I imagine nothing, Mr. Barker. But I must ask, was Mr. Douglas completely happy with your friendship with his wife?"

Barker stood for a moment, his face serious and in deep thought, then he spoke. "Poor Douglas had only one fault, and that was his jealousy. He was such a good friend, and yet, if his wife and I talked together, a kind of wave of jealousy would pass over him, and he would start saying the wildest things in a moment. But I'm sure, gentlemen, that no man ever had a more loving wife—and I can say also no friend could be more true than I!"

"You do know that the dead man's wedding ring has been taken?"

"I have no idea what it means sir, but you must never question the lady's honor."

"There is one small point," remarked Sherlock Holmes. "When you entered the room, there was only one candle lit on the table, was there not?"

"Yes, that was so."

"By its light you saw the terrible thing that had happened, and rang at once for help, which arrived speedily, did it not?"

"Within a minute or so."

"And yet when they arrived they found that the candle was out and the lamp had been lit. That seems very remarkable."

Barker looked uncomfortable and he answered after a pause. "There was very bad light. My first thought was to get a better one. The lamp was on the table, so I lit it and blew out the candle."

Holmes asked no further questions and Barker turned and left the room.

Mrs. Douglas then entered the room. Her face was pale, but her manner was calm.

"Mrs. Douglas," said the inspector. "Perhaps you can tell us something which may help. How long was it after hearing the shot were you stopped on the stairs by Mr. Barker?"

"It may have been a couple of minutes. Then Mrs. Allen took me upstairs. It was all like a bad dream."

"Can you give us any idea of how long your husband had been downstairs before you heard the shot?"

"No, I cannot say. He went from his dressing room and I did not hear him go. He went round the house every night; he was nervous of fire."

"You have known your husband only in England, have you not?"

"Yes, we have been married five years."

"Have you heard him speak of anything which occurred in America which might bring some danger to him?"

Mrs. Douglas thought carefully before she answered. "Yes," she said at last, "I have always felt that there was a danger hanging over him. He refused to discuss it with me, but I knew it by certain words that he let fall and by the way that he looked at unexpected strangers. I was certain that he had some powerful enemies and that he was always on guard against them."

"Might I ask," asked Holmes, "what the words were that you heard?"

"The Valley of Fear," the lady answered. "'I have been in the Valley of Fear. I am not out of it yet.'"

"He never mentioned any names?"

"Yes, once, when he was sick with a fever, he spoke a single name, with anger and a sort of horror. McGinty was the name — Bodymaster McGinty. I asked him when he recovered who Bodymaster McGinty was, but he would tell me nothing."

"There is one other point," said Inspector MacDonald. "You have heard, no doubt, that his wedding ring has been taken. Does that suggest anything to you?"

For a moment, I thought I saw a shadow of a smile on the woman's lips.

"I really cannot tell," she answered. "It's certainly very strange."

"Well, we will not keep you any longer," said the inspector.

Mrs. Douglas rose and swept from the room.

Holmes sat with his head on his hands, in deepest thought. Now he rose and rang the bell. "Ames," he said, when the butler entered, "can you remember what Mr. Barker was wearing on his feet last night when you joined him in the study?"

"Yes, Mr. Holmes. He had a pair of bedroom slippers, and they are still under the chair in the hall. I may say that I noticed that they were stained with blood—so were my own."

"That is natural enough, considering the state of the room. Very good, Ames."

A few minutes later we were in the study. Holmes had brought with him the slippers from the hall.

"Strange!" said Holmes, quietly. "Very strange indeed!" He placed the slipper upon the blood mark on the sill. It was exactly the same size.

"Man," cried the inspector, "Barker has marked the window himself! It's broader than any boot mark. But what's the game Mr. Holmes?"

"Ay, what's the game indeed?" my friend repeated thoughtfully.

47

Chapter 6
A Dawning Light

The three detectives were busy with the details of the case, so I took a walk in the old-world garden which surrounded the house. As I walked towards a spot hidden by bushes, I heard the sound of voices and a woman's laughter. An instant later I saw Mrs. Douglas and the man Barker before they saw me. Her appearance gave me a shock. Her eyes shone with the joy of living and he had an answering smile on his handsome face. But their faces changed when they saw me and Barker came towards me.

"Excuse me, sir," he said, "but are you Dr. Watson?"

I bowed coldly in reply.

"Dr. Watson," said Mrs. Douglas, "you know Mr. Holmes better than anyone. Supposing that a matter were to be brought secretly to his knowledge. Is it really necessary that he should tell the detectives?"

"Mr. Holmes works alone," I said. "But he would not hide anything which would help them solve the case. I can say no more."

I raised my hat and went on my way.

"I wish to hear none of their secrets," said Holmes, when I reported to him what had happened. "It would be too difficult if it comes to an arrest for murder."

"You think it will come to that?"

"My dear Watson, I don't say that we have solved it—but when we have found the missing dumb-bell—"

"The dumb-bell?"

"Dear me, Watson. What is the use of only one dumb-bell? Of course the case depends on the missing dumb-bell."

He lit his pipe and began to talk about his case, almost as if he were thinking aloud.

"A lie, Watson—the whole story told by Barker is a lie. Mrs. Douglas is lying also. But why are they lying? According to their story, the killer had less than a minute after the murder to take the ring, which was under another, from the dead man's finger, to replace the other ring—a thing he never would have done—and to put that card beside the body. Impossible! No, no, Watson, the murderer was alone with the dead man for some time with the lamp lit. Of that I have no doubt at all. Therefore, the shot must have been fired at some time earlier than we are told.

"At a quarter to eleven the servants had all gone to their rooms, except for Ames, who was in the pantry. I have found that no noise made in the study can be heard in the pantry when all the doors are shut. Mrs. Allen, who is somewhat deaf, mentioned that she did hear something like the sound of a door slamming half an hour before the alarm was given. I have no doubt that was the sound of a gunshot.

"If this is so, we have to find what Barker and Mrs. Douglas, if they are not the actual murderers, could have been doing from the time when the sound of the shot brought them down until half past eleven when they rang the bell to call the servants. What were they doing, and why did they not instantly give the alarm?"

"Do you think that Barker and Mrs. Douglas are guilty of murder?"

"My dear Watson," said Holmes, shaking his pipe at me, "I think that Mrs. Douglas and Barker know the truth about the murder, and are hiding it. I am sure they do. But, let us consider, if they are guilty, why the Valley of Fear, or the Boss McSomebody? Why the cut-off shotgun of all weapons—and an American one at that? How could they be so sure that the sound of it would not bring someone on to them? And again, if a woman and her lover murder a husband, are they going to clearly show their guilt by removing his wedding ring after his death? Does that seem likely?"

"No, it does not. So how do you propose to solve the case?"

"I think an evening alone in that study would help me much. I have arranged it with Ames. You smile, Friend Watson. Well, we shall see. By the way, may I borrow that big umbrella of yours?"

"Certainly—but what a poor weapon! If there is any danger—"

"Nothing serious, my dear Watson."

It was nightfall when Inspector MacDonald and White Mason brought some good news.

"Man, I had my doubts that there was ever an outsider," said MacDonald, "but that's all past now. We've had the bicycle identified, and we have a description of our man. Mr. Douglas had seemed nervous since the day before, when he had been at the nearby town of Tunbridge Wells. So we took the bicycle over with us and showed it at the hotels there. It was identified at once by the manager of the Eagle Commercial as belonging to a man named Hargrave, an American, who had taken a room two days before."

"Was there anything to identify this man?" asked Holmes.

"Very little. A cycle map of the country lay on his bedroom table. He had left the hotel after breakfast yesterday morning on his bicycle, and no more was heard of him."

"But what did he look like?" asked Holmes.

MacDonald looked at his notebook. "The hotel people all agreed that he was a man of about five foot nine in height, fifty or so years, with a grayish mustache, and a curved nose."

"Well, that might almost be a description of Douglas himself," said Holmes. "Did you get anything else?"

"He was dressed in a heavy gray suit with a short yellow overcoat and a soft cap. So, yesterday morning he set off for this place on his bicycle with the gun hidden in his coat, left his bicycle where it was found and waited for Mr. Douglas to come out. But, when it got dark and Mr. Douglas did not appear, he took his chance and approached the house. He slipped into the first room he saw and hid behind the curtain. He waited until half past eleven when Mr. Douglas came into the room, shot him, then escaped across the moat. He left the bicycle, which would be a clue against him, and made his way to London, or some other safe hiding place. How is that, Mr. Holmes?"

"Well Mr. Mac, my end of the story is that the crime occurred half an hour earlier than reported; that Mrs. Douglas and Barker are both hiding something; that they helped the murderer escape—or they reached the room before he escaped—and that they lied about his escape through the window, and they probably let him go themselves by lowering the drawbridge."

"But the lady has never been in America in all her life," said White Mason. "What possible connection could she have with an American murderer which would cause her to help him?"

"Yes, there are some difficulties," said Holmes. "I will make a little investigation of my own tonight, and we shall see what happens."

"Can we help you, Mr. Holmes?"

"No, no!" said Holmes mysteriously. "Darkness and Watson's umbrella are all that I will need."

48

Chapter 7
The Solution

The next morning after breakfast we found Inspector MacDonald and White Mason at the local police station.

Holmes started the conversation with some surprising words. "Mr. Mac and Mr. Mason, I wish to give you a very serious piece of advice in only four words—stop working the case!"

"What!" cried the inspector. "But the bicyclist, he must be somewhere."

"Yes, yes, and no doubt we shall get him, but don't trouble to trace the mysterious gentleman with the bicycle. I assure you that it won't help you."

"You are holding something back. It's hardly fair of you, Mr. Holmes."

"You know how my methods work, Mr. Mac. But I will hold back for the shortest time possible. I only wish to make my details clear."

"What has happened since last night to give you a completely new idea of the case?"

"Well, I spent some hours last night at the Manor House."

"What were you doing?"

"Ha! I was looking for the missing dumb-bell and I ended up finding it. I can say no more. But gentlemen, meet me here this evening without fail—without fail! And now, I would like you to write a note to Mr. Barker."

Holmes said the following words and MacDonald wrote them down, though he didn't look pleased about it.

"DEAR SIR:

"We must drain the moat, in the hope that we may find something which may help our investigation. The workmen will begin early tomorrow morning, so I thought it best to let you know beforehand.

"Now sign that, and send it by hand at about five o'clock. At that hour we shall meet again in this room," instructed Holmes.

That evening Holmes was very serious in his manner, myself very curious and the detectives clearly untrusting and a little angry.

"Well, gentlemen, it is a chill evening; so you'd better wear your warmest coats. Let us get started at once."

We passed along the border of the Manor House park, until we reached some bushes almost opposite the drawbridge. Holmes bent down behind the bushes, and we all followed his example. There was a single light over the gateway and a light in the study. Everything else was dark and still.

"How long is this to last?" asked the inspector finally. "And what is it that we are watching for?"

"That's what we're watching for!" whispered Holmes.

As he spoke we could see someone passing in front of the light in the study. Suddenly, the window was thrown open and we could see the dark outline of a man's head and shoulders, looking out into the night. Then he leaned forward and seemed to be stirring up the moat with something which he held in his hand. Then suddenly he pulled something up—a large, round object which he dragged through the window.

"Now!" cried Holmes. "Now!"

We were all upon our feet, running across the bridge and into the room which had been occupied by the man whom we had been watching.

The oil lamp, the glow we had seen from outside, was now in the hand of Cecil Barker, who held it towards us as we entered.

"What is the meaning of all this?" he cried.

Holmes glanced around and then pointed to a wet bundle which lay under the writing table.

"This is what we want, Mr. Barker—this bundle, weighted with a dumb-bell, which you have just raised from the bottom of the moat."

Barker stared at Holmes with surprise in his face. "How did you know anything about it?" he asked.

"Simply that I put it there—or perhaps I should say 'replaced' it there. You will remember, Inspector MacDonald, that I was somewhat curious about the absence of the dumb-bell. So, last night, with the help of Ames, and the crook of Watson's umbrella, I went 'fishing' and came up with this bundle."

Sherlock Holmes put the wet bundle on the table and undid the cord around it. From within he took out a dumb-bell and a pair of boots.

"American, as you see," he remarked, pointing at the toes. Then he laid a long knife on the table and finally he undid a bundle of clothing: underclothes, socks, a gray suit and a short yellow overcoat. He held the overcoat towards the light. "'Neal Outfitter, Vermissa, U.S.A.' I have found that Vermissa is a little town in one of the best known coal and iron valleys in the United States. I remember, Mr. Barker, that you associated the coal districts with Mr. Douglas's first wife. It would surely mean that the V.V. on the card by the dead body might stand for Vermissa Valley, which may be that Valley of Fear of which we have heard. And now Mr. Barker, your explanation."

Cecil Barker's face showed anger, surprise and indecision.

"Well, all I can say is that if there's any secret here it's not my secret, and I'm not the man to give it away," said Barker firmly.

A long silence was then broken by a woman's voice. Mrs. Douglas had been listening at the half opened door, and now she entered the room.

"You have done enough for now, Cecil," she said.

"Madam," said Holmes. "I would strongly urge you to tell the police everything. It may be that I am at fault for not following the hint that you gave to my friend Dr. Watson, but at that time I had every reason to believe that you were directly concerned with the crime. Now I am sure that this is not so. I strongly recommend that you ask Mr. Douglas to tell us his own story."

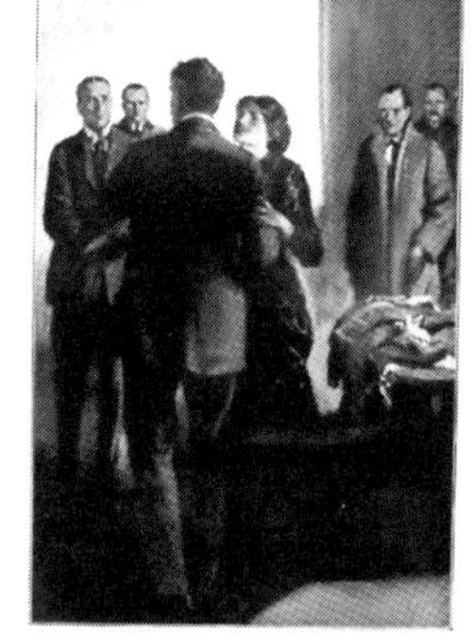

Mrs. Douglas gave a cry of surprise at Holmes's words. The detectives and I must have cried out, too, as we saw a man come toward us now from a dark corner of the room. Mrs. Douglas turned, and in an instant her arms were round him.

"It's best this way, Jack," she said.

"Indeed, yes, Mr. Douglas," said Sherlock Holmes, "I am sure that you will find it best."

The man stood with the dazed look of one who comes from the dark into the light. It was a remarkable face, clear gray eyes, a strong, short mustache, a square chin and a humorous mouth. He took a good look at us all, and then to my surprise he handed me a bundle of papers.

"I've heard of you," he said in a voice which was not quite English and not quite American. "Well, Dr. Watson, I've been in there two days, and I've spent the daylight hours putting the thing into words. There's the story of the Valley of Fear."

Inspector MacDonald had been staring at the newcomer with the greatest surprise. "Well," he cried at last. "If you are Mr. John Douglas of Birlstone Manor, then whose death have we been investigating for these last two days, and where have you come from now? You seemed to spring out of the floor."

"Ah, Mr. Mac," said Holmes, "when I found the suit of clothes in the moat, it at once became clear to me that the body we had found must have been that of the bicyclist from Tunbridge Wells. Therefore I decided that, with the help of his wife and friend, Mr. Douglas was probably hidden in the house and was awaiting quieter times when he could make his final escape."

"Well, you are about right," said Douglas. "It all came down to this: there are some men that hate me and so long as I am alive and they are alive, there is no safety in this world for me. They chased me out of America, but when I married and settled down in this quiet spot I thought my last years were going to be peaceful. I never explained to my wife how things were. She told you all that she knew, and so did Mr. Barker here; for on the night when this thing happened there was little time for explanations. She knows everything now, however. Gentlemen, the day before these happenings I was over at Tunbridge Wells, and I saw a man in the street. He was the worst enemy I had among them all. I was on my guard all that next day and never went out into the park. After the bridge was up my mind was more restful. But later when I checked the house in my dressing gown, as was my habit, I entered the study with just one candle

in my hand and he sprang at me. I saw a knife so I hit him and the knife fell to the floor. A moment later he'd got his gun from under his coat, but I got hold of it before he could fire. We fought for a minute and then the gun fired at his head. I'm afraid his own mother would not have known the face of my sworn enemy, Ted Baldwin.

"Then Barker came hurrying down. I heard my wife coming, and I ran to the door and stopped her. Barker and I waited for the servants to come along. But when there was no sign of them, we understood that they had heard nothing, and it was at that instant that an idea came to me. Baldwin's sleeve had slipped up and I saw the branded mark of the lodge upon his arm. See here!" Douglas turned up his own coat and shirt sleeve to show a brown triangle within a circle exactly like that which we had seen on the dead man. "Then there was his height and hair and figure, about the same as my own, and no one could recognize his face. I put on this suit and Barker and I put my dressing gown on him and he lay as you found him. We tied all his things into a bundle and I weighted them down with the dumb-bell and threw them out the window. The card he had meant to lay upon my body was lying beside his own. I put my other rings on his finger, but I could not remove my wedding ring. I also put a piece of plaster on him where I am wearing one myself.

"Well, that was the situation. I thought if I could hide for a while and then get away where I could be joined by my wife, we should have a chance of living in peace. If they saw in the papers that Baldwin had killed me, there would be an end to all my troubles. I went into this hiding place and Barker did the rest. He opened the window and made the mark on the sill to give an idea of how the murderer escaped. Then he rang the bell and what happened afterward you know."

There was a silence which was broken by Sherlock Holmes.

"Mr. Douglas, how did this man know that you lived here, or how to get into your house?"

"I know nothing of this."

Holmes's face was very white and serious. "The story is not over yet, I fear," he said. "You may find worse dangers than your enemies from America. I see trouble before you, Mr. Douglas. You'll take my advice and still be on your guard."

And now, my readers, I will ask you to journey back some twenty years in time, and westward some thousands of miles, to America, so that I may tell you a terrible story—so terrible that you may find it hard to believe. And when you have read it, we shall meet once more in those rooms on Baker Street, where our current story will find its end.

PART 2

The Scowrers

49

Chapter 1
The Man

IT was the fourth of February, 1875. The snow was deep but the railroad was open, and the evening train, which connected all the coal-mining towns, was slowly moving across the plain to Vermissa, a small town in a lonely corner of the country.

In the leading passenger car, a young man sat by himself. He was middle-sized, in about his thirtieth year, and had come all the way from Ireland. He had large, humorous gray eyes and it was easy to see that he wanted to be friendly to everyone.

The young traveler looked out at the dark countryside and sometimes took from his pocket a letter which he studied carefully. Once from the back of his belt, he pulled a gun which was fully loaded. He quickly put it back, but not before it had been seen by a miner who was seated nearby.

"Hullo," said the miner. "You a stranger in these parts?"

"Yes. I heard there was always work for a willing man."

"You may find you need that gun here," said the miner. "Have you any friends?"

"I am one of the Order of Freemen and where there is a lodge I will find my friends."

The miner came closer to the young traveler, sat down, and held out his hand. "I'm Brother Scanlan, Lodge 341, Vermissa Valley. Glad to see you in these parts."

"Thank you. I'm Brother Jack McMurdo, Lodge 29, Chicago."

"Where are you going now?"

"Vermissa."

"Well, I must get off now. But, there's one piece of advice I'll give you: if you're in trouble in Vermissa, go to the Union House and see Boss McGinty. He is the Bodymaster of Vermissa Lodge and he controls everything around these parts. Bye for now." With that, Scanlan left the train.

Two policemen looked at McMurdo from across the train car. "I guess you are new to this part, young man," said one of them.

"Well, what if I am?" McMurdo answered in a rude voice.

"I advise you to be careful in choosing your friends. I don't think I'd begin with Mike Scanlan if I were you."

"What the hell is it to you who are my friends!" yelled McMurdo, so that every head in the car turned to look and the policemen were rather surprised. "I'm not afraid of you! My name's Jack McMurdo—see? If you want me, you'll find me at Jacob Shafter's on Sheridan Street, Vermissa. That's so you know I'm not hiding from you!"

A few minutes later the train stopped at Vermissa and

McMurdo got off. As he started walking, one of the miners from the train came up to him.

"Well, you certainly know how to talk to the cops," the miner said with respect. "Let me show you the road. I'm passing Shafter's on my way." So the two men walked through the dirty, ugly town.

"That's the Union House," said the guide, pointing to a hotel. "Jack McGinty is the boss there."

"What sort of a man is he?" McMurdo asked.

"What! You never heard of him or the Scowrers?"

"A group of murderers, are they not?"

"Quiet!" cried the miner. "Man, you won't live long in these parts if you speak in the open streets like that." The man looked nervously around him as he spoke. "There's the house you want."

"I thank you," said McMurdo, walking up the path and knocking on the door.

It was opened by a young German woman, fair-haired, with a pair of beautiful dark eyes. McMurdo had never seen such a beautiful woman and he stood staring at her without saying a word. At last he said, "Your house was recommended to me by a friend for board."

"Come right in, sir," said

the woman. "I'm Miss Ettie Shafter, Mr. Shafter's daughter and I run the house—ah, here comes father."

A heavy, old man came up the path. In a few moments McMurdo explained his business. And so it was that McMurdo came to stay in the Shafter's house, the first step in a long train of events, ending in a far distant land.

50

Chapter 2
The Bodymaster

McMurdo was a man who made his mark quickly. Within a week he had become the most important person at Shafter's. The young Irishman's joke was always the quickest, his conversation the brightest, his song the best and he drew good humor from all around him. But he showed again and again a sudden strong anger, which made those who met him feel fear and respect.

From the first it was clear that Ettie had won his heart. On the second day he told her that he loved her, and when she talked about someone else, he would not listen.

"You can keep saying no, Ettie," he would cry, "but the day will come when you say yes, and I am young enough to wait."

McMurdo had gotten a job as a bookkeeper, for he was a well-educated man. This kept him out most of the day and he had not found time to visit the head of the lodge of the Order of Freemen.

One evening, his good German host asked the young man

into his private room and started to talk about Ettie.

"It seems to me that you are in love with my Ettie," said Mr. Shafter.

"Yes, that is so," the young man answered.

"Well, I want to tell you right now that it is no use. Someone has already decided to marry her. It is Teddy Baldwin."

"And who the devil is he?"

"He is a boss of Scowrers."

"Who are these Scowrers that you are all afraid of?"

The boarding-house keeper looked frightened and spoke quietly, as everyone did who talked of that terrible society. "The Scowrers," he said, "are the Order of the Freemen!"

The young man stared. "Why, I am a member of that order myself."

"You? I would never have had you in my house if I had known that."

"What's wrong with the order? It is for charity and good."

"Maybe in some places, but not here!"

McMurdo laughed. "That can't be true."

"If you live here long you will see. You will soon be as bad as the rest. It is bad enough that one of these people wants to marry my Ettie, and that I am too afraid to say no, but that I should have another for my boarder? You must leave this very night!"

McMurdo was shocked that he was to be pushed out of the house and away from the girl he loved. He looked for Ettie later that evening and poured his troubles out to her.

"Ettie, I have known you only a week, but you are the very breath of life to me, and I cannot live without you!"

"Oh, Mr. McMurdo," said the young woman. "I have told you that you are too late!" She put her face into her hands. "I wish to heaven that you had been first!"

He put his arms around her as she cried.

"Could you take me away?" she said through tears. "If you would escape with me, Jack, we could take father and live far from the power of these wicked men."

There was a struggle on McMurdo's face. "No, I can't leave here. No harm will come to you, Ettie. As for the wicked men, you may find that I am as bad as the worst of them before we are through. But, hullo, who's this?" A tall, mean-looking man had walked into the room.

Ettie jumped to her feet with alarm. "I'm glad to see you Mr. Baldwin," she said. "This is a friend of mine, Mr. McMurdo."

"Well, mister, this young lady is mine, and you'll find it a very fine evening for a walk."

"Thank you, but I do not feel like taking a walk," answered McMurdo.

"Don't you?" The man's eyes were filled with anger. "Maybe you feel like having a fight then!"

"That I do!" cried McMurdo, jumping to his feet.

"For God's sake, Jack!" cried poor Ettie. "Jack, he will hurt you!"

"I'll choose my own time, mister," Baldwin said as he went out the door.

For a few moments McMurdo and the young woman stood in silence. Then she threw her arms around him.

"Oh, Jack, how brave you were! But it's no use, you must go! Tonight—Jack—tonight! He will kill you. What chance do you have against a dozen of them, with Boss McGinty and all the power of the lodge behind them?"

McMurdo kissed her. "Don't fear for me. I'm a freeman myself. Maybe I am no better than the others. Perhaps you hate me now, too."

"No, Jack, I could never do that! I've heard that there is no harm in being a freeman anywhere but here. But if you are a freeman, Jack, you should go down and make a friend of Boss McGinty."

"I was thinking the same thing," said McMurdo. "I'll go right now."

The bar of McGinty's saloon was crowded as usual, for it was the favorite place of all the rougher men of the town.

McMurdo pushed open the swinging door and went in. At the far end of the bar, stood the famous McGinty himself. He was a black-haired giant and his eyes were a strange dead black color, which gave him a particularly frightening appearance. McMurdo pushed his way through the crowd.

"I'm new here, Mr. McGinty," he said boldly.

"And who told you to see me?"

"Brother Scanlan of Lodge 341, Vermissa. I recently left Chicago, where I was a member of Lodge 29. I drink your health, sir."

"We don't take folk on trust in these parts, nor do we believe all we're told neither. Come in here for a moment, behind the bar."

McGinty led him to a small room, closed the door, and sat down. For a couple of minutes there was complete silence. Suddenly he bent down and pulled out a terrible looking gun.

"This is a strange welcome," said McMurdo.

"What are you doing here?"

"Working, the same as you—but a poorer job."

"Why did you leave Chicago?"

McMurdo took a worn newspaper cutting from an inner pocket. McGinty glanced at the story of the shooting of one Jonas Pinto, in the Lake Saloon, Market Street, Chicago.

"Why did you shoot him?"

"I was making fake money. This man Pinto was helping me. Then he said he wanted to quit, so I killed him and came out here."

"Why here?"

"'Cause I read in the paper that people weren't too particular in these parts."

McGinty laughed. "Well, you'll be a very useful brother, I'm thinking. We can use a bad man or two among us, Friend McMurdo."

Suddenly Ted Baldwin burst into the room.

"So," he said with an angry look at McMurdo, "you got here first, did you? I must tell you, Boss, about this man."

"We have a new brother here, Baldwin, and it is not for us to greet him in such a way," said McGinty. "Shake hands, man."

"Never!" cried Baldwin.

"What is it then?"

"A young lady. She is free to choose for herself," McMurdo said calmly.

"Is she?" cried Baldwin.

"I should say that she is," said the Boss with a dark stare.

"You are not Bodymaster for life, Jack McGinty, and by God! When it next comes time to vote—"

The Boss sprang at Baldwin like a tiger and closed his hands around the other's neck.

"Easy, Bodymaster!" cried McMurdo, as he dragged him back.

McGinty let go, and Baldwin, shaken and feeling his throat, said, "I have nothing against you, sir."

"Well, then," cried the Boss, "we are all good friends again and that's the end of the matter. The lodge rules with a heavy hand in these parts, Brother McMurdo, if you ask for trouble."

"I surely won't do that," said McMurdo. He held out his hand to Baldwin. "I'm quick to quarrel and quick to forgive."

Baldwin had to take his hand, for the strict eye of the terrible Boss was watching. But his face showed his true feelings.

"You'll have to join Lodge 341, Brother McMurdo. We have our own ways and methods, different from Chicago. Saturday night is our meeting and I expect to see you there," said McGinty.

51

Chapter 3
Lodge 341, Vermissa

On the following day, McMurdo moved to a boarding-house on the other side of the town. Scanlan, the first man he had met on the train, moved to Vermissa and the two stayed together. Shafter let McMurdo come to meals when he liked, so he still saw Ettie and they grew closer as the weeks went by.

On a Saturday night McMurdo was introduced to the lodge. The group met in a large room at the Union House. Some sixty members met at Vermissa, but altogether there were nearly five hundred members across the whole coal district.

They were mostly older men, with lawless souls, in truth a very dangerous group of murderers who took a terrible pride in their activities. At first they had tried to keep their actions secret, but no one would dare to speak against them and the law could not stop them.

Three of the men removed McMurdo's coat and rolled up the sleeve of his right arm. Then they placed a thick, black cap right over his head and the upper part of his face, so that he could see nothing.

"Jack McMurdo," said the voice of McGinty, "is your lodge number 29, Chicago?"

"Yes, it is."

"Are you ready to be tested?"

"Yes, I am."

Then he almost screamed out, for a terrible pain shot through his right arm. He bit his lip and tightened his hands to hide the pain.

Then there was loud cheering, the cover was taken from his head. An odd mark burned red and painful on his arm, but he stood smiling among the brothers.

"One last word, Brother McMurdo," said McGinty. "You have already promised secrecy to the lodge. Do you know that the punishment for disobeying me is instant death?"

"I do," said McMurdo.

"Then I welcome you to Lodge 341. Let us drink to our new brother!"

When the drinks had all been finished, the business of the lodge proceeded.

"The first business," said McGinty, "is to send a message to our local newspaper editor, James Stanger." McGinty took a small piece of newspaper from his jacket pocket and began to read.

"LAW AND ORDER!

"TERROR IN THE COAL AND IRON DISTRICT

"Twelve years have now passed since the first killing which proved there is a criminal group among us. From that day these murders have never ceased. These lawless men are known to us. The group is public. How long are we to endure it? Are we to forever live—

Sure I've read enough of it!" cried the Boss, throwing the paper down.

"Kill him!" cried a dozen voices.

"I protest against that," said Brother Morris, a kind-looking man. "Our hand is too heavy in the valley. James Stanger is an old man and if he is struck down, that will surely bring our end."

"See here, Brother Morris, you should be more careful what you say," said the Bodymaster threateningly.

Morris turned a deadly pale. "I am sorry Eminent Bodymaster and I promise you that I will not question you again."

The Bodymaster relaxed as he listened to the humble words, "Very good, Brother Morris. I would be sad if I had to give you a lesson. And now, boys," he continued, looking round at the company, "It's true that if Stanger were killed, there would be more trouble than we need. But I guess you can give him a hard warning. Can you fix it, Brother Baldwin?"

"Sure!" said the young man, eagerly.

"How many men will you take?"

"Half a dozen, and two to guard the door."

"I think our new brother should go," said the Boss.

Ted Baldwin looked at McMurdo with eyes that showed he had not forgotten nor forgiven. "Well, he can come if he wants," he said in a rude voice.

Later that night, the men gathered in front of a high building. The words "Vermissa Herald" were printed in gold lettering between the brightly lit windows.

"Here," Baldwin said to McMurdo, "you can stand at the door and watch the street."

The other men pushed open the door of the newspaper office and went upstairs. McMurdo stayed below. From the room above came a shout, a cry for help, and then the sound of running feet and falling chairs. An instant later a gray-haired man rushed to the top of the stairs.

He was caught and half a dozen sticks struck him over and over. Baldwin kept hitting the man even after the others stopped. McMurdo rushed up the stairs and pushed him back.

"You'll kill the man," McMurdo said.

"Curse you!" answered Baldwin.

McMurdo pulled his gun from his pocket. "Didn't the Bodymaster order that he was not to be killed?"

"You'd best hurry," cried the

man below. "The windows are all lighting up and you'll have half the town here in five minutes."

Leaving the motionless body of the editor at the top of the stairs, the criminals rushed down the street. At the Union House, some of them mixed with the crowd in McGinty's saloon, whispering across the bar to the Boss that the job had been well done. Others, among them McMurdo, went by the side streets to their own homes.

52

Chapter 4
The Valley of Fear

When McMurdo awoke the next morning his head hurt with the effect of the drink and his arm was hot and sore. Because of the fake money he made, he did not regularly attend his work, so he had a late breakfast, and read the *Vermissa Herald*. It said:

> SHOCK AT THE HERALD OFFICE
> —EDITOR SERIOUSLY WOUNDED.
>
> ...The matter is now in the hands of the police; but it can hardly be hoped that there will be better results than in the past. Some of the men were recognized, so perhaps an arrest will be made. The police are even now searching for the attackers.

McMurdo was thinking about the previous evening and the editor's scared face when he received a message. It read:

> I wish to speak to you, but would rather not in your house. You will find me up on Miller Hill. If you come there now, I have something which is important for you to hear and for me to say.

He was not sure who sent it but decided to go. As he walked up the winding path to the top of the hill, he saw a man with a hat low over his face. The man looked up and McMurdo saw Brother Morris, the freeman who had made the Bodymaster angry the night before.

"I wanted to have a word with you, Mr. McMurdo," said the older man, with fear in his voice. "It seemed to me last night that you are new to the ways here and perhaps not as hard as the other men. Can I trust you?"

"Of course!"

"When you joined the Freeman's society in Chicago, did you ever imagine it would lead to crime?"

"If you call it crime."

"Of course it is crime!" cried Morris. "When I came here I was forced to join the lodge and now I can't get away; if I leave the society it means death for me. Oh, it is awful—awful!"

McMurdo smiled. "I think you are a weak man and make too much of the matter."

"Too much! Wait till you have lived here longer. Look down the valley! It is the Valley of Fear, the Valley of Death."

"Well, I'll let you know what I think when I have seen more," said McMurdo carelessly. "What you have said is safe with me. Now I'll be getting home."

"One word before you go," said Morris. "We may have been seen together. They may want to know what we have spoken about. Let us say that I offered you a job at my store."

"And I refused it. Well, goodbye, Brother Morris, and good luck for the future."

That same afternoon, as McMurdo sat smoking, the door swung open and the door frame was filled with the huge figure of Boss McGinty.

"What were you speaking to Brother Morris about on Miller Hill this morning?"

The question came so suddenly that McMurdo was glad to have his answer prepared. He laughed. "Brother Morris did not know about the fake money I make. He offered me a job at his store."

"And you refused it?"

"Sure. Couldn't I earn ten times as much in my own bedroom with four hours' work?"

"That is so. But you should not be seen too much with Brother Morris. He is not a loyal man, so don't give me reason to question your loyalty to me."

McMurdo was about to answer, but the door flew open, and three faces looked angrily at them from under police caps. Two guns were aimed at McMurdo's head. Another man came into the room. It was Captain Marvin, a police officer recently moved from Chicago.

"I thought you'd be getting into trouble, Mr. McMurdo of Chicago," he said. "Come with us."

"What am I charged with?" asked McMurdo.

"You are wanted in connection with the beating of old Editor Stanger."

"Well," cried McGinty with a laugh, "this man was with me at my saloon, playing cards up to midnight, and I can bring a dozen men to prove it."

"We will settle it in court tomorrow," said Marvin. "Come on, McMurdo."

He was taken to the police station and pushed into the common cell. Here he found Baldwin and three other criminals of the night before, all awaiting their trial the next morning.

But they had no cause for worry. It proved difficult to say who the attackers were due to poor light. The injured man had been so taken by surprise that he remembered nothing except that one man had a mustache. McGinty's clever lawyer was easily able to show that there was not enough evidence against the men. Brothers of the lodge smiled and waved. But there were others who sat with hate in their faces as the men walked free out of the courtroom.

53

Chapter 5
The Darkest Hour

Jack McMurdo's popularity increased among his fellows after the trial. But Ettie Shafter's father would have nothing more to do with him, nor would he allow him to enter the house. Ettie herself was too deeply in love to give him up completely, but she also knew she couldn't marry a criminal. She decided to go to see him, possibly for the last time.

"Give it up, Jack!" she cried, putting her arms around his neck. "For my sake, give it up!"

"How could I do it? You don't suppose that the lodge would let a man go free with all its secrets?"

"I've thought of that, Jack. Father has saved some money. He is tired of this place where the fear of these people darkens our lives. He is ready to go. We would escape together to Philadelphia or

New York, where we would be safe from them."

McMurdo laughed. "The lodge has a long arm. Do you think that they would not find us there?"

"Well then, to the West, or to England, or to Germany where father came from—anywhere to get away from this Valley of Fear!"

"I can't leave just yet, but if you give me six months, I'll work it so that we can leave here without being afraid."

The young woman laughed with joy. "Is it a promise?"

"Well, it may be seven or eight months. But within a year at the longest we will leave the valley behind us."

Ettie returned to her house more light-hearted than she had been since Jack McMurdo had come into her life.

Later that night, as the Scowrer's meeting finished, McGinty touched McMurdo on the arm and led him into the saloon's inner room.

"See here, my boy," said the Boss, "I've got a job for you at last. You can take two men with you—Manders and Reilly. You're to knock down Chester Wilcox, the head of the Iron Dike Company. Twice we've tried to get him, but had no luck, and Jim Carnaway lost his life over it. Now it's for you to try. His house is all alone on the Iron Dike road. It's no good by day because he'll see you coming. But at night, you could blow up the house using gunpowder. "

"I'll do my best," promised McMurdo.

"Very good," said McGinty, shaking him by the hand.

That very night McMurdo started off to prepare for the job.

It was daylight before he returned. The next day he explained his plan to Manders and Reilly, who were as excited as if it were a deer-hunt.

Two nights later they met outside the town, all three with guns and one of them carrying the gunpowder. It was two in the morning before they came to the lonely house. They moved forwards carefully with their guns in their hands.

McMurdo listened at the door of the house, but all was quiet within. He placed the gunpowder by the door and lit the fuse. Then he and his two companions ran quickly off before the house exploded into little bits.

But their well-organized work was all for nothing! Fearing for his safety, Chester Wilcox had moved himself and his family only the day before to some safer and less-known place, where a policeman could watch over them.

"Leave him to me," said McMurdo. "He's my man, and I'll get him sure if I have to wait a year for him."

Such were the ways of the Scowrers by which they spread their rule of fear over a wide district.

54

Chapter 6
Danger

The months went by and McMurdo was now so popular that nothing was done in the lodge without his help and advice.

It was a Saturday evening in May and McMurdo was leaving to attend the lodge meeting when Morris, the weaker brother of the order, came to see him. He looked serious and his kindly face was worried.

"I can't forget that I spoke my heart to you once, and that you kept it to yourself, even though the Boss himself came to see you about it. You are the only one I can speak to and be safe. I've got a secret, a terrible secret."

McMurdo looked at the man carefully. "Well, let me hear it."

"There's a detective on our trail."

McMurdo stared at him in surprise. "Why, man, you're crazy," he said. "The place is full of police and detectives, and they've never done us any harm."

"No, no. It's not a man of the district. You've heard of Pinkerton's, the private detective group? If a Pinkerton man is deep in this business, we will all be destroyed."

"How did you hear of him?" asked McMurdo.

"I had a store in the East before I came here. I left good friends behind me, and one of them is in the telegram service. Here's a letter that I had from him yesterday."

McMurdo read:

How are the Scowrers in your parts? Between you and me, I heard that five big companies and two railroads have decided to plan against your group. Pinkerton's best man, Birdy Edwards, is asking a lot of questions in your area. He must be stopped immediately. I learned about this from strange messages that have come through here every day from near Vermissa.

McMurdo sat in silence for some time, with the letter in his hands. Then he suddenly jumped.

"By God!" he cried, "I've got him. We will fix this Birdy Edwards before he can do any harm. See here, Morris, will you leave this matter to me?"

"Sure, if you don't mention my name. But you won't kill this man, will you?"

"The less you know, Friend Morris, the better you will sleep."

Morris shook his head sadly as he left, feeling that he would be to blame for the detective's death.

McMurdo prepared for the worst, burning every paper which would show him to be a criminal, before he left the house. On his way to the lodge he stopped at old man Shafter's. He knocked at the window and Ettie came out to him. She read trouble in his serious face.

"Something has happened! Oh, Jack, you are in danger!"

"But it is not very bad, my love. And yet we may have to move before it is worse. I had bad news tonight, and I see trouble coming. If I go, by day or by night, you must come with me! Will you come?"

"Yes, Jack, I will come."

"Now, Ettie, it will be just a word to you, and when it reaches you, you will drop everything and come right down to the waiting room at the station."

"Day or night, I'll come when you send word, Jack."

Somewhat eased in mind, now that his own preparations for escape had begun, McMurdo went on to the lodge. The noise of pleasure and welcome greeted him as he entered. He went to his place and raised his hand.

"Eminent Bodymaster," he said in a serious voice, taking the letter from his pocket, "I bring bad news this day. I have information that the richest and most powerful organizations in this state are planning to destroy us, and that there is a Pinkerton detective, one Birdy Edwards, at work here in Vermissa Valley. He's collecting the evidence that may put a rope around the necks of many of us, and send every man in this room into a prison cell."

There was a dead silence in the room.

"What is your evidence for this, Brother McMurdo?" the Boss asked.

"It is in this letter which has come into my hands," said McMurdo. He read the letter out loud.

"Does anyone know this Birdy Edwards by sight?" asked McGinty.

"Yes," said McMurdo, "I do."

There was a murmur of surprise through the hall.

"Eminent Bodymaster, I would ask the lodge to choose a small group, yourself, if I might suggest it, and Brother Baldwin here, and five more. To this group I can talk freely of what I know and of what I advise should be done."

The meeting finished early and left the top men to discuss the problem.

"I said just now that I knew Birdy Edwards," McMurdo explained. "Of course he is not here under that name. He passes under the name of Steve Wilson, and he is lodging at Hobson's Patch."

"How do you know him?"

"Because I talked with him once on the train —he said he was a reporter. Wanted to know all he could about the Scowrers for a New York newspaper. 'I'd pay you well,' he said 'if you could give me some information.' But I was giving nothing away."

"How did you know he wasn't a newspaper man?"

"He got out at Hobson's Patch, and so did I. I went into the telegram office, and he was leaving it.

"'See here,' said the telegram operator after Wilson had gone out. He'd filled in the form with stuff that might have been Chinese for all we could make of it. It was clearly a code. He's a detective all right."

"By God! I believe you're right," said McGinty, "but what do you think we should do about it?"

"He's in Hobson's Patch, but I don't know the house. I've got a plan, though, if you'll take my advice."

"Well, what is it?"

"I'll go over to Hobson's Patch tomorrow morning. I'll find him through the operator, then tell him I'm a Freeman myself. I'll offer him all the secrets of the lodge, for a price. I'll say the papers are at my house and tell him to come at ten o'clock at night to see everything. You can plan the rest yourselves. My house is set off the road with nothing nearby. All seven of you should come to me by nine o'clock. We'll get him!"

"At nine tomorrow we'll come," said the Boss. "Once you get the door shut behind him, you can leave the rest to us."

55

Chapter 7
The Trapping of Birdy Edwards

As McMurdo said, the house in which he lived was a lonely one and very well suited for such a crime as they had planned. They were hopeful that nothing of great importance had yet come to the detective's knowledge. They would find a way to make him talk before they killed him.

McMurdo went to Hobson's Patch as agreed. He was back from his trip in the afternoon, and reported to Boss McGinty at the Union House.

"I took his money, and he promised to give me much more when he has seen all my papers."

"What papers?"

"Well, there are no papers, but I lied and told him about books of rules and forms of Freeman membership. If we handle it right, they can never prove we killed him. Now, see here, Boss, I'll tell you my plan. He will come at ten and will knock three times. You will all be in the other room. I'll show him into the parlor beside the door and leave him there while I get the papers. That will give me time to tell you how things are. Then I will go back to him with some faked papers. As he is reading them, I will grab him. I'll call out and you'll rush in."

"It's a good plan," said McGinty. "The lodge will owe you for this."

When McMurdo had returned home he made his own preparations for the evening in front of him. First, he cleaned and loaded his gun. Then he discussed the matter with his housemate Scanlan. Though he was a Scowrer himself, Scanlan was secretly shocked by the actions of the lodge members, and said that he would gladly leave for the evening.

The lodge men came around nine, as planned. On the outside they were respectable citizens, but their faces showed that there was little hope for Birdy Edwards. McGinty and Ted Baldwin were among the men who gathered that night for the killing of the Pinkerton detective. McMurdo's manner was cool, though he had planned a deadly trap for Birdy Edwards.

They all sat still. Then three loud knocks suddenly sounded at the door.

"Hush! Not a sound!" whispered McMurdo, as he went from the room, closing the door carefully behind him.

The murderers waited. Then they heard the outer door open. There were a few words of greeting. An instant later came the slam of the door and the turning of the key in the lock. He was safe within their trap. Ted Baldwin laughed, and the Boss clapped his great hand across his mouth.

"Be quiet, you fool!" he whispered.

There was the sound of conversation from the next room. Then the door opened, and McMurdo appeared, his finger on his lip.

He came to the end of the table and looked slowly around at them all. His manner had changed to that of one who has important work to do.

"Well!" cried the Boss at last. "Is he here? Is Birdy Edwards here?"

"Yes," McMurdo answered slowly. "Birdy Edwards is here. I am Birdy Edwards!"

There were ten seconds during which there was a deep silence. Seven white faces were motionless with terror. Then with a sudden breaking of glass, gun barrels broke through each window, pointing at the lodge men.

At the sight Boss McGinty gave the roar of a wounded bear and jumped for the half-opened door. A gun aiming at him and the cold blue eyes of Captain Marvin met him at the door. The Boss fell back in his chair.

"You're safer there," said the man whom they had known as McMurdo. "There are forty armed men around this house, so you have no chance. Take their guns, Marvin!" The shocked men could do nothing.

"I'd like to say a word

before we separate," said the man who had trapped them. "You know me now for what I am. I am Birdy Edwards of Pinkerton's. I was chosen to break up your gang. It was a hard and dangerous game to play. Only Captain Marvin and my employers knew about it. But it's over tonight, thank God, and I am the winner!"

Seven pale faces looked up at him as he continued. "I never killed a man in Chicago, nor made a fake dollar in my life. But I knew the way into your good wishes, so I pretended that I was running from the law. Maybe people will say that I am as bad as you. But what is the truth? The night I joined you to beat up old man Stanger I could not warn him, but I held your hand, Baldwin, when you would have killed him. I also gave Chester Wilcox warning, so that when I blew up his house he and his family were in hiding."

"You traitor!" cried McGinty.

"Ay, Jack McGinty, you and your likes have been the enemy of God and man in these parts. I had to stay until I had every man and every secret right here in my hand. But I had to act quickly in the end because a letter had come that would have let you know about it."

There is little more to tell. In the early morning hours, Miss Ettie Shafter and Mr. Birdy Edwards boarded a special train out of the land of danger. It was the last time that Ettie or her lover set foot in the Valley of Fear. Ten days later they were married in Chicago, with old Jacob Shafter as witness of the wedding.

The trial of the Scowrers was held far from Vermissa. McGinty was hung along with eight of his chief followers and fifty others were put in prison. The work of Birdy Edwards was complete.

And yet, the game was not over. Ted Baldwin and others were not hung and there came a day when they were freed from prison.

Birdy Edwards was chased out of Chicago after the remaining Scowrers almost killed him. He changed his name and moved to California, and it was there that the light went out in his life for a time when Ettie Edwards died. He started a business with an Englishman named Barker and made a lot of money. But again there came another warning, and he left—just in time—for England. And so he became the John Douglas who for the second time married and lived for five years as a Sussex county gentleman.

56

Epilogue

The Trial of John Douglas finally resulted in his freedom. It was clearly self-defense, the jury found.

"Get him out of England at any cost," Holmes wrote to Mrs. Douglas. "There are forces here which may be more dangerous than those he has escaped. There is no safety for your husband in England."

Late last night our landlady brought up a message that a gentleman wished to see Holmes, and that the matter was very important. Into the room walked Cecil Barker, our friend of the moated Manor House. His face was drawn and tired.

"I've bad news—terrible news, Mr. Holmes. It's poor Douglas. I told you that they started out for South Africa three weeks ago. The ship reached Cape Town last night. I received this telegram from Mrs. Douglas this morning:

"'Jack has been lost overboard in a storm off St. Helena. No one knows how the accident occurred.'

"'IVY DOUGLAS.'"

"So, it came like that, did it?" said Holmes thoughtfully. "Well, I've no doubt it was well planned."

"You mean you think he was murdered?" Barker asked.

"Surely!"

"Oh, those terrible Scowrers—" I started.

"No, no, my friend. This was done by Moriarty. This crime is from London, not from America."

"But for what reason?"

"I can only say that we first heard of this business through one of his associates. These Americans were well advised. They became partners with Moriarty, a great man of crime. From that moment poor Douglas had no chance."

"Don't tell me there is nothing we can do," said Barker angrily.

"No," said Holmes, and his eyes seemed to be looking far into the future. "I don't say that he can't be beat. But you must give me time—you must give me time!"

Word List

・本文で使われている語のうち、中学校レベル以外の全ての語を掲載しています。

・語形が規則変化する語の見出しは原形で示しています。不規則変化語は本文中で使われている形になっています。

・一般的な意味を紹介していますので、一部の語で本文で実際に使われている品詞や意味と合っていないことがあります。

・品詞は以下のように示しています。

名 名詞	代 代名詞	形 形容詞	副 副詞	動 動詞	助 助動詞	前 前置詞	接 接続詞	間 間投詞
冠 冠詞	略 略語	俗 俗語	熟 熟語	頭 接頭語	尾 接尾語	記 記号	関 関係代名詞	

A

□ **a ～ or two** 1～か2～，2，3の

□ **aback** 熟 **be taken aback** あっけにとられる，不意を突かれる

□ **Abdullah Khan** アブドーラ・カーン《人名》

□ **Abel White** アベル・ホワイト《人名》

□ **ability** 名 ①できること，(～する)能力 ②才能

□ **about** 熟 **as no one was about** 周囲に誰もいなかったので **be about to** まさに～しようとしている，～するところだ **be worried about** (～のことで)心配している，～が気になる［かかる］ **care about** ～を気に掛ける **hear about** ～について聞く **How about ～?** ～はどうですか。 **speak about** ～について話す **What about ～?** ～についてあなたはどう思いますか。～はどうですか。 **worry about** ～のことを心配する

□ **above all** 何よりも

□ **absence** 名 欠席，欠如，不在

□ **accept** 動 ①受け入れる ②同意する，認める

□ **accident** 名 ①(不慮の)事故，災難 ②偶然

□ **accompany** 動 ①ついていく，つきそう ②(～に)ともなって起こる ③伴奏をする **be accompanied by** ～を伴って

□ **according** 副《－to ～》～によれば［よると］

□ **account** 名 説明，報告，記述 **on that account** そのような訳で

□ **accustom** 動《－to ～》～に慣れさせる **accustomed to** ～に慣れて

□ **Achmet** 名 アクメット《人名》

□ **across** 熟 **come across** ～に出くわす，～に遭遇する **go across** 横断する，渡る **run across** 走って渡る **walk across** ～を歩いて渡る

□ **act** 名 行為，行い **in the act** 現行犯で，最中に 動 行動する

□ **active** 形 ①活動的な ②積極的な ③活動［作動］中の

□ **activity** 名 活動，活気

□ **actual** 形 実際の，現実の

□ **actually** 副 実際に，本当に，実は

□ **ad** 名 広告

□ **add** 動 ①加える，足す ②足し算をする ③言い添える

□ **address** 名 住所，アドレス 動 あて名を書く

□ **administrator** 名 経営者，理事，管理者

□ **admiral** 名 海軍提督，艦隊司令官 **Admiral Baskerville** バスカヴィル海軍少将

□ **admire** 動 感心する，賞賛する

□ **admit** 動 認める，許可する，入れる

□ **adopted** 形 養子［養女］になった

□ **advance** 名 進歩，前進 **in advance** 前もって，あらかじめ

□ **advantage** 名 有利な点［立場］，強み，優越

□ **adventure** 名 冒険

□ **advice** 名 忠告，助言，意見

□ **advise** 動 忠告する，勧める

□ **affair** 名 事柄，事件 **love affair** 恋愛（関係），浮気

□ **affect** 動 影響する

□ **affection** 名 愛情，感情

□ **afford** 動《can－》～することができる，～する(経済的・時間的な)余裕がある

□ **Afghanistan** 名 アフガニスタン《国》

□ **afraid** 熟 **be afraid of** ～を恐れる，～を怖がる **I'm afraid (that)** 残念ながら～，悪いけれど～

□ **Africa** 名 アフリカ《大陸》 **South Africa** 南アフリカ

□ **after** 熟 **after all** やはり，結局のところ **after all the fun I have had at their expense** さんざん彼らをだしにして笑った後に **after a while** しばらくして **after that** その後 **be after** ～の後をつける **go after** ～の後を追う **hill after hill** 小山に次ぐ小山 **look after** ～の世話をする，～に気をつける **run after** ～を追いかける **the man we are after** 私たちが後をつけた男

□ **afterward** 副 その後，のちに

□ **afterwards** 副 その後，のちに

□ **again** 熟 **again and again** 何度も繰り返して **once again** 再度，もう一度 **over and over again** 何度も繰り返して

□ **against** 熟 **against the wall** 壁を背にして **against us** 私たちに敵対する **go against** 合わない，反する **score a point against** ～をやり込める **turn against** ～に敵対する

□ **agate** 名 メノウ

□ **agent** 名 ①代理人 ②代表者

□ **ago** 熟 **long ago** ずっと前に，昔

□ **Agra** 名 アグラ《インドの都市の名前》

□ **Agra Fort** アーグラ城塞

□ **agree with** (人)に同意する

□ **agreement** 名 ①同意，合意，協定 ②一致

□ **ah** 間《驚き・悲しみ・賞賛などを表して》ああ，

やっぱり

□ **ahead** 熟 **ahead of** ～より先［前］に，～に先んじて **pull ahead** 前にでる

□ **aid** 動 援助する，助ける，手伝う **aided by** ～によって援助［支援］される

□ **aim** 動 ①（武器・カメラなどを）向ける ②ねらう，目指す

□ **Akbar** 名（ドスト・）アクバル《人名》

□ **alarm** 名 ①警報，目覚まし時計 ②驚き，突然の恐怖

□ **Alice** 名 アリス《人名》

□ **alive** 熟 **no man alive** 誰ひとり（～ない）

□ **all** 熟 **above all** 何よりも **after all** やはり，結局のところ **all alone** ただ独りで **all around** 全体的に，あらゆる点で **all day** 一日中 **all day and night** 昼も夜も **all day long** 一日中，終日 **all for nothing** いたずらに，無駄に **all one's life** ずっと，生まれてから **all over** ～中で，全体に亘って，～の至る所で，全て終わって，もうだめで **all right** 大丈夫で，よろしい，申し分ない，わかった，承知した **all the time** ずっと，いつも，その間ずっと **all the way** ずっと，はるばる，いろいろと **at all** とにかく《肯定文で》，そもそも《疑問文で》 **by all means** なんとしても，ぜひとも **first of all** まず第一に **in all probability** たぶん，おそらく **not at all** 少しも～でない **not ～ at all** 少しも［全然］～ない **sit up all night** 徹夜する **That's all right.** いいんですよ。 **with all** ～がありながら **worst of all** 一番困るのは，最悪なことに

□ **Allen, Mrs.** 名 アレン夫人

□ **allow** 動 ①許す，《－… to ～》…が～するのを可能にする，…に～させておく ②与える

□ **all-powerful** 形 全能の，全権力を握って

□ **all-seeing** 形 全てお見通しの

□ **almanac** 名 年鑑

□ **alone** 熟 **all alone** ただ独りで **leave ～ alone** ～をそっとしておく

□ **along** 熟 **along the way** 途中で，これまでに，この先，ここに至るまでに **along with** ～と一緒に **come along** ①一緒に来る，ついて来る ②やって来る，現れる **drive along**（車で）走行する **run along** おいとまする，立ち去る **walk along**（前へ）歩く，～に沿って歩く

□ **aloud** 副 大声で，（聞こえるように）声を出して

□ **although** 接 ～だけれども，～にもかかわらず，たとえ～でも

□ **altogether** 副 まったく，全然，全部で

□ **always** 熟 **not always** 必ずしも～であるとは限らない

□ **amazement** 名 びっくりすること，驚愕

□ **amazing** 形 驚くべき，見事な

□ **America** 名 アメリカ《国名・大陸》

□ **American** 形 アメリカ（人）の 名 アメリカ人

□ **American Exchange** 米国証券取引所

□ **Ames** 名 エームズ《人名》

□ **amongst** 前 ～の間に［を・で］

□ **amount** 名 ①量，額 ②《the －》合計 **no amount of** 最大限の～でさえ…ない

□ **amuse** 動 楽しませる

□ **amusement** 名 おもしろさ，おかしさ

□ **ancient** 形 昔の，古代の

□ **and so** そこで，それだから，それで

□ **and so on** ～など，その他もろもろ

□ **and yet** それなのに，それにもかかわらず

□ **Andaman Islands** アンダマン諸島

□ **Andamans** 名 アンダマン諸島

□ **angel** 名 ①天使 ②天使のような人 **Avenging Angels** 報復の天使《モルモン教の武装組織，教えに背いた教徒を罰する》

□ **anger** 名 怒り **white with anger** 怒りで白くなる 動 怒る，～を怒らせる

□ **angrily** 副 怒って，腹立たしげに

□ **angry** 熟 **be angry at** ～に腹を立てている **get angry** 腹を立てる

□ **animal-like** 形 動物のような

□ **annoyed** 形 いらいらした，怒った

□ **another** 熟 **one another** お互い

□ **answering** 名 応答

□ **Anthony** 名 アンソニー《人名》

□ **anxious** 形 ①心配な，不安な ②切望して **be anxious for** ～を切望している

□ **anxiously** 副 心配［切望］して

□ **any** 熟 **any time** いつでも **at any moment** 今すぐにも **can be of any help to** ～の役に立つことができる **not ～ any longer** もはや～でない［～しない］ **not ～ any more** もう［これ以上］～ない

□ **anyhow** 副 ①いずれにせよ，ともかく ②どんな方法でも

□ **anymore** 副《通例否定文，疑問文で》今はもう，これ以上，これから

□ **anyone** 代 ①《疑問文・条件節で》誰か ②《否定文で》誰も（～ない） ③《肯定文で》誰でも

□ **anything but** ～のほかは何でも，少しも～でない

□ **anything else** ほかの何か

☐ **anyway** 副 ①いずれにせよ，ともかく ②どんな方法でも

☐ **anywhere** 副 どこかへ[に]，どこにも，どこへも，どこにでも

☐ **apart** 副 ①ばらばらに，離れて ②別にして，それだけで **apart from** ～を除いては

☐ **apartment** 名 アパート

☐ **appear** 動 ①現れる，見えてくる ②(～のように)見える，～らしい **appear to** ～するように見える

☐ **appearance** 名 ①現れること，出現 ②外見，印象

☐ **apply** 動 ①申し込む，志願する，問い合わせる ②あてはまる ③適用する **apply for** ～を求める

☐ **appointment** 名 (会合などの)約束，予約

☐ **approach** 動 ①接近する ②話を持ちかける 名 接近，(～へ)近づく道

☐ **argue** 動 ①論じる，議論する ②主張する

☐ **argument** 名 議論，論争

☐ **armchair** 名 ひじ掛けいす，ひじ置き

☐ **armed** 形 武装した

☐ **army** 名 軍隊，《the －》陸軍

☐ **around** 熟 **all around** 全体的に，あらゆる点で **bring around** 連れて[持って]くる **carry around** 持ち歩く **come around** ぶらっと訪れる **go around** 動き回る，あちらこちらに行く，回り道をする，(障害)を回避する **lie around** そこらへんに転がっている **look around** まわりを見回す **look around for** ～を捜し求める **run around** 走り回る **turn around** 振り向く，向きを変える，方向転換する **walk around** 歩き回る，ぶらぶら歩く

☐ **arouse** 動 (感情などを)起こす，刺激する

☐ **arrange** 動 ①並べる，整える ②取り決める ③準備する，手はずを整える

☐ **arrangement** 名 ①準備，手配 ②取り決め，協定 ③整頓，配置

☐ **arrest** 動 逮捕する 名 逮捕 **under arrest** 逮捕されて

☐ **arrival** 名 ①到着 ②到達

☐ **arrive at** ～に着く，～に至る

☐ **arrive in** ～に着く

☐ **Arthur Charpentier** アーサー・シャルパンティエ《人名》

☐ **article** 名 (新聞・雑誌などの)記事，論文

☐ **artist** 名 芸術家

☐ **as** 熟 **as a matter of duty** 職務上 **as A so B** Aと同様にB **as ～ as ever** 相変わらず，これまでのように **as ～ as one can** できる限り～ **as ～ as possible** できるだけ～ **as clear as day** 昼のように明るい，明々白々な **as ever** 相変わらず，これまでのように **as far as** ～と同じくらい遠く，～まで，～する限り(では) **as far as one can** できるだけ **as for** ～に関しては，～はどうかと言うと **As I did so** そうしているうちに **as if** あたかも～のように，まるで～みたいに **as is** その[現状の]ままで **as long as** ～する以上は，～である限りは **as much as** ～と同じだけ **as no one was about** 周囲に誰もいなかったので **as of now** 今のところ **as soon as** ～するとすぐ，～するや否や **as though** あたかも～のように，まるで～みたいに **as time goes by** 時間が過ぎるにつれて **as to** ～に関しては，～については，～に応じて **as usual** いつものように，相変わらず **as well** なお，その上，同様に **as well as** ～と同様に **as you know** ご存知のとおり **as you wish** 望み通りに **It is as well that he is** 彼がいるに越したことはない **just as** (ちょうど)であろうとおり **see ～ as …** ～を…と考える **so long as** ～する限りは **such as** たとえば～，～のような **such ～ as …** …のような～ **the same ～ as …** …と同じ(ような) ～

☐ **ash** 名 灰

☐ **ashore** 副 岸に，陸上に **put ～ ashore** ～を上陸させる

☐ **aside** 副 わきへ(に)，離れて

☐ **ask ～ if** ～かどうか尋ねる

☐ **ask for the hand of** ～に結婚を申し込む

☐ **asleep** 形 眠って(いる状態の) **fall asleep** 眠り込む，寝入る

☐ **assist** 動 手伝う，列席する，援助する

☐ **associate** 動 ①連合[共同]する，提携する ②～を連想する **associate ～ with** ～と…を結び付ける 名 仲間，組合員

☐ **assume** 動 仮定する，当然のことと思う

☐ **assure** 動 ①保障する，請け負う ②確信をもって言う

☐ **astonishment** 名 驚き

☐ **at** 熟 **at a distance** 少し離れて **at all** とにかく《肯定文で》，そもそも《疑問文で》 **at any moment** 今すぐにも **at best** せいぜい，よくても **at ease** 安心して，ホッとして **at fault** 誤って，非難されるべき **at first** 最初は，初めのうちは **at home** 自宅で，在宅して **at last** ついに，とうとう **at least** 少なくとも **at once** すぐに，同時に **at one time** ある時には，かつては **at one's mercy** ～のなすがままになって **at peace** 平和に，安らかに，心穏やかで **at present** 今のところ，現在は，目下 **at that moment** その時に，その瞬間に **at that time**

その時 **at the end of** ～の終わりに **at the moment** 今は **at (the) most** せいぜい, 多くても **at the time** そのころ, 当時は **at the time of** ～の時[際]に **at this** これを見て, そこで(すぐに) **at this moment** 現在のところ, 現段階[時点]では **at this point** 現在のところ **at this time** 現時点では, このとき **at times** 時々 **at work** 働いて, 仕事中で, 職場で

□ **Athelney Jones** アセルニー・ジョーンズ《人名》

□ **attach** 動 ①取り付ける, 添える ②付随する, 帰属する **attach importance to** ～を重要視する

□ **attached** 形 ついている, 結びついた, 《be – to ～》～に未練[愛着]がある

□ **attack** 動 ①襲う, 攻める ②非難する ③(病気が)おかす 名 ①攻撃, 非難 ②発作, 発病 **heart attack** 心臓麻痺

□ **attacker** 名 攻撃者, 敵

□ **attempt** 動 試みる, 企てる 名 試み, 企て, 努力

□ **attend** 動 ①出席する ②世話をする, 仕える ③伴う ④《– to ～》～に注意を払う, 専念する, ～の世話をする

□ **attention** 名 ①注意, 集中 ②配慮, 手当て, 世話 **attract attention** 注意を引く

□ **attitude** 名 姿勢, 態度, 心構え

□ **attract** 動 ①引きつける, 引く ②魅力がある, 魅了する **attract attention** 注意を引く

□ **Aurora** 名 オーロラ号《蒸気船の名》

□ **author** 名 著者, 作家

□ **available** 形 利用[使用・入手]できる, 得られる

□ **Avenging Angels** 報復の天使《モルモン教の武装組織, 教えに背いた教徒を罰する》

□ **avenue** 名 ①並木道 ②《A-, Ave.》～通り, ～街

□ **average** 形 平均の, 普通の

□ **avoid** 動 避ける, (～を)しないようにする

□ **await** 動 待つ, 待ち受ける

□ **awake** 形 目が覚めて

□ **aware** 形 ①気がついて, 知って ②(～の)認識のある

□ **away** 熟 **back away** 後ずさりする **come away** ～から離れて行く **far away** 遠く離れて **get away** 逃げる, 逃亡する, 離れる **give away** ただで与える, 贈る, 譲歩する, 手放す **go away** 立ち去る **keep away from** ～に近寄らない **move away** ①立ち去る ②移す, 動かす **put away** 片づける, 取っておく **right away** すぐに **run away** 走り去る, 逃げ出す **run away from** ～から逃れる **stay away from** ～から離れている **straight away** すぐに **take away** ①連れ去る ②取り上げる, 奪い去る ③取り除く **take someone away** (人)を連れ出す **turn away** 向こうへ行く, 追い払う, (顔を)そむける, 横を向く **walk away** 立ち去る, 遠ざかる **worn away** 摩耗する

□ **awful** 形 ①ひどい, 不愉快な ②恐ろしい

□ **awoke** 動 awake (目覚めさせる)の過去

□ **ay** 間 ああ, やれやれ

B

□ **back** 熟 **back and forth** あちこちに, 前後に **back away** 後ずさりする **back end** 後端 **back file** バックナンバーのファイル **bring back** 戻す, 呼び戻す, 持ち帰る **come back** 戻る **come back to** ～へ帰ってくる, ～に戻る **drive back** 車で引き返す **fall back** 後退する, 戻る, 退却する, 後ろ向きに倒れる **get back** 戻る, 帰る **get ～ back** ～を取り返す[戻す] **give back** (～を)返す **go back to** ～に帰る[戻る], (中断していた作業に)再び取り掛かる **hold back** (事実・本心などを)隠す, (感情を)抑える, 自制する **lean back** 後ろにもたれる **push back** 押し返す, 押しのける **put back** (もとの場所に)戻す, 返す **take back** ①取り戻す ②(言葉, 約束を)取り消す, 撤回する **turn back** 元に戻る

□ **background** 名 背景, 前歴, 生い立ち

□ **backward** 形 ①後方(へ)の, 逆の ②遅れた 副 後方へ, 逆に, 後ろ向きに

□ **backwards** 形 ①後方(へ)の, 逆の ②遅れた 副 後方へ, 逆に, 後ろ向きに

□ **bad luck** 災難, 不運, 悪運

□ **badly** 副 ①悪く, まずく, へたに ②とても, ひどく

□ **Baker Street** ベーカー街《ロンドンの地名, ホームズとワトソンの住む家がある》

□ **Baker Street irregulars** ベーカー街非正規隊

□ **bald** 形 ①はげた ②すり減った, (木に)葉がない

□ **bald-headed** 形 頭のはげた

□ **Baldwin** 名 ボールドウィン《人名》

□ **band** 名 ①ひも, 帯 ②楽団, 団(party)

□ **bank** 名 土手, 川岸

□ **bar** 名 酒場

□ **barely** 副 ①かろうじて, やっと ②ほぼ, もう

少しで

☐ **bargain** 名駆け引き

☐ **bark** 名ほえる声，どなり声 動ほえる，どなる

☐ **Barker** 名バーカー《人名》

☐ **baronet** 名準男爵

☐ **barrel** 名たる，1たるの分量 **gun barrel** 銃身

☐ **barrow** 名（土まんじゅう形の）塚 **High Barrow** ハイ・バロー《地名》

☐ **Barrymore the butler** 名バリモア執事

☐ **Bartholomew Sholto** バーソロミュー・ショルトー《人名》

☐ **Baskerville** 名バスカヴィル《人名》 **Baskerville Hall** バスカヴィル邸

☐ **battle** 名戦闘，戦い

☐ **bear** 動①運ぶ ②支える ③耐える **bear the name of** ～の名前がある **bear up** 支える 名熊

☐ **beard** 名あごひげ

☐ **bearded** 形あごひげを生やした

☐ **beast** 名①動物，けもの ②けもののような人，非常にいやな人［物］

☐ **beat** 動①打つ，鼓動する ②打ち負かす **beat anything** 無比無類である **beat up**（人を）めった打ちにする 名①鼓動，脈 ②（警察官などの）巡回区域

☐ **beaten** 動beat（打つ）の過去分詞 形打たれた，打ち負かされた，疲れ切った

☐ **beating** 名たたくこと，殴打

☐ **beauty** 名美，美しい人［物］

☐ **because of** ～のために，～の理由で

☐ **become of** ～はどうなるのか

☐ **bed** 熟**go to bed** 床につく，寝る

☐ **bedroom** 名寝室

☐ **bedside** 名寝台のそば，まくら元

☐ **before** 熟**the day before** 前の日 **the night before** 前の晩

☐ **beforehand** 副①あらかじめ，前もって ②早まって

☐ **beg** 動懇願する，お願いする **I do beg your pardon.** 大変失礼いたしました。

☐ **begin** 熟**to begin with** はじめに **We end where we began.** 我々は振り出しのところでおしまいだ。

☐ **beginning** 名初め，始まり

☐ **behalf** 名利益 **on behalf of** ～のために，～に代わって

☐ **behind** 前①～の後ろに，～の背後に ②～に遅れて，～に劣って **close ～ behind** …… を～の後ろで閉める 副①後ろに，背後に ②遅れて，劣って **leave behind** あとにする，～を置き去りにする **stay behind** 後ろにつく，後に残る，留守番をする

☐ **belief** 名信じること，信念，信用

☐ **believe in** ～を信じる

☐ **believer** 名信じる人，信奉者，信者

☐ **bell** 名ベル，鈴，鐘

☐ **belong** 動《－to ～》～に属する，～のものである

☐ **below** 前①～より下に ②～以下の，～より劣る 副下に［へ］

☐ **Benares metal-work** バラナシの金属細工

☐ **bend** 動①曲がる，曲げる ②屈服する［させる］ **bend over** かがむ，腰をかがめる，～に身をかがめる **bend down** かがみこむ

☐ **Bender** ベンダー《人名》

☐ **beneath** 前～の下に［の］，～より低い 副下に，劣って

☐ **bent** 動bend（曲がる）の過去，過去分詞 形①曲がった ②熱中した，決心した

☐ **Bernstone Edwards** バーンストン・エドワーズ《人名》

☐ **Beryl** 名ベリル《人名》**Beryl Garcia** ベリル・ガルシア **Beryl Stapleton** ベリル・ステイプルトン

☐ **beside** 前①～のそばに，～と並んで ②～と比べると ③～とはずれて

☐ **besides** 前①～に加えて，～のほかに ②《否定文・疑問文で》～を除いて 副その上，さらに

☐ **best** 熟**at best** せいぜい，よくても **do one's best** 全力を尽くす **try one's best** 全力を尽くす

☐ **best-preserved** 形保存状態の極めて良い

☐ **bet** 動賭ける

☐ **better** 熟**feel better** 気分がよくなる **get better**（病気などが）良くなる **I'd better** ～した方がよさそうだ **had better** ～したほうが身のためだ，～しなさい

☐ **beyond** 前～を越えて，～の向こうに **beyond the reach of** ～の力の及ばない，～の手の届かない 副向こうに

☐ **Bible** 名①《the -》聖書 ②《b-》権威ある書物，バイブル

☐ **bicyclist** 名自転車乗り

☐ **Billy, the page** ボーイのビリー

☐ **Birdy Edwards** バーディ・エドワーズ《人名》

☐ **Birlstone** 名バールストン《地名》

☐ **Birlstone Manor** バールストン荘

☐ **Birlstone police** バールストン警察

☐ **bit** 動bite（かむ）の過去，過去分詞 名①小片，少量 ②《a –》少し，ちょっと

☐ **bite** 動かむ，かじる **bite off** かみ切る 名かむこと，かみ傷，ひと口

☐ **bitter** 形①にがい ②つらい

☐ **black oak** クロガシ

☐ **black or blue** 人種や肌の色に関係なく《blue=「青人」はインド人やアジア人を指す軽蔑語》

☐ **Black Tor** 黒い丘《ダートムア国立公園にある丘の名前》

☐ **black-bearded** 形黒いあごひげを生やした

☐ **black-haired** 形黒髪の

☐ **blackness** 名暗さ，暗黒

☐ **Blair Island** ブレア島

☐ **blame** 動とがめる，非難する

☐ **blanket** 名毛布

☐ **bleed** 動出血する，血を流す［流させる］

☐ **bless** 動神の加護を祈る，～を祝福する **God bless you.** 神のご加護がありますように。おやまあ。

☐ **blessing** 名①（神の）恵み，加護 ②祝福の祈り **blessing in disguise** 不幸中の幸い

☐ **blew** 動blow（吹く）の過去

☐ **blind** 動①目をくらます ②わからなくさせる

☐ **blindly** 副盲目的に，むやみに

☐ **blink** 動目をパチパチさせる

☐ **blonde** 形（女性が）金髪の，ブロンドの

☐ **blood** 名血，血液 **blood stain** 血痕 **make one's blood run cold**（人）をゾッとさせる，血の気を引かせる

☐ **bloodmark** 名血の跡

☐ **blood-red** 形血で赤く染まった

☐ **blood-relation** 名血族の者

☐ **bloodstain** 名血痕

☐ **bloody** 形血だらけの，血なまぐさい，むごい

☐ **blow** 動①（風が）吹く，（風が）～を吹き飛ばす ②息を吹く，（鼻を）かむ ③破裂する **blow out** 吹き消す **blow up** 破裂する［させる］ 名打撃

☐ **blowpipe** 名吹き筒

☐ **blow-pipe** 名吹き筒

☐ **blue** 名青人《インド人やアジア人を指す軽蔑語》**black or blue** 人種や肌の色に関係なく

☐ **board** 名①板 ②まかない **get on board** 乗る 動①乗り込む ②下宿する

☐ **boarder** 名下宿人

☐ **boarding** 名まかない

☐ **boarding-house** 名宿，下宿屋

☐ **boat-length** 名艇身

☐ **boatman** 名（貸し）ボート屋，ボートの漕ぎ手，船頭

☐ **bodyguard** 名ボディーガード，護衛

☐ **Bodymaster** 名（自由民団の）支部長

☐ **boldly** 副大胆に，厚かましく

☐ **bone** 名骨

☐ **bony** 形①骨のような，骨質の ②（人が）骨太の，やせた

☐ **Book of Life**『生命の書』

☐ **bookcase** 名本箱

☐ **bookkeeper** 名帳簿係

☐ **boot** 名《-s》長靴，ブーツ

☐ **border** 名境界，へり，国境

☐ **bored** 形うんざりした，退屈した

☐ **boring** 形うんざりさせる，退屈な

☐ **boss** 名上司，親方，監督

☐ **both A and B** AもBも

☐ **both of them** 彼ら［それら］両方とも

☐ **bother** 動悩ます，困惑させる

☐ **bottom** 名①底，下部，すそ野，ふもと，最下位，根底 ②尻

☐ **bottomless** 形底なしの

☐ **bound** 動境を接する，制限する **bounded by** ～によって囲まれた

☐ **bow** 動（～に）お辞儀する **bow down** 屈服する，甘んじて従う

☐ **boxer** 名拳闘家

☐ **boy** 熟**my boy**（親しい）友達《呼びかけ》

☐ **Bradley** 名ブラッドリー《タバコ会社の名前，または商標》

☐ **brain** 名①脳 ②知力

☐ **branded** 形焼き印を押された

☐ **brave** 形勇敢な

☐ **bravery** 名勇敢さ，勇気ある行動

☐ **break** 熟**break in** 口をはさむ，割り込む **break into** 急に～する **break into a smile (laugh)** 急に笑みを浮かべる（笑う） **break open**（金庫などを）こじ開ける **break out** 発生する，急に起こる，（戦争が）勃発する **break someone's heart**（人）の心を打ち砕く **break** through ～を打ち破る break up ばらばらになる, 解散させせる

□ **breath** 名息, 呼吸

□ **breathe** 動呼吸する

□ **breathing** 名呼吸, 息づかい

□ **breathtaking** 形息をのむような, 美しい

□ **breed** 名品種, 血統

□ **brick** 名レンガ

□ **brief** 形簡単な

□ **briefly** 副短く, 簡潔に

□ **Brigham Young** ブリガム・ヤング《モルモン教徒の開拓者たちを率いたリーダー, 1801–1877》

□ **brighten** 動輝かせる, 快活にさせる

□ **brightly** 副明るく, 輝いて, 快活に

□ **bring** 熟 **bring around** 連れて［持って］くる **bring back** 戻す, 呼び戻す, 持ち帰る **bring justice to** ～に裁きを受けさせる **bring out** (物)をとりだす, 引き出す **bring ～ out into the open** ～を明るみに出す **bring someone down** (人)を倒す **bring up** ～を持ってくる

□ **British** 形①英国人の ②イギリス英語の 名英国人

□ **Brixton** 名ブリクストン《ロンドンの地名》 **Brixton Road** ブリクストン街

□ **broad** 形幅の広い

□ **brother** 名〔男性の〕同胞, 同志, 兄弟分, 同組合員 **foster brother** 乳兄弟

□ **build** 名体格

□ **builder** 名建設者

□ **building** 名建物, 建造物, ビルディング

□ **bullet** 名銃弾, 弾丸状のもの

□ **bully** 動いじめる, おどす

□ **bump** 動①ドスン［バン］と当たる ②ぶつかる, ぶつける

□ **bundle** 名束, 包み, 一巻き

□ **burial** 名埋葬

□ **buried** 形埋められた

□ **burn with** ～を強く感じる

□ **burned** 形焼けた, 黒焦げになった

□ **burning** 形燃えている

□ **burst** 動①爆発する［させる］ ②破裂する［させる］ **burst in** 急に入る, 乱入する **burst into** ～に飛び込む, 急に～する **burst into tears** 急に泣き出す **burst out laughing** 爆笑する 名①破裂, 爆発 ②突発

□ **bury** 動①埋葬する, 埋める ②覆い隠す **She shall not be buried in that.** こんなものをつけたまま彼女を埋葬させるものか。

□ **bush** 名低木, 茂み, やぶ, 未開墾地

□ **business** 熟 **on business** 仕事で

□ **busy with** 《be –》 ～で忙しい

□ **but** 熟 **anything but** ～のほかは何でも, 少しも～でない **not ～ but …** ～ではなくて… **nothing but** ただ～だけ, ～にすぎない, ～のほかは何も…ない

□ **butler** 名執事

□ **by** 熟 **by God** 神にかけて, 本当に **by Heaven** 神にかけて **by all means** なんとしても, ぜひとも **by chance** 偶然, たまたま **by day** 昼間は, 日中は **by God** 神かけて, 本当に **by Heaven** 神にかけて **by now** 今のところ, 今ごろまでには **by oneself** 一人で, 自分だけで, 独力で **by the look of** ～の様子から判断して **by the time** ～する時までに **by the way** ところで, ついでに, 途中で **by then** その時までに **by this time** この時までに, もうすでに **By whom?** 誰に？ **drop by** 立ち寄る **get by** どうにかやっていく, 生き残る **go by** ①(時が)過ぎる, 経過する ②～のそばを通る ③～に基づいて［よって］行う **one by one** 1つずつ, 1人ずつ **side by side** 並んで **stand by** そばに立つ, 傍観する, 待機する **stop by** 途中で立ち寄る, ちょっと訪ねる **take someone by surprise** (人)をびっくりさせる, 不意打ちを食らわす **walk by** 通りかかる

C

□ **C.C.H.** 略 **Charing Cross Hospital** チャリング・クロス病院

□ **cab** 名辻馬車(現代のタクシー) **get a cab to** ～まで辻馬車で行く

□ **cabdriver** 名辻馬車の運転手

□ **cabin** 名(丸太作りの)小屋, 船室, キャビン

□ **cabman** 名辻馬車の運転手

□ **Calcutta** 名カルカッタ《地名。現在のコルカタ》

□ **California** 名カリフォルニア《米国の州》

□ **Californian** 名カリフォルニア州の人

□ **call** 熟 **call for** ～を求める, 訴える, ～を呼び求める, 呼び出す **call in** ～を呼ぶ, ～に立ち寄る **call on** 呼びかける, 招集する, 求める, 訪問する **call out** 叫ぶ, 呼び出す, 声を掛ける **call to** ～に声をかける **call upon** 求める, 頼む, 訪問する **to be left until called for** (郵便物の)局留め

□ **caller** 名訪問者, 電話をかける人

□ **calm** 形穏やかな，落ち着いた 動静まる，静める **calm down** 落ち着く，沈静化する

□ **calmly** 副落ち着いて，静かに

□ **Camberwell** 名キャンバーウェル《地名》 **Camberwell Road** キャンバーウェル街

□ **camp** 名野営（地），キャンプ

□ **campfire** 名キャンプファイア，たき火

□ **can** 熟 **as far as one can** できるだけ **as ~ as one can** できる限り～ **can be of any help to** ～の役に立つことができる **can do nothing** どうしようもない **can hardly** とても～できない **Can you ~?** ～してくれますか。

□ **Canada** 名カナダ《国名》

□ **candle** 名ろうそく

□ **canoe** 名カヌー

□ **capable** 形①《be – of ~［~ing］》～の能力［資質］がある ②有能な

□ **Cape Town** ケープタウン《南アフリカの地名》

□ **captain** 名（警察の）警部，陸軍大尉 **Captain Marvin** マーヴィン警部 **Captain Morstan** モースタン大尉

□ **care** 熟 **care about** ～を気に掛ける **care for** ～の世話をする，～を扱う，～が好きである，～を大事に思う **take care** 気をつける，注意する **take care of** ～の世話をする，～の面倒を見る，～を管理する

□ **careless** 形不注意な，うかつな

□ **carelessly** 副不注意にも，ぞんざいに

□ **carpet** 名じゅうたん，敷物 **carpet slipper** 家庭用スリッパ

□ **carriage** 名①馬車 ②乗り物，車

□ **carry around** 持ち歩く

□ **carry into** ～の中に運び入れる

□ **carry off** 誘かいする，さらって行く，運び去る

□ **carry on** 続ける

□ **carry out** 外へ運び出す，［計画を］実行する

□ **Carson city** カーソンシティ《アメリカの地名，ユタ州のとなりのネバダ州にある街》

□ **Cartwright** 名カートライト《人名》

□ **case** 熟 **have a case** 告訴する **in case** ～だといけないので，念のため，万が一 **in case of** ～の場合には，～に備えて **in nine out of ten cases** 十中八九 **in that case** もしそうなら **on the case** その事件を捜査中で **The case is closed.** 事件は一件落着です。

□ **cash** 名現金

□ **catch hold of** ～をつかむ，捕らえる

□ **catch sight of** ～を見つける，～を見かける

□ **catch up with** ～に追いつく

□ **cattle** 名畜牛，家畜

□ **cattleman** 名牛飼い，牧夫

□ **cattlemen** 名 cattleman（牛飼い，牧夫）の複数

□ **caught** 熟 **get caught** 逮捕される

□ **cease** 動やむ，やめる，中止する

□ **Cecil Barker** セシル・バーカー《人名》

□ **ceiling** 名天井

□ **celebration** 名①祝賀 ②祝典，儀式

□ **cell** 名小室，独房 **prison cell** 刑務所の監房

□ **Celtic** 形ケルト（人）の **Celtic nose** 鷲鼻

□ **central** 形中央の，主要な

□ **certain** 形①確実な，必ず～する ②（人が）確信した ③ある ④いくらかの

□ **certainly** 副①確かに，必ず ②《返答に用いて》もちろん，そのとおり，承知しました

□ **challenge** 動挑む，試す

□ **chance** 熟 **by chance** 偶然，たまたま **slightest chance** わずかな可能性 **take a chance** 一か八かやってみる

□ **chapter** 名（書物の）章

□ **character** 名①特性，個性 ②品性，人格

□ **charge** 動①（代金を）請求する ②（～を…に）負わせる ③命じる 名①請求金額，料金 ②責任 ③非難，告発 **in charge of** ～を任されて，～を担当して，～の責任を負って

□ **Charing Cross** チャリング・クロス《地名》 **Charing Cross Hospital** チャリング・クロス病院

□ **charity** 名①慈善（行為） ②思いやり

□ **Charles Baskerville** チャールズ・バスカヴィル《人名》

□ **charm** 名魅力，魔力 動魅了する

□ **charming** 形魅力的な，チャーミングな

□ **Charpentier** 名シャルパンティエ《人名》

□ **chase** 動①追跡する，追い［探し］求める ②追い立てる

□ **check** 動①照合する，検査する ②阻止［妨害］する ③（所持品を）預ける **check into** チェックインする，調査する **check on** ～を調べる 名①照合，検査 ②小切手 ③（突然の）停止，阻止（するもの） ④伝票，勘定書

□ **cheerful** 形上機嫌の，元気のよい，（人を）気持ちよくさせる

□ **cheerfully** 副陽気に，快活に

□ **cheering** 名歓声, 喝采

□ **chemical** 形化学の, 化学的な **chemical laboratory** 化学実験室

□ **chest** 名 ①大きな箱, 戸棚, たんす ②金庫 ③胸, 肺

□ **Chester Wilcox** チェスター・ウィルコックス《人名》

□ **Chicago** 名シカゴ《地名》

□ **chief** 名頭, 長, 親分 **police chief** 警察署長 形最高位の, 第一の, 主要な

□ **childish** 形子どもっぽい, 幼稚な

□ **chill** 形冷え冷えとした.

□ **chin** 名あご

□ **Chinese** 形中国(人)の 名 ①中国人 ②中国語

□ **choice** 名選択(の範囲・自由), えり好み, 選ばれた人[物]

□ **Chosen Valley** 選ばれし谷《モルモン教徒たちが放浪の末に住みかに定めた地域》

□ **church-going** 形教会通いの

□ **churchman** 名牧師

□ **cigar** 名葉巻

□ **cigarette** 名(紙巻)たばこ

□ **cipher** 名暗号文

□ **circle** 名 ①円, 円周, 輪 ②仲間, サークル **stone circle** 環状列石

□ **circumstance** 名 ①(周囲の)事情, 状況, 環境 ②《-s》(人の)境遇, 生活状態 **under the circumstance** そんな事情なので

□ **citizen** 名 ①市民, 国民 ②住民, 民間人

□ **civilian** 名一般市民, 民間人

□ **claim** 動 ①主張する ②要求する, 請求する 名 ①主張, 断言 ②要求, 請求

□ **clap** 動(手を)たたく

□ **Clayton** 名クレイトン《人名》

□ **clean-faced** 形きれいにひげを剃った

□ **clean-living** 形清く正しい生き方の

□ **clean-shaven** 形ひげのない

□ **clear** 形 ①はっきりした, 明白な ②澄んだ ③(よく)晴れた 動 ①はっきりさせる ②片づける ③晴れる **clear up** きれいにする, 片付ける, (疑問, 問題を)解決する

□ **clearly** 副 ①明らかに, はっきりと ②《返答に用いて》そのとおり

□ **Cleveland** 名クリーブランド《米国の地名》

□ **clever** 形 ①頭のよい, 利口な ②器用な, 上手な

□ **climb on** ～の上によじ登る

□ **climb out** (～から)降りる

□ **climb over** ～を乗り越える

□ **close** 熟 **be close to** ～に近い **close ～ behind …** …を～の後ろで閉める **close upon** ～に迫る **closer and closer** どんどん近づく **get close** 近づく **get close to** ～に近づく, 接近する **The case is closed.** 事件は一件落着です。

□ **closely** 副 ①密接に ②念入りに, 詳しく ③ぴったりと

□ **closing time** 閉店[終業]時間

□ **clothing** 名衣類, 衣料品

□ **clue** 名手がかり, 糸口

□ **coal** 名石炭

□ **coal-mining town** 炭鉱町

□ **coast** 名海岸, 沿岸

□ **cocaine** 名コカイン

□ **code** 名暗号 動暗号にする

□ **coded message** 暗号文

□ **cold** 熟 **run cold** 冷たくなる

□ **cold-blooded** 形冷血な, 血も涙もない

□ **coldly** 副冷たく, よそよそしく

□ **colleague** 名同僚, 仲間, 同業者

□ **collection** 名収集, 収蔵物

□ **column** 名 ①コラム, (新聞などの)欄 ②(新聞などの)縦の段[行・列]

□ **come** 熟 **come across** ～に出くわす, ～に遭遇する **come along** ①一緒に来る, ついて来る ②やって来る, 現れる **come and** ～しに行く **come around** ぶらっと訪れる **come away** ～から離れて行く **come back** 戻る **come back to** ～へ帰ってくる, ～に戻る **come down** 下りて来る, 田舎へ来る **come for** ～に向かって来る, ～の目的で来る, ～を取りに来る **come from** ～の生まれ[出身]である **come in** 中にはいる, やってくる **come into** ～に入ってくる **come loose** 抜ける, 緩む **come of** ～の結果として生ずる **come on** いいかげんにしろ, もうよせ, さあ来なさい **come out** 出てくる, 出掛ける, 姿を現す **come out friends** 友人になる **come out of** ～から出てくる **come over** やって来る **come over someone's face** 〔表情などが〕(人)の顔に表れる **come over to** ～にやって来る **come someone's way** (人)の身に降りかかる **come this far** ここまで来る **come through** 通り抜ける, 成功する **come to an end** 終わる **come true** 実現する **come up** 近づいてくる, 階上に行く, 浮上する, 水面へ上ってくる, 発生する, 昇る, 現れる **come up with** ～に追いつく, ～を思いつく, 考え出す,

見つけ出す **come upon** (人) に偶然出合う

□ **comfort** 名 ①快適さ, 満足 ②慰め ③安楽

□ **comfortable** 形 快適な, 心地いい **make oneself comfortable** くつろぐ

□ **command** 名 命令, 指揮(権)

□ **commander** 名 司令官, 指揮官

□ **comment** 名 論評, 解説, コメント 動 論評する, 注解する, コメントする

□ **commercial** 名 コマーシャル **Eagle Commercial** イーグル・コマーシャル《ホテル名》

□ **commit** 動 ①委託する ②引き受ける ③(罪などを) 犯す **commit a crime** 犯罪を犯す

□ **common** 熟 **common sense** 常識, 共通感覚 **House of Commons** 庶民院, 下院 **in common use** 一般的に使われて[用いられて]いる

□ **companion** 名 ①友, 仲間, 連れ ②添えもの, つきもの

□ **compare** 動 ①比較する, 対照する ②たとえる

□ **complete** 形 完全な, まったくの, 完成した

□ **completely** 副 完全に, すっかり

□ **concern** 動 ①関係する,《be -ed in [with] ～》～に関係している ②心配させる 名 ①関心事 ②関心, 心配 ③関係, 重要性

□ **concerned** 形 ①関係している, 当事者の ②心配そうな, 気にしている

□ **concert** 名 ①音楽[演奏]会, コンサート ②一致, 協力

□ **conclusion** 名 結論, 結末

□ **condition** 名 ①(健康) 状態, 境遇 ②《-s》状況, 様子 ③条件 **on the condition that** もし～なら

□ **confess** 動 (隠し事などを) 告白する, 打ち明ける, 白状する

□ **confession** 名 告白, 自白

□ **confidence** 名 ①自信, 確信, 信頼, 信用度 ②秘密, 打ち明け話 **in confidence** 極秘で, 内密に

□ **confident** 形 自信のある, 自信に満ちた

□ **confident-looking** 形 自信に満ちて見える

□ **confidently** 副 確信して, 自信をもって, 大胆に

□ **confirm** 動 確かめる, 確かにする

□ **confirmed** 形 確認された

□ **confused** 形 困惑した, 混乱した **get confused** まごつく, 当惑する

□ **congratulate** 動 祝う, 祝辞を述べる

□ **congratulation** 名 祝賀, 祝い,《-s》祝いの言葉

□ **connect** 動 関係づける, つなぐ

□ **connected** 形 結合した, 関係のある

□ **connection** 名 ①つながり, 関係 ②縁故

□ **consent** 名 同意, 承諾, 許可

□ **consider** 動 ①考慮する, ～しようと思う ②(～と) みなす ③気にかける, 思いやる

□ **construction** 名 建設, 工事, 建物

□ **consulting** 形 ①相談の ②診察の ③顧問の **consulting detective** 探偵

□ **contain** 動 ①含む, 入っている ②(感情などを) 抑える **contain oneself** 自分(感情) を抑える

□ **container** 名 容器, 入れ物

□ **continent** 名 大陸 **North American Continent** 北米大陸

□ **continuation** 名 ①継続, 続行 ②続編

□ **continuous** 形 連続的な, 継続する, 絶え間ない

□ **control** 動 ①管理[支配]する ②抑制する, コントロールする 名 ①管理, 支配(力) ②抑制 **have control over** ～を支配コントロールする **in control** ～を支配して, ～を掌握している

□ **convenient** 形 便利な, 好都合な

□ **conversation** 名 会話, 会談

□ **convict** 名 罪人, 囚人

□ **convince** 動 納得させる, 確信させる

□ **cooking** 名 料理(法), クッキング

□ **coolly** 副 冷静に, 冷たく

□ **Coombe Tracey** クーム・トレーシー《地名》

□ **cop** 名 警官

□ **Copenhagen** 名 コペンハーゲン《地名, デンマークの首都》

□ **copy** 名 ①コピー, 写し ②(書籍の) 一部, 冊

□ **cord** 名 ひも

□ **correct** 形 正しい, 適切な, りっぱな

□ **cost** 名 ①値段, 費用 ②損失, 犠牲 **at any cost** 何を犠牲にしても, どうあっても 動 (金・費用が) かかる, (～を) 要する, (人に金額を) 費やさせる

□ **Costa Rican** 形 コスタリカ(人) の

□ **cotton** 名 ①綿, 綿花 ②綿織物, 綿糸

□ **could** 熟 **could have done** ～だったかもしれない《仮定法》 **Could you ～?** ～してくださ

いますか。 **How could ～?** 何だって～なんてことがありえようか? **If +《主語》+ could** ～できればなあ《仮定法》

□ **council** 名 会議，評議会，議会

□ **Council of Four** 四人評議会《モルモン教の指導者4人による評議会》

□ **count** 動 ①数える ②(～を…と)みなす

□ **countryside** 名 地方，田舎

□ **county** 名 郡，州

□ **couple** 名 ①2つ，対 ②夫婦，一組 ③数個 **a couple of** 2，3の

□ **course** 熟 **in the course of** ～しているうちに **of course** もちろん，当然

□ **court** 名 法廷，裁判所

□ **courtroom** 名 法廷

□ **cover** 動 ①覆う，包む，隠す ②扱う，(～に)わたる，及ぶ ③代わりを務める ④補う **be covered with** ～でおおわれている 名 覆い，カバー

□ **cover-up** 名 隠蔽，もみ消し

□ **cow** 名 雌牛，乳牛

□ **co-worker** 名 同僚，仕事仲間

□ **Cowper** 名 クーパー《人名》

□ **cracked** 形 砕けた，ひび割れた

□ **crazily** 副 気の狂ったように

□ **crazy** 形 ①狂気の，ばかげた，無茶な ②夢中の，熱狂的な

□ **create** 動 創造する，生み出す，引き起こす

□ **creature** 名 (神の)創造物，生物，動物

□ **credit** 名 信用，評判，名声 **take credit** 手柄を取る，評価を得る

□ **creosote** 名 クレオソート《防腐薬，鎮痛薬などに用いられる化学物質》

□ **crime** 名 ①(法律上の)罪，犯罪 ②悪事，よくない行為 **commit a crime** 犯罪を犯す

□ **criminal** 形 犯罪の，罪深い，恥ずべき **criminal case** 刑事事件 名 犯罪者，犯人

□ **Criterion** 名 クライテリオン《ロンドンにある飲食店》

□ **crocodile** 名 クロコダイル

□ **crook** 名 曲がった部分

□ **crowd** 動 群がる，混雑する **get crowded out** 締め出しを食らう，押し出される 名 群集，雑踏，多数，聴衆

□ **crowded** 形 混雑した，満員の

□ **crown** 名 冠

□ **cruel** 形 残酷な，厳しい

□ **crush** 動 押しつぶす，砕く，粉々にする

□ **cry out** 叫ぶ

□ **cry over** ～を嘆く

□ **crying** 形 泣き叫ぶ

□ **cupboard** 名 食器棚，戸棚

□ **curiosity** 名 ①好奇心 ②珍しい物[存在]

□ **curious** 形 好奇心の強い，珍しい，奇妙な，知りたがる

□ **curl** 名 巻き毛，渦巻状のもの

□ **curly** 形 巻き毛の

□ **curly-haired** 形 縮れ毛の

□ **current** 形 現在の，目下の

□ **curse** 動 のろう，ののしる **Curse you.** この野郎。 名 のろい(の言葉)

□ **curve** 名 曲線，カーブ

□ **curved** 形 曲がった，湾曲した

□ **cut out** 切り取る，切り抜く

□ **cut-off** 名 切り離すこと

□ **cut-out** 名 切り抜き

□ **cycle** 名 ①周期，循環 ②自転車，オートバイ **cycle map** 自転車地図

D

□ **dare** 動《– to ～》思い切って[あえて]～する 助 思い切って[あえて]～する **how dare** よくもぬけぬけと～できるものだ

□ **dark** 熟 **get dark** 暗くなる

□ **darkblack** 形 真っ黒な

□ **darken** 動 暗くする[なる]

□ **darkness** 名 暗さ，暗やみ

□ **darling** 名 ①最愛の人 ②あなた《呼びかけ》

□ **dart** 名 ダート《狩猟用の短い矢で，手で投げるか吹き矢として使われた》

□ **Dartmoor** 名 ダートムア《地名》

□ **date** 動 年代を定める

□ **dawning** 形 始まりの，夜明けの

□ **day** 熟 **all day** 一日中 **all day and night** 昼も夜も **all day long** 一日中，終日 **by day** 昼間は，日中は **day and night** 昼も夜も **full day** 丸一日 **good day** こんにちは **one day** (過去の)ある日，(未来の)いつか **the day before** 前の日 **these days** このごろ

□ **daybreak** 名 夜明け

□ **daylight** 名 ①日光，昼の明かり，昼間 ②夜明け

□ **daytime** 名昼間
□ **dazed** 形放心状態の，ぼうぜんとした
□ **dead** 熟 **fall dead** 倒れて死ぬ **in the dead of night** 真夜中に
□ **deadly** 形命にかかわる，痛烈な，破壊的な
□ **deaf** 形耳が聞こえない
□ **deal** 動 ①分配する ②《－with［in］～》～を扱う 名 ①取引，扱い ②（不特定の）量，額 **a good［great］deal（of ～）** かなり［ずいぶん・大量］（の～），多額（の～）
□ **dealing** 名取引
□ **Dear me!** おや！，まあ！《驚きを表す》
□ **dearie** 名愛しい人，あなた
□ **death** 名 ①死，死ぬこと ②《the－》終えん，消滅 **meet one's death** 最後を遂げる，死ぬ **to death** 死ぬまで，死ぬほど
□ **decision** 名 ①決定，決心 ②判決
□ **deck** 名（船の）デッキ，甲板，階，床
□ **decoration** 名装飾，飾りつけ
□ **deduce** 動推論する
□ **deduction** 名 ①差し引き（額）②推論 **science of deduction** 推理の科学
□ **deductive** 形推理の，推論的な
□ **deeply** 副深く，非常に
□ **deer-hunt** 名鹿狩りをすること
□ **defeat** 動打ち破る，負かす
□ **defend** 動防ぐ，守る，弁護する
□ **defendant** 名被告（人）
□ **definite** 形限定された，明確な，はっきりした
□ **delay** 動遅らせる，延期する 名遅延，延期，猶予
□ **delight** 名喜び，愉快
□ **delighted** 形喜んでいる，うれしそうな
□ **delightful** 形楽しい，愉快にさせる
□ **deliver** 動配達する，伝える
□ **demand** 動 ①要求する，尋ねる ②必要とする
□ **demonstration** 名 ①論証，証明 ②デモンストレーション，実演
□ **Denmark** 名デンマーク《国名》
□ **Dennis** 名デニス《人名》
□ **deny** 動否定する，断る，受けつけない
□ **depart** 動出発する
□ **departure** 名 ①出発，発車 ②離脱
□ **depend** 動《－on［upon］～》①～を頼る，～をあてにする ②～による
□ **depressed** 形がっかりした，落胆した
□ **describe** 動（言葉で）描写する，特色を述べる，説明する
□ **description** 名（言葉で）記述（すること），描写（すること）
□ **desert** 名砂漠，不毛の地
□ **deserted** 形人影のない，さびれた
□ **deserve** 動（～を）受けるに足る，値する，（～して）当然である
□ **design** 名デザイン
□ **designer** 名デザイナー，設計者
□ **desire** 動強く望む，欲する 名欲望，欲求，願望
□ **Desmond** 名デズモンド《人名》
□ **despair** 名絶望，自暴自棄
□ **desperate** 形 ①絶望的な，見込みのない ②ほしくてたまらない，必死の
□ **desperately** 副絶望的に，必死になって
□ **despite** 前～にもかかわらず
□ **destined** 形運命づけられた，定められた
□ **destroy** 動破壊する，絶滅させる，無効にする
□ **detail** 名 ①細部，《-s》詳細 ②《-s》個人情報 **in great detail** 極めて詳細に，綿密に
□ **detect** 動見つける
□ **detection** 名発見，探知，検出
□ **detective** 名探偵，刑事 **make a detective** 刑事に出世する **private detective** 私立探偵 形探偵の
□ **determination** 名決心，決定
□ **determined** 形決心した，決然とした
□ **develop** 動 ①発達する［させる］②開発する
□ **development** 名 ①発達，発展 ②開発
□ **devilish** 形 ①悪魔のような ②のろわしい，極悪な
□ **Devon** 名デボンシャー（Devonshire）《地名》
□ **Devonshire** 名デボンシャー《地名》
□ **diamond** 名ダイヤモンド
□ **diary** 名日記
□ **die away** 次第に静まる
□ **die of** ～がもとで死ぬ
□ **different from** 《be－》～と違う
□ **difficulty** 名 ①むずかしさ ②難局，支障，苦情，異議
□ **dig** 動 ①掘る ②小突く ③探る

□ **dine** 動食事をする，ごちそうする

□ **dining** 名食事，夕食をとること **dining room** 食堂

□ **dip** 動ちょっと浸す，さっとつける

□ **direct** 形まっすぐな，直接の，率直な，露骨な

□ **directed** 形指令［指導］された

□ **direction** 名①方向，方角 ②《-s》指示，説明書 ③指導，指揮 **in the direction of** ～の方向に

□ **directly** 副①じかに ②まっすぐに ③ちょうど

□ **directory** 名住所氏名録 **Medical Directory** 医師録

□ **dirt** 名①汚れ，泥，ごみ ②土

□ **dirty** 形①汚い，汚れた ②卑劣な，不正な

□ **disagree** 動異議を唱える，反対する

□ **disappear** 動見えなくなる，姿を消す，なくなる

□ **disappearance** 名見えなくなること，消失，失踪

□ **disappointed** 形がっかりした，失望した

□ **disappointment** 名失望

□ **disbelief** 名不信，疑惑，不信仰 **in desbelief** 信じられない様子で

□ **discomfort** 名不快（なこと），辛苦，つらさ

□ **discourse** 動話をする

□ **discoverer** 名発見者

□ **discovery** 名発見

□ **discuss** 動議論［検討］する

□ **disease** 名①病気 ②（社会や精神の）不健全な状態

□ **disguise** 動変装させる，隠す 名変装（すること），見せかけ **blessing in disguise** 不幸中の幸い **in the disguise** 変装して

□ **dishonored** 形名誉を汚された

□ **dislike** 動嫌う

□ **disloyal** 形不実な

□ **dismiss** 動却下する

□ **disobey** 動服従しない，違反する

□ **distance** 名距離，隔たり，遠方 **at a distance** 少し離れて **in the distance** 遠方に

□ **distant** 形遠い，隔たった

□ **district** 名①地方，地域 ②行政区

□ **distrustful** 形不信の念を抱いている

□ **disturbed** 形かき乱された，動揺した，不安な

□ **divide** 動分かれる，分ける，割れる，割る **be divided into** 分けられる **divide into** ～に分かれる

□ **divided** 形分けられた，分かれた

□ **division** 名分割

□ **divorce** 名離婚，分離

□ **doctor** 熟**go to the doctor** 医者に診てもらいに行く

□ **door** 熟**knock at/on the door** ドアをノックする（音）

□ **doorbell** 名玄関の呼び鈴［ベル］

□ **doorman** 名（ホテルの）ドアマン

□ **door-step** 名戸口の踏み段上がり段

□ **doorway** 名戸口，玄関，出入り口

□ **Dost Akbar** ドスト・アクバル《人名》

□ **dot** 名①点，小数点 ②水玉（模様）

□ **double** 形①2倍の，二重の ②対の

□ **doubt** 名①疑い，不確かなこと ②未解決点，困難 **no doubt** きっと，たぶん **have no doubt** 疑いなく思っている，信じている 動疑う

□ **Douglas** 名ダグラス《人名》

□ **Douglas, Mrs.** ダグラス夫人

□ **down** 熟**bring someone down**（人）を倒す **come down** 下りて来る，田舎へ来る **down in the south** 南の方で **down on one's luck** 運が傾いて，つきに見放されて **down the river** 川下に **get down** 降りる，身をかがめる，ひざまずく **go down** 下に降りる **halfway down** ～の途中で **hang down** ぶら下がる **hunt down** 追い詰める，追跡して捕らえる **hurry down** 急いで下りる［駆け込む］ **lay down** ①下に置く，横たえる ②裏切る **lie down** 横たわる，横になる **look down** 見下ろす **look down at** ～に目［視線］を落とす **look down on** ～を見下す **look down upon** 見下ろす，俯瞰する **put down** 下に置く，下ろす **run down** 駆け下りる **run up and down** かけずり回る **rush down** 猛然と～に駆け寄る **settle down** 落ち着く，興奮がおさまる **struck down** 倒れる **take down** 下げる，降ろす **throw down** 投げ出す，放棄する **track down** 見つけ出す，追跡して捕らえる **turn down**（音量などを）小さくする，弱くする，拒絶する **up and down** 上がったり下がったり，行ったり来たり，あちこちと **walk up and down** 行ったり来たりする **weigh down** 圧迫する **write down** 書き留める

□ **downstairs** 副階下で，下の部屋で 形階下の 名階下

□ **dozen** 名1ダース，12（個）

□ **Dr.** 名～博士，《医者に対して》～先生

□ **drag** 動①引きずる ②のろのろ動く［動かす］

□ **drain** 動水抜きをする, 排出させる
□ **drama** 名劇, 演劇, ドラマ, 劇的な事件
□ **draw** 動①引く, 引っ張る ②描く ③引き分けになる［する］ **draw out** 聞き出す,（情報などを）引き出す
□ **drawbridge** 名跳ね橋
□ **drawn** 動draw（引く）の過去分詞
□ **dream of** ～を夢見る
□ **dreamland** 名夢の国, 眠り
□ **dreamy** 形夢を見る, 空想にふける
□ **Drebber** 名ドレバー《人名》
□ **dressing** 名着付け, 身支度 **dressing room** 更衣室 **dressing gown** ドレッシングガウン
□ **drew** 動draw（引く）の過去
□ **dried** 動dry（乾燥する）の過去, 過去分詞 形乾燥した
□ **drinking shop** 飲み屋, 居酒屋
□ **drive along**（車で）走行する
□ **drive around** 車を走らせる
□ **drive back** 車で引き返す
□ **drive off** 車で走り去る
□ **drive out** 追い払う
□ **drive up** 車でやって来る
□ **drive up and down** 車で行ったりきたりする
□ **driven** 動drive（車で行く）の過去分詞
□ **driver** 名①運転手 ②（馬車の）御者
□ **drop** 熟**with a mighty drop on one side** 片側が激しい落下
□ **drop by** 立ち寄る
□ **drop off** ～から（取れて）落ちる
□ **drop someone off at home**（人）を車で家まで送る
□ **drop to one's knees** がっくりと両ひざをつく
□ **drove** 動drive（車で行く）の過去
□ **drug** 名薬, 麻薬
□ **drunk** 形（酒に）酔った, 酔っぱらった **get drunk** 酔う, 酩酊する 名酔っ払い
□ **drunken** 形酔っ払った
□ **dry-land** 名乾燥地 **dry-land marker stick** 乾燥地の目印棒
□ **dryly** 副無味乾燥に, 冷淡に
□ **duck** 名カモ, アヒル
□ **due** 形予定された, 期日のきている, 支払われるべき **due to** ～によって, ～が原因で
□ **dug** 動dig（掘る）の過去, 過去分詞
□ **dull** 形退屈な, 鈍い, くすんだ, ぼんやりした
□ **dumb-bell** 名ダンベル, 鉄アレイ
□ **Duncan Street** ダンカン通り《ロンドンの地名》
□ **dust** 名ちり, ほこり, ごみ, 粉
□ **dusty** 形ほこりだらけの
□ **duty** 名①義務（感）, 責任 ②職務, 任務, 関税 **as a matter of duty** 職務上 **off duty** 非番で **public duty** 公務
□ **dying** 形死にかかっている, 消えそうな

E

□ **each one** 各自
□ **each other** お互いに
□ **each side**《on －》それぞれの側に
□ **eager** 形①熱心な ②《be － for ～》～を切望している,《be － to ～》しきりに～したがっている
□ **eagerly** 副熱心に, しきりに
□ **eagerness** 名熱心, 熱望
□ **eagle** 名ワシ（鷲）
□ **Eagle Commercial** イーグル・コマーシャル《ホテル名》
□ **earn** 動①儲ける, 稼ぐ ②（名声を）博す
□ **earth** 熟**earth floor** 土間 **How on earth ～?** 一体どうやったら **on earth** いったい
□ **ease** 名安心, 気楽 **at ease** 安心して, ホッとして 動安心させる, 楽にする, ゆるめる
□ **easily** 副①容易に, たやすく, 苦もなく ②気楽に
□ **edge** 名①刃 ②端, 縁
□ **editor** 名編集者, 編集長
□ **educated** 形教養のある, 教育を受けた
□ **effect** 名影響, 効果, 結果
□ **effort** 名努力（の成果）
□ **eh** 間《略式》えっ（何ですか）, もう一度言ってください《驚き・疑いを表したり, 相手に繰り返しを求める》
□ **either** 熟**either A or B** AかそれともB **either side of** ～の両側に **on either side** 両側に
□ **elbow** 動ひじで突く［押す］, 押し分けて進む **elbow out** ～を追い出す
□ **elder** 形先輩の, 年長の 名（教会の）長老

□ **eldest** 形最年長の

□ **electric** 形電気の, 電動の

□ **else** 熟 anything else ほかの何か no one else 他の誰一人として〜しない or else さもないと

□ **emerald** 名エメラルド

□ **eminent** 形 (身分などが) 高い, 名高い, 高名な

□ **emotion** 名感激, 感動, 感情

□ **emotional** 形 ①感情の, 心理的な ②感情的な, 感激しやすい

□ **employer** 名雇主, 使用[利用]する人

□ **enable** 動 (〜することを) 可能にする, 容易にする

□ **encourage** 動 ①勇気づける ②促進する, 助長する

□ **end** 熟 at the end of 〜の終わりに back end 後端 come to an end 終わる in the end とうとう, 結局, ついに meet one's end 命を落とす We end where we began. 我々は振り出しのところでおしまいだ。

□ **endanger** 動危険にさらす, 脅かす

□ **endure** 動 ①我慢する, 耐え忍ぶ ②持ちこたえる

□ **enemy** 名敵

□ **energetic** 形エネルギッシュな, 精力的な, 活動的な

□ **England** 名 ①イングランド ②英国

□ **Englishman** 名イングランド人, イギリス人

□ **enjoyment** 名楽しむこと, 喜び

□ **Enoch J. Drebber** イーノック・J・ドレバー《人名》

□ **enough** 熟 be kind enough to 親切にも〜する enough of 〜はもうたくさん enough to do 〜するのに十分な sure enough 思ったとおり, 確かに well enough かなり上手に

□ **entire** 形全体の, 完全な, まったくの

□ **entirely** 副完全に, まったく

□ **entry** 名入ること, 入り口

□ **envelope** 名封筒, 包み

□ **epilogue** 名 ① (劇の) 納め口上, エピローグ ②終章, 終節

□ **episode** 名挿話, 出来事

□ **equal** 名同等のもの[人]

□ **equally** 副等しく, 平等に

□ **error** 名誤り, 間違い, 過失

□ **escape** 動逃げる, 免れる, もれる 名逃亡, 脱出, もれ

□ **escaper** 名逃亡者

□ **established** 形落ち着いて, 納まって

□ **Ettie Shafter** エティー・シャフター《人名》

□ **Europe** 名ヨーロッパ

□ **European** 名ヨーロッパ人 形ヨーロッパ (人) の

□ **Euston** 名ユーストン《ロンドンの地名》

□ **Euston Station** ユーストン駅

□ **even if** たとえ〜でも

□ **even though** 〜であるけれども, 〜にもかかわらず

□ **evening paper** 夕刊

□ **ever** 熟 as ever 相変わらず, これまでのように as 〜 as ever 相変わらず, これまでのように ever since それ以来ずっと

□ **every time** 〜するときはいつも

□ **everyone** 代誰でも, 皆

□ **everything** 代すべてのこと[もの], 何でも, 何もかも

□ **everywhere** 副どこにいても, いたるところに

□ **evidence** 名 ①証拠, 証人 ②形跡

□ **evil** 形 ①邪悪な ②有害な, 不吉な 名 ①邪悪 ②害, わざわい, 不幸

□ **evil-looking** 形不気味な

□ **exact** 形正確な, 厳密な, きちょうめんな

□ **examination** 名試験, 審査, 検査, 診察

□ **examine** 動試験する, 調査[検査]する, 診察する

□ **example** 熟 for example たとえば

□ **excellent** 形優れた, 優秀な

□ **except** 前〜を除いて, 〜のほかは except for 〜を除いて, 〜がなければ 接〜ということを除いて

□ **exchange** 動交換する

□ **excited** 形興奮した, わくわくした

□ **excitedly** 副興奮して

□ **excitement** 名興奮 (すること)

□ **exciting** 形興奮させる, わくわくさせる

□ **exclaim** 動 ① (喜び・驚きなどで) 声をあげる ②声高に激しく言う

□ **excuse oneself** 辞退する

□ **exist** 動存在する, 生存する, ある, いる

□ **expect** 動予期[予測]する, (当然のこととして) 期待する

□ **expense** 名 ①出費, 費用 ②犠牲, 代価 after

all the fun I have had at their expense さんざん彼らをだしにして笑った後に

□ **experiment** 名実験，試み

□ **expert** 名専門家，熟練者，エキスパート

□ **explanation** 名 ①説明，解説，釈明 ②解釈，意味

□ **explode** 動爆発する［させる］

□ **expression** 名 ①表現，表示，表情 ②言い回し，語句

□ **extra** 形余分の，臨時の

□ **extreme** 形極端な，極度の，いちばん端の

□ **extremely** 副非常に，極度に

□ **eye** 熟keep an eye on ～から目を離さない

□ **eyebrow** 名まゆ（眉）

□ **eyeglasses** 名メガネ

F

□ **face** 熟come over someone's face〔表情などが〕（人）の顔に表れる

□ **fact** 熟in fact つまり，実は，要するに

□ **fail** 動 ①失敗する，落第するさせる ②《－to ～》～し損なう，～できない ③失望させる never not fail to ～ 必ず～する

□ **faint** 動気絶する

□ **fair** 形 ①正しい，公平［正当］な ②色白の，金髪の

□ **fair-haired** 形金髪の

□ **faith** 名 ①信念，信仰 ②信頼，信用

□ **faithful** 形忠実な，正確な

□ **faithfully** 副忠実に，正確に yours faithfully 敬具《手紙で使う礼儀正しい結びの表現》

□ **fake** 名にせもの fake money 偽金 fake dollar 偽ドル

□ **faked** 形捏造した faked paper 偽札

□ **fall** 熟fall asleep 眠り込む，寝入る fall back 後退する，戻る，退却する，後ろ向きに倒れる fall dead 倒れて死ぬ fall in love 恋におちる fall in love with 恋におちる fall over ～につまずく，～の上に倒れかかる fall to the ground 転ぶ fall upon ～の上にかかる

□ **fallen** 動fall（落ちる）の過去分詞

□ **falling** 形落下する

□ **false** 形うその，間違った，にせの，不誠実な

□ **falsely** 副不当に

□ **familiar** 形 ①親しい，親密な ②《be－with ～》～に精通している ③普通の，いつもの，おなじみの

□ **family** 熟set up a family 家族（家庭）を作る

□ **famous for** 《be－》～で有名である

□ **fancy** 動 ①心に描く，（～と）考える ②好む，引かれる

□ **far** 熟as far as ～と同じくらい遠く，～まで，～する限り（では） as far as one can できるだけ come this far ここまで来る far away 遠く離れて far from ～から遠い，～どころか far into ずっと far off ずっと遠くに，はるかかなたに far side 向こう側，反対側 far too あまりにも～過ぎる how far どのくらいの距離か so far 今までのところ，これまでは

□ **farmer** 名農民，農場経営者

□ **farmhouse** 名農場内の家屋，農家

□ **farmland** 名農地

□ **fasten** 動固定する，結ぶ，締まる

□ **fat** 形太った

□ **fate** 名運命，宿命

□ **fault** 名 ①欠点，短所 ②過失，誤り at fault 誤って，非難されるべき find fault with ～のあら探しをする

□ **favor** 熟find favor with（人）に気に入られる，愛顧を得る

□ **fear** 名 ①恐れ ②心配，不安 for fear that ～ではないかと心配で with fear 怖がって 動 ①恐れる ②心配する

□ **fearful** 形 ①恐ろしい ②心配な，気づかって

□ **fearfully** 副おそるおそる，怯えながら

□ **feather** 名羽，《-s》羽毛

□ **feature** 名 ①特徴，特色 ②顔の一部，《-s》顔立ち

□ **feel** 熟feel better 気分がよくなる feel for ～に同情する，～を手さぐりで探す feel like ～がほしい，～したい気がする，～のような感じがする feel sick 気分が悪い feel sorry for ～をかわいそうに思う not feel like doing ～する気になれない

□ **feeling** 名 ①感じ，気持ち ②触感，知覚 ③同情，思いやり，感受性 形感じる，感じやすい，情け深い

□ **feet** 熟get to one's feet 立ち上がる jump to one's feet 飛び起きる，はじかれたように立ち上がる leap to one's feet サッと立ち上がる on one's feet 立っている状態で to one's feet 両足で立っている状態に spring to one's feet サッと立ち上がる

□ **fellow** 名 ①仲間，同僚 ②人，やつ fine fellow だんなさん 形仲間の，同士の

□ **female** 名婦人，雌

□ **fence** 名囲み, さく
□ **Fernworthy** 名ファーンワージー《地名》
□ **Ferrier** 名フェリアー《人名》
□ **fever** 名①熱, 熱狂 ②熱病
□ **field** 熟 **gold field** 金鉱
□ **fierce** 形どう猛な, 荒々しい, すさまじい, 猛烈な
□ **fierce-looking** 形猛猛しい
□ **fiery** 形①火の, 燃えさかる ②火のように赤い
□ **figure** 名人[物]の姿, 形
□ **file** 名ファイル, 書類綴じ, 縦 **back file** バックナンバーのファイル
□ **fill in** ～に記入する
□ **filled with** 《be－》～でいっぱいになる
□ **final** 形最後の, 決定的な
□ **find favor with** (人)に気に入られる, 愛顧を得る
□ **find one's way** たどり着く
□ **find out** 見つけ出す, 気がつく, 知る, 調べる, 解明する
□ **find someone guilty** (人)を有罪と評決する
□ **finding** 名発見
□ **fine** 熟 **that's fine by me** 私は構いませんよ **fine fellow** だんなさん **fine points** 詳細
□ **fingernail** 名指の爪
□ **finish doing** ～するのを終える
□ **finished** 形①終わった, 仕上がった ②洗練された ③もうだめになった
□ **fireplace** 名暖炉
□ **firm** 形堅い, しっかりした, 断固とした
□ **firmly** 副しっかりと, 断固として
□ **first** 熟 **at first** 最初は, 初めのうちは **first of all** まず第一に **for the first time** 初めて **in the first place** 第一に, そもそも
□ **first-class** 形①一流の, (乗り物の)一等の ②(郵便で)第一種の 副一等で, 第一種郵便で
□ **firstly** 副初めに, まず第一に
□ **fishing** 名釣り, 魚業
□ **fist** 名こぶし, げんこつ
□ **fit** 形①適当な, 相応な ②体の調子がよい **be physically fit** 身体が健康である 動合致[適合]する, 合致させる
□ **fitness** 名体の健康
□ **five-pound note** 5ポンド紙幣
□ **fix** 動①固定する[させる] ②修理する ③決定する ④用意する, 整える **fix on** ～にくぎ付けになる
□ **fixed** 形①固定した, ゆるぎない ②八百長の
□ **flame** 名炎, (炎のような)輝き
□ **flash** 名閃光, きらめき 動閃光を発する
□ **flight** 名逃走, 脱出
□ **float** 動浮く, 浮かぶ
□ **floor** 熟 **earth floor** 土間 **ground floor** 1階
□ **flow** 動流れ出る, 流れる, あふれる
□ **fly open** 突然開く
□ **flyleaf** 名(本の)見返し
□ **fog** 名濃霧
□ **foggy** 形霧の多い, 霧の立ちこめた
□ **fold** 動①折りたたむ, 包む ②(手を)組む
□ **folk** 名(生活様式を共にする)人々
□ **follow up** (人)の跡を追う
□ **followed by** その後に～が続いて
□ **follower** 名信奉者, 追随者
□ **following** 形《the－》次の, 次に続く
□ **fool** 名①ばか者, おろかな人 ②道化師 **make a fool of ～** ～をばかにする 動ばかにする, だます, ふざける
□ **foolish** 形おろかな, ばかばかしい
□ **foolishly** 副おろかに
□ **foot** 熟 **foot marks** 足跡 **foot of a hill** 丘のふもと **on foot** 歩いて
□ **foothold** 名足がかり, 足場
□ **footmark** 名足跡
□ **footprint** 名足型, 足跡
□ **footstep** 名足音, 歩み
□ **for** 熟 **all for nothing** いたずらに, 無駄に **as for** ～に関しては, ～はどうかと言うと **for God's sake** お願いだから **for a moment** 少しの間 **for a moment or two** ほんの少しの間 **for a time** しばらく, 一時の間 **for a while** しばらくの間, 少しの間 **for example** たとえば **for long** 長い間 **for nothing** ただで, 無料で, むだに **for now** 今のところ, ひとまず **for oneself** 独力で, 自分のために **for some time** しばらくの間 **for that matter** ついでに言えば **for the first time** 初めて **for the moment** 差し当たり, 当座は **for this reason** そういったわけで **for years** 何年も
□ **force** 名力, 勢い **police force** 警官隊 動①強制する, 力ずくで～する, 余儀なく～させる ②押しやる, 押し込む **force one's way through** ～を強行突破する **force one's way**

into ～に押し入る
☐ **forceful** 形力強い, 説得力のある
☐ **forefinger** 名人差し指
☐ **foresee** 動予見[予測]する
☐ **foreseen** 動 foresee (予見する) の過去分詞
☐ **forever** 熟 **now and forever** 今もずっと
☐ **forgetful** 形忘れっぽい, 無頓着な
☐ **forgive** 動許す **may God forgive you** 神があなたを許しますように《あなたはなんてひどいことをするのか, という意味》
☐ **forgiven** 動 forgive (許す) の過去分詞
☐ **form** 名 ①形, 形式 ②書式 **telegraph form** 電報を送るときに使う書込み用紙 動形づくる
☐ **formal** 形正式の, 公式の, 形式的な, 格式ばった
☐ **former** 形 ①前の, 先の, 以前の ②《the –》(二者のうち) 前者の
☐ **formerly** 副元は, 以前は
☐ **Forrester** 名フォレスター《人名》
☐ **fort** 名砦, 要塞
☐ **forth** 副前へ, 外へ **back and forth** あちこちに, 前後に
☐ **fortune** 名 ①富, 財産 ②幸運, 繁栄, チャンス ③運命, 運勢
☐ **forward** 形 ①前方の, 前方へ向かう ②将来の ③先の 副 ①前方に ②将来に向けて ③先へ, 進んで **rush forward** 突進する
☐ **foster** 形里親の **foster brother** 乳兄弟
☐ **Foulmire** 名ファウルマイア《農家》
☐ **founder** 名創立者, 設立者
☐ **four-wheeled** 四輪の
☐ **frame** 名骨組み, 構造, 額縁
☐ **France** 名フランス《国名》
☐ **Frankland** 名フランクランド《人名》
☐ **frankly** 副率直に, ありのままに
☐ **Fred Porlock** フレッド・ポーロック《人名》
☐ **free** 熟 **go free** 自由の身になる **set free** (人) を解放する, 釈放される, 自由の身になる
☐ **free-born** 形自由の身に生まれた
☐ **freedom** 名 ①自由 ②束縛がないこと
☐ **freely** 副自由に, 障害なしに
☐ **freeman** 名自由民団の一員
☐ **freemen** 名 freeman (自由民団の一員) の複数 **Order of Freemen** 自由民団
☐ **French** 形フランス (人・語) の
☐ **frequent** 形ひんぱんな, よく訪れる
☐ **freshly** 副新しく, ～したてで
☐ **friend** 熟 **a friend of mine** 友人の1人 **come out friends** 友人になる **make friends with** ～と友達になる
☐ **friendless** 形友のない
☐ **friendly** 形親しみのある, 親切な, 友情のこもった
☐ **friendship** 名友人であること, 友情
☐ **fright** 名恐怖, 激しい驚き **give someone a fright** (人) を怖がらせる
☐ **frighten** 動驚かせる, びっくりさせる
☐ **frightened** 形おびえた, びっくりした
☐ **frightening** 形恐ろしい, どきっとさせる
☐ **from** 熟 **apart from** ～を除いては **be different from** ～と違う **far from** ～から遠い, ～どころか **from now** 今から, これから **from now on** 今後 **from time to time** ときどき **hear from** ～から手紙[電話・返事]をもらう **keep away from** ～に近寄らない **keep someone from** ～から (人) を阻む **run away from** ～から逃れる **stay away from** ～から離れている **take from** ～から引く, 選ぶ
☐ **front** 熟 **front desk** [ホテルの] フロント **get in front of** ～の正面に出る **in front of** ～の前に, ～の正面に
☐ **fuel** 名燃料
☐ **full** 形完全な, 不足していない **be full of** ～で一杯である **full day** 丸一日
☐ **full-blooded** 形多血質の
☐ **fully** 副十分に, 完全に, まるまる
☐ **fund** 名 ①資金, 基金, 財源 ②金 ③公債, 国債 **common fund** 共有資金
☐ **funeral** 名葬式, 葬列
☐ **funny** 形 ①おもしろい, こっけいな ②奇妙な, うさんくさい
☐ **furniture** 名家具, 備品, 調度
☐ **further** 形いっそう遠い, その上の, なおいっそうの **further on** これより先, もっと先で **nothing seem further** 何も変化が見えない 副いっそう遠く, その上に, もっと
☐ **fuse** 名 (電気の) ヒューズ, 信管, 導火線
☐ **future** 熟 **in the future** 将来は

G

☐ **gain** 動 ①得る, 増す ②進歩する, 進む
☐ **gang** 名 ①群れ, 一団 ②ギャング, 暴力団
☐ **Ganges** 名ガンジス川

☐ **gap** 名ギャップ, 隔たり, すき間

☐ **Garcia** 名ガルシア《人名》

☐ **gardenhouse** 名庭園にある小さな建物

☐ **gatekeeper** 名門番, 守衛

☐ **gateway** 名出入り口, 道

☐ **gather** 動 ①集まる, 集める ②生じる, 増す ③推測する **gather up** 一箇所に集める

☐ **gem** 名宝石, 宝玉, すばらしいもの

☐ **general** 形 ①全体の, 一般の, 普通の ②おおよその ③(職位の)高い, 上級の **in general** 一般に, たいてい 名大将, 将軍

☐ **generally** 副 ①一般に, だいたい ②たいてい

☐ **generous** 形 ①寛大な, 気前のよい ②豊富な

☐ **gentle** 形 ①優しい, 温和な ②柔らかな

☐ **German** 形ドイツ(人・語)の 名 ①ドイツ人 ②ドイツ語

☐ **Germany** 名ドイツ《国名》

☐ **get** 熟 **get a job** 職を得る **get angry** 腹を立てる **get at** 届く, 入手する **get away** 逃げる, 逃亡する, 離れる **get back** 戻る, 帰る **get ～ back** ～を取り返す[戻す] **get better** (病気などが)良くなる **get by** どうにかやっていく, 生き残る **get caught** 逮捕される **get close** 近づく **get close to** ～に近づく, 接近する **get confused** まごつく, 当惑する **get crowded out** 締め出しを食らう, 押し出される **get dark** 暗くなる **get down** 降りる, 身をかがめる, ひざまずく **get drunk** 酔う, 酩酊する **get hold of** ～を手に入れる, ～をつかむ **get home** 家に着く[帰る] **get in** 中に入る, 乗り込む **get in front of** ～の正面に出る **get into** ～に入る, 入り込む, (服などを)着る **get into trouble** 面倒を起こす, 困った事になる, トラブルに巻き込まれる **get into trouble with** ～とトラブルを起こす **get mixed up** かかわり合いになる, 巻き添えを食う **get near** 接近する **get off** (～から)降りる **get on** (電車などに)乗る **get on board** 乗る **get out** 外に出る, 出て行く, 逃げ出す **get out of** ～から下車する, ～から取り出す, ～から外へ出る[抜け出る] **get ready** 用意[支度]をする **get revenge** 復しゅうする **get someone into trouble** (人)に迷惑を掛ける, 困らせる **get started** 始める **get there** そこに到着する, 目的を達成する, 成功する **get through** 乗り切る, ～を通り抜ける **get to** (事)を始める, ～に達する[到着する] **get to do** ～できるようになる, ～できる機会を得る **get to one's feet** 立ち上がる **get up** 起き上がる, 立ち上がる **get used to** ～になじむ, ～に慣れる **get worse** 悪化する

☐ **giant** 名巨人, 大男 形巨大な

☐ **gift** 名贈り物

☐ **give** 熟 **give ～ a ride** ～を車で送る **give away** ただで与える, 贈る, 譲歩する, 手放す **give back** (～を)返す **give in** 降参する, 屈する, (書類などを)提出する **give ～ in return for** …の見返りに～を与える **give out** 分配する **give someone a fright** (人)を怖がらせる **give someone a lesson** (人)を懲らしめる **give someone one's word** (人)に約束する **give up** あきらめる, やめる, 引き渡す **give way** 道を譲る, 譲歩する, 負ける **I give you my word.** 約束するよ。保証するよ。

☐ **glad to** 《be –》～してうれしい, 喜んで～する

☐ **gladly** 副喜んで, うれしそうに

☐ **glance** 動ちらりと見る

☐ **glorious** 形 ①栄誉に満ちた, 輝かしい ②荘厳な, すばらしい

☐ **glory** 名栄光, 名誉, 繁栄

☐ **glow** 動(火が)白熱して輝く 名白熱, 輝き

☐ **go** 熟 **as time goes by** 時間が過ぎるにつれて **far gone** ひどく酔っ払って, 泥酔して **go across** 横断する, 渡る **go after** ～の後を追う **go against** (主義などに)合わない, 反する **go and** ～しに行く **go around** 動き回る, あちらこちらに行く, 回り道をする, (障害)を回避する **go away** 立ち去る **go back to** ～に帰る[戻る] **go by** ①(時が)過ぎる, 経過する ②～のそばを通る ③～に基づいて[よって]行う **go days without** ～なしで何日も過ごす **go doing** ～をしに行く **go down** 下に降りる **go for** ～に出かける, ～を追い求める, ～に襲いかかる **go for a walk** 散歩に行く **go free** 自由の身になる **go home** 帰宅する **go in** 中に入る, 開始する **go into** ～に入る **go off** ①出かける, 去る, 出発する ②始める, 突然～しだす **go off upon** ～を頼りにいく **go on** 続く, 続ける, 進み続ける, 起こる, 発生する **go on one's way** 道を進む, 立ち去る **go on to** ～に移る, ～に取り掛かる **go on to say** さらに続けて～と言う **go out** 外出する, 外へ出る **go out of** ～から出る[消える] **go over to** ～の前に[へ]行く, ～に出向いて行く **go round** ～の周りを進む, 歩き回る, 回って行く **go shopping** 買い物に行く **go through** 通り抜ける, 一つずつ順番に検討する **go to bed** 床につく, 寝る **go to sleep** 寝る **go to the doctor** 医者に診てもらいに行く **go up** ①～に上がる, 登る ②～に近づく, 出かける **go up to** ～まで行く, 近づく **go wrong** 失敗する, 道を踏みはずす, 調子が悪くなる **let go** 手を放す, 行かせる **off you go** 散れ, 出て行け **ready to go** すっかり準備が整った **there goes** チャンスなどが行ってしまう

☐ **God** 熟 **by God** 神にかけて, 本当に **for**

God's sake お願いだから God bless you. 神のご加護がありますように。おやまあ。 may God forgive you 神があなたを許しますように《あなたはなんてひどいことをするのか，という意味》 My God. おや，まあ Thank God. ありがたい thanks God 神よ感謝します《ああ助かった，ああよかった，という意味》

□ **godless** 形 神を否定した，神を恐れぬ

□ **gold** 名 金，金貨，金製品，金色 形 金の，金製の，金色の

□ **gold field** 金鉱

□ **golden** 形 ①金色の ②金製の

□ **good** 熟 **a good many** かなり多くの **Good day.** こんにちは，ご機嫌よう。 **Good heavens!** しまった！，おやまあ！ **good wishes** 好意，厚情 **make a good husband** よい夫になる

□ **good-bye** 間 さようなら 名 別れのあいさつ

□ **good-looking** 形 顔立ちのよい，ハンサムな，きれいな

□ **good-night** 間 さようなら!，お休みなさい

□ **got** 熟 **got to** ～しなければならない（**have**) **got to** ～しなければならない **have got** 持っている

□ **gotten** 動 get（得る）の過去分詞

□ **government** 名 政治，政府，支配

□ **governor-general** 名（植民地などの）総督

□ **gown** 名 ガウン，室内着 **dressing gown** ドレッシングガウン

□ **grab** 動 ①ふいにつかむ，ひったくる ②横取りする

□ **gradually** 副 だんだんと

□ **grass** 名 草，牧草（地），芝生 動 草［芝生］で覆う［覆われる］

□ **grassy** 形 草で覆われた，草のような

□ **grateful** 形 感謝する，ありがたく思う

□ **grave** 名 墓

□ **gray-haired** 形 白髪頭の

□ **grayish** 形 灰色がかった

□ **great** 熟 **a great deal of** 多量の，大量の **a great number of** 非常に多くの **great deal** 多量に，大いに，ずっと

□ **Great Mogul** ムガール皇帝《ダイヤモンドの名前》

□ **greatly** 副 大いに

□ **greed** 名 どん欲，欲張り

□ **greet** 動 ①あいさつする ②（喜んで）迎える

□ **greeting** 名 あいさつ（の言葉），あいさつ（状）

□ **Gregson** 名 グレグソン《人名》

□ **Greuze** 名 ジャン＝バティスト・グルーズ《Jean-Baptiste Greuze, フランスの画家，1725–1805》

□ **Grimpen** 名 グリンペン《地名》 **Grimpen Mire** グリンペン大沼 **Grimpen Road** グリンペン街道

□ **groan** 動 ①うめく，うなる ②ぶうぶう言う 名 うめき声

□ **ground** 熟 **fall to the ground** 転ぶ **ground floor** 1階 **on the ground** 地面に

□ **grove** 名 木立，林 **Holland Grove** ホランド・グローブ《ロンドンの地名》

□ **grow -er and -er** ～にますます～する

□ **grow into** 成長して～になる

□ **grow up** 成長する，大人になる

□ **guard** 名 ①警戒，見張り ②番人 **be on one's guard** 気を付ける，警戒する 動 番をする，監視する，守る

□ **guarded** 形 防護されている

□ **guardman** 名 ガードマン（見張り）

□ **guess at** ～を推測する

□ **guess-work** 名 当てずっぽう，当て推量

□ **guest** 名 客，ゲスト

□ **guiding stick** 目印の棒

□ **guilt** 名 罪，有罪，犯罪

□ **guilty** 形 有罪の，やましい **find someone guilty**（人）を有罪と評決する

□ **gun** 名 銃，大砲 **gun barrel** 銃身

□ **gunpowder** 名 火薬

□ **gunshot** 名 射撃，発砲

H

□ **ha** 間 ほう，まあ，おや《驚き・悲しみ・不満・喜び・笑い声などを表す》

□ **habit** 名 習慣，癖，気質

□ **had** 熟 **had better** ～したほうが身のためだ，～しなさい **I wish I had been there.** 自分がそこにいられればよかったのに。

□ **hairy** 形 毛むくじゃらの，毛製の

□ **half-opened** 形 半開きの

□ **half-past** 名 ～時半すぎ

□ **half-pound** 名 半ポンド

□ **half-smile** 名 半笑い，かすかな微笑み

□ **half-starved** 形 半分餓死状態の

☐ **halfway** 副中間［中途］で，不完全に **halfway down** ～の途中で **halfway up** ～の半ばまで 形中間［中途］の，不完全な

☐ **hall** 名公会堂，ホール，大広間，玄関 **Baskerville Hall** バスカヴィル邸 **Lafter Hall** ラフターホール

☐ **Halliday's Private Hotel** ハリデーズ・プライベート・ホテル《英国のホテル》

☐ **hallway** 名玄関，廊下

☐ **halting** 形言葉がつかえる，もたつく

☐ **Hampstead** 名ハムステッド《地名》

☐ **hand** 熟 **ask for the hand of** ～に結婚を申し込む **hand over** 手渡す，引き渡す，譲渡する **in the hands of** ～の手中に **put up one's hand** 手を挙げる **shake hands** 握手をする **take the law into one's own hand** 私的制裁を与える **with a rough hand** 粗い筆跡で **written by hand** 手書き

☐ **handcuff** 名手錠 動手錠をかける

☐ **handcuffed** 形手錠をかけられた

☐ **hand-gun** 名ハンドガン，拳銃

☐ **handkerchief** 名ハンカチ

☐ **handle** 動①手を触れる ②操縦する，取り扱う

☐ **handprint** 名手形

☐ **handsome** 形端正な（顔立ちの），りっぱな，（男性が）ハンサムな

☐ **handwriting** 名①手書き，肉筆 ②筆跡，書体

☐ **hang** 動かかる，かける，つるす，ぶら下がる **hang down** ぶら下がる **hang off** 垂れ下がる **hang on** ～につかまる，しがみつく **hang up** つるす，電話を切る

☐ **happen to** たまたま～する，偶然～する

☐ **happening** 名出来事，事件

☐ **happily** 副幸福に，楽しく，うまく，幸いにも

☐ **happiness** 名幸せ，喜び

☐ **happy to** 《be－》～してうれしい，喜んで～する

☐ **hard of hearing** 耳の不自由な，耳の遠い

☐ **hard time** 《a－》つらい時期

☐ **hard to** ～し難い

☐ **harden** 動固める，固くする，頑固にする

☐ **hard-looking** 形厳しい，荒々しい，無慈悲な

☐ **hardly** 副①ほとんど～でない，わずかに ②厳しく，かろうじて **can hardly** とても～できない

☐ **hardship** 名（耐えがたい）苦難，辛苦

☐ **hard-working** 形よく働く

☐ **hardy** 名①頑丈な，耐えられる ②大胆な

☐ **Hargrave** 名ハーグレイヴ《人名》

☐ **harm** 名害，損害，危害 動傷つける，損なう

☐ **harmless** 形無害の，安全な

☐ **harvest** 名①収穫（物），刈り入れ ②成果，報い

☐ **hate** 動嫌う，憎む，（～するのを）いやがる 名憎しみ

☐ **hateful** 形憎らしい，忌まわしい

☐ **hatred** 名憎しみ，毛嫌い

☐ **have** 熟 **could have done** ～だったかもしれない《仮定法》 **had better** ～したほうが身のためだ，～しなさい **have a case** 告訴する **have control over** ～を支配コントロールする **have a talk** 話をする **have got** 持っている **have got to** ～しなければならない **have no doubt** 疑いなく思っている，信じている **have no idea** わからない **have no time to do** ～する時間がない **have nothing to do with** ～と何の関係もない **have someone ～** 人に～してもらう **have to do with** ～と関係がある **should have done** ～すべきだった（のにしなかった）《仮定法》 **will have done** ～してしまっているだろう《未来完了形》 **would have … if ～** もし～だったとしたら…しただろう **you have my word** 約束しますよ

☐ **head for** ～に向かう，～の方に進む

☐ **head of** ～の長

☐ **head off for** ～を目指して進む

☐ **heading** 名表題，見出し

☐ **healthy** 形健康な，健全な，健康によい

☐ **hear about** ～について聞く

☐ **hear from** ～から手紙［電話・返事］をもらう

☐ **hear of** ～について聞く

☐ **hearing** 名聞くこと，聴取，聴力 **hard of hearing** 耳の不自由な，耳の遠い

☐ **heart** 熟 **break someone's heart** （人）の心を打ち砕く **heart attack** 心臓麻痺 **heart of** ～の中心 **lose heart** 落胆する，失望する **win someone's heart** （人）のハートを射止める

☐ **heartless** 形無情な，残酷な

☐ **heat** 名熱，暑さ

☐ **heatedly** 副興奮して，激して

☐ **heaven** 名天国 **by Heaven** 神にかけて **Good heavens!** しまった！，おやまあ！

☐ **heavily** 副①重く，重そうに，ひどく ②多量に

☐ **height** 名高さ, 身長
☐ **heir** 名相続人, 後継者
☐ **Helena, St.** セントヘレナ《島名》
☐ **hell** 名地獄, 地獄のようなところ［状態］
☐ **hell-hound** 名地獄の番犬
☐ **hello** 熟 **say hello to** ～によろしく言う
☐ **help** 熟 **can be of any help to** ～の役に立つことができる **help someone up** ひとを助け起こす, ささえる **help ～ to …** ～が…するのを助ける **help ～ with …** …を～の面で手伝う **with the help of** ～の助けにより, ～のおかげで
☐ **helper** 名助手, 協力者, 助けになるもの
☐ **helpful** 形役に立つ, 参考になる
☐ **helpless** 形無力の, 自分ではどうすることもできない
☐ **Henry Baskerville** ヘンリー・バスカヴィル《人名》
☐ **Herald** 名（バーミッサ・）ヘラルド《新聞（社）の名》
☐ **herd** 名（大型動物の）一群, 群集, 民衆
☐ **here** 熟 **here and there** あちこちで **here are ～** こちらは～です。 **here is ～** こちらは～です。 **Here it is.** はい, どうぞ。 **Look here.** ほら。ねえ。 **over here** こっちへ［に］; ほら, さあ《人の注意を引く》
☐ **hesitate** 動ためらう, ちゅうちょする
☐ **hid** 動 hide（隠れる）の過去, 過去分詞
☐ **hidden** 動 hide（隠れる）の過去分詞 形隠れた, 秘密の
☐ **hide** 動隠れる, 隠す, 隠れて見えない, 秘密にする
☐ **hiding place** 隠れ場所
☐ **high and low** あらゆるところを, くまなく
☐ **High Barrow** ハイ・バロー《地名》
☐ **high-pitched** 形かん高い
☐ **hill after hill** 小山に次ぐ小山
☐ **hillside** 名丘の中腹［斜面］
☐ **hilltop** 名丘の頂上
☐ **Hindu** 名ヒンドゥー人, インド人
☐ **hint** 名暗示, ヒント, 気配
☐ **hire** 動雇う, 賃借りする
☐ **hitting sound** ぶつかる音
☐ **hmm** 間ふむ, ううむ《熟考・疑問・ためらいなどを表す》
☐ **hmmm** 間ふうむ, なるほど
☐ **hobby** 名趣味, 得意なこと
☐ **Hobson's Patch** ホブソンズ・パッチ《地名》
☐ **hold** 熟 **catch hold of** ～をつかむ, 捕らえる **get hold of** ～を手に入れる, ～をつかむ **hold back**（事実・本心などを）隠す,（感情を）抑える, 自制する **hold in**（動かないように）押さえる **hold out** 差し出す,（腕を）伸ばす **hold up** ①維持する, 支える ②～を持ち上げる
☐ **Holland Grove** ホランド・グローブ《ロンドンの地名》
☐ **Holmes** 名ホームズ《人名》**Sherlock Holmes** シャーロック・ホームズ《人名》
☐ **holy** 形聖なる, 神聖な
☐ **home** 熟 **at home** 自宅で, 在宅して **drop someone off at home**（人）を車で家まで送る **get home** 家に着く［帰る］ **go home** 帰宅する **on one's way home** 帰り道で **take someone home**（人）を家まで送る
☐ **homely** 形①家庭的な, 飾らない ②器量のよくない, 質素な, 素朴な
☐ **honest** 形①正直な, 誠実な, 心からの ②公正な, 感心な **honest soul** 良心的な人
☐ **honestly** 副正直に
☐ **honesty** 名正直, 誠実
☐ **honor** 名①名誉, 光栄, 信用 ②節操, 自尊心 **do someone honor**（人）に敬意を表する **honor of doing** ～する光栄［栄誉］ **in honor of** ～に敬意を表して, ～を記念して 動尊敬する, 栄誉を与える
☐ **honorable** 形①尊敬すべき, 立派な ②名誉ある ③高貴な
☐ **hook** 名止め金, 釣り針
☐ **hop** 動（片足で）ぴょんと飛ぶ, 飛び越える, 飛び乗る
☐ **Hope Town** ホープ・タウン《地名》
☐ **Hope** 名ホープ《人名》
☐ **hopeful** 形希望に満ちた, 望みを抱いて（いる）, 有望な
☐ **hopeless** 形①希望のない, 絶望的な ②勝ち目のない
☐ **horrible** 形恐ろしい, ひどい
☐ **horror** 名①恐怖, ぞっとすること ②嫌悪
☐ **horse-drawn** 形馬が引く
☐ **horseman** 名乗馬の名手, 騎兵, 騎手
☐ **horsemen** 名 horseman（騎兵, 騎手）の複数
☐ **host** 名客をもてなす主人
☐ **hound** 名猟犬
☐ **Houndsditch** 名ハウンズディッチ《ロンドンの地名》
☐ **hour** 熟 **in one hour** 1時間で, 1時間以内に

☐ **House of Commons** 庶民院, 下院

☐ **house-doctor** 名住込み医師

☐ **household** 名家族, 世帯 **set up a household** 所帯を構える, 家庭を持つ

☐ **housekeeper** 名家政婦

☐ **housemate** 名同居人

☐ **how** 熟 **How about ～?** ～はどうですか。 **How could ～?** 何だって～なんてことがありえようか? **how far** どのくらいの距離か **How on earth ～?** 一体どうやったら **how to** ～する方法 **no matter how** どんなに～であろうとも

☐ **however** 副たとえ～でも 接けれども, だが

☐ **Hudson, Mrs.** ハドソン夫人

☐ **huge** 形巨大な, ばく大な

☐ **Hugo Baskerville** ヒューゴ・バスカヴィル《人名》

☐ **hullo** 間やあ, おや

☐ **humanly** 副人道的に

☐ **humble** 形つつましい, 粗末な

☐ **humbly** 副腰を低くして, 恐れ入って

☐ **humor** 名ユーモア

☐ **humorous** 形こっけいな, ユーモアのある

☐ **hundreds of** 何百もの～

☐ **hung** 動 hang (かかる) の過去, 過去分詞

☐ **hunger** 名空腹, 飢え

☐ **hunt** 動狩る, 狩りをする, 探し求める **hunt down** 追い詰める, 追跡して捕らえる 名狩り, 追跡

☐ **hunter** 名狩りをする人, 狩人, ハンター

☐ **hunting whip** 狩猟用むち

☐ **hurry** 熟 **hurry down** 急いで下りる[駆け込む] **in a hurry** 急いで, あわてて

☐ **husband** 熟 **make a good husband** よい夫になる

☐ **hush** 間しっ! 静かに!

☐ **hut** 名簡易住居, あばら屋, 山小屋

I

☐ **I give you my word.** 約束するよ。保証するよ。

☐ **idea** 熟 **have no idea** わからない

☐ **ideal** 形理想的な, 申し分のない

☐ **identify** 動 (本人・同一と) 確認する, 見分ける

☐ **if** 熟 **as if** あたかも～のように, まるで～みたいに **ask ～ if** ～かどうか尋ねる **even if** たとえ～でも **If +《主語》+ could** ～できればなあ《仮定法》 **if not the world** 世界でとはいわないまでも **if you please** よろしければ **see if** ～かどうかを確かめる **what if** もし～だったらどうなるだろうか **wonder if** ～ではないかと思う **would have … if ～** もし～だったとしたら…しただろう **would ～ if …** もし…なら～でしょう **Would you mind if ～?** ～してもかまいませんか。

☐ **illegal** 形違法な, 不法な

☐ **ill-health** 名体調不良

☐ **Illinois** 名イリノイ州《アメリカの地名》

☐ **illness** 名病気

☐ **imagination** 名想像 (力), 空想

☐ **imagine** 動想像する, 心に思い描く **I would imagine that** ～だと思う

☐ **immediate** 形さっそくの, 即座の, 直接の

☐ **immediately** 副すぐに, ～するやいなや

☐ **impatient** 形我慢できない, いらいらしている

☐ **importance** 名重要性, 大切さ

☐ **importantly** 副重大に, もったいぶって

☐ **impress** 形感銘を受けて

☐ **improve** 動改善する[させる], 進歩する

☐ **in** 熟 **in a hurry** 急いで, あわてて **in a moment** ただちに **in a way** ある意味では **in advance** 前もって, あらかじめ **in all probability** たぶん, おそらく **in an instant** たちまち, ただちに **in case** ～だといけないので, 念のため, 万が一 **in case of** ～の場合には, ～に備えて **in charge of** ～を任されて, ～を担当して, ～の責任を負って **in common use** 一般的に使われて[用いられて]いる **in control** ～を支配して, ～を掌握している **in fact** つまり, 実は, 要するに **in front of** ～の前に, ～の正面に **in honor of** ～を祝って **in one hour** 1時間で, 1時間以内に **in front of** ～の前に **in nine out of ten cases** 十中八九 **in one place** 一ヶ所に **in peace** 平和のうちに, 安心して **in public** 人前で, 公然と **in question** 問題の, 論争中の **in print** 紙上に **in return** お返しとして **in return for** ～に対する見返りとして, ～の交換条件として **in sight** 視野に入って **in silence** 黙って, 沈黙のうちに **in some way** 何とかして, 何らかの方法で **in spite of** ～にもかかわらず **in that case** もしそうなら **in the dead of night** 真夜中に **in the direction of** ～の方向に **in the distance** 遠方に **in the end** とうとう, 結局, ついに **in the future** 将来は **in the mail** 郵送される **in the meantime** それまでは, 当分は **in the middle** of ～の真ん中［中ほど］に **in the world** 世界で **in this way** このようにして **in time** 間に合って，やがて **in touch** 連絡を取って **in trouble** 面倒な状況で，困って **in turn** 順番に，立ち代わって **pull in**（網を）引く **show someone in** 人を中に案内する，招き入れる

□ **inch** 名 ①インチ《長さの単位。1/12フィート，2.54cm》②少量

□ **include** 動 含む，勘定に入れる

□ **including** 前 ～を含めて，込みで

□ **income** 名 収入，所得，収益

□ **incorrect** 形 正しくない，間違った

□ **increase** 動 増加［増強］する，増やす，増える

□ **indecision** 名 優柔不断，ためらい

□ **indeed** 副 ①実際，本当に ②《強意》まったく 間 本当に，まさか

□ **India** 名 インド《国名》

□ **Indian** 名 インド人 形 インド（人）の

□ **indicate** 動 指す，示す，（道などを）教える

□ **Indies** 名 インド諸島 **West Indies** 西インド諸島

□ **indigo-planter** 名 藍農場主

□ **individual** 形 独立した，個性的な，個々の 名 個体，個人

□ **influence** 名 影響，勢力

□ **inform** 動 ①告げる，知らせる ②密告する

□ **initial** 名 頭文字

□ **injure** 動 痛める，傷つける

□ **injured** 形 負傷した，（名誉・感情などを）損ねられた

□ **injury** 名 けが **do oneself an injury**（自分で）具合を悪くする

□ **ink** 名 インク

□ **inner** 形 ①内部の ②心の中の

□ **inquire** 動 尋ねる，問う

□ **inquiry** 名 ①質問，探求，問い合わせ ②事実を求めること

□ **insect** 名 虫，昆虫 **insect net** 捕虫網

□ **insist** 動 ①主張する，断言する ②要求する

□ **inspect** 動 検査する，調べる

□ **inspector** 名（英国の）警部補

□ **instant** 形 即時の，緊急の，即席の 名 瞬間，寸時 **in an instant** たちまち，ただちに

□ **instantly** 副 すぐに，即座に

□ **instead** 副 その代わりに **instead of** ～の代わりに，～をしないで

□ **instruct** 動 ①教える，教育する ②指図［命令］する

□ **intake** 名 吸い込み

□ **intelligent** 形 頭のよい，聡明な

□ **intend** 動《– to ～》～しようと思う，～するつもりである

□ **intention** 名 ①意図，（～する）つもり ②心構え

□ **interested** 形 興味を持った，関心のある **be interested in** ～に興味［関心］がある

□ **interesting** 形 おもしろい，興味を起こさせる

□ **interrupt** 動 さえぎる，妨害する，口をはさむ

□ **invaluable** 形 とても有益な

□ **invent** 動 ①発明［考案］する ②ねつ造する

□ **investigate** 動 研究する，調査する，捜査する

□ **investigation** 名（徹底的な）調査，取り調べ

□ **involve** 動 関連を持つ，関わる

□ **involved** 形 ①巻き込まれている，関連する ②入り組んだ，込み入っている

□ **Ireland** 名 アイルランド《国名》

□ **Irishman** 名 アイルランド（系）人

□ **iron** 名 鉄，鉄製のもの 形 鉄の，鉄製の **iron hand** 冷酷な組織支配

□ **Iron Dike Company** アイアン・ダイク・カンパニー《会社名》

□ **Iron Dike road** アイアン・ダイク道路

□ **irregular** 形 不規則な，ふぞろいの 名《-s》不正規軍［兵］

□ **islander** 名 島の住民

□ **isolated** 形 隔離した，孤立した

□ **it** 熟 **That's it.** それだけのことだ。

□ **It is ～ for someone to ...**（人）が…するのは～だ

□ **It is ～ of A to ...** Aが…するのは～だ

□ **item** 名 ①項目，品目 ②（新聞などの）記事

□ **itself** 代 それ自体，それ自身

□ **Ivy Douglas** アイビー・ダグラス《人名》

J

□ **Jack** 名 ジャック《人名》

□ **Jack McGinty** ジャック・マギンティ《人名》

□ **Jack McMurdo** ジャック・マクマードー《人名》

□ **jacket** 名 短い上着

- □ **Jacob Shafter** ジェイコブ・シェフター《人名》
- □ **Jacobson's Yard** ジョイコブソンズ造船所
- □ **jail** 名 刑務所
- □ **James** 名 ジェームズ《人名》
- □ **James Desmond** ジェームズ・デズモンド《人名》
- □ **James Mortimer** ジェームズ・モーティマー《人名》
- □ **James Stanger** ジェームズ・ステンジャー《人名》
- □ **jaw** 名 ①あご ②《-s》あご状のもの
- □ **jealousy** 名 嫉妬, ねたみ
- □ **Jean Baptiste Greuze** ジャン＝バティスト・グルーズ《フランスの画家, 1725–1805》
- □ **Jefferson Hope** ジェファーソン・ホープ《人名》
- □ **jewel** 名 宝石, 貴重な人[物]
- □ **jewelry** 名 宝石, 宝飾品類
- □ **Jiddah** 名 ジッダ《サウジアラビアの地名》
- □ **Jim** 名 ジム《人名》
- □ **Jim Carnaway** ジム・カーナウェイ《人名》
- □ **job** 熟 **get a job** 職を得る
- □ **John Clayton** ジョン・クレイトン《人名》
- □ **John Douglas** ジョン・ダグラス《人名》
- □ **John Ferrier** ジョン・フェリアー《人名》
- □ **John H. Watson** ジョン・H・ワトソン《人名》
- □ **John Rance** ジョン・ランス《人名》
- □ **John Sholto, Major** ジョン・ショルトー少佐
- □ **John Underwood and sons** ジョン・アンダーウッド・アンド・サンズ《ロンドンにある衣料品店》
- □ **Johnny** ジョニー《人名》
- □ **Johnston** ジョンストン《人名》
- □ **joke** 名 冗談, ジョーク 動 冗談を言う, ふざける, からかう
- □ **jokingly** 副 冗談に, しゃれて
- □ **Jonas Pinto** ジョナス・ピント《人名》
- □ **Jonathan Small** ジョナサン・スモール《人名》
- □ **Jones** 名 ジョーンズ《人名》
- □ **Joseph Smith** ジョセフ・スミス・ジュニア《末日聖徒イエス・キリスト教会(モルモン教)の設立者, 1805–1844》
- □ **Joseph Stangerson** ジョセフ・スタンガーソン《人名》
- □ **journey** 名 ①(遠い目的地への)旅 ②行程
- □ **joy** 名 喜び, 楽しみ
- □ **joyfully** 副 うれしそうに, 喜んで
- □ **judge** 動 判決を下す, 裁く, 判断する, 評価する **be any judge** なんらかの判断をする 名 裁判官, 判事, 審査員
- □ **judgment** 名 ①判断, 意見 ②裁判, 判決
- □ **jump** 熟 **jump to one's feet** 飛び起きる, はじかれたように立ち上がる **jump out** 飛び出る **jump out of** ～から飛び出す **jump over** ～の上を飛び越える **jump to one's feet** 飛び起きる **jump up** 素早く立ち上がる **jump upon** 飛び乗る
- □ **jury** 名 陪審, 陪審員団
- □ **just as** (ちょうど)であろうとおり
- □ **just in time** いよいよというときに, すんでのところで, やっと間に合って
- □ **just then** そのとたんに
- □ **justice** 名 ①公平, 公正, 正当, 正義 ②司法, 裁判(官) **bring justice to** ～に裁きを受けさせる

K

- □ **keep** 熟 **keep an eye on** ～から目を離さない **keep away from** ～に近寄らない **keep on** そのまま続ける **keep one's promise** 約束を守る **keep someone from** ～から(人)を阻む **keep up** 上げたままにしておく
- □ **keeper** 名 保護者, 後見人
- □ **Kemball** 名 ケンボール《人名》
- □ **keyhole** 名 かぎ穴
- □ **Khan** 名 カーン《人名》
- □ **killer** 名 殺人者[犯]
- □ **killing** 名 殺害, 殺人
- □ **kind** 熟 **be kind enough to** 親切にも～する **be kind to** ～に親切である **it is kind of ～ to** …してくれるなんて～は親切である **kind of** ある程度, いくらか, ～のようなもの[人] **that is very kind of you** ご親切にどうも
- □ **kind-looking** 形 親切そうな
- □ **kindly** 形 親切な, 情け深い, 思いやりのある 副 親切に, 優しく
- □ **kiss** 名 キス 動 キスする
- □ **kitchen-maid** 名 下働きのメイド
- □ **km** 名 キロメートル《単位》
- □ **knee** 名 ひざ **drop to one's knees** がっくり

と両ひざをつく

□ **kneel** 動ひざを曲げる, ひざまずく **kneel down** ひざまずく

□ **Kneller** 名ゴドフリー・ネラー《Sir Godfrey Kneller, 肖像画家, 1646–1723》

□ **knelt** 動kneel (ひざまずく) の過去, 過去分詞

□ **knife** 名ナイフ, 小刀, 包丁, 短剣

□ **knife-wound** 刃物による刺し傷

□ **knock** 動ノックする, たたく, ぶつける **knock at/on the door** ドアをノックする (音) 名打つこと, 戸をたたくこと [音]

□ **know** 熟**as you know** ご存知のとおり **know nothing of** ～のことを知らない **know of** ～について知っている **little know** 分かっていない **you know** ご存知のとおり, そうでしょう

□ **knowingly** 副すべてお見通しだという顔つきで

□ **knowledge** 名知識, 理解, 学問

□ **known to** 《be –》～に知られている

L

□ **laboratory** 名実験室, 研究室 **chemical laboratory** 化学実験室

□ **lack** 動不足している, 欠けている

□ **ladder** 名はしご, はしご状のもの

□ **Lafter Hall** ラフターホール

□ **laid** 動lay (置く) の過去, 過去分詞

□ **Lake Saloon** レイク・サルーン《酒場の名》

□ **Lal Rao** ラル・ラオ《人名》

□ **lamp** 名ランプ, 灯火

□ **landlady** 名女家主, 女主人

□ **lantern** 名手提げランプ, ランタン

□ **last** 動続く 名最後 **at last** ついに **take one last look** ～を見納めする **the last time** この前～したとき

□ **late** 形最近死んだ, 故…

□ **lately** 副近ごろ, 最近

□ **latest** 形最新の, 最近の

□ **laugh** 熟**break into a lagh** 急に笑いだす **burst out laughing** 爆笑する **laugh to oneself** 一人笑いをする **make someone laugh** (人) を笑わせる

□ **laughter** 名笑い (声)

□ **Laura Lyons** ローラ・ライオンズ《人名》

□ **Lauriston Gardens** ローリストン・ガーデン《ロンドンの地名》

□ **law** 熟**take the law into one's own hand** 私的制裁を与える

□ **law and order** 治安, 法と秩序

□ **lawful** 形合法な

□ **lawless** 形①法律のない, 不法な ②無法な, 手に負えない

□ **lawman** 名法務官

□ **lawyer** 名弁護士, 法律家

□ **lay** 動①置く, 横たえる, 敷く ②整える ③卵を産む ④lie (横たわる) の過去 **lay down** ①下に置く, 横たえる ②裏切る **lay one's hand on** ～を捕まえる **lay off** レイオフする, 一時解雇する **lay out** ①説明する, 明確に述べる ②きちんと並べる, 陳列する

□ **layer** 名層, 重ね

□ **lazy** 形怠惰な, 無精な

□ **lead into** (ある場所) へ導く

□ **lead out onto** ～の方へ導く

□ **lead the way** 先に立って導く, 案内する, 率先する

□ **lead to** ～に至る, ～に通じる, ～を引き起こす

□ **leading** 形主要な, 指導的な, 先頭の

□ **lean** 動①もたれる, 寄りかかる ②傾く, 傾ける **lean back** 後ろにもたれる **lean over** ～にかがみ込む

□ **leap** 動①跳ぶ ②跳び越える **leap to one's feet** サッと立ち上がる

□ **leapt** 動leap (跳ぶ) の過去, 過去分詞

□ **learning** 名学問, 学識

□ **least** 名最小, 最少 **at least** 少なくとも **in the least** ちっとも, 少しも

□ **leather** 名皮革, 皮製品

□ **leave** 熟**leave A to B** AをBに託す, 任せる **leave ～ alone** ～をそっとしておく **leave behind** あとにする, ～を置き去りにする **leave for** ～に向かって出発する **leave ～ for …** …を～のために残しておく **leave in** ～をそのままにしておく **make someone leave** 退校 [職] させる **on leave** 休暇中で

□ **led** 動lead (導く) の過去, 過去分詞

□ **left** 熟**to be left until called for** (郵便物の) 留め置き

□ **left-hand** 形①左側の, 左方向の ②左手の, 左利きの

□ **length** 名長さ, 縦, たけ, 距離 **at full length** 十分に, 全身を伸ばして **at length** ついに, 詳しく **length of steps** 歩幅

☐ **less** 副 ～より少なく，～ほどでなく **less and less** だんだん少なく～，ますます～でなく **no less than** ～と同じだけの，～も同然 **not less than** ～以下ではなく，～にまさるとも劣らない

☐ **less-known** 形 あまり知られていない

☐ **lesson** 熟 **give someone a lesson** (人)を懲らしめる

☐ **Lestrade** 名 レストレード《人名》

☐ **let go** 手を放す，行かせる，釈放する

☐ **Let me see.** ええと。

☐ **let nothing stand between** ～との間の疑問を何一つ放置しない

☐ **let us** どうか私たちに～させてください

☐ **lettering** 名 書いた［刻んだ］文字，銘

☐ **level** 名 水準

☐ **lid** 名 (箱，なべなどの)ふた

☐ **lie** 動 ①うそをつく ②横たわる，寝る ③(ある状態に)ある，存在する **lie around** そこらへんに転がっている **lie down** 横たわる，横になる 名 うそ，詐欺 **tell a lie** うそをつく

☐ **life** 熟 **all one's life** ずっと，生まれてから **run for one's life** 死に物狂いで走る，一目散に逃げる **value one's life** 命を大切にする **way of life** 生き様，生き方，暮らし方

☐ **lifeless** 形 ①生物の住まない ②生命のない ③活力のない

☐ **lifetime** 名 ①一生，生涯 ②寿命

☐ **lift** 動 持ち上げる，上がる

☐ **light sleeper** 眠りの浅い人

☐ **light-hearted** 形 気楽な，快活な

☐ **lightly** 副 ①軽く，そっと ②軽率に

☐ **likable** 形 好ましい，感じのよい

☐ **like** 熟 **feel like** ～がほしい，～したい気がする，～のような感じがする **like this** このような，こんなふうに **like of** ～のような(人) **look like** ～のように見える，～に似ている **not feel like doing** ～する気になれない **Now this is more like it.** こいつはいいぞ。 **would like** ～がほしい **would like to** ～したいと思う **Would you like ～?** ～はいかがですか。

☐ **likeable** 形 好ましい

☐ **likely** 形 ①ありそうな，(～)しそうな ②適当な 副 たぶん，おそらく **very likely** たぶん

☐ **likewise** 副 同じように

☐ **liking** 名 好み，趣味 **take a liking to** ～を好きになる

☐ **limb** 名 手足，四肢

☐ **limit** 名 限界，《-s》範囲，境界

☐ **line of** 熟 一連の～，～の系統，血筋

☐ **line up**《号令で》整列

☐ **line with** ～で顔にしわをよせる

☐ **lined with**《be –》～が立ち並ぶ

☐ **link** 名 ①(鎖の)輪 ②リンク ③相互［因果］関係 **missing link** ミッシングリンク《つながりが分断された部分》

☐ **lip** 名 唇，《-s》口

☐ **liquid** 名 液体

☐ **list** 名 名簿，目録，一覧表

☐ **lit** 動 light (火をつける)の過去，過去分詞

☐ **liter** 名 リットル，リッター

☐ **literature** 名 文学，文芸

☐ **little more than** ～と大差ない，ほとんど～

☐ **little way**《a –》少し

☐ **live out** 生き延びる，離れて暮らす

☐ **live out the future that** ～という運命(将来)を生きる

☐ **live to see** ～のために生きる

☐ **lively** 形 ①元気のよい，活発な ②鮮やかな，強烈な，真に迫った

☐ **Liverpool** 名 リバプール《英国の地名》

☐ **living** 名 生計，生活 形 ①生きている，現存の ②使用されている ③そっくりの **not a (living) soul** 人っ子一人いない

☐ **load** 動 ①(荷を)積む ②弾を込める，装てんする

☐ **loaded** 形 荷を積んだ，詰め込んだ

☐ **locate** 動 ①置く，居住する［させる］ ②～の居場所をつきとめる

☐ **lock** 熟 **lock up** 鍵をかける，～を閉じ込める **under lock and key** 厳重に管理して

☐ **lodge** 名 〔組合などの組織の〕支部 動 泊まる，泊める，下宿する［させる］

☐ **lodging** 名 ①宿泊，宿 ②《-s》下宿

☐ **London** 名 ロンドン《英国の首都》

☐ **lonely** 形 ①孤独な，心さびしい ②ひっそりした，人里離れた

☐ **long** 熟 **all day long** 一日中，終日 **as long as** ～する以上は，～である限りは **for long** 長い間 **long ago** ずっと前に，昔 **long since** ずっと以前に **long way** はるかに **so long as** ～する限りは

☐ **longer** 熟 **no longer** もはや～でない［～しない］ **not ～ any longer** もはや～でない［～しない］

☐ **long-haired** 形 長毛の

□ **look** 熟 **by the look of** 〜の様子からして **look after** 〜の世話をする，〜に気をつける **look around** まわりを見回す **look around for** 〜を捜し求める **look down** 見下ろす **look down at** 〜に目［視線］を落とす **look down on** 〜を見下す **look down upon** 見下ろす，俯瞰する **look for** 〜を探す **Look here.** ほら。ねえ。 **look in** 中を見る，立ち寄る **look into** ①〜を検討する，〜を研究する ②〜の中を見る，〜をのぞき込む **look like** 〜のように見える，〜に似ている **look on** 傍観する，眺める **look out** ①外を見る ②気をつける，注意する **look out of** （窓などから）外を見る **look out over** 〜をはるかに見渡す **look over at** 〜の方を見る **look through** 〜をのぞき込む **look to be** 〜になりそうである **look up** 見上げる，調べる **look up to** 〜を仰ぎ見る **look upon** 〜を見る，見つめる **take one last look** 〜を見納めする

□ **lookout** 名 ①見張り，警戒 ②見込み

□ **loose** 形 自由な，ゆるんだ，あいまいな **come loose** 抜ける，緩む

□ **loosely** 副 ①ゆるく，おおざっぱに ②だらしなく

□ **lord** 名 首長，主人，領主，貴族，上院議員

□ **lose heart** 落胆する，失望する

□ **loss** 名 ①損失（額・物），損害，浪費 ②失敗，敗北 **at a loss** 途方に暮れて

□ **lots of** たくさんの〜

□ **love** 熟 **be in love with** 〜に恋して，〜に心を奪われて **fall in love** 恋におちる **fall in love with** 恋におちる **love affair** 恋愛（関係），浮気

□ **lovely** 形 愛らしい，美しい，すばらしい

□ **lover** 名 ①愛人，恋人 ②愛好者

□ **loving** 形 愛する，愛情のこもった

□ **lower** 形 もっと低い，下級の，劣った 動 下げる，低くする

□ **loyal** 形 忠実な，誠実な

□ **loyalty** 名 忠義，忠誠

□ **luck** 熟 **bad luck** 災難，不運，悪運 **down on one's luck** 運が傾いて，つきに見放されて **out of luck** ついていない

□ **luckily** 副 運よく，幸いにも

□ **lucky for** （人）にとってラッキーだったことには

□ **Lucy Ferrier** ルーシー・フェリアー《人名》

□ **lumber** 名 材木，用材

□ **Lyceum Theatre** ライシーアム劇場

□ **lying** 形 ①うそをつく，虚偽の ②横になっている

□ **Lyons** 名 ライオンズ《人名》

M

□ **M.R.C.S.** 略 **Membership of the Royal College of Surgeons** 王立外科医学協会準会員

□ **Mac** 名 マック《人名，マクドナルドの愛称》

□ **MacDonald, Inspector** マクドナルド警部補

□ **mad** 形 ①気の狂った ②逆上した，理性をなくした ③ばかげた ④（〜に）熱狂［熱中］して，夢中の

□ **madam** 名《ていねいな呼びかけ》奥様，お嬢様

□ **Madame Charpentier** シャルパンティエ夫人

□ **maddening** 形 ひどくいらいらさせる

□ **made up of** 《be –》〜で構成されている

□ **madman** 名 ①狂人 ②常軌を逸した人

□ **Madras** 名 マドラス《地名，現在のチェンナイ》

□ **magic** 名 ①魔法，手品 ②魔力

□ **magnifying glass** 虫眼鏡，拡大鏡

□ **Mahomet Singh** マホメット・シン《人名》

□ **maid** 名 お手伝い，メイド

□ **mail** 熟 **in the mail** 郵送される

□ **main** 形 主な，主要な

□ **mainly** 副 主に

□ **major** 名 陸軍少佐

□ **make** 熟 《**be**》**made up of** 〜で構成されている **make … 〜** …に〜させる **make a ditective** 刑事になる **make a good husband** よい夫になる **make a mistake** 間違いをする **make friends with** 〜と友達になる **make money** お金を儲ける **make noise** 音を立てる **make of** 〜を考える，理解する **make one's blood run cold** （人）をゾッとさせる，血の気を引かせる **make one's way** 進む，行く，成功する **make one's way into** 〔部屋など〕に入る，進入する **make oneself comfortable** くつろぐ **make out** 作り上げる，認識する，立証する **make someone laugh** （人）を笑わせる **make someone leave** 退校［職］させる **make sure** 確かめる，確認する **make up** 作り出す，考え出す，〜を構成［形成］する **make up one's mind** 決心する **We shall make something of you yet.** 君への評価を改めなければならないな。

□ **man of science** 科学者

□ **manage** 動 ①動かす，うまく処理する ②経営［管理］する，支配する ③どうにか〜する **manage to** 〜を成し遂げる，達成する

□ **manager** 名 経営者，支配人，支店長，部長

□ **Manders** 名 マンダーズ《人名》

□ **manner** 名 ①方法, やり方 ②態度, 様子 ③《-s》行儀, 作法, 生活様式

□ **manor** 名 ①荘園 ②警察の管轄区

□ **manor house** 領主の館

□ **manuscript** 名 原稿, 手書き原稿, 写本

□ **many** 熟 **many a** いくつもの〜, 数々の〜 **so many** 非常に多くの

□ **mark** 名 ①印, 記号, 跡 ②点数 ③特色 動 印［記号］をつける

□ **marked** 形 印のある, マークされた

□ **marker** 熟 **dry-land marker stick** 乾燥地の目印棒

□ **marriage** 名 結婚(生活・式)

□ **married** 形 結婚した, 既婚の

□ **marry** 動 結婚する

□ **Marvin, Captain** マーヴィン警部

□ **Mary Morstan** メアリー・モースタン《人名》

□ **Mason** 名 メイソン《人名》

□ **mass** 名 ①固まり, (密集した)集まり ②多数, 多量

□ **master** 名 主人, 雇い主

□ **match** 名 ①試合, 勝負 ②相手, 釣り合うもの ③マッチ(棒) 動 ①〜に匹敵する ②調和する, 釣り合う ③(〜を…と)勝負させる **match up to** 〜と合致匹敵する

□ **matter** 熟 **a matter of** 〜の問題 **as a matter of duty** 職務上 **for that matter** ついでに言えば **no matter how** どんなに〜であろうとも **no matter what** たとえ何があろう［起ころう］と **not matter** 問題にならない

□ **maximum** 名 最大(限), 最高

□ **May I 〜?** 〜してもよいですか。

□ **McGinty** 名 マギンティ《人名》

□ **McGregor** 名 マクレガー《人名》

□ **McMurdo** 名 マクマードー《人名》

□ **McSomebody** 名 マックなんとかという人

□ **meaning** 名 意味, 趣旨

□ **mean-looking** 形 意地の悪そうな, たちの悪そうな

□ **means** 熟 **by all means** なんとしても, ぜひとも

□ **meantime** 名 合間, その間 **in the meantime** それまでは, 当分は

□ **meanwhile** 副 それまでの間, 一方では

□ **measure** 動 ①測る, (〜の)寸法がある ②評価する 名 計量器, 物差し.

□ **measurement** 名 ①測定 ②寸法

□ **medical** 形 ①医学の ②内科の **Medical Directory** 医師録 **Medical Officer** 医官

□ **meet one's end** 命を落とす

□ **meet one's death** 最後を遂げる, 死ぬ

□ **meet up** 会う

□ **meet with** 〜に出会う

□ **meeting** 名 集まり, ミーティング, 面会

□ **membership** 名 会員, 会員資格

□ **memory** 名 記憶(力), 思い出

□ **mend** 動 直す, 繕う, よくなる **mend one's way** 悔い改める, 改心する

□ **mental** 形 心の, 精神の

□ **mentally** 副 心で, 精神的に

□ **mention** 動 (〜について)述べる, 言及する **Don't mention it.** どういたしまして。

□ **merchant** 名 商人, 貿易商

□ **mercy** 名 ①情け, 哀れみ, 慈悲 ②ありがたいこと, 幸運 **at one's mercy** 〜のなすがままになって

□ **mere** 形 単なる, ほんの, まったく〜にすぎない **mere sight of** 〜を見ただけで

□ **merely** 副 単に, たかが〜に過ぎない

□ **Merripit House** メリピット・ハウス

□ **merry** 形 陽気な, 愉快な, 快活な

□ **message** 熟 **get a message to** 〜に連絡を取る **take a message** 伝言をうけたまわる

□ **messenger** 名 使者, (伝言・小包などの)配達人, 伝達者 **messenger office** メッセンジャー会社

□ **metal** 名 金属, 合金

□ **metal-work** 名 金属細工品

□ **meter** 名 メートル《長さの単位》

□ **method** 名 方法, 手段

□ **middle** 名 中間, 最中 **in the middle of** 〜の真ん中［中ほど］に 形 中間の, 中央の

□ **middle-aged** 形 中高年の

□ **middle-sized** 形 中背の

□ **mid-forties** 名 40代半ば

□ **midnight** 名 夜の12時, 真夜中, 暗黒

□ **might** 助《mayの過去》①〜かもしれない ②〜してもよい, 〜できる **try as he might** 彼がどんなに試そうとも

□ **mighty** 形 強力な, 権勢のある, 壮大な, 非常な **with a mighty drop on one side** 片側が激しい落下

□ **Mike Scanlan** マイク・スキャンラン《人名》

□ **mile** 名 ①マイル《長さの単位。1,609m》 ②《-s》かなりの距離

□ **milk boy** 牛乳配達の少年

□ **Miller Hill** ミラー・ヒル《地名》

□ **mind** 名 ①心, 精神, 考え ②知性 **make up one's mind** 決心する **set mind** 決意する, 心に決める 動 ①気にする, いやがる ②気をつける, 用心する **Never mind.** 気にするな。 **Would you mind if ～?** ～してもかまいませんか。

□ **mine** 熟 **a friend of mine** 友人の1人

□ **mine** 名 鉱坑

□ **miner** 名 炭鉱労働者, 坑夫

□ **minute** 熟 **by the minute** 刻々と, どんどん

□ **mire** 名 沼地 **Grimpen Mire** グリンペン大沼

□ **misfortune** 名 不運, 不幸, 災難

□ **miss** 動 ①逃す, 取りそこなう **miss out on** ～のチャンスを逃す ②～がないのを惜しむ 名 ①失敗 ②《M-》～嬢, ～さん

□ **missing** 形 欠けている, 行方不明の **missing link** ミッシングリンク《つながりが分断された部分》

□ **mistake** 熟 **make a mistake** 間違いをする

□ **mistaken** 形 誤った

□ **mister** 名《男性に対して》～さん, ～氏

□ **mix** 動 ①混ざる, 混ぜる ②(～を)一緒にする **mix up** ごちゃ混ぜにする 名 混合(物)

□ **mixed** 形 混合の, 混ざった **get mixed up** かかわり合いになる, 巻き添えを食う

□ **moat** 名 堀

□ **moated** 形 堀のある

□ **modern** 形 現代[近代]の, 現代的な, 最近の 名 現代[近代]人

□ **Mogul, Great** ムガール皇帝《ダイヤモンドの名前》

□ **mole** 名 モグラ

□ **moment** 名 ①瞬間, ちょっとの間 ②(特定の)時, 時期 **at any moment** 今すぐにも **at that moment** その時に, その瞬間に **at the moment** 今は **at this moment** 現在のところ, 現段階[時点]では **big moment** 重大事(件) **for a moment** 少しの間 **for a moment or two** ほんの少しの間 **for the moment** 差し当たり, 当座は **in a moment** ただちに **one moment** ちょっとの間

□ **money** 熟 **fake money** 偽金 **make money** お金を儲ける

□ **monkey-faced** 形 猿のような顔をした

□ **monthly** 形 月1回の, 毎月の

□ **mood** 名 気分, 機嫌, 雰囲気, 憂うつ

□ **moonlight** 名 月明かり, 月光

□ **moor** 名 原野, 沼地

□ **more** 熟 **more of** ～よりもっと **more than** ～以上 **Now this is more like it.** こいつはいいぞ。 **no more** もう～ない **no more than** ただの～にすぎない **not ～ any more** もう[これ以上]～ない **once more** もう一度 **the more ～ the more …** ～すればするほどますます…

□ **moreover** 副 その上, さらに

□ **Moriarty, Professor** モリアーティ教授

□ **Mormon** 名 モルモン教《キリスト教の流れを汲む新興宗教》, モルモン教徒

□ **morning** 熟 **morning paper** 朝刊 **one morning** ある朝

□ **Morris** 名 モリス《人名》

□ **Morstan** 名 モースタン《人名》

□ **Morstan, Captain** モースタン大尉

□ **Mortimer** 名 モーティマー《人名》

□ **most** 熟 **at (the) most** せいぜい, 多くても

□ **mostly** 副 主として, 多くは, ほとんど

□ **motionless** 形 動きのない, 静止の

□ **mountain pass** 山道, 峠

□ **mountain peak** 山頂

□ **move** 熟 **move away** ①立ち去る ②移す, 動かす **move in** 引っ越す **move off** 立ち去る **move on** 先に進む **move to** ～に引っ越す

□ **movement** 名 ①動き, 運動 ②変動

□ **moving** 形 動いている

□ **much** 熟 **as much as** ～と同じだけ **not much** たいしたものではない **that much** それだけ **too much** 過度の **too much of** あまりに～過ぎる

□ **muddy** 形 泥だらけの, ぬかるみの

□ **murder** 名 人殺し, 殺害, 殺人事件 動 殺す

□ **murderer** 名 殺人犯

□ **murderous** 形 残忍な

□ **murmur** 名 つぶやき, かすかな音

□ **murmuring** 形 うめく(音)

□ **muscle** 名 筋肉, 腕力

□ **mustache** 名《-s》口ひげ

□ **My God.** おや, まあ

□ **mysterious** 形 神秘的な, 謎めいた

□ **mysteriously** 副 神秘的に, 不思議に

□ **mystery** 名 ①神秘, 不可思議 ②推理小説, ミステリー

N

□ **nail** 名爪

□ **name** 動名前をあげる 名名前 **bear the name of** ～の名前がある

□ **narrow** 形狭い

□ **narrowly** 副かろうじて

□ **natural scientist** 自然科学者, 博物学者

□ **naturalist** 名①自然主義者 ②博物学者

□ **nature** 熟**nature of which** ものごとの本質 **second nature** 習性, 第二の天性

□ **Nauvoo** 名ノーブー《米国イリノイ州の地名》

□ **Neal** 名ニール《店名》

□ **near** 熟**get near** 接近する **near miss** 目標までもう一歩のところ

□ **nearby** 形近くの, 間近の 副近くで, 間近で

□ **nearly** 副ほとんど, もう少しで

□ **necessary** 形必要な, 必然の **if necessary** もし必要ならば

□ **needle** 名針, 針状のもの

□ **neighborhood** 名近所(の人々), 付近

□ **neighboring** 形隣の, 近所の

□ **neither** 形どちらの～も…でない 代(2者のうち)どちらも～でない 副《否定文に続いて》～も…しない **neither ～ nor …** ～も…もない

□ **nephew** 名おい(甥)

□ **nerve** 名①神経 ②気力, 精力

□ **nervous** 形①神経の ②神経質な, おどおどした **nervous breakdown** 神経衰弱, ノイローゼ

□ **nervously** 副神経質に, いらいらして

□ **net** 熟**insect net** 捕虫網

□ **Nevada** 名ネバダ州《米国の地名》

□ **Never have I seen ...** 《倒置》I never have seen ...

□ **Never mind.** 気にするな。

□ **New York** ニューヨーク《米国の都市；州》

□ **newcomer** 名新しく来た人, 初心者

□ **news** 名報道, ニュース, 便り, 知らせ

□ **newspaper** 名新聞(紙) **newspaper type** 新聞書体

□ **next time** 次回に

□ **next to** ～のとなりに, ～の次に

□ **next to nothing** ほとんどなきに等しい

□ **night** 熟**all day and night** 昼も夜も **day and night** 昼も夜も **in the dead of night** 真夜中に **sit up all night** 徹夜する **the night before** 前の晩

□ **nightclothes** 名ねまき

□ **nightfall** 名夕暮れ

□ **no** 熟**have no idea** わからない **have no time to do** ～する時間がない **no doubt** きっと, たぶん **no longer** もはや～でない[～しない] **no matter how** どんなに～であろうとも **no matter what** たとえ何があろう[起ころう]と **no more** もう～ない **no more than** ただの～にすぎない **no one** 誰も[一人も]～ない **no one else** 他の誰一人として～しない **no sooner** ～するや否や **no use** 役に立たない, 用をなさない **of no use** 使われないで **there is no way** ～する見込みはない **There's no point in** ～しても意味がない

□ **nobody** 代誰も1人も～ない 名とるに足らない人

□ **nod** 動うなずく, うなずいて～を示す

□ **no-good** 形何の価値もない, 最低の

□ **noise** 名騒音, 騒ぎ, 物音 **make noise** 音を立てる

□ **noisy** 形騒々しい, やかましい

□ **nom-de-plume** 名筆名, ペンネーム

□ **non-believer** 名無信仰な人, 信じない人

□ **none** 代(～の)何も[誰も・少しも]…ない **none other than** ほかならぬ～

□ **nonsense** 名ばかげたこと, ナンセンス

□ **nor** 接～もまたない **neither ～ nor …** ～も…もない

□ **normal** 形普通の, 平均の, 標準的な

□ **normally** 副普通は, 通常は

□ **North American Continent** 北米大陸

□ **northern** 形北の, 北向きの, 北からの

□ **Northumberland Hotel** ノーサンバーランド・ホテル

□ **Norwood** 名ノーウッド《地名》

□ **nosy** 形おせっかいな

□ **not** 熟**not always** 必ずしも～であるとは限らない **not ～ any longer** もはや～でない[～しない] **not ～ any more** もう[これ以上]～ない **not at all** 少しも～でない **not ～ at all** 少しも[全然]～ない **not ～ but …** ～ではなくて… **not feel like doing** ～する気になれない **not matter** 問題にならない **not quite** まったく～だというわけではない **not yet** まだ～してない **whether or not** ～かどうか

□ **note** 名①メモ, 覚え書き ②注釈 ③注意, 注目 ④手形, 紙幣 **five-pound note** 5ポンド紙幣

□ **notebook** 名ノート, 手帳

□ **nothing** 熟 **all for nothing** いたずらに，無駄に **can do nothing** どうしようもない **for nothing** ただで，無料で，むだに **have nothing to do with** ～と何の関係もない **know nothing of** ～のことを知らない **let nothing stand between someone** 疑問を何一つ放置せず **next to nothing** ほとんどなきに等しい **nothing but** ただ～だけ，～にすぎない，～のほかは何も…ない

□ **notice** 名 ①注意 ②通知 ③公告 動 ①気づく，認める ②通告する

□ **Notting Hill** ノッティング・ヒル《ロンドンの地名》

□ **now** 熟 **as of now** 今のところ **by now** 今のところ，今ごろまでには **for now** 今のところ，ひとまず **from now** 今から，これから **from now on** 今後 **now and forever** 今もずっと **now that** 今や～だから，～からには **Now this is more like it** こいつはいいぞ **right now** 今すぐに，たった今 **up to now** これまで

□ **nugget** 名 (貴金属の)かたまり，貴重なもの

□ **number of** 《a－》いくつかの～，多くの～ **a great number of** 非常に多くの

O

□ **oak** 名 オーク《ブナ科の樹木の総称》**black oak** クロガシ 形 オーク(材)の

□ **obey** 動 服従する，(命令などに)従う

□ **object** 名 ①物，事物 ②目的物，対象

□ **observant** 形 すぐ気がつく，目ざとい

□ **observation** 名 観察(力)，注目

□ **observe** 動 ①観察[観測]する，監視[注視]する ②気づく

□ **occasion** 名 ①場合，(特定の)時 ②機会，好機 ③理由，根拠 **on occasion** 時折，時々

□ **occasionally** 副 時折，時たま

□ **occupy** 動 ①占領する，保有する ②占める

□ **occur** 動 (事が)起こる，生じる，(考えなどが)浮かぶ

□ **odd** 形 奇妙な

□ **oddly** 副 奇妙なことに

□ **of** 熟 **of course** もちろん，当然 **of no use** 使われないで **of one's own** 自分自身の **of use** 役に立って **of which** ～の中で

□ **off** 熟 **carry off** 誘かいする，さらって行く，運び去る **cut-off** 切断された **drop off** ～から(取れて)落ちる **drop someone off at home** (人)を車で家まで送る **far off** ずっと遠くに，はるかかなたに **get off** (～から)降りる **go off** ①出かける，去る，出発する ②始める，突然～しだす **move off** 立ち去る **off duty** 非番で **off you go** 散れ，出て行け **pull off** 離れる，去る，(衣服などを)脱ぐ **put off** ～から逃れる，延期する，要求をそらす，不快にさせる，やめさせる **run off** 走り去る，逃げ去る **set off** 出発する **start off** 出発する **take off** (衣服を)脱ぐ，取り去る，～を取り除く **walk off** 立ち去る

□ **offer** 動 申し出る，申し込む，提供する

□ **office** 名 **messenger office** メッセンジャー会社

□ **officer** 名 役人，公務員，警察官 **Medical Officer** 医官 **police officer** 警察官

□ **Ohio** 名 オハイオ州《米国の地名》

□ **oil** 名 油，石油

□ **OK** 名 許可，承認

□ **old-world** 形 旧世界の

□ **on** 熟 **and so on** ～など，その他もろもろ **be on one's guard** 気を付ける，警戒する **call on** 呼びかける，招集する，求める，訪問する **carry on** 続ける **come on** いいかげんにしろ，もうよせ，さあ来なさい **from now on** 今後 **further on** これより先，もっと先で **get on** (電車などに)乗る **go on** 続く，続ける，進み続ける，起こる，発生する **keep on** そのまま続ける **look on** 傍観する，眺める **move on** 先に進む **on behalf of** ～のために，～に代わって **on business** 仕事で **on each side** それぞれの側に **on earth** いったい **on either side** 両側に **on foot** 歩いて **on one's feet** 立っている状態で **on one's way** 途中で，出て行く，出かける **on one's way home** 帰り道で **on one's way to** ～に行く途中で **on the condition that** もし～なら **on the ground** 地面に **on the spot** その場で，ただちに **on the way** 途中で **on the way to** ～へ行く途中で **on top of** ～の上(部)に **on which** = where **take on** 帯びる，持つようになる，～と戦う **try on** 試着してみる **turn on** ①～の方を向く ②(スイッチなどを)ひねってつける，出す

□ **once** 熟 **at once** すぐに，同時に **once again** 再度，もう一度 **once more** もう一度

□ **one** 熟 **at one time** ある時には，かつては **each one** 各自 **in one hour** 1時間で，1時間以内に **in one place** 一ヶ所に **no one** 誰も[一人も]～ない **no one else** 他の誰一人として～しない **one another** お互い **one by one** 1つずつ，1人ずつ **one day** (過去の)ある日，(未来の)いつか **one moment** ちょっとの間 **one morning** ある朝 **one of** ～の1つ[人] **one side** 片側 **this one** これ，こちら

□ **oneself** 熟 **by oneself** 一人で，自分だけで，独力で **excuse oneself** 辞退する **for oneself** 独力で，自分のために **make oneself** comfortable くつろぐ **put oneself in the position of** 自分を～の立場に置く，～の立場になって考える

□ **onto** 前 ～の上へ［に］ **lead out onto** ～の方へ導く

□ **open** 熟 **break open**（金庫などを）こじ開ける

□ **open-air** 形 野外の，戸外の

□ **opening** 名 ①開始，始め ②開いた所，穴

□ **open-mouthed** 形 口を開けた

□ **operator** 名 オペレーター，交換手

□ **opportunity** 名 好機，適当な時期［状況］

□ **oppose** 動 反対する，敵対する

□ **opposite** 形 反対の，向こう側の

□ **or** 熟 **a ～ or two** 1～か2～，2，3の **either A or B** AかそれともB **for a moment or two** ほんの少しの間 **or else** さもないと **or so** ～かそこらで **sooner or later** 遅かれ早かれ **whether or not** ～かどうか

□ **order** 熟 **in order to** ～するために，～しようと **in perfect order** 完璧な状態で **in what order** どのような順序で

□ **Order of Freemen** 自由民団

□ **ordinary** 形 ①普通の，通常の ②並の，平凡な 名 普通の状態 **out of the ordinary** 並外れた

□ **organization** 名 組織(化)，編成，団体，機関

□ **organize** 動 組織する

□ **original** 形 始めの，元の，本来の

□ **originally** 副 元は，元来

□ **other** 熟 **each other** お互いに

□ **ought** 助《－to ～》当然～すべきである，きっと～するはずである

□ **out** 熟 **be out** 外出している，〔火・電灯などが〕消えて **break out** 発生する，急に起こる，（戦争が）勃発する **bring out**（物）をとりだす，引き出す **burst out laughing** 爆笑する **call out** 叫ぶ，呼び出す，声を掛ける **carry out** 外へ運び出す，［計画を］実行する **come out** 出てくる，出掛ける，姿を現す **come out friends** 友人になる **come out of** ～から出てくる **cry out** 叫ぶ **cut out** 切り取る，切り抜く **draw out** 引き抜く **find out** 見つけ出す，気がつく，知る，調べる，解明する **get out** 外に出る，出て行く，逃げ出す **get out of** ～から下車する，～から取り出す，～から外へ出る［抜け出る］ **give out** 分配する **go out** 外出する，外へ出る **go out of** ～から出る［消える］ **hold out** 差し出す，（腕を）伸ばす **jump out** 飛び出る **jump out of** ～から飛び出す **lay out** きちんと並べる，陳列する **lead out onto** ～の方へ導く **live out** 生き延びる，離れて暮らす **look out** ①外を見る ②気をつける，注意する **look out of**（窓などから）外を見る **look out over** ～をはるかに見渡す **make out** 作り上げる，認識する，立証する **out of** ①～から外へ，～から抜け出して ②～から作り出して，～を材料として ③～の範囲外に，～から離れて ④（ある数）の中から **out of luck** ついていない **out of reach** 手の届かないところに **out of sight** 見えないところに **point out** 指し示す，指摘する **pour out** どっと出てくる，～に注ぎだす，吐き出す **pull out** 引き抜く，引き出す，取り出す **push out** 突き出す **put out** ①外に出す，（手など）を（差し）出す ②（明かり・火を）消す **read out** 声を出して読む，読み上げる **rush out of** 急いで～から出てくる **sell out** 売り切る，裏切る **send out** 使いに出す，派遣する，発送する **set out** 出発する **speak out** はっきり遠慮なく言う **stare out** ～をじっと見つめる **stretch out** ①手足を伸ばす，背伸びする ②広がる **take out** 取り出す，取り外す，連れ出す，持って帰る **throw out** 放り出す **turn out** ～と判明する，（結局～に）なる **walk out of** ～から出る **way out** 出口，逃げ道，脱出方法，解決法 **work out** うまくいく，何とかなる，（問題を）解く，考え出す，答えが出る，～の結果になる **worn out** 擦り切れた

□ **outburst** 名 爆発，噴出

□ **outdo** 動 ～にまさる，～をしのぐ **outdo each other** お互い張り合う

□ **outdoors** 名《the－》戸外，野外

□ **outer** 形 外の，外側の

□ **outfitter** 名 洋服店

□ **outline** 名 ①外形，輪郭 ②概略

□ **outrun** 動 走って逃れる

□ **outsider** 名 よそ者，部外者，門外漢

□ **over** 熟 **all over** ～中で，全体に亘って，～の至る所で，全て終わって，もうだめで **be over** 終わる，〔向こう側に〕渡って，〔量や年齢などが〕越えて **bend over** かがむ，腰をかがめる，～に身をかがめる **climb over** ～を乗り越える **come over** やって来る **come over someone's face**〔表情などが〕（人）の顔に表れる **come over to** ～にやって来る **cry over** ～を嘆く **fall over** ～につまずく，～の上に倒れかかる **go over to** ～の前に［へ］行く，～に出向いて行く **hand over** 手渡す，引き渡す，譲渡する **jump over** ～の上を飛び越える **lean over** ～にかがみ込む **look out over** ～をはるかに見渡す **look over at** ～の方を見る **over and over** 何度も繰り返して **over and over again** 何度も繰り返して **over here** こっちへ［に］；ほら，さあ《人の注意を引く》 **over there** あそこに **run over to** ～へ急いでやってくる，ひと走りする **sweep over** 押し寄せる **take** over 引き継ぐ **talk over** ～について議論する **turn over** ひっくり返る［返す］, (ページを)めくる, 思いめぐらす, 引き渡す **walk over to** ～の方に歩いていく **watch over** 見守る, 見張る

- □ **overboard** 副船外へ
- □ **overcoat** 名オーバー, 外套
- □ **overcome** 動勝つ, 打ち勝つ, 克服する
- □ **overjoyed** 形大喜びして, 狂喜して
- □ **overlook** 動見落とす
- □ **overpower** 動圧倒する, 征服する
- □ **overtake** 動①追いつく ②上回る ③車を追い越す
- □ **owe** 動①(～を)負う, (～を人の)お陰とする ②(金を)借りている, (人に対して～の)義務がある
- □ **own** 熟 **of one's own** その人自身の **take the law into one's own hand** 私的制裁を与える
- □ **owner** 名持ち主, オーナー
- □ **Oxford Street** オックスフォード街

P

- □ **pace** 名歩調, 速度
- □ **pack** 動荷造りする, 詰め込む
- □ **package** 名包み, 小包, パッケージ
- □ **Paddington** 名パディントン駅
- □ **paid** 動pay (払う)の過去, 過去分詞 形雇われの, 有給の, 支払い済みの
- □ **pain** 熟 **put out of pain** 痛みから解放する, 楽にする
- □ **painful** 形①痛い, 苦しい, 痛ましい ②骨の折れる, 困難な
- □ **painter** 名画家
- □ **painting** 名絵(をかくこと), 絵画, 油絵
- □ **pair** 名(2つから成る)一対, 一組, ペア
- □ **pale** 形(顔色・人が)青ざめた, 青白い
- □ **palm** 名手のひら(状のもの)
- □ **pantry** 名食品貯蔵室
- □ **paper** 熟 **evening paper** 夕刊 **faked paper** 偽札 **morning paper** 朝刊 **unsigned police paper** 署名なしの逮捕状
- □ **pardon** 熟 **I do beg your pardon.** 大変失礼いたしました。
- □ **parlor** 名客間
- □ **part** 熟 **part of** ～の一部分 **part with** ～を手放す **play a part** 役目を果たす **take part in** ～に参加する
- □ **parted lips** 形半ば開いた唇
- □ **particular** 形①特別の ②詳細な 名事項, 細部, 《-s》詳細
- □ **particularly** 副特に, とりわけ
- □ **parting** 名別離, 別れ, 分離 **parting shot** 捨て台詞
- □ **partner** 名仲間, 同僚
- □ **party** 熟 **other party** 他の関係者 **third party** 第三者, 部外者
- □ **pass** 熟 **mountain pass** 山道, 峠 **pass along** ～を通る **pass for** ～で通る **pass out** 倒れる, 卒倒する **pass through** ～を通る, 通行する
- □ **passage** 名①通過, 通行, 通路 ②一節, 経過
- □ **passenger** 名乗客, 旅客
- □ **passing** 形通り過ぎる, 一時的な
- □ **passion** 名情熱, (～への)熱中, 激怒
- □ **passionately** 副激しく, 吐き出すように
- □ **password** 名合言葉, パスワード
- □ **past** 形過去の, この前の 名過去(の出来事) 前《時間・場所》～を過ぎて, ～を越して 副通り越して, 過ぎて
- □ **patch** 名小さな町, 村 **Hobson's Patch** ホブソンズ・パッチ《地名》
- □ **path** 名①(踏まれてできた)小道, 歩道 ②進路, 通路
- □ **pathway** 名小道, 通路
- □ **patience** 名我慢, 忍耐(力), 根気
- □ **patient** 形我慢［忍耐］強い, 根気のある
- □ **pattern** 名①決まった型, パターン, 柄, 型, 模様 ②手本, 模範
- □ **pause** 名①(活動の)中止, 休止 ②区切り 動休止する, 立ち止まる
- □ **pay** 動①支払う, 払う, 報いる, 償う ②割に合う, ペイする **pay a visit** ～を訪問する 名給料, 報い
- □ **peace** 熟 **at peace** 平和に, 安らかに, 心穏やかで **in peace** 平和のうちに, 安心して
- □ **peaceful** 形平和な, 穏やかな
- □ **peacefully** 副平和に, 穏やかに
- □ **peak** 名頂点, 最高点, 山頂, 峰 **mountain peak** 山頂
- □ **pearl** 名真珠
- □ **Peckham** 名ペッカム《ロンドンの地名》
- □ **Pennsylvania Small Arms Company** ペンシルバニア小火器会社
- □ **perfectly** 副完全に, 申し分なく

□ **performance** 名 ①実行, 行為 ②成績, できばえ, 業績
□ **perfume** 名 香り, 香水
□ **perhaps** 副 たぶん, ことによると
□ **Perkins** 名 パーキンス《人名》
□ **permission** 名 許可, 許し
□ **Pershore** 名 パーショア《地名》
□ **personal** 形 ①個人の, 私的な ②本人自らの ③容姿の
□ **persuade** 動 説得する, 促して～させる
□ **persuasion** 名 ①説得（力） ②信念, 信仰
□ **Pete** 名 ピート《人名》
□ **Philadelphia** 名 フィラデルフィア《地名》
□ **phosphorous** 名 リン
□ **photograph** 名 写真
□ **physical** 形 身体の, 肉体の
□ **physically** 副 肉体的に, 身体的に **be physically fit** 身体が健康である
□ **Piccadilly** 名 ピカデリー《ロンドンの地名》
□ **pick** 動 選ぶ, 拾いあげる **the pick of a bad lot** 無能の中から選んだまだマシな人, もの **pick up** 拾い上げる, 車で迎えに行く
□ **pile** 名 積み重ね, 堆積, （～の）山
□ **pill** 名 錠剤, ピル
□ **pillar** 名 ①柱, 支柱, 支え ②根幹
□ **pin** 名 ピン, 飾りピン, 細い留め具 動 ①ピンで留める ②くぎ付けにする
□ **Pinkerton's** 名 ピンカートン探偵局
□ **Pinto** 名 ピント《人名》
□ **pipe** 名 管, 筒, パイプ
□ **pity** 名 哀れみ, 同情, 残念なこと
□ **place** 熟 **in one place** 一ヶ所に **in the first place** 第一に, そもそも **take one's place** （人と）交代する, （人）の代わりをする, 後任になる **take place** 行われる, 起こる
□ **plain** 形 ①明白な, はっきりした ②簡素な, 無地の, 装飾のない ③平らな ④不細工な, 平凡な 名 高原, 草原
□ **plan to** ～するつもりである
□ **planning** 名 立案, 開発計画
□ **plantation** 名 大農園, 植林地
□ **plaster** 名 ①しっくい, 壁土, 石膏 ②ばんそうこう, 膏薬
□ **play a part** 役目を果たす, 加担する
□ **player** 名 ①競技者, 選手, 演奏者, 俳優 ②演奏装置
□ **pleasant** 形 ①（物事が）楽しい, 心地よい ②快活な, 愛想のよい
□ **please** 熟 **be pleased to** ～してうれしい **be pleased with** ～が気に入る **if you please** よろしければ
□ **pleased** 形 喜んだ, 気に入った **pleased with oneself** いい気になる, 満足する
□ **pleasing** 形 心地のよい, 楽しい
□ **pleasure** 名 喜び, 楽しみ, 満足, 娯楽 **(It's) my pleasure.** どういたしまして。
□ **plenty** 名 十分, たくさん, 豊富 **plenty of** たくさんの～
□ **pocketbook** 名 ①札入れ, ハンドバッグ ②手帳 ③文庫本
□ **point** 熟 **at this point** 現在のところ **fine points** 詳細 **point of view** 考え方, 視点 **point out** 指し示す, 指摘する **score a point against** ～をやり込める **There's no point in** ～しても意味がない **to the point** 要領を得た
□ **poison** 名 ①毒, 毒薬 ②害になるもの 動 毒を盛る, 毒する
□ **poisonous** 形 有毒な, 有害な
□ **poker** 名 火かき棒
□ **pole** 名 棒, さお, 柱
□ **police** 熟 **police chief** 警察署長 **police force** 警官隊 **police officer** 警察官 **unsigned police paper** 署名なしの逮捕状
□ **police-boat** 名 港湾警察が使用する船
□ **policeman** 名 警察官
□ **policemen** 名 policeman（警察官）の複数
□ **political** 形 ①政治の, 政党の, 政治的な ②策略的な
□ **politics** 名 政治（学）, 政策
□ **Pondicherry Lodge** ポンディシェリー荘
□ **pool** 名 水たまり, プール
□ **popularity** 名 人気, 流行
□ **population** 名 人口, 住民（数）
□ **Porlock** 名 ポーロック《人名（ペンネーム）》
□ **portrait** 名 肖像画
□ **pose** 動 ①ポーズをとる［とらせる］ ②気取る, 見せかける
□ **position** 名 ①位置, 場所, 姿勢 ②地位, 身分, 職 ③立場, 状況 **put oneself in the position of** 自分を～の立場に置く, ～の立場になって考える
□ **positive** 形 積極的な, 前向きな, 肯定的な, 好意的な
□ **possession** 名 ①所有（物） ②財産, 領土

□ **possibility** 名可能性, 見込み, 将来性

□ **possible** 形①可能な ②ありうる, 起こりうる **as ~ as possible** できるだけ~ **if possible** できるなら

□ **possibly** 副①あるいは, たぶん ②《否定文, 疑問文で》どうしても, できる限り, とても, なんとか

□ **post** 名駐屯地, 警戒区域

□ **postcard** 名(郵便)はがき

□ **post-marked** 形消印済みの

□ **postmaster** 名郵便局長

□ **pound** 名①ポンド《英国の通貨単位》②ポンド《重量の単位。453.6g》動①どんどんたたく, 打ち砕く ②ドクンドクンと波打つ

□ **pour** 動①注ぐ, 浴びせる ②流れ出る, 流れ込む ③ざあざあ降る **pour out** どっと出てくる, ~に注ぎだす, 吐き出す

□ **power** 熟 **in one's power** 手中に, 思いのままに

□ **powerful** 形力強い, 実力のある, 影響力のある

□ **powerful-looking** 形屈強そうな

□ **powerless** 形力のない, 頼りない, 弱い

□ **practical** 形①実際的な, 実用的な, 役に立つ ②経験を積んだ

□ **practice** 名(医者の)開業場所, 診療所

□ **praise** 動ほめる, 賞賛する **praise to the sky** 褒めちぎる 名賞賛

□ **precious** 形①貴重な, 高価な ②かわいい, 大事な

□ **prediction** 名予言, 予報, 予測

□ **prefer** 動(~のほうを)好む, (~のほうが)よいと思う

□ **preparation** 名①準備, したく ②心構え

□ **prepare for** ~の準備をする

□ **prepared** 形準備[用意]のできた

□ **presence** 名①存在すること ②出席, 態度

□ **present** 熟 **at present** 今のところ, 現在は, 目下

□ **press** 動①圧する, 押す, プレスする ②強要する, 迫る **press on** どんどん進める, 続行する

□ **pretend** 動①ふりをする, 装う ②あえて~しようとする

□ **prevent** 動①妨げる, じゃまする ②予防する, 守る, 《- ~ from …》~が…できない[しない]ようにする

□ **previous** 形前の, 先の

□ **price** 名値段, 代価

□ **pride** 名誇り, 自慢, 自尊心

□ **Princetown** 名プリンスタウン《地名》

□ **Princetown Prison** プリンスタウン刑務所

□ **print** 熟 **in print** 紙上に

□ **printed word** 活字

□ **prison** 名①刑務所, 監獄 ②監禁 **prison cell** 刑務所の監房

□ **prisoner** 名囚人, 捕虜

□ **private** 形①私的な, 個人の ②民間の, 私立の ③内密の, 人里離れた **private detective** 私立探偵

□ **privately** 副内密に, 非公式に, 個人的に

□ **probability** 名見込み, 可能性 **in all probability** たぶん, おそらく

□ **probably** 副たぶん, あるいは

□ **proceed** 動進む, 進展する, 続ける

□ **process** 名①過程, 経過, 進行 ②手順, 方法, 製法, 加工

□ **professor** 名教授, 師匠

□ **Professor Moriarty** モリアーティ教授

□ **progress** 名①進歩, 前進 ②成り行き, 経過

□ **promise** 熟 **keep one's promise** 約束を守る

□ **proof** 名証拠, 証明

□ **proper** 形適した, 適切な, 正しい

□ **properly** 副適切に, きっちりと

□ **property** 名財産, 所有物[地]

□ **prophet** 名予言者, 預言者

□ **proportion** 名①割合, 比率, 分け前 ②釣り合い, 比例 **in proportion to** ~に比例して

□ **propose** 動①申し込む, 提案する ②結婚を申し込む

□ **protection** 名保護, 保護するもの[人]

□ **protest** 動①主張[断言]する ②抗議する, 反対する

□ **proud** 形①自慢の, 誇った, 自尊心のある ②高慢な, 尊大な

□ **prove** 動①証明する ②(~であることが)わかる, (~と)なる

□ **proven** 動prove(証明する)の過去分詞

□ **provided** 接もし~ならば, 仮に~とすれば

□ **province** 名①州, 省 ②地方, 田舎

□ **psst** 間ちょっと, おい

□ **public** 名一般の人々, 大衆 **in public** 人前で, 公然と 形公の, 公開の **public duty** 公務

□ **publicly** 副公に, 公然と, 人前で, 世間に

□ **publish** 動 ①発表[公表]する ②出版[発行]する

□ **puddle** 名 ①水たまり ②こね土

□ **pull in** (網, 釣り糸を)引く

□ **pull off** 離れる, 去る, (衣服などを)脱ぐ

□ **pull out** 引き抜く, 引き出す, 取り出す

□ **pull up** ①立ち止まる ②引っ張りあげる **pull up outside** (建物などの)外に止まる, 車などを止める

□ **punish** 動罰する, ひどい目にあわせる

□ **punishment** 名 ①罰, 処罰 ②罰を受けること

□ **purpose** 熟 **to the purpose** 目的にかなって

□ **purse** 名 ①財布, 小銭入れ ②小物入れ

□ **push back** 押し返す, 押しのける

□ **push on** 続行する, 継続する

□ **push one's way through** かき分けて前に出る

□ **push out** 突き出す

□ **push through** (人ごみなどを)かき分ける

□ **put** 熟 **put ~ ashore** ~を上陸させる **put away** 片づける, 取っておく **put back** (もとの場所に)戻す, 返す **put down** 下に置く, 下ろす **put in** ~の中に入れる **put ~ into …** ~を…の状態にする, ~を…に突っ込む **put off** ~から逃れる, 延期する, 要求をそらす, 不快にさせる, やめさせる **put on** ①~を身につける, 着る ②~を…の上に置く **put oneself in the position of** 自分を~の立場に置く, ~の立場になって考える **put out** ①外に出す, (手など)を(差し)出す ②(明かり・火を)消す **put out of pain** 痛みから解放する, 楽にする **put up one's hand** 手を挙げる **put up with** ~を我慢する

□ **puzzle** 名 ①難問, なぞ, 当惑 ②パズル 動迷わせる, 当惑する[させる]

□ **puzzled** 形当惑した, 困惑した

□ **puzzlement** 名当惑, 困惑

Q

□ **quality** 名 ①質, 性質, 品質 ②特性 ③良質

□ **quantity** 名 ①量 ②《-ties》多量, たくさん

□ **quarrel** 動けんかする, 口論する

□ **quarter** 名 ①4分の1, 25セント, 15分, 3カ月 ②方面, 地域 ③部署 **quarter to** ~時15分前

□ **queen** 名女王, 王妃

□ **queer** 形奇妙な, あやしい, 気分が悪い

□ **question** 熟 **in question** 問題の, 論争中の

□ **questioning** 形尋ねるような, 不審そうな

□ **quickly** 副敏速に, 急いで, すぐに

□ **quietly** 副 ①静かに ②平穏に, 控えめに

□ **quiet-natured** 形静かな, 穏やかな, 内気な

□ **quit** 動やめる, 辞職する, 中止する

□ **quite** 熟 **not quite** まったく~だというわけではない

R

□ **rabbit** 名ウサギ

□ **race** 名人種, 民族

□ **RACHE** 死体のそばの壁に血文字で書かれていた謎のことば

□ **Rachel** 名レイチェル《女性の名前》

□ **ragged** 形 ①ぼろぼろの, ぼろを着た ②ぎざぎざの, ごつごつした

□ **railroad** 名鉄道, 路線

□ **raincoat** 名レインコート

□ **raise** 動 ①上げる, 高める ②起こす ③~を育てる ④(資金を)調達する

□ **rajah** 名ラジャ《〔インドの〕国王, 支配者》

□ **Rance** 名ランス《人名》

□ **rang** 動 ring (鳴る)の過去

□ **range** 名列, 連なり, 範囲

□ **rare** 形 ①まれな, 珍しい, 逸品の ②希薄な ③(肉が)生焼けの, レアの

□ **rather** 副 ①むしろ, かえって ②かなり, いくぶん, やや ③それどころか逆に **rather than** ~よりむしろ **would rather** ~する方がよい **would rather ~ than …** …よりむしろ~したい

□ **reach** 熟 **beyond the reach of** ~の力の及ばない, ~の手の届かない **out of reach** 手の届かないところに **reach for** ~に手を伸ばす, ~を取ろうとする **within reach of** ~の手の届くところに

□ **react** 動反応する, 対処する

□ **read out** 声を出して読む, 読み上げる

□ **reader** 名 ①読者 ②読本, リーダー

□ **reading** 名読書, 読み物, 朗読

□ **ready** 熟 **be ready for** 準備が整って, ~に期待する **be ready to** すぐに[いつでも]~できる, ~する構えで **get ready** 用意[支度]をする

ready to go すっかり準備が整った

□ **realize** 動理解する, 実現する

□ **rear** 形後ろの

□ **reason for** ～の理由

□ **reasonable** 形筋の通った, 分別のある

□ **reasoning** 名推理

□ **rebellion** 名反乱, 反抗, 謀反, 暴動

□ **rebuilt** 動rebuild (再建する) の過去, 過去分詞

□ **recall** 動思い出す, 思い出させる, 呼び戻す

□ **recent** 形近ごろの, 近代の

□ **recently** 副近ごろ, 最近

□ **reckon** 動～だと思う, 推測する

□ **recognizable** 動見覚えがある, 認識できる

□ **recognize** 動認める, 認識[承認]する

□ **recommend** 動①推薦する ②勧告する, 忠告する

□ **reconsider** 動考え直す, 再検討する

□ **record** 名①記録, 登録, 履歴 ②(音楽などの) レコード off the record 非公式で, オフレコで on record 記録されて, 公表されて

□ **recover** 動①取り戻す, ばん回する ②回復する

□ **reddish** 形赤みがかかった

□ **red-faced** 形赤ら顔の

□ **rediscovery** 名再発見

□ **redness** 名赤み

□ **refer** 動①《-to ～》～に言及する, ～と呼ぶ ②～を参照する, ～に問い合わせる

□ **refreshed** 形さわやかになって, 再び元気づいて

□ **refuse** 動拒絶する, 断る

□ **regard** 動①(～を…と) 見なす ②尊敬する, 重きを置く ③関係がある

□ **Regent Street** リージェント街

□ **region** 名①地方, 地域 ②範囲

□ **registered post** 書留郵便

□ **regular** 形①規則的な, 秩序のある ②定期的な, 一定の, 習慣的

□ **regularly** 副整然と, 規則的に

□ **Reilly** 名ライリー《人名》

□ **rejoin** 動復帰する, 再び一緒になる

□ **relate** 動①関連がある, かかわる, うまく折り合う ②物語る

□ **relation** 名①(利害) 関係, 間柄 ②親戚

□ **relative** 名親戚, 同族

□ **relax** 動①くつろがせる ②ゆるめる, 緩和する

□ **release** 動解き放す, 釈放する

□ **relief** 名(苦痛・心配などの) 除去, 軽減, 安心, 気晴らし

□ **religion** 名宗教, ～教, 信条

□ **rely** 動(人が…に) 頼る, 当てにする rely on ～を頼り[当て]にする, ～を信頼する

□ **remain** 動①残っている, 残る ②(～の) ままである[いる]

□ **remaining** 形残った, 残りの

□ **remark** 名①注意, 注目, 観察 ②意見, 記事, 批評

□ **remarkable** 形①異常な, 例外的な ②注目に値する, すばらしい

□ **remarkably** 副目立って, きわだって

□ **remind** 動思い出させる, 気づかせる

□ **reminder** 名思い出させるもの

□ **remove** 動①取り去る, 除去する ②(衣類を) 脱ぐ

□ **renew** 動(～を) 再び始める, 取り戻す

□ **repair** 動修理[修繕]する 名修理, 修繕 repair yard 修理場

□ **repeat** 動繰り返す

□ **replace** 動①取り替える, 差し替える ②元に戻す

□ **reply** 名答え, 返事, 応答

□ **reporter** 名レポーター, 報告者, 記者

□ **represent** 動①表現する ②意味する ③代表する

□ **reprint** 名増刷, 再版, 復刻版

□ **reproduce** 動①再生する, 再現する ②複写する

□ **rescue** 動救う 名救助, 救出

□ **rescuer** 名救助者

□ **rescuing** 形救助する

□ **resistance** 名抵抗, 反抗, 敵対

□ **respect** 名①尊敬, 尊重 ②注意, 考慮 win respect 敬意を得る 動尊敬[尊重]する

□ **respectable** 形①尊敬すべき, 立派な ②(量など) 相当な

□ **respectfully** 副うやうやしく, つつしんで, 丁重に

□ **responsible** 形責任のある, 信頼できる, 確実な make responsible for ～を引き受ける

□ **restful** 形安らかな, 落ち着いた

□ **restless** 形落ち着かない, 不安な

□ **restore** 動元に戻す, 復活させる

□ **result** 名結果, 成り行き, 成績 **as a result** その結果(として) **as a result of** ～の結果(として) 動(結果として)起こる, 生じる, 結局～になる

□ **retire** 動引き下がる, 退職[引退]する

□ **retold** 動retell(再び語る)の過去, 過去分詞

□ **return** 熟**give ～ in return for** …の見返りに～を与える **in return** お返しとして **in return for** ～に対する見返りとして, ～の交換条件として **return to** ～に戻る, ～に帰る

□ **reveal** 動明らかにする, 暴露する, もらす

□ **revenge** 名復讐 **get revenge** 復しゅうする

□ **review** 動①批評する ②再調査する ③復習する

□ **reward** 動報いる, 報酬を与える

□ **Reynolds** 名ジョシュア・レイノルズ《Sir Joshua Reynolds, 肖像画家, 1723–1792》

□ **ribbon of** リボン状に長く延びる

□ **Richmond** 名リッチモンド《地名》

□ **ride** 熟**give ～ a ride** ～を車で送る

□ **rider** 名(馬などの)乗り手, ライダー

□ **rifle** 名ライフル銃

□ **right** 熟**all right** 大丈夫で, よろしい, 申し分ない, わかった, 承知した **right away** すぐに **right now** 今すぐに, たった今 **That's all right.** いいんですよ。

□ **rightful** 形正当な, 当然の

□ **ring** 名輪, 円形, 指輪 動鳴る, 鳴らす

□ **ringing** 名(鐘がなる)音

□ **risen** 動rise(昇る)の過去分詞

□ **risk** 動危険にさらす, 賭ける, 危険をおかす

□ **river** 熟**down the river** 川下に

□ **riverside** 名川辺

□ **roadway** 名車道

□ **roar** 動①ほえる ②(人が)わめく 名うなり声, ほえ声, 怒号

□ **rob** 動奪う, 金品を盗む, 襲う **rob ～ of …** ～から…を奪う

□ **rocky** 形①岩の多い ②ぐらぐら揺れる, ぐらつく

□ **rode** 動ride(乗る)の過去

□ **Rodger Baskerville** ロジャー・バスカヴィル《人名》

□ **roll** 動①転がる, 転がす ②(波などが)うねる, 横揺れする **roll up** 巻き上げる

□ **romance** 名恋愛(関係・感情), 恋愛[空想・冒険]小説

□ **romantic** 形ロマンチックな, 空想的な

□ **roof** 名屋根(のようなもの)

□ **room** 熟**dining room** 食堂 **dressing room** 更衣室 **take a room** (宿で)部屋を取る

□ **rope** 名綱, なわ, ロープ

□ **rosy** 形バラのような, バラ色の, (顔色が健康的に)赤い

□ **rough** 形①(手触りが)粗い ②荒々しい, 未加工の **with a rough hand** 粗い筆跡で

□ **rough-looking** 形見かけの粗野な

□ **round** 熟**go round** ～の周りを進む, 歩き回る, 回って行く **walk round** ブラブラ歩き回る

□ **route** 名道, 道筋, 進路, 回路

□ **row** 名論争, 騒ぎ

□ **rub** 動こする

□ **ruby** 名ルビー

□ **rudder** 名〔船の〕かじ

□ **rude** 形粗野な, 無作法な, 失礼な

□ **ruin** 動破滅させる

□ **run** 熟**make one's blood run cold** (人)をゾッとさせる, 血の気を引かせる ②運営する ③(話などが)書いてある ④(ひも状のものが)ひろがる, 延びる **run across** 走って渡る **run after** ～を追いかける **run along** おいとまする, 立ち去る **run around** 走り回る **run away** 走り去る, 逃げ出す **run away from** ～から逃れる **run cold** 冷たくなる **run down** 駆け下りる **run for one's life** 死に物狂いで走る, 一目散に逃げる **run in** 走って入る **run into** (思いがけず)～に出会う, ～に駆け込む, ～の中に走って入る **run off** 走り去る, 逃げ去る **run out** 尽きる, なくなる **run over to** ～へ急いでやってくる, ひと走りする **run through** 走り抜ける **run up** ～に走り寄る **run up and down** かけずり回る

□ **rush** 動突進する, せき立てる **rush down** 猛然と～に駆け寄る **rush forward** 突進する **rush in** ～に突入する, ～に駆けつける **rush out of** 急いで～から出てくる **rush over** 急いでやってくる 名突進, 突撃, 殺到

□ **Russia** 名ロシア《国名》

□ **Rutland Island** ラットランド島

S

□ **saddened** 形悲しみに包まれた

□ **sadly** 副悲しそうに, 不幸にも

□ **sadness** 名悲しみ, 悲哀

□ **safeguard** 動 守る, 保護する
□ **safely** 副 安全に, 間違いなく
□ **safety** 名 安全, 無事, 確実
□ **sahib** 名 閣下, 殿, だんな
□ **sailing** 名 船旅, 出航
□ **sailor** 名 船員, (ヨットの) 乗組員
□ **saint** 名 聖人, 聖徒
□ **sake** 名 (〜の) ため, 利益, 目的 **for God's sake** お願いだから
□ **salary** 名 給料
□ **Sally** 名 サリー《人名》
□ **saloon** 名 ①大広間, 談話室 ②酒場 **Lake Saloon** レイク・サルーン《酒場の名》
□ **same** 熟 **the same 〜 as …** …と同じ(ような)〜
□ **sank** 動 sink (沈む) の過去
□ **sapphire** 名 サファイア
□ **satisfaction** 名 満足
□ **satisfied** 形 満足した
□ **satisfy** 動 ①満足させる, 納得させる ②(義務を) 果たす, 償う
□ **satisfying** 形 満足を与える, 十分な
□ **Sawyer** 名 ソーヤー《人名》
□ **say** 熟 **go on to say** さらに続けて〜と言う **say hello to** 〜によろしく言う **What do you say to 〜?** 〜はいかがですか。
□ **Scanlan** 名 スキャンラン《人名》
□ **scare** 動 こわがらせる, おびえる
□ **scared** 形 おびえた, びっくりした
□ **scarf** 名 スカーフ
□ **scarlet** 名 緋色, 深紅
□ **scatter** 動 ①ばらまく, 分散する ②《be -ed》散在する
□ **scene** 名 ①現場, 風景 ②大騒ぎ, 騒動
□ **scenery** 名 風景, 景色
□ **schoolmaster** 名 ①先生 ②校長
□ **science** 熟 **man of science** 科学者 **science of deduction** 推理の科学
□ **scientific** 形 科学の, 科学的な
□ **scientist** 熟 **natural scientist** 自然科学者, 博物学者
□ **score** 動 (競技で) 得点する, 採点する **score a point against** 〜をやり込める
□ **Scotland Yard** ロンドン警視庁の通称, 愛称
□ **Scotsman** 名 スコットランド人
□ **Scowrers** 名 スカウラーズ《秘密結社の名》
□ **scratch** 名 ひっかき傷
□ **scream** 名 金切り声, 絶叫 動 叫ぶ, 金切り声を出す
□ **seal** 動 印を押す, ふたをする, 密閉する
□ **search** 動 捜し求める, 調べる 名 捜査, 探索, 調査
□ **searchlight** 名 サーチライト, 探照灯
□ **seat** 熟 **take a seat** 席にすわる
□ **secrecy** 名 秘密であること
□ **secret** 形 秘密の, 隠れた 名 秘密
□ **secretary** 名 秘書, 書記
□ **secretly** 副 秘密に, 内緒で
□ **see** 熟 **I see** なるほど, そうか **Let me see.** ええと。 **live to see** 〜のために生きる **see 〜 as …** 〜を…と考える **see for yourself** 自分で確かめる **see if** 〜かどうかを確かめる **See you.** ではまた。 **you see** あのね, いいですか
□ **seeker** 名 追求者
□ **seem** 動 (〜に) 見える, (〜のように) 思われる **seem to be** 〜であるように思われる
□ **Selden** 名 セルデン《名》
□ **self-defense** 名 自衛, 自己防衛, 正当防衛
□ **selfish** 形 わがままな, 自分本位の, 利己主義の
□ **sell out** 売り切る, 裏切る
□ **send for** 〜を呼びにやる, 〜を呼び寄せる
□ **send off** (メッセージを) 送る
□ **send out** 使いに出す, 派遣する, 発送する
□ **sender** 名 送り主, 荷主, 発信人
□ **sense** 名 ①感覚, 感じ ②《-s》意識, 正気, 本性 ③常識, 分別, センス ④意味 **common sense** 常識, 共通感覚 **in a sense** ある意味では **make sense** 意味をなす, よくわかる
□ **sentence** 名 文
□ **separate** 動 ①分ける, 分かれる, 隔てる ②別れる, 別れさせる
□ **separately** 副 離れて, 独立して, 別々に
□ **separation** 名 分離(点), 離脱, 分類, 別離
□ **sergeant** 名 軍曹, 巡査部長
□ **serious** 形 ①まじめな, 真剣な ②重大な, 深刻な, (病気などが) 重い
□ **serious-looking** 形 しかつめらしい
□ **seriously** 副 ①真剣に, まじめに ②重大に
□ **servant** 名 召使, 使用人, しもべ
□ **serve** 動 ①仕える, 奉仕する ②(役目を) 果たす, 務める, 役に立つ

☐ **service** 名 ①勤務, 業務 ②奉仕, 貢献 **be of service to** ～の手助けになる

☐ **set free** (人)を解放する, 釈放される, 自由の身になる

☐ **set mind** 決意する, 心に決める

☐ **set off** 出発する

☐ **set out** 出発する

☐ **set up** 設ける, 始める **set up a family** 家族(家庭)を作る **set up a household** 所帯を構える, 家庭を持つ

☐ **setting** 名 設定, 周囲の環境

☐ **settle** 動 ①安定する[させる], 落ち着く, 落ち着かせる ②《- in ～》～に移り住む, 定住する **settle down** 落ち着く, 興奮がおさまる

☐ **settled** 形 固定した, 落ち着いた, 解決した

☐ **seventeenth** 名 17, 17人[個] 形 17の, 17人[個]の

☐ **shadow** 名 ①影, 暗がり ②亡霊

☐ **shadowy** 形 影のある, 陰の多い, 暗い, おぼろげな

☐ **Shafter** 名 シェフター《人名》

☐ **shake** 動 ①振る, 揺れる, 揺さぶる, 震える ②動揺させる **shake hands** 握手をする **shake one's head** 首を振る ②動揺させる, 狼狽させる 名 振ること

☐ **shaken** 動 shake (振る)の過去分詞 **be shaken to the soul** 心の底から震える

☐ **shall** 熟 **Shall I ～?** (私が) ～しましょうか。**Shall we ～?** (一緒に) ～しましょうか。**She shall not be buried in that.** こんなものをつけたまま彼女を埋葬させるものか。**We shall make something of you yet.** 君への評価を改めなければならないな。

☐ **shamefully** 副 恥ずかしくも, 不面目に

☐ **shape** 名 ①形, 姿, 型 ②状態, 調子

☐ **shaped** 形 (～の)形をした

☐ **sharp** 形 ①鋭い, とがった ②刺すような, きつい ③鋭敏な ④急な

☐ **sharper-eyed** 名 目のいい人

☐ **sharply** 副 鋭く, 激しく, はっきりと

☐ **shave** 動 (ひげ・顔を)そる, 削る

☐ **sheep** 名 羊

☐ **sheet** 名 ①シーツ ②(紙などの)1枚

☐ **shelf** 名 棚

☐ **shelter** 名 ①避難所, 隠れ家 ②保護, 避難

☐ **Sheridan Street** シェラディン通り

☐ **Sherlock Holmes** シャーロック・ホームズ《観察力と推理力に優れた探偵》

☐ **shilling** 名 シリング《英国の旧通貨単位。1/20ポンド》

☐ **shine** 動 ①光る, 輝く ②光らせる, 磨く

☐ **shipmate** 名 同じ船の船員仲間

☐ **shocked** 形 ～にショックを受けて, 憤慨して

☐ **shocking** 形 衝撃的な, ショッキングな

☐ **shoe** 名 ①靴 ②(馬の)蹄鉄

☐ **shoeless** 形 靴をはかない, 靴なしの

☐ **Sholto** 名 ショルトー《人名》

☐ **shone** 動 shine (光る)の過去, 過去分詞

☐ **shook** 動 shake (振る)の過去

☐ **shooting** 名 射殺

☐ **shopping** 名 買い物 **go shopping** 買い物に行く

☐ **shore** 名 岸, 海岸, 陸

☐ **shorten** 動 短くする, 縮める

☐ **shorthand** 形 速記の

☐ **short-handed** 形 人手不足の

☐ **shortly** 副 まもなく, すぐに

☐ **shotgun** 名 散弾銃

☐ **should have done** ～すべきだった(のにしなかった)《仮定法》

☐ **shoulder** 名 肩 動 肩にかつぐ

☐ **show someone in** [人を]中に案内する, 招き入れる

☐ **shown** 動 show (見せる)の過去分詞

☐ **shut** 動 ①閉まる, 閉める, 閉じる ②たたむ ③閉じ込める ④shutの過去, 過去分詞

☐ **shy** 形 内気な, 恥ずかしがりの, 臆病な

☐ **sick** 熟 **feel sick** 気分が悪い

☐ **sickness** 名 病気

☐ **side** 名 側, 横, そば, 斜面 **either side of** ～の両側に **far side** 向こう側, 反対側 **on each side** それぞれの側に **on either side** 両側に **one side** 片側 **side by side** 並んで 形 ①側面の, 横の ②副次的な

☐ **sideburn** 名 男性の顔の耳の前に生えているひげ

☐ **sigh** 動 ため息をつく, ため息をついて言う 名 ため息

☐ **sight** 熟 **catch sight of** ～を見つける, ～を見かける **in sight** 視野に入って **mere sight of ～** ～を見ただけで **out of sight** 見えないところに

☐ **signal** 名 信号, 合図

☐ **Sikh** 名 シーク教徒

☐ **silence** 名 沈黙, 無言, 静寂 **in silence** 黙って,

沈黙のうちに
□ **silent** 形 ①無言の, 黙っている ②静かな, 音を立てない ③活動しない
□ **silently** 副 静かに, 黙って
□ **silk** 形 絹の, 絹製の
□ **sill** 名〔窓・戸などの〕敷居
□ **silver** 名 銀, 銀貨, 銀色 形 銀製の
□ **similar** 形 同じような, 類似した, 相似の
□ **simply** 副 ①簡単に ②単に, ただ ③まったく, 完全に
□ **sin** 名（道徳・宗教上の）罪
□ **since** 熟 **ever since** それ以来ずっと **long since** ずっと以前に
□ **Singapore** 名 シンガポール《国名》
□ **Singh** 名 シン《人名》
□ **single** 形 たった1つの **single visit** 一度きりの訪問
□ **single-handed** 形 単独の, 自力の
□ **sink** 名（台所の）流し
□ **sit on** ～の上に乗る, ～の上に乗って動けないようにする
□ **sit still** じっとしている, じっと座っている
□ **sit up** 起き上がる, 上半身を起こす, 寝ないで起きている
□ **sit up all night** 徹夜する
□ **sitting room** 居間, お茶の間
□ **sitting-room** 名 居間, お茶の間
□ **situation** 名 ①場所, 位置 ②状況, 境遇, 立場
□ **skill** 名 ①技能, 技術 ②上手, 熟練
□ **skilled** 形 熟練した, 腕のいい, 熟練を要する
□ **skillful** 形 熟練した, 腕利きの
□ **sky** 熟 **praise to the sky** 褒めちぎる
□ **slam** 動 ばたんと閉まる, 急に閉る 名 ばたん（という音）
□ **slamming** 名 バタンと閉めること
□ **sleep** 熟 **go to sleep** 寝る **sleep in** 寝床に入る, 住み込む **sleep well** よく眠る
□ **sleeper** 名 眠っている人［動物, 植物］ **light sleeper** 眠りの浅い人
□ **sleepily** 副 眠そうに
□ **sleeping** 形 眠っている, 休止している
□ **sleeve** 名 袖, たもと, スリーブ
□ **slid** 動 slide（滑る）の過去, 過去分詞
□ **slight** 形 ①わずかな ②ほっそりして ③とるに足らない
□ **slightly** 副 わずかに, いささか
□ **slip** 動 ①滑る, 滑らせる, 滑って転ぶ ②するっと着ける, 装着させる **slip up** ずり上がる
□ **slipper** 名《通例-s》部屋ばき, スリッパ **carpet slipper** 家庭用スリッパ
□ **sloping** 形 傾斜した, 勾配のある
□ **slowly** 副 遅く, ゆっくり
□ **Small** 名 スモール《人名》
□ **smart** 形 ①利口な, 抜け目のない ②きちんとした, 洗練された
□ **smelt** 動 smell（においがする）の過去, 過去分詞
□ **smile at** ～に微笑みかける
□ **smiling** 形 微笑する, にこにこした
□ **Smith** 名 スミス《人名》
□ **smoke** 動 喫煙する, 煙を出す **smoke out** いぶり出す, 明るみに出す 名 煙, 煙状のもの
□ **smoker** 名 喫煙家, たばこを吸う人
□ **smoking** 形 煙っている, 喫煙の **smoking room** 喫煙室
□ **smooth** 形 滑らかな, すべすべした
□ **snow-capped** 形 雪を頂いた, 雪をかぶった
□ **so** 熟 **and so** そこで, それだから, それで **and so on** ～など, その他もろもろ **As I did so** そうしているうちに **or so** ～かそこらで **so far** 今までのところ, これまでは **so long as** ～する限りは **so many** 非常に多くの **so that** ～するために, それで, ～できるように **so ～ that …** 非常に～なので…
□ **so-called** 形 いわゆる
□ **society** 名 社会, 世間
□ **sock** 名《-s》ソックス, 靴下
□ **sofa** 名 ソファー
□ **soften** 動 柔らかくなる［する］, 和らぐ
□ **softly** 副 柔らかに, 優しく, そっと
□ **soil** 名 土, 土地
□ **soldier** 名 兵士, 兵卒
□ **sole** 名 足の裏, 靴底
□ **solid** 形 ①固体［固形］の ②頑丈な
□ **Salt Lake City** ソルトレイクシティー《ユタ州の州都》
□ **solution** 名 解決, 解明
□ **solve** 動 解く, 解決する
□ **some** 熟 **for some time** しばらくの間 **in some way** 何とかして, 何らかの方法で **some time** いつか, そのうち, しばらく
□ **somebody** 代 誰か, ある人
□ **somehow** 副 ①どうにかこうにか, ともかく,

何とかして ②どういうわけか

□ **someone** 代 ある人, 誰か

□ **Somerton, Dr.** ソマートン医師

□ **something** 代 ①ある物, 何か ②いくぶん, 多少 **be on to something** 何かにありつく

□ **sometime** 副 時々

□ **sometimes** 副 時々, 時たま

□ **somewhat** 副 いくらか, やや, 多少

□ **somewhere** 副 ①どこかへ[に] ②いつか, およそ

□ **soon** 熟 **as soon as** ～するとすぐ, ～するや否や **no sooner** ～するや否や **sooner or later** 遅かれ早かれ **would sooner ～ than …** …するよりはむしろ～した方がマシだ

□ **sore** 形 痛い, 傷のある

□ **sorrow** 名 悲しみ, 後悔

□ **sorry** 熟 **be sorry for** ～をすまないと思う **feel sorry for** ～をかわいそうに思う

□ **sort** 名 種類, 品質 **a sort of** ～のようなもの, 一種の～ **what sort of** どういう

□ **soul** 名 ①魂 ②精神, 心 **be shaken to the soul** 心の底から震える

□ **south** 熟 **down in the south** 南の方で

□ **South Africa** 南アフリカ

□ **southwest** 形 南西の, 南西向きの

□ **spaniel** 名 スパニエル犬

□ **spare** 動 ①取っておく ②(～を)惜しむ, 節約する ③免れる

□ **speak about** ～について話す

□ **speak of** ～を口にする

□ **speak out** はっきり遠慮なく言う

□ **speak to** ～と話す

□ **speak up** 率直に話す, はっきりしゃべる

□ **speaking** 形 話す, ものを言う 名 話すこと, 談話, 演説

□ **speciality** 名 専門, 本職, 得意

□ **specialty** 名 得意なこと, 十八番

□ **sped** 動 speed (急ぐ) の過去, 過去分詞

□ **speechless** 形 無言の, 口がきけない

□ **speed** 名 速力, 速度

□ **speedily** 副 早く, 急いで

□ **spirit** 名 ①霊 ②精神, 気力

□ **spite** 名 悪意, うらみ **in spite of** ～にもかかわらず

□ **splash** 動 (水・泥を)はね飛ばす

□ **spoil** 動 ①台なしにする, だめになる ②甘やかす

□ **spot** 名 ①地点, 場所, 立場 ②斑点, しみ **on the spot** その場で, ただちに 動 ①～を見つける ②点を打つ, しみをつける

□ **spotlight** 名 スポットライト

□ **sprang** 動 spring (跳ねる) の過去

□ **spring to one's feet** サッと立ち上がる

□ **spy** 動 ひそかに見張る, スパイする

□ **square** 名 四角い広場, (市外の)一区画 形 正方形の, 四角な, 直角な, 角ばった

□ **square-toed** 形 つま先が四角い

□ **sshh** 間 しーっ

□ **St. Helena** セントヘレナ《島名》

□ **St. Louis** セントルイス《米国の地名》

□ **St. Oliver's Private scool** セント・オリバー私立学校

□ **stab** 動 (突き)刺す

□ **staff** 名 職員, スタッフ

□ **stage** 名 段階

□ **stain** 名 しみ, よごれ **blood stain** 血痕

□ **stained** 動 stain (汚す, 傷つける) の過去形

□ **stair** 名 ①(階段の)1段 ②《-s》階段, はしご

□ **staircase** 名 階段

□ **Stamford** 名 スタンフォード《人名》

□ **stamp** 名 ①印 ②切手 動 踏みつける

□ **stand** 熟 **let nothing stand between** ～との間の疑問を何一つ放置しない **stand against** 刃向かう, 敵対する **stand by** ①そばに立つ ②傍観する **stand for** ～を意味する **stand up** 立ち上がる

□ **Stanger** 名 ステンジャー《人名》

□ **Stangerson** 名 スタンガーソン《人名》

□ **Stapleton** 名 ステープルトン《人名》

□ **stare** 動 じっと[じろじろ]見る **stare out** ～をじっと見つめる 名 じっと見ること, 凝視

□ **staring** 形 じっと見る, 凝視する

□ **start** 熟 **get started** 始める **start doing** ～し始める **start off** 出発する

□ **starve** 動 餓死する, 飢えさせる

□ **state** 名 ①あり様, 状態 ②国家, (アメリカなどの)州 ③階層, 地位 動 述べる, 表明する

□ **statement** 名 声明, 供述, 述べること

□ **stay** 熟 **stay at** (場所)に泊まる **stay away from** ～から離れている **stay behind** 後ろにつく, 後に残る, 留守番をする **stay in** 家にいる, (場所)に泊まる, 滞在する **stay up** 起きている **stay with** ～の所に泊まる

□ **steadily** 副しっかりと
□ **steady** 形 ①しっかりした, 安定した, 落ち着いた ②堅実な, まじめな
□ **steal** 動盗む
□ **stealing** 名窃盗
□ **steamboat** 名蒸気船
□ **steamship** 名汽船, 蒸気船
□ **steep** 形険しい
□ **step over** またぐ
□ **step up** (低いところから)上がる
□ **Steve Wilson** スティーブ・ウィルソン《人名》
□ **steward** 名 ①給仕 ②スチュワード, 乗客係
□ **stick** 名棒, 杖 **dry-land marker stick** 乾燥地の目印棒 **guiding stick** 目印の棒 **walking stick** 杖, ステッキ
□ **sticky** 形くっつく, 粘着性の
□ **stiff** 形 ①堅い, 頑固な ②堅苦しい
□ **stiffly** 副硬く, 堅苦しく, きごちなく
□ **still** 熟 **sit still** じっとしている, じっと座っている
□ **stir** 動動かす, かき回す, 奮起させる **stir up** 荒立てる, 引き起こす
□ **stole** 動 steal (盗む)の過去
□ **stolen** 動 steal (盗む)の過去分詞
□ **stomach** 名 ①胃, 腹 ②食欲, 欲望, 好み
□ **stone** 名石, 小石 **stone circles** 環状列石 形石の, 石製の
□ **stop by** 途中で立ち寄る, ちょっと訪ねる
□ **stop doing** ~するのをやめる
□ **stop to** ~しようと立ち止まる
□ **storekeeper** 名店主, 店長, 小売り商人
□ **storm** 名嵐, 暴風雨
□ **stormy** 形嵐の, 暴風の
□ **storyteller** 名物語をする人, 物語作家
□ **straight** 熟 **straight away** すぐに **things straight** 物事をありのままに
□ **Strand** 名ストランド《ロンドンの地名》
□ **strangely** 副奇妙に, 変に, 不思議なことに, 不慣れに
□ **stranger** 名 ①見知らぬ人, 他人 ②不案内[不慣れ]な人
□ **street** 熟 **Oxford Street** オックスフォード街 **Regent Street** リージェント街
□ **strength** 名 ①力, 体力 ②長所, 強み ③強度, 濃度
□ **strengthen** 動強くする, しっかりさせる
□ **strengthened** 形強くする, 丈夫にする
□ **stretch** 動引き伸ばす, 広がる, 広げる **stretch out** ①手足を伸ばす, 背伸びする ②広がる
□ **strict** 形厳しい, 厳密な
□ **strike** 動 ①打つ, ぶつかる ②(災害などが)急に襲う **strike back** 打ち返す, 仕返しする **strike off** 削除する, 除名する **strike on** ~を思いつく **struck down** 倒れる
□ **striking** 形著しい, 目立つ
□ **string** 名ひも, 糸, 弦
□ **strip** 名 (細長い)1片
□ **strong-looking** 形強そうに見える, 頑健そうな
□ **strongly** 副強く, 頑丈に, 猛烈に, 熱心に
□ **strong-willed** 形意志の強い
□ **struck** 動 strike (打つ)の過去, 過去分詞 **struck down** 倒れる
□ **struggle** 動もがく, 奮闘する 名もがき, 奮闘 **death struggle** 死闘
□ **stubborn** 形頑固な, 強情な
□ **stuck** 動 stick (刺さる)の過去, 過去分詞
□ **study** 名研究, 書斎
□ **stuff** 名 ①材料, 原料 ②もの, 持ち物
□ **stump** 名木の切り株, 切れ端
□ **stupid** 形ばかな, おもしろくない
□ **substance** 名 ①物質, 物 ②実質, 中身, 内容
□ **succeed** 動 ①成功する ②(~の)跡を継ぐ
□ **success** 名成功, 幸運, 上首尾
□ **successful** 形成功した, うまくいった
□ **such ~ that ...** 非常に~なので…
□ **such a** そのような
□ **such as** たとえば~, ~のような **such ~ as ...** …のような~
□ **sudden** 形突然の, 急な
□ **suffer** 動 ①(苦痛・損害などを)受ける, こうむる ②(病気に)なる, 苦しむ, 悩む
□ **suggest** 動 ①提案する ②示唆する
□ **suggestion** 名 ①提案, 忠告 ②気配, 暗示
□ **suit** 名 ①スーツ, 背広 ②訴訟 ③ひとそろい, 一組 動 ①適合する[させる] ②似合う
□ **suitable** 形適当な, 似合う, ふさわしい
□ **suited** 形適して
□ **sum** 名 ①総計 ②金額 動 ①合計する ②要約する **sum up** 要約する, まとめる

☐ **sunburned** 動 sunburn（日焼けする）の過去，過去分詞 形 日焼けした

☐ **sunk** 動 sink（沈む）の過去分詞

☐ **supernatural** 名 超自然の

☐ **supper** 名 夕食，晩さん，夕飯

☐ **supply** 動 供給［配給］する，補充する 名 供給（品），給与，補充

☐ **supply-boat** 名 補給船

☐ **support** 動 ①支える，支持する ②養う，援助する 名 ①支え，支持 ②援助，扶養

☐ **suppose** 動 ①仮定する，推測する ②《be -d to ～》～することになっている，～するものである

☐ **sure** 熟 **Are you sure ～?** 本当に～なのですか？ **be sure to** 必ず～する **make sure** 確かめる，確認する **sure enough** 思ったとおり，確かに

☐ **surely** 副 ①（疑問文で確認の意味を込めて）確か ②確実に

☐ **surprise** 熟 **take someone by surprise**（人）をびっくりさせる，不意打ちを食らわす **to one's surprise** ～が驚いたことに

☐ **surprised** 形 驚いた **be surprised to** ～して驚く

☐ **surprising** 形 驚くべき，意外な

☐ **surprisingly** 副 驚くほど（に），意外にも

☐ **surround** 動 囲む，包囲する

☐ **surrounding** 形 周囲の

☐ **suspect** 動 疑う，（～ではないかと）思う **be suspected of** ～の容疑をかけられる 名 容疑者，注意人物

☐ **suspicion** 名 ①容疑，疑い ②感づくこと

☐ **Sussex** 名 サセックス《地名》

☐ **swam** 動 swim（泳ぐ）の過去

☐ **swear** 動 ①誓う，断言する ②はっきり～であると言える ③口汚くののしる

☐ **sweep over** 押し寄せる

☐ **swept** 動 sweep（さっと通る）の過去，過去分詞

☐ **swimming** 名 水泳

☐ **swing** 動 ①揺り動かす，揺れる ②回転する，ぐるっと回す

☐ **swinging door** スイングドア《ドアパネルが前後両方向に回動開閉するドア》

☐ **swordsman** 名 剣客，剣術の使い手

☐ **swore** 動 swear（誓う）の過去

☐ **sworn** 動 swear（誓う）の過去分詞

☐ **swung** 動 swing（回転する）の過去，過去分詞

☐ **symbol** 名 シンボル，象徴

☐ **sympathy** 名 ①同情，思いやり，お悔やみ ②共鳴，同感

T

☐ **tablet** 名 ①錠剤，タブレット ②便箋，メモ帳 ③銘板

☐ **tail** 名 尾，しっぽ

☐ **take** 熟 **in the time it take for** ～の間に **It takes someone ～ to …**（人）が…するのに～（時間など）がかかる **take a chance** 一か八かやってみる **take a liking to** ～を好きになる **take a message** 伝言をうけたまわる **take a room**（宿で）部屋を取る **take a seat** 席にすわる **take a walk** 散歩をする **take away** ①連れ去る ②取り上げる，奪い去る ③取り除く **take back** ①取り戻す ②（言葉，約束を）取り消す，撤回する **take care** 気をつける，注意する **take care of** ～の世話をする，～の面倒を見る，～を管理する **take down** ①下げる，降ろす ②記録する，書き付ける **take from** ～から引く，選ぶ **take in** 取り入れる，取り込む，（作物・金などを）集める **take into** 手につかむ，中に取り入れる **take it in** すべてを理解する **take off**（衣服を）脱ぐ，取り去る，～を取り除く **take on** 帯びる，持つようになる，～と戦う **take one last look** ～を見納めする **take one's place**（人と）交代する，（人）の代わりをする，後任になる **take out** 取り出す，取り外す，連れ出す，持って帰る **take over** 引き継ぐ **take part in** ～に参加する **take place** 行われる，起こる **take someone away**（人）を連れ出す **take someone by surprise**（人）をびっくりさせる，不意打ちを食らわす **take someone home**（人）を家まで送る **take the law into one's own hand** 私的制裁を与える **take ～ to …** ～を…に連れて行く **take up** 取り上げる，拾い上げる

☐ **taken by**《be －》～に連れられている，～に魅せられる，熱中する，

☐ **tale** 名 ①話，物語 ②うわさ，悪口

☐ **talk** 熟 **have a talk** 話をする **talk of** ～のことを話す **talk over** ～について議論する

☐ **talker** 名 話す人 **quite a talker** 非常におしゃべりな人

☐ **target** 名 標的，目的物，対象

☐ **task** 名（やるべき）仕事，職務，課題

☐ **taste** 名 ①味，風味 ②好み，趣味 動 味がする，味わう

☐ **tax** 名 ①税 ②重荷，重い負担

☐ **taxi** 名 タクシー

□ **teaching** 名①教えること，教授，授業 ②《-s》教え，教訓

□ **tear** 熟 **burst into tears** 急に泣き出す **tear at** ～を引き裂こうとする

□ **tear-stained** 形涙にぬれた，涙のあとが残る

□ **Ted Baldwin** テッド・ボールドウィン《人名》

□ **Teddy Baldwin** テディ・ボールドウィン《人名》

□ **teenager** 名10代の人，ティーンエイジャー《13歳から19歳》

□ **telegram** 名電報

□ **telegraph** 名電報，電信 **telegraph form** 電報を送るときに使う書込み用紙

□ **telescope** 名望遠鏡

□ **tell ~ to …** ～に…するように言う

□ **tell a lie** うそをつく

□ **tell of** ～について話す［説明する］

□ **temper** 名①気質，気性，気分 ②短気 **keep one's temper** 平静さを保つ **lose one's temper** かんしゃくを起こす

□ **temple** 名寺，神殿，教会堂

□ **term** 名①期間，期限 ②語，用語 ③《-s》条件 ④《-s》関係，仲

□ **terrace** 名台地，テラス，バルコニー

□ **terribly** 副ひどく

□ **terrified** 形おびえた，こわがった

□ **territory** 名①領土，縄張り ②（広い）地域，範囲，領域

□ **terror** 名①恐怖 ②恐ろしい人［物］

□ **Thaddeus Sholto** サディアス・ショルトー《人名》

□ **than** 熟 **more than** ～以上 **no more than** ただの～にすぎない **rather than** ～よりむしろ **than usual** いつもより **would rather ~ than …** …よりむしろ～したい

□ **thank ~ for** ～に対して礼を言う

□ **Thank God.** ありがたい，助かった

□ **thankful** 形ありがたく思う

□ **that** 熟 **after that** その後 **at that moment** その時に，その瞬間に **at that time** その時 **for that matter** ついでに言えば **in that case** もしそうなら **now that** 今や～だから，～からには **so that** ～するために，それで，～できるように **so ~ that …** 非常に～なので… **such ~ that …** 非常に～なので… **That's all right.** いいんですよ。 **That's it.** それだけのことだ。

□ **theater** 名劇場

□ **theatre** 名劇場

□ **then** 熟 **by then** その時までに **just then** そのとたんに **there and then** ただちに，その場で

□ **theorist** 名理論家

□ **theorize** 動理論を立てる，説を立てる

□ **theory** 名①理論，学説 ②仮説

□ **there** 熟 **get there** そこに到着する，目的を達成する，成功する **here and there** あちこちで **I wish I had been there.** 自分がそこにいられればよかったのに。 **over there** あそこに **there and then** ただちに，その場で **there goes** チャンスなどが行ってしまう **there is no way** ～する見込みはない **There's no point in** ～しても意味がない **up there** あそこで

□ **therefore** 副したがって，それゆえ，その結果

□ **these days** このごろ

□ **thick** 形厚い，密集した，濃厚な

□ **thick-necked** 形首の太い

□ **thief** 名泥棒，強盗

□ **thieves** 名thief（泥棒）の複数

□ **thin** 形薄い，細い，やせた，まばらな

□ **think** 熟 **think of** ～のことを考える，～を思いつく，考え出す **be well thought of** 評判がいい

□ **thinker** 名思想家，考える人

□ **thinking** 名考えること，思考 形思考力のある，考える

□ **third** 形第3の **third party** 第三者，部外者 名（カレンダーの）3日

□ **thirst** 名（のどの）渇き，（～に対する）渇望，切望

□ **thirteenth** 形第13番目の

□ **thirtieth** 形①《the –》30番目の ②30分の1の

□ **this** 熟 **at this** これを見て，そこで（すぐに） **at this moment** 現在のところ，現段階［時点］では **at this point** 現在のところ **at this time** 現時点では，このとき **by this time** この時までに，もうすでに **in this way** このようにして **like this** このような，こんなふうに **this one** これ，こちら **this way** このように

□ **thorn** 名とげ，とげのある植物，いばら

□ **Thorsley** 名トースリー《地名》

□ **those who** ～する人々

□ **though** 接①～にもかかわらず，～だが ②たとえ～でも **as though** あたかも～のように，まるで～みたいに **even though** ～であるけれども，～にもかかわらず 副しかし

□ **thoughtfully** 副考え[思いやり]深く
□ **thousand and first** 1001番目
□ **thousand to one** まず間違いない
□ **thousands of** 何千という
□ **thread** 名糸, 糸のように細いもの
□ **threat** 名おどし, 脅迫
□ **threateningly** 副脅迫的に, 脅して
□ **three-foot** 形3フィートの
□ **thrilling** 形スリル満点の, ぞくぞくする
□ **throat** 名のど, 気管
□ **through** 熟 break through ～を打ち破る come through 通り抜ける, 成功する get through 乗り切る, ～を通り抜ける go through 通り抜ける, 一つずつ順番に検討する look through ～をのぞき込む pass through ～を通る, 通行する push one's way through かき分けて前に出る push through (人ごみなどを)かき分ける run through 走り抜ける
□ **throw down** 投げ出す, 放棄する
□ **throw out** 放り出す
□ **throw up** 跳ね上げる
□ **thrown** 動 throw (投げる)の過去分詞
□ **thus** 副①このように ②これだけ ③かくて, だから
□ **tie up** ひもで縛る, 縛り上げる, つなぐ, 拘束する
□ **tiger** 名①トラ(虎) ②あばれ者
□ **tight** 形堅い, きつい, ぴんと張った
□ **tighten** 動①ぴんと張る, 堅く締める ②余裕がなくなる ③厳しくなる
□ **tightly** 副きつく, しっかり, 堅く
□ **tile** 名タイル, 瓦
□ **till** 前～まで(ずっと) 接～(する)まで
□ **time** 熟 a hard time つらい時期 all the time ずっと, いつも, その間ずっと any time いつでも at one time ある時には, かつては at that time その時 at the time そのころ, 当時は at the time of ～の時[際]に at this time 現時点では, このとき at times 時々 by the time ～する時までに by this time この時までに, もうすでに closing time 閉店[終業]時間 every time ～するときはいつも for a time しばらく, 一時の間 for some time しばらくの間 for the first time 初めて from time to time ときどき have no time to do ～する時間がない in my time これまでに in the time it take for ～の間に in time 間に合って, やがて just in time いよいよというときに, すんでのところで, やっと間に合って next time 次回に some time いつか, そのうち, しばらく the last time この前～したとき
□ **Times** 名タイムズ《新聞》
□ **timing** 名タイミング
□ **tiny** 形ちっぽけな, とても小さい
□ **tip** 名先端, 頂点
□ **tire out** (人)をへとへとに疲れさせる
□ **tired** 形①疲れた, くたびれた ②あきた, うんざりした be tired of ～に飽きて[うんざりして]いる
□ **tiredness** 名疲労, 倦怠
□ **tiring** 形①疲れる, 骨の折れる ②退屈させる
□ **title** 名①題名, タイトル ②肩書, 称号 ③権利, 資格
□ **to** 熟 to begin with はじめに, まず第一に to death 死ぬまで, 死ぬほど to one's feet 両足で立っている状態に to one's surprise ～が驚いたことに to the point 要領を得た to the purpose 目的にかなって
□ **tobacco** 名たばこ
□ **Tobias Gregson** トバイアス・グレッグソン《人名》
□ **Toby** 名トビー《犬の名》
□ **toe** 名足指, つま先
□ **Tom Dennis** トム・デニス《人名》
□ **tone** 名音, 音色, 調子
□ **Tonga** 名トンガ《人名》
□ **tongue** 名①舌 ②弁舌 ③言語
□ **too** 熟 far too あまりにも～過ぎる too much 過度の too much of あまりに～過ぎる too ～ to … …するには～すぎる
□ **tool** 名道具, 用具, 工具
□ **top** 熟 on top of ～の上(部)に
□ **top-coat** 名薄手のコート, 外套
□ **tor** 名ゴツゴツした岩山 Black Tor 黒い丘《ダートムア国立公園にある丘の名前》
□ **torn** 動 tear (裂く)の過去分詞
□ **Torquay Terrace** トーキー・テラス《ロンドンの地名》
□ **total** 形総計の, 全体の, 完全な
□ **touch** 熟 in touch 連絡を取って
□ **trace** 名①跡 ②(事件などの)こん跡 動たどる, さかのぼって調べる
□ **tracing** 名跡を追う[尋ねる]こと
□ **track** 名①跡, 足跡 ②(思考や行動の)流れ, 道筋 動追跡する track down 見つけ出す, 追跡して捕らえる
□ **trade** 名取引, 貿易, 商業, 職業

□ **trading ship** 交易船
□ **tragedy** 名悲劇, 惨劇
□ **trail** 名(通った)跡
□ **train of** 一連の
□ **trained** 形訓練された, 熟練した
□ **traitor** 名反逆者, 裏切り者
□ **trap** 名わな, 策略 動わなを仕掛ける, わなで捕らえる
□ **trapdoor** 名はねぶた, 揚げぶた, 落とし戸
□ **trapping** 名わな
□ **traveler** 名旅行者
□ **treasure** 名財宝, 貴重品, 宝物
□ **treasure-seeker** 名宝探し家
□ **treat** 動①扱う ②治療する ③おごる 名①おごり, もてなし, ごちそう ②楽しみ
□ **treatment** 名①取り扱い, 待遇 ②治療(法)
□ **tree-lined** 形並木のある
□ **trembling** 形震えている
□ **trial** 名裁判
□ **triangle** 名三角形
□ **Trichinopoly** 名トリチノポリ《地名, 現在のティルチラーパッリ県》
□ **Trichinopoly cigar** トリチノポリ産の葉巻
□ **trick** 名①策略 ②いたずら, 冗談 ③手品, 錯覚 動だます
□ **trouble** 熟**be troubled by** ～に悩まされている **get into trouble** 面倒を起こす, 困った事になる, トラブルに巻き込まれる **get into trouble with** ～とトラブルを起こす **get someone into trouble** (人)に迷惑を掛ける, 困らせる **in trouble** 面倒な状況で, 困って
□ **troubled** 形不安[心配]そうな
□ **true** 熟**come true** 実現する **true to** 忠実に
□ **truly** 副①全く, 本当に, 真に ②心から, 誠実に
□ **trust** 動信用[信頼]する, 委託する 名信用, 信頼, 委託
□ **trusted** 形信頼されている
□ **trusting** 形信じている, (信じて)人を疑わない
□ **trusty** 形信頼できる
□ **truth** 名①真理, 事実, 本当 ②誠実, 忠実さ **get at the truth** 真相を解明する **to tell the truth** 実は, 実を言えば
□ **truthful** 形正直な, 真実の
□ **try and do** ～しようとする
□ **try as he might** 彼がどんなに試そうとも
□ **try on** 試着してみる
□ **try one's best** 全力を尽くす
□ **Tunbridge Wells** タンブリッジ・ウェルズ《地名》
□ **turban** 名ターバン
□ **turn** 熟**in turn** 順番に, 立ち代わって **turn against** ～に敵対する **turn around** 振り向く, 向きを変える, 方向転換する **turn away** 向こうへ行く, 追い払う, (顔を)そむける, 横を向く **turn back** 元に戻る **turn down** (音量などを)小さくする, 弱くする, 拒絶する **turn in** 向きを変える, (向きを変えてわき道になどに)入る, 床につく **turn into** 進路を～へ向ける **turn on** ①～の方を向く ②(スイッチなどを)ひねってつける, 出す **turn out** ～と判明する, (結局～に)なる **turn over** ひっくり返る[返す], (ページを)めくる, 思いめぐらす, 引き渡す **turn the light around** 明かりをつけて周りを照らす **turn to** ～の方を向く, ～に頼る, ～に変わる **turn up** 生じる, 姿を現す, (袖を)折り返して短くする **turn white** 青ざめる, 血の気が引く
□ **twin** 名双子の一方, 双生児 形双子の, 1対の
□ **twinkling** 形きらきら光る
□ **two** 熟**a ～ or two** 1～か2～, 2, 3の **for a moment or two** ほんの少しの間
□ **tying** 動tie(結ぶ)の現在分詞
□ **type** 名活字, 字体**newspaper type** 新聞書体
□ **typewriter** 名タイプライター

U

□ **U.S.A.** 略米国
□ **ugly** 形①醜い, ぶかっこうな ②いやな, 不快な, 険悪な
□ **um** 間ううん, ううむ
□ **unable to** 《be –》～することができない
□ **unaware** 形無意識の, 気づかない
□ **unbelievable** 形信じられない(ほどの), 度のはずれた
□ **unbelievably** 副信じられないほど
□ **unbroken** 形完全な, 途切れのない
□ **uncertain** 形不確かな, 確信がない
□ **uncomfortable** 形心地よくない
□ **uncomfortably** 副心地悪く
□ **uncommon** 形珍しい, まれな
□ **unconcerned** 形無関心な, 心配しない
□ **uncover** 動ふたを取る, 覆いを取る, あばく
□ **under arrest** 逮捕されて

□ **under lock and key** 厳重に閉じ込めて
□ **underclothes** 名下着, 肌着
□ **undergone** 動undergo (経験する) の過去分詞
□ **underlie** 動基礎となる, 下に横たわる
□ **understanding** 名理解, 意見の一致, 了解
□ **Underwood** 名(ジョン・)アンダーウッド(・アンド・サンズ)《ロンドンにある衣料品店》
□ **undid** 動undo (ほどく) の過去
□ **undiscovered** 形発見されていない
□ **undo** 動①ほどく, はずす ②元に戻す, 取り消す
□ **uneasy** 形不安な, 焦って
□ **unemotional** 形感情的でない
□ **unexpected** 形思いがけない, 予期しない
□ **unfair** 形不公平な, 不当な
□ **unfold** 動①(折りたたんだものを) 広げる, 開く ②(計画などを) 知らせる, 明らかになる
□ **unfortunate** 形不運な, あいにくな, 不適切な
□ **unfortunately** 副不幸にも, 運悪く
□ **ungodly** 副邪悪な
□ **unguarded** 形うっかりとした, 不注意な
□ **unhappy** 形不運な, 不幸な
□ **unimpressed** 形感動していない, 感銘を受けていない
□ **union** 名①結合, 合併, 融合 ②連合国家
□ **Union House** ユニオン・ハウス
□ **unique** 形唯一の, ユニークな, 独自の
□ **United States** アメリカ合衆国《国名》
□ **unknown** 形知られていない, 不明の
□ **unless** 接もし〜でなければ, 〜しなければ
□ **unlikely** 形ありそうもない, 考えられない
□ **unlock** 動かぎを開ける, 解く
□ **unmarried** 形未婚の, 独身の
□ **unnatural** 形不自然な, 異常な
□ **unnaturally** 副異常に, 不自然に
□ **unofficial** 形非公式な, 私的な
□ **unpleasant** 形不愉快な, 気にさわる, いやな, 不快な
□ **unprotected** 形①無防備な ②保護のない
□ **unsigned** 形無署名の, 署名のない **unsigned police paper** 署名なしの逮捕状
□ **unsmiling** 形にこりともしない
□ **unspoken** 形言外の, 暗黙の
□ **unsteadily** 副ふらつく, 不安定な
□ **unsteady** 形不安定な, 不規則な, ふらついた
□ **unsure** 形確かでない, 自信がない
□ **untie** 動ほどく, 解放する
□ **untouched** 形①そのままの, 触られていない ②無垢な
□ **untrusting** 形明らかに不信で
□ **unusual** 形普通でない, 珍しい, 見[聞き]慣れない
□ **unwrap** 動包装を解く, 包みを開ける
□ **up** 熟**be made up of** 〜で構成されている **blow up** 破裂する[させる] **break up** ばらばらになる, 解散させる **bring up** ①育てる, 連れて行く ②(問題を) 持ち出す **catch up with** 〜に追いつく **clear up** きれいにする, 片付ける, (疑問, 問題を) 解決する **come up** 近づいてくる, 階上に行く, 浮上する, 水面へ上ってくる, 発生する **come up with** 〜に追いつく, 〜を思いつく, 考え出す, 見つけ出す **drive up** 車でやって来る **follow up** (人) の跡を追う **get mixed up** かかわり合いになる, 巻き添えを食う **get up** 起き上がる, 立ち上がる **give up** あきらめる, やめる, 引き渡す **go up** ①〜に上がる, 登る ②〜に近づく, 出かける **go up to** 〜まで行く, 近づく **grow up** 成長する, 大人になる **help someone up** ひとを助け起こす, ささえる **hold up** ①維持する, 支える ②〜を持ち上げる **jump up** 素早く立ち上がる **keep up** 上げたままにしておく **lock up** 〜を閉じ込める **look up** 見上げる, 調べる **look up to** 〜を仰ぎ見る **make up** 作り出す, 考え出す, 〜を構成[形成]する **make up one's mind** 決心する **pick up** 拾い上げる, 車で迎えに行く **pull up** 引っ張り上げる **put up one's hand** 手を挙げる **put up with** 〜を我慢する **roll up** 巻き上げる **run up** 〜に走り寄る **run up and down** かけずり回る **set up** 配置する, セットする, 据え付ける, 設置する **sit up** 起き上がる, 上半身を起こす **sit up all night** 徹夜する **slip up** ずり上がる **speak up** 率直に話す, はっきりしゃべる **stand up** 立ち上がる **step up** (低いところから) 上がる **stir up** 荒立てる, 引き起こす **take up** 取り上げる, 拾い上げる **throw up** 跳ね上げる **tie up** ひもで縛る, 縛り上げる, つなぐ, 拘束する **turn up** 生じる, 姿を現す, (袖を) 折り返して短くする **up and down** 上がったり下がったり, 行ったり来たり, あちこちと **up there** あそこで **up to** 〜まで, 〜に至るまで, 〜に匹敵して **up to now** これまで **wake up** 起きる, 目を覚ます **walk up** 歩み寄る, 歩いて上る **walk up and down** 行ったり来たりする **walk up to** 〜に歩み寄る
□ **upbringing** 名①しつけ, 育て方 ②生い立ち

□ **upon** 前 ①《場所・接触》～(の上)に ②《日・時》～に ③《関係・従事》～に関して, ～について, ～して **call upon** 求める, 頼む, 訪問する **come upon** (人)に偶然出合う **depend upon** ～に頼る **fall upon** ～の上にかかる **look down upon** 見下ろす, 俯瞰する **look upon** ～を見る, 見つめる

□ **upper** 形上の, 上位の, 北方の **upper floor** 上階

□ **uprising** 名 ①起床, 起立 ②反乱, 暴動, 謀反

□ **upset** 形 ①うろたえて, 動揺して **get onself upset** 取り乱す ②憤慨して 動気を悪くさせる

□ **upstairs** 副2階へ[に], 階上へ 形2階の, 階上の

□ **upwards** 副上の方へ, 上向きに

□ **urge** 動 ①せき立てる, 強力に推し進める, かりたてる ②《－… to ～》…に～するよう熱心に勧める 名衝動, かりたてられるような気持ち

□ **urgent** 形緊急の, 差し迫った

□ **USA** 略 アメリカ合衆国(=United States of America)

□ **use** 熟 **be of use** 役に立つ **in common use** 一般的に使われて[用いられて]いる **no use** 役に立たない, 用をなさない **of no use** 使われないで **of use** 役に立って

□ **used** 動 ①use(使う)の過去, 過去分詞 ②《－to》よく～したものだ, 以前は～であった 形 ①慣れている, 《get [become] － to》～に慣れてくる ②使われた, 中古の

□ **useless** 形役に立たない, 無益な

□ **usual** 形通常の, いつもの, 平常の, 普通の **as usual** いつものように, 相変わらず **than usual** いつもより

□ **Utah** 名ユタ州《米国の地名》

□ **utter** 動(声・言葉を)発する

V

□ **valley** 名谷, 谷間

□ **valuable** 形貴重な, 価値のある, 役に立つ

□ **value** 名価値, 値打ち, 価格 **of value** 貴重な, 価値のある 動評価する, 値をつける, 大切にする **value one's life** 命を大切にする

□ **Vandeleur** 名ヴァンデリュル《人名》

□ **variety** 名 ①変化, 多様性, 寄せ集め ②種類

□ **various** 形変化に富んだ, さまざまの, たくさんの

□ **Vermissa** 名バーミッサ《地名》

□ **Vermissa Herald** バーミッサ・ヘラルド《新聞(社)の名》

□ **Vermissa Lodge** バーミッサ支部

□ **Vermissa Valley** バーミッサ谷

□ **very likely** たぶん

□ **very well** 結構, よろしい

□ **victory** 名勝利, 優勝

□ **view** 熟 **point of view** 考え方, 視点

□ **villager** 名村人, 田舎の人

□ **villain** 名悪党, 悪者, 罪人

□ **violence** 名 ①暴力, 乱暴 ②激しさ **man of violence** 乱暴そうな男

□ **violent** 形暴力的な, 激しい

□ **violently** 副激しく, 猛烈に, 暴力的に

□ **violin** 名バイオリン

□ **visit** 熟 **make a single visit** 一回きりの訪問をする **pay a visit** ～を訪問する

□ **visitor** 名訪問客

□ **volume** 名 ①本, 巻, 冊 ②《-s》たくさん, 多量 ③量, 容積

□ **vote** 動投票する, 投票して決める

□ **voyage** 名航海, 航行, 空の旅

W

□ **wage** 名賃金, 給料, 応酬

□ **wager** 動賭ける **wager two to one** 二対一で賭ける, 負けたら倍払う

□ **wagon** 名荷馬車, ワゴン(車)

□ **waist** 名ウエスト, 腰のくびれ

□ **waist-belt** 名腰ベルト

□ **wait for** ～を待つ

□ **waiting** 形待っている, 仕えている

□ **wake up** 起きる, 目を覚ます

□ **walk** 熟 **go for a walk** 散歩に行く **take a walk** 散歩をする **walk across** ～を歩いて渡る **walk along** (前へ)歩く, ～に沿って歩く **walk around** 歩き回る, ぶらぶら歩く **walk away** 立ち去る, 遠ざかる **walk by** 通りかかる **walk off** 立ち去る **walk out of** ～から出る **walk over** ～の方に歩いていく **walk over to** ～の方に歩いていく **walk round** ブラブラ歩き回る **walk through** 通り抜ける **walk to** ～まで歩いて行く **walk up** 歩み寄る, 歩いて上る **walk up and down** 行ったり来たりする **walk up to** ～に歩み寄る **walk upon** ～の上を歩く

□ **walking stick** 杖, ステッキ

□ **wall** 熟 **against the wall** 壁を背にして, 壁に

向かって

□ **wallpaper** 名壁紙

□ **wander** 動①さまよう, 放浪する, 横道へそれる ②放心する

□ **wanderer** 名さまよう人, 放浪者

□ **wandering** 名[-s]放浪, 流浪の旅

□ **warm** 動熱が入る, 熱中する

□ **warmly** 副温かく, 親切に, 熱心に, 心から

□ **warmth** 名暖かさ, 思いやり

□ **warn** 動警告する, 用心させる **warn of** ～を警告する

□ **warning** 名警告, 警報

□ **waste-basket** 名くずかご

□ **wastepaper** 名紙くず

□ **watch over** 見守る, 見張る

□ **watchfulness** 名用心深さ, 油断のなさ

□ **watchman** 名夜警, 警備員

□ **watchmen** 名watchman（夜警）の複数

□ **Waterloo Station** ウォータールー駅

□ **Watson** 名ワトソン《人名》

□ **wave** 名①波 ②（手などを）振ること 動①揺れる, 揺らす, 波立つ ②（手などを振って）合図する

□ **way** 熟**a little way** 少し **all the way** ずっと, はるばる, いろいろと **along the way** 途中で, これまでに, この先 **by the way** ところで, ついでに, 途中で **find one's way** たどり着く **give way** 道を譲る, 譲歩する, 負ける **go on one's way** 道を進む, 立ち去る **in a way** ある意味では **in some way** 何とかして, 何らかの方法で **in this way** このようにして **lead the way** 先に立って導く, 案内する, 率先する **long way** はるかに **make one's way** 進む, 行く, 成功する **make one's way into**〔部屋など〕に入る, 進入する **on one's way** 途中で, 出て行く, 出かける **on one's way home** 帰り道で **on one's way to** ～に行く途中で **on the way** 途中で **on the way to** ～へ行く途中で **one's way to** ～への途中で **push one's way through** かき分けて前に出る **some way** しばらく **there is no way** ～する見込みはない **this way** このように **way of** ①～の手口, 習性 ②～する方法 **way of life** 生き様, 生き方, 暮らし方 **way out** 出口, 逃げ道, 脱出方法, 解決法 **way to** ～する方法, ～に行く道

□ **weaken** 動弱くなる, 弱める, 弱らせる

□ **weakly** 副弱々しく

□ **weakness** 名①弱さ, もろさ ②欠点, 弱点

□ **wealth** 名①富, 財産 ②豊富, 多量

□ **wealthy** 形裕福な, 金持ちの

□ **weapon** 名武器, 兵器

□ **wear** 動すり減る

□ **weary** 形とても疲れた, あきあきした

□ **wed** 動結婚させる, 結婚する

□ **wedding** 名結婚式, 婚礼 **wedding ring** 結婚指輪

□ **weigh** 動①（重さを）はかる ②重さが～ある ③圧迫する, 重荷である **weigh down** 圧迫する

□ **weight** 動①重みをつける ②重荷を負わせる

□ **well** 熟**all very well** 大変けっこうなこと, ちっとも構いません **as well** なお, その上, 同様に **as well as** ～と同様に **be well -ed** よく［十分に］～された **be well thought of** 評判がいい **do well** 成績が良い, 成功する **It is as well that he is** 彼がいるに越したことはない **sleep well** よく眠る **very well** 結構, よろしい **well done** うまくやった **well enough** かなり上手に

□ **well-being** 名快適な暮らし, 幸福, 福祉

□ **well-booted** 形高価な靴をはいた

□ **well-built** 形がっちりした, よい体格の

□ **well-dressed** 形よい身なりの, 上等な服を着た

□ **well-educated** 形教養のある

□ **well-known** 形よく知られた, 有名な

□ **well-organized** 形よく組織された, うまくまとまった

□ **well-played** 形上手な

□ **well-trained** 形よく訓練された

□ **West Indies** 西インド諸島

□ **Westminster Stairs** ウェストミンスター・ステアズ《テムズ川に沿ってある階段の一つ》

□ **Westmoreland** 名ウエストモアランド《地名》

□ **Westville Arms** ウェストビル・アームズ《宿泊先の名》

□ **westward** 形西へ, 西方に

□ **wet** 形ぬれた, 湿った

□ **wharf** 名波止場, 埠頭

□ **what** 熟**in what order** どのような順序で **no matter what** たとえ何があろう［起ころう］と **What about ～?** ～についてあなたはどう思いますか。～はどうですか。 **What do you say to ～?** ～はいかがですか。 **What (～) for?** 何のために, なぜ **what if** もし～だったらどうなるだろうか **what sort of** どういう **what … for** どんな目的で **What's the matter?** どう

したんですか。 **what's up with you** どうしたんだ

□ **whatever** 代 ①《関係代名詞》～するものは何でも ②どんなこと[もの]が～とも 形 ①どんな～でも ②《否定文・疑問文で》少しの～も，何らかの

□ **whatsoever** 代 どんなものであれ，とにかく何であれ

□ **wheat** 名 小麦

□ **wheel** 名 輪，車輪

□ **where to** どこで～すべきか

□ **whereabout** 名 [-s] 行方，所在

□ **whereabouts** 名 所在，ゆくえ，ありか.

□ **whereas** 接 ～であるのに対して[反して]，～である一方

□ **whether** 接 ～かどうか，～かまたは…，～であろうとなかろうと **whether or not** ～かどうか

□ **which** 熟 **of which** ～の中で **on which** = where

□ **whichever** 代 いったいどれが，どちら(どれ)でも，どちらが～しようとも

□ **while** 熟 **after a while** しばらくして **all the while** その間ずっと **for a while** しばらくの間，少しの間

□ **whip** 名 むち **hunting whip** 狩猟用むち

□ **whiskey** 名 ウイスキー

□ **whisky** 名 ウイスキー

□ **whisper** 動 ささやく，小声で話す 名 ささやき，ひそひそ話，うわさ

□ **whistle** 名 口笛

□ **white** 熟 **turn white** 青ざめる，血の気が引く **white with anger** 怒りで白くなる

□ **White Hart Hotel** ホワイト・ハート・ホテル《ロンドンにあるホテル》

□ **White Mason** ホワイト・メーソン《人名》

□ **white-faced** 形 青ざめた，白い顔の

□ **white-haired** 形 白髪の

□ **who** 熟 **those who** ～する人々

□ **whoa** 間 おっと，うわっ

□ **whoever** 代 ～する人は誰でも，誰が～しようとも

□ **whole** 形 全体の，すべての，完全な，満～，丸～ 名《the －》全体，全部 **as a whole** 全体として **on the whole** 全体として見ると

□ **whom** 代 ①誰をに ②《関係代名詞》～するところの人，そしてその人を **By whom?** 誰に？

□ **Why don't you ～?** ～したらどうだい，～しませんか。

□ **Why not?** どうしてだめなのですか。いいですとも。ぜひそうしよう！

□ **wicked** 形 悪い，不道徳な

□ **wide** 形 幅の広い，広範囲の，幅が～ある 副 広く，大きく開いて

□ **widely** 副 広く，広範囲にわたって

□ **widen** 動 広くなる[する]，大きく開く

□ **Wiggins** 名 ウィギンズ《人名》

□ **wild-looking** 形 乱れた格好の

□ **wildly** 副 荒々しく，乱暴に，むやみに，狂乱して

□ **will** 名 遺言(状)

□ **will have done** ～してしまっているだろう《未来完了形》

□ **Will you ～?** ～してくれませんか，～しませんか，～する意思はありますか

□ **William Baskerville** ウィリアム・バスカヴィル《人名》

□ **willing** 形 ①喜んで～する，～しても構わない，いとわない ②自分から進んで行う

□ **Wilson, Sergeant** ウィルソン巡査部長

□ **win respect** 敬意を得る

□ **win someone's heart** (人)のハートを射止める

□ **winding** 形 曲がりくねった

□ **wine** 名 ワイン，ぶどう酒

□ **wing** 名 翼，羽

□ **winner** 名 勝利者，成功者

□ **wire** 名 電信

□ **wish** 熟 **as you wish** 望み通りに **good wishes** 好意，厚情 **I wish I had been there.** 自分がそこにいられればよかったのに。 **wish for** 所望する

□ **with** 熟 **agree with** (人)に同意する **along with** ～と一緒に **be busy with** ～で忙しい **be covered with** ～でおおわれている **be filled with** ～でいっぱいになる **be in love with** ～に恋して，～に心を奪われて **be pleased with** ～が気に入る **be wrong with** (～にとって)よくない，～が故障している **begin with** ～で始まる **burn with** ～を強く感じる **catch up with** ～に追いつく **come up with** ～に追いつく，～を思いつく，考え出す，見つけ出す **do with** ～を処理する **fall in love with** 恋におちる **get into trouble with** ～とトラブルを起こす **have nothing to do with** ～と何の関係もない **have to do with** ～と関係がある **help ～ with …** …を～の面で手伝う **lined with**《be

–》～が立ち並ぶ **make friends with** ～と友達になる **meet with** ～に出会う **part with** ～を手放す **put up with** ～を我慢する **stay with** ～の所に泊まる **to begin with** はじめに, まず第一に **white with anger** 怒りで白くなる **with a mighty drop on one side** 片側が激しい落下 **with all** ～がありながら **with fear** 怖がって **with the help of** ～の助けにより, ～のおかげで

□ **withdraw** 動引っ込める, 取り下げる, (預金を)引き出す

□ **within** 前 ①～の中[内]に, ～の内部に ②～以内で, ～を越えないで **within reach of** ～の手の届くところに 副中[内]へ[に], 内部に

□ **without** 熟 **do without** ～なしですませる

□ **witness** 名 ①証拠, 証言 ②目撃者

□ **wives** 名 wife (妻) の複数

□ **woke** 動 wake (目が覚める) の過去

□ **wonder** 動 ①不思議に思う, (～に)驚く ②(～かしらと)思う **wonder if** ～ではないかと思う

□ **wooden** 形木製の, 木でできた

□ **wooden-legged** 形木の義足の

□ **wool** 名羊毛, 毛糸, 織物, ウール

□ **Worcestershire** 名ウースターシャー《地名》

□ **word** 熟 **give someone one's word** (人) に約束する **I give you my word.** 約束するよ。保証するよ。 **printed word** 活字 **word for word** 一字一句違わず **you have my word** 約束しますよ

□ **work** 熟 **at work** 働いて, 仕事中で, 職場で **work in** ～の分野で働く, ～に入り込む **work of** ～の仕業 **work on** ～で働く, ～に取り組む, ～を説得する, ～に効く **work out** うまくいく, 何とかなる, (問題を)解く, 考え出す, 答えが出る, ～の結果になる

□ **worker** 名仕事をする人, 労働者

□ **working** 形働く, 作業の, 実用的な

□ **workman** 名労働者, 職人

□ **workmanship** 名細工(品)

□ **workmen** 名 workman (労働者) の複数

□ **world** 熟 **if not the world** 世界でとはいわないまでも **in the world** 世界で

□ **worn away** 摩耗する

□ **worn out** 疲弊した

□ **worried** 形心配そうな, 不安げな **be worried about** (～のことで)心配している, ～が気になる[かかる]

□ **worry about** ～のことを心配する

□ **worse** 形いっそう悪い, より劣った, よりひどい **get worse** 悪化する

□ **worst** 形《the –》最も悪い, いちばんひどい **worst of all** 一番困るのは, 最悪なことに

□ **worth** 形(～の)価値がある, (～)しがいがある **It is more than my life is worth to be seen talking to you.** 君と話しているところを見られたら私の命にかかわる。

□ **worthy** 形価値のある, 立派な

□ **would** 熟 **would have … if ～** もし～だったとしたら…しただろう **would like** ～がほしい **would like to** ～したいと思う **would rather** ～する方がよい **would rather ～ than …** …よりむしろ～したい **would sooner ～ than …** …するよりはむしろ～した方がマシだ **Would you ～?** ～してくださいませんか。 **Would you like ～?** ～はいかがですか。 **Would you mind if ～?** ～してもかまいませんか。

□ **wouldn't** would notの短縮形

□ **wound** 名傷

□ **wounded** 形傷ついた

□ **wrapping** 名包み

□ **wrinkle** 名しわ

□ **write down** 書き留める

□ **write to** ～に手紙を書く

□ **writer** 名書き手, 作家

□ **writing** 名 ①書くこと, 作文, 著述 ②筆跡 ③書き物, 書かれたもの, 文書

□ **written by hand** 手書き

□ **wrong** 熟 **be wrong with** (～にとって)よくない, ～が故障している **go wrong** 失敗する

Y

□ **yard** 名ヤード《長さの単位。0.9144m》

□ **year** 熟 **for years** 何年も **for ～ years** ～年間, ～年にわたって

□ **yell** 動大声をあげる, わめく

□ **yet** 熟 **and yet** それなのに, それにもかかわらず **not yet** まだ～してない

□ **yew tree** イチイ

□ **York** 名ヨーク《地名》

□ **Yorkshire** 名ヨークシャー《地名》

□ **you** 熟 **as you know** ご存知のとおり **as you wish** 望み通りに **if you please** よろしければ **you know** ご存知のとおり, そうでしょう **you see** あのね, いいですか

- □ **Young** 名ヤング《人名》
- □ **younger brother** 弟
- □ **youngster** 名少年, 若者, 子ども
- □ **yourself** 熟 **see for yourself** 自分で確かめる
- □ **yourselves** 代 yourself（あなた自身）の複数
- □ **youth** 名若さ, 元気, 若者
- □ **youthful** 形若々しい

英語で読む
シャーロック・ホームズ珠玉長編4作品

2023年12月2日　第1刷発行

原著者　コナン・ドイル

発行者　浦　晋亮

発行所　IBCパブリッシング株式会社
〒162-0804 東京都新宿区中里町29番3号 菱秀神楽坂ビル
Tel. 03-3513-4511　Fax. 03-3513-4512
www.ibcpub.co.jp

印刷所　株式会社シナノパブリッシングプレス

Printed in Japan

ISBN978-4-7946-0789-8